A PLAN FOR LIFE

Praise for A Plan for Life

A highly informative manual for getting the most from your life.

"Eric Wentworth has done the impossible; he has condensed a broad range of critical life-enhancing information into a comprehensive, entertaining and highly informative manual for getting the most from your life."

— Peter Engler, author of *Your Crystal Clear Career Action Plan.*

The guidance, tools, and resources to create a new plan for your life.

"Reinvention is the key to leading a fulfilling life in the years to come. Eric has provided the guidance, tools, and resources to create a new plan for your life."

— Dee McCrorey, author of *Innovation in a Reinvented World.*

A masterful blend of new information and timeless inspiration.

"Those of us who answer our calling, show up every day for the work of developing our potential, do our best to prepare for the journey ahead, are rewarded with successful, productive, and satisfying lives. If I had to choose just one book to take along as a guide, it would be A Plan for Life. A masterful blend of new information and timeless inspiration, this book is a stepping-stone for confidently crossing the rivers of uncertainty-and a surfboard for gracefully riding the waves of change in the 21st Century."

— Dave Lent, Producer, author of *The 5 Keys to Mastery* and *Video Rules.*

A "Must Read" Book that will shift your mindset.

"A Plan for Life is a Must Read Book that will shift your mindset. Most people spend their time and energy doing course-corrections as they wander somewhat aimlessly through life. But life these days is more complicated and challenging than ever. Eric's book provides the information you likely didn't get in school, but is necessary to create a successful plan for your own life."

— Darren Jacklin, World-class professional speaker, corporate trainer, angel investor.

Your roadmap to a successful life.

"More than ever your life is what you make of it. It's important for everyone to continue growing and learning in order to evolve in our fast-changing world. A Plan for Life is your roadmap to a successful life."

— Ron Nash, author of *TheInAcademy.*

Every page contains tips and suggestions that can change your life.

"Life is difficult in the 21st Century. Accelerating change is making it harder and harder to keep up and stay relevant. A Plan for Life offers practical guidance to maintain balance and thrive in our interconnected world. Nearly every page contains tips and suggestions that can change your life for the better!"

— Patrick Schwerdtfeger, author of *Marketing Solutions for the Self-Employed.*

Everybody needs to read this book!

"A profound resource on how to live a good life. Everybody needs to read this book."

— Patti Wilson, CEO, The Career Company.

A clear path to creating a life well lived.

"A 360-degree look at the world we live in and a clear path to creating a life well lived, A Plan for Life: The 21st Century Guide to Success in Health, Wealth, Career, Education, Place, Love...and You! is a cross between Dr. Oz's You! The Owner's Manual and a modern-day encyclopedia of helpful hints, great tips, and thought-provoking insights. Eric has done the research so you don't have to!"

— Joy Nordenstrom, MBA, CMM, Founder/CEO of Joy of Romance, Inc.

Learn to make better choices.

"Every day is stacked with decisions that can be life-altering. Learn to make better choices with fewer regrets and greater happiness...with A Plan for Life."

— Mike O'Neil, President, Integrated Alliances, *Forbes* Top 50 Social Media Power Influencer - 2012 and 2013.

Immediately begin improving your life.

"A Plan for Life goes beyond the typical motivational book about successful living to provide a wealth of resources and information that can immediately begin improving your life."

— Randy Williams, Founder/CEO, Keiretsu Forum, world's largest angel investor organization.

A PLAN *for* LIFE

The 21st Century Guide to Success in Wealth, Health, Career, Education, Love, Place... and You!

ERIC C. WENTWORTH

Charles Stephen Publishing
1 Blackfield Drive, Suite 175
Tiburon, CA 94920
415-516-9342

First Print Edition
Cover design by Fabrizio Romano

Library of Congress Cataloging-in-Publication Data
Wentworth, Eric
A Plan for Life: The 21st Century Guide to Success in Health, Wealth, Career, Education, Place, Love...and You!

Includes index.
ISBN-10 0991198301
ISBN-13 978-0-9911983-0-6
1. Success—Guidance and resources. 2. Health. 3. Personal finances. 4. Career
5. Love. 6. Motivation. 7. Education. I. Title

LCCN 2014905550

Acknowledgements

As this book took several thousand hours to research and write, I want to thank all those friends and relatives who supported and encouraged me along the way...and those thought-leaders who provided their time, practical knowledge or inspiration. It's a more valuable book for their participation.

Many thanks to my wife Carol Ann, who believed in the value of this work from the beginning, for her never-wavering support and love. Also, thank you to my bright and beautiful children Jack, Cristina, and Trent...all of whom are already meeting the challenges of the 21st Century with creativity and courage.

I'm especially thankful to my friends and family: Michael Wentworth, Bill Howard, Ron Nash, Larry Mindel, Greg Jones, Lee Shonka, Nancy and David Padberg, Steve Allen, Mara Quigley, Peter Engler, Bruce Janigan (aka Avery Mann), Randy Williams, Dee McCrorey, Marci and Dick Bolles, Peter Kleinbrodt, Del Langdon, Patti Wilson, Fabrizio Romano, Debra and Richard Barta, Patrick Schwerdtfeger, LeiAn Lynch, Debby and Jerry Derloshon, Violet and Charles Wentworth, Eileen Wentworth, Dorothy and Harold Stenzinger, Michelle Van Otten, John Blecka, Steve Grant, Teri Wentworth, Joy Nordenstrom, Christy Shonka, Marsha and Chuck Rauenhorst, Dave Lent, Cheri Charland, Susan Burgess, Joanne Fine, Joshua Engle, Jerry Jampolsky MD, Diane Cirincione Ph.D., Steve and Mary Beth Garber, Mike O'Neill, Mike Rose, Mary O'Mara, Sally Williamson, Brad Frederickson, Victor Hugo Zayas, Carter Bennett, John Benus, Elaine and Bill Petrocelli, Caral Newman, Marky Stein, Jacqueline Wentworth, Amy Frost, Amanda Pirot, Jett and Dan Gulbronsen, Sarah Hyde, Mia and Jeffrey Allenstein, David Bennett, David Varnai, Holly Seeler, Lynn and Mark Garay, Neal Gibson, Nancy and Mark de Gorter, Richard Feola, Janet Bonanno, Sandra Kurtz, Susan and Kenneth Vonderahe, Rita Becker, Tony Mariscal, Helene de Boissier-Swanson, Mary Beth Bond, Todd Padberg, David Varnai, Kimberly and Peter Brooks, Dave Duffin, Nancy and Jim Palazola, Marla Burgess, Ann Grassel, Deborah Royston, Jeremiah Treacy, Darren Jacklin, Paolo Salcida, Eric Hammel, Christine Torrington, Terri and Tom Bednarcyzk, Jeffrey Axelrod, Ciji Ware, Peggy and Dan Shonka, Ron Filson, Francie Rehwald, Steve Banks, Dr. Lynn Joseph, Mark Lion, Cory and Sarah Henke, Teddy Shonka, Diane Tishkoff...and to several key authors and thought-leaders, including Po Bronson, John Kremer, Clark Howard, Anthony Robbins, Lori Marrero, Seth Godin, Guy Kawasaki, David Schwartz, Dr. Martha Stout, Zig Ziglar, Jack Canfield, Tim Ferriss, Jim Carrey, Eckhart Tolle, Richard Florida, Michael Pollen, John Gray, Roger Ebert, Ryan D'Agostino, Dr. Mehmet Oz, Daniel Solin, Thomas Friedman, Brian Tracy, Larry Winget, John C. Maxwell, Nolan Bushnell, Dr. Jonny Bowden, Robert Shiller...and to Steve Allen Media, North Bay Networking Group, University of Missouri School of Journalism, Santa Barbara Writer's Conference, California Writers Club, Bay Area Independent Publishers Association, and my good writer friends of Algonquin West.

CONTENTS

Author's Notes

Everyone wants to live their best life. The need for love, good health, wealth, an interesting career, adventure, knowledge, and a meaningful existence is a universal quest. It's also an elusive quest, one that few will fully attain.

- According to a recent Gallup poll, **fewer than 6% of all people are happy with every area of their life**...and only 2 in 3 are happy in one of the major categories that make a fulfilling life: Health, Wealth, Career, Education, Place, Love and, of course, You.

The only hope of realizing your dreams is to have the knowledge and resources available to make it happen.

And a plan.

For life.

Life has become exponentially more complicated in the 21st century, which is why A Plan for Life is a very big book...with hundreds of support resources, including links to websites, videos, apps, and recommended books for more information or support. You'll find what you need to create your own personal plan in A Plan for Life and at www.APlanForLife.com.

A Plan for Life is offered as both an ebook and in a print version. Every year the book will be updated with new information. Anything in the book that is outdated or found to be incorrect will be changed.

For continual updates of new information on each of the subjects in A Plan for Life, go to www.APlanForLife.com. Also, you may want to subscribe to our Twitter feed @APlanForLife, "like" our Facebook page, "follow" our LinkedIn page, and find valuable resources on Pinterest and Tumblr.

My goal is to provide you with the latest information, tools, resources, and guidance to make your life more successful in every way in the 21st Century.

A big trend now is crowdsourcing and interactive communication. In this book I recommend many other books, websites, and blogs that feature new ideas and information that can help you adapt to the fast-changing realities of 21st Century life. I encourage you to check out what these thought-leaders have to say. If you have any comments, helpful suggestions, new information or constructive criticism that will make A Plan for Life more valuable to my readers, email me at eric@APlanForLife.com. Let's face the future together.

Introduction

"This is your one and only precious life. Someone is going to decide how it is going to be lived. That person had better be you." — Stan Slap

2000. It seems so long ago.

Since the beginning of the 21st Century the world has fundamentally changed. Forever. Nothing will ever be the same as we knew it just a few short years ago.

The Great Recession. Facebook. GMOs. Twitter. Government gridlock. Apps. Smartphones. LinkedIn. Ebooks. Crowdsourcing. Skype. You Tube. Instagram. Outsourcing. The Tea Party. Pinterest. Selfies. Barack Obama. Ebooks. Blogging. Wars in Iraq and Afghanistan. Drones. Video games. Texting. Osama bin Ladin. Nintendo Wii. Climate change. Online education. Texting. iTunes. Tumblr. Internet dating. iPad. Tesla. HD flat–screen TV. Student debt. Online porn. Legal marijuana. Gay marriage. GPS. Spotify. The Affordable Care Act. Sony Playstation 3. Wall Street crooks. 9–11.

And so on. So far the 21st Century is proving to be a wild ride. Imagine what the years ahead will bring.

- Americans face more disruptive change than at any other time since the Industrial Revolution.
- A convergence of macro forces in the next 20 years will fundamentally change the world.

✓ During the next 20 years the population of the world will increase by 2 billion…as many people as were on the planet just a hundred years ago.

✓ Increased automation, technical efficiency, and the use of robots will eliminate tens of millions of jobs as the technological revolution continues at breakneck pace. The 2013 McKinsey Global Institute study estimates that 230 million white collar jobs will disappear or be transformed in the next decade.

- ✓ The price of food, land, healthcare, housing, transportation…nearly everything…will increase at the same time that most wages remain stagnant.
- ✓ The upper 1% of the world's wealth–holders will continue to see their fortunes increase…with less for the bottom 99%.

The massive changes that have occurred since the 21st Century began will pale in comparison to what is ahead. Those who adapt to these changes will thrive. Those who don't face a bleak future.

A Plan for Life is your guide to making the future work for you.

A PLAN FOR LIFE…IT'S NOT YOUR FATHER'S SELF–HELP BOOK

My former teacher at the University of Chicago, the Pulitzer Prize film critic Roger Ebert, once said, "Have you ever noticed how many self–help books are limited to the insight expressed in their titles? You look at the cover, you know everything inside. The rest is just writing."

It's true that many of the "self–help" books take a single theme and work it to death. It's because there isn't much substance beyond the promise of the book's title. To paraphrase Gertrude Stein, "There isn't much there there." Most books of this genre provide only a few actionable directions or resources to help you plan and live life at a time when living is more complex than at any other time in history.

Most self–help, motivational, and "inspirational" books keep you tantalizingly out of reach of achieving what you want in life. It's a never–ending quest. And another opportunity for the author to sell you a book, give another seminar or conduct another workshop. Actual life–changing results are elusive.

A Plan for Life is designed to provide the guidance and resources to make real change happen in your life…so that you can meet the challenging 21st Century head–on, armed with the knowledge and tools to make it a success. And create your own plan for a successful life.

Admittedly, real change isn't always easy to do. It takes discipline and sustained effort. If you are a self-help "junkie" who doesn't want to put in the self-examination and hard work to really change your life, this book may not be for you.

THERE'S NO "SECRET" TO A SUCCESSFUL LIFE

"Life isn't about finding yourself. Life is about creating yourself."
— George Bernard Shaw

Po Bronson, bestselling author of *What Do You Want To Do With Your Life?* said this about *The Secret,* the international bestselling book and video that features an array of self-help gurus talking about the Law of Attraction. "*The Secret* makes false claims that you can just dust off your fantasies and live your dream. This is selling transformation irresponsibly." He calls these wishful thinking books "the modern dream machine industry."

Be honest with yourself for a moment. If people could simply use their mind to "attract" fame, fortune, and good health, wouldn't we all be famous, rich, and perfect? But we're not. And that's why the "self-help" industry rakes in nearly $12 billion annually. To feed those fantasies.

Well, the 21st Century isn't a time for wishful thinking, it's a time for purposeful doing.

"You need a plan to build a house. To build a life it's even more important to have a plan." — Zig Ziglar

Liz Gilbert, author of *Eat, Pray, Love*, mirrors my own feelings when she said, "I'm very wary of anyone who comes along with a message and says, 'It's very easy. All you have to do is read my book and take my seminar, and change your manner of thinking. I think if that was necessarily true, then none of us would ever have lost a loved one to cancer. There would be no death, there would be no suffering, and there would be no injustice. When people read the book or take a seminar they get that first wave of euphoria where they think, 'Oh I want to change my attitude. I want to change my life,' then two weeks later, surprise, their life is still the same. Then they feel worse about themselves." Gilbert continues, "There are self-help books that are beneficial to people and there are self-help books that are written by opportunistic idiots who do nothing."

"Without goals, and plans to reach them, you are like a ship that sets sail with no destination." — Fitzhugh Dodson

A Plan for Life offers something that is in short supply in 95% of the self–help, self–improvement, empowerment books—sound, factual, logical advice, resources, and direction to help you achieve control over the key areas of your life.

✓ Advice that is proven to work.

✓ Advice from the top experts—past and present.

✓ Advice that will make a real difference in your life.

✓ Advice you can use **now** to create <u>your</u> Plan for Life.

THE BEST THINKING OF THE BEST MINDS

"Employ your time in improving yourself by other men's writings so that you shall gain easily what others have labored so hard for."
— Plato

A Plan for Life includes sound advice and cutting–edge resources to achieve success in the seven key areas of your life: HEALTH, WEALTH, EDUCATION, CAREER, LOVE, PLACE, and YOU.

✓ You will learn how to spot and avoid the people who can ruin your life…the narcissists, toxic personalities, sociopaths, the boss from hell, and emotionally unstable.

✓ Discover how to get control of your finances and earn more money.

✓ Enjoy satisfying relationships.

✓ Get fit and healthy.

✓ Why it's important to be a continual student in order to succeed.

✓ Why your "personal brand" is important—and how to develop one that works for you.

✓ Find out why where you live can be the most important decision of your life.

✓ Learn what it takes to succeed in your career during the 21st Century.

YOU CAN'T LIVE LIKE YOU'VE LIVED BEFORE

"There is a time when we must firmly choose the course we will follow, or the relentless drift of events will make the decisions for you."
— Herbert Prochnow

The world is changing in fundamental, significant ways that will impact everything you will do for the rest of your life. Many of the old rules no longer apply. Those who do not adapt to the new way of living in the 21st Century may squander their life. You cannot just hope for the best. You cannot close your eyes to the change that's going on all around you.

"If we worked on the assumption that what is accepted as true really is true, then there would be little hope for advance." — Orville Wright

- Jim Rohn, author of *7 Strategies for Wealth and Happiness*, writes, "Your life does not get better by chance, it gets better by change." This will require an acceptance to self–examine your deepest held beliefs and ingrained habits.
- Deepak Chopra, author of *Super Brain*, has said, "Every time you are tempted to react in the same old way, ask if you want to be a prisoner of the past or a pioneer of the future."

"It is not the strongest of the species that survive, nor the most intelligent, but the one most responsive to change." — Charles Darwin

Succeeding in the 21st Century will be more challenging than at any time in modern history. You'll need to constantly gather information, ask questions, evaluate your actions, and adjust your goals…like a sharpshooter hits a target by adjusting his sight for wind, elevation, distance, and weather conditions. Your Plan for Life must be flexible enough to change as change occurs.

SCHOOLS DO A LOUSY JOB OF TEACHING YOU ABOUT LIFE

"Experience is a hard teacher because she gives the test first and the lesson afterward." — Vernon Sanders Law

Most of our schools, colleges, and universities do a poor job (or none at all) of teaching students about the life skills that will affect their future success and happiness. Traditional schooling is rooted in the 20th century, not the new realities of the 21st Century. As a result, a large percentage of graduates have no clue about what it takes to succeed in life.

They've likely never been taught how to effectively look for a job (and then succeed in it) or how to avoid the major pitfalls of life like divorce or choosing the wrong career. Few learn how to create a career based on their passion. They don't know how to stay healthy and fit or manage their finances. They have no idea how to create a winning personality...or a distinctive personal "brand." They've been programmed from childhood by the established rules of our society to choose a linear path...school, job, marriage, kids, retirement, etc...so that most people rarely question their life journey.

PARENTS LACK THE SKILLS TO TEACH THEIR CHILDREN HOW TO SUCCEED

Parents often lack the knowledge to teach their children important life skills. They frequently model poor examples for their kids to follow. Young people are often left to fend for themselves in an increasingly complex world. Millions face broken dreams, shorter lives, disappointing careers, unsatisfying relationships, and financial distress. They feel their life has little or no purpose. And the cycle of diminished dreams continues into another generation.

YOU'LL NEED TO BREAK OUT OF YOUR COMFORT ZONE

"Re-examine all you have been told at school or church or in any book, dismiss whatever insults your own soul." — Walt Whitman

Often people refuse to consider any input that contradicts their firmly held (and safe) beliefs. Psychologists call this "confirmation bias." It's the tendency to notice data that confirms your existing attitudes and beliefs and ignore or discredit information that challenges them. It is the primary reason why we make poor choices in life.

"Open your mind and clear it of all thoughts that would deceive."
— *A Course in Miracles* by Dr. Helen Schucman

John Krumboltz Ph.D., a Stanford professor, has demonstrated that beliefs and cognitions play an important role in success. In his book *Luck is No Accident: Making the Most of Happenstance in Your Career and Life*, he argues that being open and flexible to new ideas and changing circumstances provides the most opportunity to succeed.

Do your beliefs, habits, and attitudes serve you well in the pursuit of your dreams? Or are they holding you back?

YOUR EMOTIONS CAN SIDETRACK YOU

When humans encounter new information they usually see it first with their eyes. It is then processed through the limbic system where it is infused with emotions and sent to the brain for final sorting and analysis. It's at the emotional stage that you can be sidetracked. It's here where fear, indecision, resistance, and poor decisions are formed.

To break the patterns of thought and behavior created by your parents and schoolteachers you'll need to overcome natural human cognitive dissonance—the emotional discomfort in holding two conflicting beliefs—that resists new information, new ways of living, and challenges to your ingrained, safe beliefs.

JUST WHO ARE YOU ANYWAY?

"If I were required to put it into a single sentence of my own explanation of the state of our hearts, heads and nerves, I would do it this way: We are vaguely wretched because we are leading half-lives, half-hearted, and with only one-half of our minds actively engaged in making contact with the universe around us."
— From *The Decline of Pleasure* by Walter Kerr

Honest self-examination is the first step to break the bonds of ingrained beliefs and habits that may no longer be relevant to your life. Cognitive therapy with a skilled psychologist or life coach is one method to "step outside yourself."

"People don't want to hear the truth because they don't want their illusions destroyed." — Frederich Nietzsche

If that isn't an option, write down every belief about yourself and others that you think define who you are as a person. Then question each one rigorously. Most people will discover that they are who they are because that's how they were raised. If you're a Democrat it's likely your parents were as well. If you hate minorities, it's likely your family or friends do too. If you are lazy, I'll bet most of your relatives and friends are non–achievers too.

Everyone is born a blank slate that society begins writing on as soon as you take your first breaths. If you want to change your life, it's essential to wipe that slate clean of anything that is holding you back from achieving your dreams. As Socrates said, *"A life unexamined is a life not worth living."*

IT'S NEVER TOO LATE TO START THE REST OF YOUR LIFE

"The two most important days in someone's life are the day that they are born and the day they discover why." — John Maxwell, author of *The 15 Invaluable Laws of Growth: Live Them and Reach Your Potential*

Don't let age deter you from achieving your dreams. It's never too late to begin. The average age of entrepreneurs who start successful ventures is 39. If you are 40 you likely haven't even hit the halfway mark in your life…and have at least another forty years to live the life you've always dreamed of living.

THERE'S NEVER BEEN A MORE IMPORTANT TIME TO GET IT RIGHT IN LIFE

"The only person you are destined to become is the person you decide to be." — Ralph Waldo Emerson

When I first began researching this book in 2006, the American economy was in expansion mode and employment was a low 4.5%. Americans had weathered the 2000 recession, the Dot Com Bubble, and terrorist attacks on the World Trade Center and Pentagon. Life in the United States wasn't perfect, but the American Dream seemed to still be alive and kicking. The storm clouds on the horizon—the impending economic meltdown—went largely unnoticed, even by the "experts."

In hindsight, many worrisome signs and indicators pointed to serious future problems, but America was too distracted to see them. Almost without exception, America's 30,000 economists and highly paid financial gurus were as clueless about the real state of the economy as the average person on Main Street.

The nation was sucker-punched by the most serious economic crisis since the Great Depression, with millions suddenly losing their job or being ejected from their foreclosed upon home. Once formidable corporate names like Lehman Brothers, Circuit City, and Arthur Anderson went bankrupt with alarming speed. Even General Motors, once the largest auto manufacturer in the world, nearly went out of business (only to be successfully bailed out by U.S. taxpayers). As the old maxim proclaims "As General Motors goes, so goes the country." Unfortunately, it was true.

Seemingly overnight household wealth in the United States declined by an astonishing $11,200,000,000,000—that's eleven trillion, two hundred billion dollars. The economy of the United States—and the rest of the world—teetered on total collapse. While it's possible the economy could relapse in the next few years, it now seems more likely that what we face will be slow uneven growth, economic stagnation, and high unemployment.

POOR IS THE NEW MIDDLE CLASS

- Fully 77% of Americans say it is Very Difficult or Difficult to get ahead, according to a 2012 Pew Research Center survey.
- 1 in 3 now self-identify as being in the "lower class" as do 39% of Americans 18 – 29.

Millions have lost their homes in foreclosure. Millions more have lost their jobs. Millions receive unemployment assistance. Millions have been forced into bankruptcy. And millions depend upon food stamps for enough food to survive. Welcome to the 21st Century.

➢ Census data released in December, 2011 show that 48% of Americans have fallen into the poor or low-income categories...146.4 million people. It's so bad that nearly 1.6 million children experienced homelessness at some time in 2011 (the highest in U.S. history), according to the National Center on Family Homelessness.

➢ A Washington Post/ABC poll in 2012 found that only 1% of the population thought our economy is in Excellent condition (most likely the 1% of Americans who now own about half the wealth of the nation). 84% of Americans thought the economy is Not So Good or Poor.

NEARLY HALF OF AMERICA IS STRUGGLING

"Bad times have a scientific value. These are occasions a good learner would not miss." — Ralph Waldo Emerson

Henry Blodgett, CEO of *Business Insider*, believes it will be 20 – 25 years before the U.S. economy fully recovers...and that's if our leaders do everything right. The amount of debt from corporate, private, and government sectors, according to Blodgett, is near $50 trillion dollars. That is a LOT of debt to pay down.

Yahoo Finance reported in 2012 that many economists now consider an unemployment rate of 7% – 8% to be the "new normal." A report issued by former President Bill Clinton's economic commission estimates that we may not see a significant change in the unemployment rate until 2023!

America has BIG problems to solve, yet our government is beset by mediocre career politicians who seem to be unable to get beyond their corporate sponsors, ideology or personal ambition to actually do what's best for America. Don't expect help from the government—your life is up to you alone.

AMERICANS ARE WORKING HARDER BUT GETTING LESS

America has the most valuable workforce in the world. But in the aftermath of the multi–trillion dollar economic meltdown, this national resource is being wasted.

- Millions are out of work.
- Millions are under–employed in jobs that don't fully utilize their skills.
- Millions have seen their savings and investments vanish—resources they could have used to create greater abundance for us all by purchasing goods and services, starting new businesses, or developing new products—the very things that create jobs.

And while the top 1% gets richer, the rest of the population gets poorer. The typical American's take–home wages are flat or have declined during the past 30 years.

- The combined income of the 500 richest people in America exceeds the total income of the lowest 50% of America—155 million people.

The Walton family alone, heirs to the Walmart fortune, are worth as much as the bottom 41.5% of America. The richest 225 people in the world are worth $1.5 trillion! Nobel Prize winning economist Robert Schiller believes income inequality is one of America's top long-term challenges.

GOOD CHOICES = GOOD LIFE – BAD CHOICES = BAD LIFE

"It is our choices that show what we truly are, far more than our abilities."
— J.K. Rowling, author of *Harry Potter and the Chamber of Secrets*

Much of this collective grief and pain could have been avoided by making more intelligent choices in life. In the Bernie Madoff scandal, it is mind-boggling that so many people trusted their entire future (and the fortune of others under their direction) to just one poorly understood investment.

While Wall Street, corrupt government, and greedy big businesses get the brunt of the blame for the economic problems in America, many millions of ordinary people are also complicit—for being greedy enough to suspend their intelligence to gain a few percentage points more return on an investment or purchase a house they could not reasonably afford or buy luxury goods with credit cards to impress their friends. Millions of poorly considered decisions created a "perfect storm" of economic problems we now call the Great Recession.

HEADING IN THE WRONG DIRECTION

As all this financial strife is occurring, Americans are going through other, often self-induced, crises.

- More people are unhappy in their career than at any time in recent history—nearly half want a different job.
- Healthcare costs are the highest in the world, in part due to poor nutrition and lack of exercise.
- Obesity rates are at the highest level ever—2/3 of the population are overweight.
- Americans spend tens of billions treating depression—more than 1

in 10 adults take prescription antidepressants.

- The average 65–year old takes three or more prescription drugs. America is the most medicated nation in the world.
- Despite being the wealthiest nation in the world (even with the Recession) more people are unhappy than ever before—America is the most depressed advanced nation in the world.
- Internet match–making sites are used by millions to meet their "perfect" mate, yet nearly half of all marriages end in divorce.
- The amount of sex enjoyed by adults in the U.S. has declined precipitously in the past decade (although watching others have sex online is at record levels).
- Education in America is in crisis mode—nearly half of all students don't graduate from high school.
- Our standard of living is declining for the first time since the Great Depression…young Americans will be the first in nearly a hundred years who will likely experience less success than the preceding generation.

For many the American Dream is becoming a nightmare.

I don't want to scare you, but facts are facts. In 21st Century America (2011):

- 1 in 6 Americans lives in poverty.
- Half of American families are now classified as poor or low–income.
- Among advanced nations, only Mexico has a higher rate of child poverty (U.S. 21.9% vs 24.8% for Mexico).
- Only college grads have seen real wages increase since 1979.
- CEO pay was 39 times the average worker's in 1979. Today it is 425 times.
- The average annual compensation for Fortune 500 CEOs was $40 million dollars in 2010.
- Nearly three–quarters of a million people (771,000) have simply given up looking for work.

- There are 610,042 homeless people in the U.S (2013).
- For 68% of seniors Social Security is their primary source of support—averaging $1,200 a month.
- 73% opt to take Social Security early, mostly for financial reasons.
- 40% of Americans ages 36 and older are at risk of running out of money in retirement.
- 92% of Americans agree that the U.S. retirement system is facing a crisis.
- There have been more than a million bankruptcies every year since 2000.
- 1 in 6 Americans do not know where their next meal will come from (1 in 4 children).
- 2 million Americans are in prison or jail.
- 7 million Americans are on probation.
- Every week 54 children are expelled from school for bringing a gun to class.
- While social programs and education are experiencing deep cuts, the defense budget has increased to more than half a trillion dollars a year.
- America spends more money on "defense" than all other nations in the world combined.

Sources: Stanford University, Pew Research, and the U.S. Census Bureau.

Depressing, isn't it. But it doesn't have to be this way.

IF YOU DON'T PLAN YOUR LIFE, SOMEONE ELSE WILL DO IT FOR YOU

"Always dream and shoot higher than you know you can do. Try to be better than yourself." — William Faulkner

If you don't create your own *Plan for Life*, chances are you'll end up living someone else's plan for you. Without a plan, you become a captive of random events.

- Economist Laurence J. Kotlikoff and financial writer Scott Burns, authors of *Spend 'til The End: The Revolutionary Guide to Raising Your Living Standard—Today* and *When You Retire and The Clash of Generations: Saving Ourselves, Our Kids, and Out Economy*, say "Collectively, we like to fly blind. We hop into our life, gun the engine, race down the runway, and take off without any notion of where we are going—or how we will get there."

Not only do people rush headlong into life with little practical knowledge, only rarely do they set goals or make life plans. The vast majority drift through life like a leaf in a stream following the current to wherever it happens to take them—and occasionally getting hung up on a rock. Or, all too often, sink to the bottom.

A MAN (OR WOMAN) WITH A PLAN—CAN

"It's a sad day when you find out that it's not accident or time or fortune but just yourself that kept things from you." — Lillian Hellman

It's well established that people with a definite plan for their lives are happier and more successful than those who do not. Yet fewer than 3% set goals or make plans, according to Brian Tracy, author of *The Life Planning Process*. And just 1% review their goals and plans daily.

There are many reasons for indecision when it comes to making the hard choices in life—fear, laziness, and lack of knowledge about how to face the many challenges ahead. It's why so many take the easy path and simply do nothing, hoping that "luck" will take care of their life. It's the lottery approach to life—with the same odds for success.

PLAN TO SUCCEED IN LIFE

"If you don't know where you're going, you'll end up someplace else."
— Yogi Berra

More than four dozen major studies have confirmed the importance of setting goals and making plans in order to achieve success. People with goals and plans succeed 50% more often than those who just wing it, according to a 2012 Dominican University study.

In his book *The Slight Edge*, author and motivational superstar Jeff Olson says "there is no magic bullet, quick fix, or quantum leap method to success." Americans want things fast. Patience is a lost virtue. But what works are incremental improvements over time following a set of goals and a plan with specific, measurable action steps.

THE DIFFERENCE BETWEEN SUCCESS AND FAILURE IS ALMOST NO DIFFERENCE

"Successful living requires that you devote yourself to fulfilling a worthy life plan." — D. Robert Anthony, author of *Think Big* and *The Ultimate Secrets of Total Self-Confidence*

It's important to remember that the margin of difference in skill, ability, intelligence, and physical capabilities between those who succeed and those who fail in life is actually very small. Even a little extra edge will make you a winner. A well thought out and applied plan can give you that edge.

- The difference between a gold medal and a bronze in the 2009 Olympic freestyle swimming competition was just $1/100^{th}$ of a second.
- The 2011 Indy 500 winner was just 2 seconds ahead of the second place driver.
- The top four finishers at the 2013 Freedom 100 race at Indianapolis Motor Speedway were separated by 0.443 second. Peter Dempsey, the winner, won by 0.0026 second.

It's often the little extra effort, the additional phone call or the few minutes of extra time that makes the difference—that winning edge. A Plan for Life can give you that edge.

ADVICE FROM THE GREATEST MINDS IN HISTORY

"Learn all you can from the mistakes of others. You can't live long enough to make them all yourself." — Eleanor Roosevelt

In the course of researching and writing *A Plan for Life* I read more than 500 books by some of the worlds' greatest thinkers—from Sophocles to Thoreau to Tony Robbins. I read countless blogs and websites. I examined more than a thousand research reports. And I interviewed dozens of experts and ordinary people.

It would take the average busy American many years to find the information that is in this book. And that is one of the primary values of *A Plan for Life*. The "heavy lifting" has been done for you. This book will help you make the decisions that will determine the quality of your life with inspired guidance, hundreds of tools and resources, and the most recent scientifically supported data.

"Men are born to succeed, not fail." — Henry David Thoreau

It's said that to continue doing things the same way and expecting different results is the definition of being crazy. But many people simply don't have the tools or guidance that could change their lives—even when they want to change.

WE ARE WHAT WE MAKE OF OURSELF

"To let oneself be carried on passively through life is unthinkable."
— Virginia Woolf

Ralph Waldo Emerson once said that we are the sum of every decision, large and small, that we make in our life. We are what we make of ourselves. We can't blame our lack of success or achievement or happiness on anyone else—although it's a common enough human trait to do so. And while it's true that a person's life can turn on what appears to be an insignificant choice or a chance encounter, for most people the course of life is a result of our minor and major decisions applied consistently over time—a life plan.

REINVENTING YOURSELF IN A CHANGED WORLD

"Men never plan to fail; they simply fail to plan."
— William Arthur Ward, author of *Fountains of Faith*

Millions of Baby Boomers are now finding that the retirement they have dreamed of is not likely to happen. College grads are discovering that the promise of a good life is only that…a promise, not a guarantee. World events and the changing economy have combined to force a reset to many ambitions. Those with a Plan for Life will be more able to reinvent themselves.

When an architect builds a home the work is guided by a blueprint—a plan. But a good architect always realizes that the owners may want to make the kitchen larger or add another bath or make the windows bigger as their dream home evolves. Think of your plan as your blueprint for life...a guide to building a successful life that is well thought out but flexible enough to adapt to changing circumstances.

THE SEVEN LIFE DECISIONS

"Never look back—unless you're planning to go that way."
— Henry David Thoreau

The seven areas you'll need to make good decisions in to live a successful life include:

1. **Health**

Without good health and fitness it will be difficult for you to achieve success in the other key areas of your life.

2. **Wealth**

People think about money more than anything else in their life—even more than sex. Making it, keeping it, and growing it are important skills that will impact everything you do. Your relationship with money is a key ingredient in a successful life.

3. **Love**

People date haphazardly, even though dating inevitably leads to marriage. Yet, marriage is a decision that can seriously affect your happiness, health, and wealth. Of all the life decisions people make, it's the one that is often made for the wrong reasons.

4. **Career**

The choice of a career is all too often left to chance. Few people understand the importance of career management, how to find the dream job, what it takes to succeed on the job, or how to launch their own business. Yet, your career will be a major factor in determining your lifelong fulfillment and happiness.

5. **Education**

Education is the stepping stone to success for many people. But a college degree isn't a guarantee of success. For many people a college degree isn't even a necessity to living a successful life. However, lifelong learning is now essential to success in our rapidly evolving world.

6. **Place**

Where to live is a decision that most people never give much thought to, even though it can be a major factor in your success and happiness. Too often people just live where they were born (1 in 4 people, according to Pew Research) or happen to find themselves by chance. However, your environment will affect your future significantly, and it ought to be a conscious choice.

YOU

You can have wealth, health, education, and good looks—but if your personality is unattractive or ineffectual you'll find it hard to achieve what you want in life.

If you attain a reasonable amount of success in all these areas, you'll likely be successful in the 21st Century. These determine how happy you will be, how much money you'll make, and even how long you will live.

CREATE YOUR DREAM LIST

"The indispensable first step to getting the things you want out of life is this: Decide what you want." — Ben Stein

First, create your DreamList. These are all the things you would like to do, achieve or experience in life—no matter how outrageous, implausible or unattainable they may seem. Ideally, this should be a list of 50 to 100 things—your "bucket list."

You may want to create a "dream board" that includes photos and quotes to keep you focused and motivated. I suggest Oprah Winfrey's "O Dream Board" or setting up a Pinterest www.Pinterest.com account with "boards" for each key area of life (e.g. Health, Career, Love). Pinning photos and links to more information or resources will enable you to digitally create a rich dream board. Visualization is a key component in making your dreams a reality.

GOALS AND CONTROLS

"Goals are the fuel in the furnace of achievement."
— Tom Hopkins, author of *How to Master the Art of Selling*

I'm a big fan of the late Zig Ziglar, who is perhaps the "father" of practical motivation and goal-setting. Ziglar advocates creating plans from goals with specific action steps and utilizing tracking mechanisms...controls... to monitor progress.

Popular author, speaker, and thought-leader Seth Godin has written that following Zig Ziglar's advice on setting goals literally transformed his life. Godin also references the comprehensive 2002 work by Edwin Locke and Gary Latham, *Building a Practically Useful Theory of Goal Setting and Task Motivation* that reviewed 35 years of empirical research on goal setting, selection, management, and measurement. The conclusion? Goal setting is a vital component to success.

Create three levels of goals.

1. Long-term life goals.
2. Medium term goals (1 – 3 year goals).
3. Short-term goals (Monthly and daily).

Then...

1. Prioritize each goal.
2. List specific Action Steps that can help you reach your goal.
3. Put Due Dates to each Action Step so that you give yourself a deadline to achieve them.

THE PATH YOU TAKE CAN LEAD TO SUCCESS...OR FAILURE

"He who every morning plans the transactions of the day and follows out that plan, carries a thread that will guide him through the maze of the most busy life. But where no plan is laid, where the disposal of time is surrendered merely to the chance of incidence, chaos will soon reign."
— Victor Hugo

BRAD

Don't we all know someone like Brad? Brad couldn't decide on a major in college because he really didn't know what he wanted to do in life. After graduation he spent the money he had received from his relatives wandering aimlessly around the country with a couple buddies. When the money finally ran out Brad took a job at a car rental agency in his home town in order to eat and have a roof over his head. He didn't much like the job and the pay was lousy, but Brad figured it was acceptable employment until he decided what he really wanted to do in life.

One of the other employees was a young girl who had dropped out of high school because of a drug problem. Emily had kicked cocaine but didn't have any other aspirations in life other than hooking up with guys for fun weekends. Brad thought she was cute and had a sexy body. They began dating. Soon Brad and Emily moved in together, reasoning that they could get a better apartment with their combined incomes.

The apartment was a bit depressing, so Brad and Emily overspent furnishing it with nice things they bought on credit. They also purchased—on credit—two expensive new cars. It was an indulgence but they rationalized, "you're only young once."

Emily learned she was pregnant just six months after moving in with Brad. They drifted into marriage mostly at the insistence of Emily's mother. The baby was born healthy but Emily had to quit her job to take care of the infant. Brad soon found it was expensive raising a family and was forced to take a second job working as a security guard.

Brad began drinking and eating to help calm his frazzled nerves. When he wasn't out with the guys at a bar he collapsed on the sofa and watched TV. He gained 40 pounds. Emily also gained a lot of weight. To Brad she looked worn out, frumpy, and plain. She was not the "hottie" he'd dated just a couple years ago. They stopped having sex. Emily was too fatigued. And frankly, neither found the other attractive anymore.

Brad began sleeping with one of the girls he met at the bar he now frequented most nights of the week. The girl wasn't attractive but she was easy and she was available. He couldn't stand the idea of going home to a messy apartment, a colicky crying baby, and a drab wife.

Brad was constantly tired. He began making mistakes at work and missing days. One day he reported to work only to be asked to pack up his personal belongings and leave. The company gave him two weeks pay as severance.

That same day Emily informed him that she was pregnant again.

The story only gets worse from here. But you get the point. Brad made thoughtless, stupid decisions that cost him his life. Perhaps literally.

BRENDEN

Contrast Brad with Brenden. In high school Brenden decided that he wanted to be a home builder. Everything about it excited him—working with an architect to create a beautiful design, locating property to build on, planning the construction. He decided to get both a contractor's license and become an architect—after graduating from college.

Brenden worked with school counselors and his family to select the best university to further his career goals. They found a school that had both a recognized architectural program and also could fast-track him to obtain a contractor's license. Brad applied for, and was granted, a partial scholarship. He augmented this by working summers on a builder's work crew, gaining valuable hands-on experience.

Brenden always put aside 10% of what he earned. By the time he graduated (with honors) he had accumulated enough money to move to Austin. Brenden chose Austin because he liked the small city lifestyle and many recreational activities. He also liked the free-spirited, entrepreneurial people who settled in Austin. It was a market, among many he had researched, that would soon explode in growth.

Brenden researched the major home builders in town and approached the one he felt was doing the highest quality work. He was hired immediately, based upon his grades at school and his clear-minded presentation to them of what he wanted to do with his life.

He soon made many friends and joined several organizations, from the golf club to the leading charity for the homeless. It was there he met David, an older real estate developer who would become his lifelong mentor. David liked Brenden's easy style, ambition, and focus. Brenden reminded him of himself when he was young. David offered him a job soon after they met, but Brenden felt he needed to learn more at the company he was at. Besides, after just six months on the job, he felt he owed it to his company to stay on longer. David expressed disappointment, but secretly admired Brenden for his loyalty and solid character.

About this time Brenden purchased his first home, using some of the money he'd saved as a down payment. It was a small "fixer upper" house, but the mortgage payments were easy to handle from his current income. He used his building skills to plan a restoration that would make the house more livable and add considerable value to it.

Brenden exercised regularly, ate a nutritious diet, didn't smoke, and only drank socially. He made sure he spent plenty of relaxation time with family and friends. He lived a healthy lifestyle, physically and emotionally. It was reflected in his fit physique and high energy level.

Brenden dated several of the young women he met at charity functions or the golf club, but never seriously. He had decided that marriage could wait until he met just the right person and when the timing was right.

Meanwhile, the friendship between Brenden and his mentor David deepened. Despite their age difference, they shared many of the same philosophies about life and business. When Brenden was 25 David approached him with an offer to go into business together. Because he had gotten to know David over time and had come to respect him both personally and as a businessman, Brenden felt confident the two could work together as partners. Brenden and David discussed the pitfalls of partnership, drew up an agreement that covered every possibility they could think of, and then hired an attorney to convert it into a legal arrangement that was fair to both men.

Brenden, unencumbered by a family, and with savings he could now use to support his involvement in their business, was able to focus on making the partnership a success. Within two years the business began showing increased profits. In year three both men earned more money than they had in the previous five years. By year four Brenden was a millionaire.

Their business continued to prosper. Brenden invested steadily in real estate, not understanding or totally trusting the stock market. Soon he owned hundreds of apartments, two shopping centers, and raw land that lay right in the path of Austin's rapid expansion.

Comfortably wealthy by 35, Brenden was still young, full of confidence, free of stress, and able to pursue his many interests. He joined the boards of several charitable organizations, figuring it was his responsibility to give back to a society that had supported his dreams. One organization made micro-loans to qualified, but needy, families. Many of these families purchased their first home from Brenden's company. He became the chairman of the regional food bank, helping less fortunate families get enough to eat. He helped many of the people he met go back to school and get jobs, changing their lives forever. It was very gratifying work. Brenden, without trying to do so, became a pillar of the community, a person who was respected by all.

It was during a food-drive that he met Camille. Of course, Brenden was considered a "catch" by most single women. Despite the many changes in gender relations, a powerful, wealthy, attractive man still appeals to women at a strong primal level.

Brenden and Camille began dating. Camille's beauty, charm, and sensuality appealed to Brenden. He could easily have fallen for her—the physical attraction was extremely strong. But Brenden took his time getting to know Camille. They shared a variety of activities together. He spent time with her family and friends. He admired her keen wit and intelligence, attributes he had long ago decided were important in a future mate. He liked her easy manner, the kindness she frequently displayed, and her personal style. They discussed everything from politics to religion to their feelings about family and children. After several months they slept together, careful to take the necessary precautions.

After two years of steady dating and many shared experiences, the initial heady experience of "falling in love" was replaced by true, deep love. Brenden thought that Camille would make a great lifelong friend and companion as well as a passionate lover and responsible mother to their children. She was mature, educated, and respected. She had a career of her own as an attorney and was financially independent and responsible. Any serious personality flaws would have surfaced by now—and none had.

He asked Camille to marry him and she accepted. A few years later they started a family. After 15 years they are as happy as ever. Their children are well-adjusted, attending good schools, and are exposed to many of the wide range of interests pursued by their parents. Brenden has achieved what nearly everyone wants in life—success, love, a happy family, dynamic career, an interesting life, the satisfaction of giving back, and the ability to live out his life feeling as if it has true meaning.

There are many morals to these stories. But first and foremost, Brenden was smart and responsible about his life. His priorities were in order. He didn't make rash decisions. He had the discipline to do the right thing at each crucial step along the path he had chosen. He knew what he wanted and he went after it intelligently. He had a plan for his life.

Contrast Brenden's life to most others.

- ✓ The majority of people don't get the education they need to realize their dreams. If they go to college at all, the average person graduates with little idea of what they want to do in life.
- ✓ The first job that comes along becomes their career track.
- ✓ They date a few people they meet at random and decide to marry one based upon reasons that range from being "turned on" by the person to "it's time to get married."
- ✓ Children come when they get pregnant, often accidentally and at inopportune times.
- ✓ Money is usually spent on frivolous things, frittered away on unnecessary "stuff" or, in many cases, used to cover a lifestyle they can't afford.
- ✓ Savings are left for the future—which never seems to come.
- ✓ Poor lifestyle choices such as smoking, drinking, and drugs prevent many people from ever having a chance to achieve financial freedom.
- ✓ Instead of using their time to work toward a better life, the average person spends up to 45 hours a week watching television—time that does little or nothing to move them toward their dreams.

DON'T LEAVE YOUR LIFE TO CHANCE

"Since the mind is a specific bio-computer, it needs specific instructions and directions. The reason most people never reach their goals is that they don't define them, or ever seriously consider them as believable or achievable. Winners can tell you where they are going, what they plan to do along the way, and who will be sharing the adventure with them." — Denis Waitley, author of *Psychology of Success: Finding Meaning in Work and Life*

CHAPTER 1
HEALTH AND FITNESS

WHEN YOU'VE GOT YOUR HEALTH, YOU'VE GOT EVERYTHING

"Health is like money, we never have a true idea of its value until we lose it." — Josh Billings

The old maxim "When you've got your health, you've got everything" is still true today. This book leads off with health and fitness because it affects everything you do—from the spouse you attract to job promotions to how long...and how well...you will live. Good health is essential to success in the 21st Century.

Good health is simple. It's mostly a matter of diet, exercise, and good genes. But in the 21st Century it's also become very difficult to stay healthy. In the 20th century we knew little about GMOs, organic food, trans-fats, laboratory-created processed products, factory farmed chickens and eggs, antibiotic injected cows, high fructose corn syrup or the thousands of artificial additives in our food. But now we do.

AMERICA IS A SICK NATION

"The average man has 43.2 pounds of body fat."
— *Men's Health* magazine, 2012

You might be surprised at just how sick our country has become. More than half the population has one or more chronic health problems: cancer, diabetes, heart disease, hypertension, stroke, mental disorder, pulmonary disorder.

Source: Milken Institute, 2003

These chronic health problems cost the U.S. economy $277 billion a year and more than $1 trillion in lost productivity. Most can be mitigated or avoided altogether with simple diet and lifestyle changes.

90% of Americans think they eat a nutritional diet, according to *Consumer Reports* (2010). In reality only 12% do.

A big part of the problem is a national ignorance when it comes to diet and nutrition.

➢ A 2012 survey sponsored by The Associated Press and NORC Center for Public Affairs Research found that an abysmally low number of people are aware of the health risks of obesity...America's #1 health problem.

✓ 1 in 4 people believe you can be both obese and healthy.

✓ Only 15% recognize that obesity contributes to arthritis.

✓ Just 7% know that obesity can cause cancer.

✓ A mere 5% understand that obesity is a major factor in respiratory disease.

✓ Few know that obesity is a major contributing factor in high blood pressure, high cholesterol, and strokes.

✓ Not a single survey participant knew that obesity can result in infertility.

The American diet has morphed in recent years into an over-processed, high-fat, high-carb, low-fiber, sugar-coated disaster. And most people today "live" on this diet without giving a thought to what is happening to their body.

Our nation is so nutritionally illiterate that few people realize that a typical meal at McDonald's (Cheeseburger—500 to 750 calories, large fries—570 calories, large Coke—370 calories) takes an entire day of hard labor to work off. It takes *3 ½ hours* of brisk walking just to burn off the 500 calories in a single piece of cherry pie. Or 5 hours to walk off the 780 calories (and 47 grams of fat) in just two slices of Domino's pepperoni pizza.

This deep and pervasive ignorance about personal health is one reason why the United States now ranks #50 in longevity among the worlds' nations. Despite the highest per capita health care expenditures in the world, America is essentially a sick nation.

TAKE CONTROL OF YOUR HEALTH

Most of the things you have the highest odds of dying from are also things you have the most control over. More than half (55.8%) of Americans, according to the Milken Institute, will die from one or more of these seven diseases: cancer, diabetes, heart disease, hypertension, pulmonary disease, and stroke.

Most healthcare experts agree that only about 40% of your health, rate of aging, and longevity are a result of your genes. The other 60% is in your control. The quality of your life...and even when you leave this life...is in your hands.

START WITH THE BASICS

Let's start with the basics of good health.

- Eat right and not too much—mostly vegetables, fruit, whole grains, and fish (and a little lean meat). Organic. Non-genetically modified. No, no, no, fast food or "fake" manufactured food.
- Maintain the ideal weight for your age, height, and body type. This is likely less than you currently weigh.
- Be physically active and incorporate both cardiovascular exercises and resistance exercise into your life—and do this at least five days a week.
- Get plenty of sleep and restorative rest—seven hours minimum (30% of Americans get six hours or less).
- Practice good hygiene. Wash your hands—and other parts.
- Take a good quality multi-vitamin, some extra Vitamin D, and a high-quality fish oil capsule a few times a week. More is not better with vitamin supplements.
- If your doctor recommends it, take a baby aspirin (81mg) every day

after the age of 45. Elderly people who took an aspirin a day for more than two years had a 55% lower rate of dementia, 44% fewer heart attacks, and certain types of cancer were cut by 50%.

- Drive a safe car, fasten your seat belt (15% still don't...resulting in nearly 13,000 unnecessary deaths annually), don't drive fast (nearly 10,000 died from speeding accidents), avoid distractions (more than 3,000 deaths and 400,000 injuries...1.3 million accidents—23% of total collisions—involve cellphone use), and never drive under the influence of drugs or alcohol (9,878 deaths). Total auto traffic deaths: 34,080. Sources: National Highway Traffic Safety Administration, National Safety Council, National Transportation Safety Board (2011)
- Don't work as a fisherman, coal miner, farmer, construction worker, truck driver or lion tamer. More than 4,430 people (nearly all men) died on the job in 2009 (the lowest since 1992 due to the high unemployment rate).
- Exercise caution when doing anything that has the potential to kill you—even climbing a ladder to clean out the rain gutters (falls from ladders kill more than 400 people a year).
- Get married to the right person and stay married (easier said than done).
- Find a career that suits your talents and personality—and potentially compensates you well. And where you feel you have some control over your destiny.
- Learn the basics of money management and invest/spend wisely so that you are financially secure—unlike the 76% of Americans who in 2013 live "paycheck to paycheck."
- Don't smoke (the #1 way to ruin your health).
- Stay away from illegal drugs and potentially dangerous prescription pharmaceuticals (more than 100,000 deaths every year).
- Own a dog or cat (dog owners are more fit, less stressed).
- Live where the air is clean (sorry Los Angeles).
- Live where the water is clean (sorry Jacksonville).

- Live where the crime rate is low (sorry Detroit).
- Don't have more than two or three alcoholic drinks a week (3 in 10 abuse alcohol).
- Get your teeth checked by a competent dentist once a year (only 62% do), brush your teeth at least twice a day (only about half do), and always use dental floss (18% never do).
- See your doctor for a checkup every year or so (78% do). Be aware of any genetic predispositions toward disease. Consider getting a DNA profile (about $99).
- Drink at least five glasses of purified water a day (75% are chronically dehydrated).
- Practice safe sex (only 56% say they always do with a casual partner) and 62% of HIV–positive men have unprotected sex, according to the Centers for Disease Control. Have lots of sex (1 in 5 live in a sexless marriage, 30% of men and 28% of women haven't had sex in the past year).
- Laugh a lot (it boosts your immune system).
- Continue to learn all your life to keep your mind sharp and adapt to the changing economy (75% will need significant retraining in their career).
- Listen to music (reduces stress and anxiety while improving your brain function).
- Do good deeds for others (it can expand mental capacity).
- Meditate or take up yoga (can increase mental capacity).
- Get massages (1 in 4 had one in the past year).
- Make time to relax, engage in a hobby, or just play (lowers stress, increases happiness).

Oh, and be consistent.

That's it. Now you can skip reading the rest of the chapter (I'm kidding—there's lots of great stuff and even a few surprises ahead). Do these things regularly and you have an excellent chance of living a vibrant, injury and disease-free life for eighty or ninety years. This is a pretty good return on your investment, an investment anyone on their death bed wishes they had made.

Ah, but it's not that easy. Human beings have a self-destructive bent that sometimes defies all reason. Put simply, people don't always (seldom?) do the right thing.

WE HAVE MET THE ENEMY...AND IT IS US

Americans are their own worst enemy.

- ✓ More than a third of all Americans—adults and children—are obese—the highest rate in the industrialized world. And we keep getting FATTER every year.
- ✓ Even now, despite overwhelming evidence that smoking is harmful, 20.5% of men and 15.8% of women adults smoke, according to the Centers for Disease Control (2012). Because, you know, throat cancer is so cool. Fortunately, the trend is toward not smoking.
- ✓ About 10,000 people will die on the road because they thought it was OK to drive while intoxicated or drugged. Another 10,000 thousand will perish because they like to speed or run red lights or play chicken at the train crossing.
- ✓ Texting while driving will kill thousands more (pretty sad when your last words are LOL). You are 23 times more likely to be in an accident if you text while driving, according to the Institute for Highway Safety.
- ✓ Some will fall asleep at the wheel...and never wake up. By the way, your lifetime odds of dying in an auto accident are pretty high...1 in 98...and more than 2 million are injured annually, according to the National Safety Council (2012). The average person will be in an auto accident every 18 years of driving, according to the Property Casualty Insurers Association of America.
- ✓ More than 106,000 people will die this year from prescription drug misuse. That's like 83 fully loaded 747's crashing every day of the year. Now if that happened, don't you think there would be outrage, demands for change, and Federal investigations? But year after year, the

pharmaceutical industry gets a free pass. Why? Because prescription drug companies have the most well-funded lobbyists of any industry.

✓ Another 30,000 will kill themselves on purpose (jumping off the Golden Gate Bridge being the perennial favorite...1,000+ and counting) because they didn't get the mental health support they needed.

YOUR HEALTH COSTS

Maintaining good health will affect your financial health in many ways. For example, obesity costs men an average of $2,600 a year in extra healthcare expenses. For women the cost is more than $4,000 a year. The obese spend 42% more on medical care, 77% more on drugs, and 48% more time in the hospital than normal weight people, according to the Centers for Disease Control and Prevention. That's enough to make you sick just thinking about it. Being healthy and fit will save you tens of thousands of dollars in healthcare and insurance costs over your lifetime.

Overweight people also earn less than their slimmer colleagues. When a friend attended a 25-year high school reunion, he realized afterward that the most successful people from his school were all slim and fit. It was a revelation...and gives new meaning to "survival of the fittest."

Unfortunately, employers don't pay by the pound. Yeah its prejudice, but there's not much you can do about it in the real world. Fat is just not where it's at. You are less likely to get a job, a promotion, or make it to a top position if you are overweight...especially if you are a woman.

Add it all up and the costs of an unhealthy lifestyle can be staggering.

AS YOUR WEIGHT GOES UP, YOUR SEX LIFE GOES DOWN (LITERALLY)

"The part can never be well until the whole is well." — Plato

Being overweight can seriously affect your sex life—especially for men. When men gain weight, metabolic changes occur—particularly in hormone levels—that may cause fatigue, mild depression, and ennui—all of these affect bedroom performance.

One study found that 40% of obese men had low testosterone levels. Obese men were also 2 ½ times more likely to suffer from erectile dysfunction than normal weight men. Erectile dysfunction is a precursor (the canary in the coal mine) to heart disease. Poor blood flow elsewhere usually means poor blood flow "down there".

Sexual function for obese women is a problem too. A 2011 study found that overweight women were far less likely than normal weight women to have had any sexual activity in the previous 12 months. In fact, the amount of sex women are having is declining...and tracks the rise in obesity.

Obese women also report a very high level of poor self-esteem, a factor in sexual desire. There's some truth to why overweight women have a poor self-image. One study found that 84% of men would not date an obese woman.

Other studies indicate that being overweight decreases a man's appeal to woman by half. Like men, most women think obesity is a deal killer in a potential mate.

PHYSICAL FITNESS = EMOTIONAL FITNESS

"Exercise is good for your mind, body, and soul." — Pliny the Younger

Physically fit people have fewer emotional and psychological problems—problems that can negatively affect every aspect of life. They suffer from fewer personality disorders than healthy people. They have lower levels of drug addiction, alcoholism, and compulsive disorders. On nearly every level of emotional health there is a positive correlation with physical health.

Healthy people live longer too...between 3 and 10 years on average...giving you more time to achieve what you want in your brief time here on earth. Being fit provides the energy and stamina you need to achieve your dreams...in everything from your career to your sex life (reason enough to stay in good shape!).

Healthy, fit people also marry more successfully. It's imbedded in our genetic makeup to select a mate who is attractive, healthy, and fit. It's Nature's way of insuring the successful propagation of the human species—survival of the fittest. A happy marriage can produce an array of life-enhancing benefits—from how long you live to how successful your career will be.

Everything you do in life is affected by how fit and healthy you are. So it's vitally important to begin your *Plan for Life* with a healthy foundation.

YOU DON'T HAVE TO BE ANOTHER DEPRESSING STATISTIC

"Those who think they have not time for exercise will sooner or later have to find time for illness."
— Edward Stanley, 19th century British statesman

A successful life is all about choosing to live intelligently. The consequences of making poor decisions in your life can be severe. Here's how many years on average you can deduct from your lifespan if you are guilty of doing these:

- Heavy smoking — Deduct 8.7 years
- Inactive lifestyle — Deduct 5.3 years
- Heavy drinking — Deduct 4.7 years
- Obesity — Deduct 2.0 years

Add it up. These negative lifestyle choices can take more than two decades off your life—over 7,300 days. What were you doing two decades ago? Yeah, it's a LONG time.

AMERICA, THE LAND OF THE BUBBLE PEOPLE

Take a look sometime at the photos of World War II army recruits. They are all lean and fit. Compare it to the blubbery teens that join the armed forces today. Today's youth are so out of shape the army has been forced to create a pre–boot camp (known as the Pork Chop Brigade) just to shape them up for boot camp! Record numbers of recruits simply cannot make the grade under any circumstances, already suffering from diabetes, heart disease, and other maladies previously reserved for the elderly.

The three major factors why people were so lean and fit in 1940 are:

1. Americans in the 40's did not eat as much as we do today...in fact, about a third of the population was malnourished by today's standards.
2. There were very few "manufactured" foods, almost no snacks, few sugared drinks, and candy or cake was considered a rare treat.
3. The majority of the population expended more calories working, tending to the house chores, and walking.

In 1950 fewer than 100 million people in the world were obese. Now it's 1.6 billion. In the U.S. alone we have more than 100 million overweight citizens.

In Europe, the locals often describe American tourists as the "Bubble People." It's easy to spot Americans at a train station from the many tourists passing through from other parts of the world. They're the ones with the pillow-size guts, huge rumbling butts, bloated faces, and legs that look like small tree trunks.

1/3 OF ALL AMERICANS ARE OBESE

- In 2012, 1 in 3 adults is obese (10% or more above their healthy weight)...a 70% increase just since 2000.
- More than 1 in 4 children are obese.
- Obesity rates are rising in 31 states. In some states the obesity rate is nearly 50%.
- Five of the most obese states are also among the ten poorest states, an indication that poor nutrition results from lack of knowledge and financial ability to purchase healthy foods.

Obesity is (no pun intended) a growing problem. In places like Mississippi, where 44% of the population are obese, being fat is becoming the norm. Many TV commercials now cast for "overweight" people because they want to depict the "typical" American family.

SIGNS OF RISING OBESITY ARE EVERYWHERE

Beyond dry statistics how do you really know that obesity is a BIG problem in America? That's easy, because the signs are everywhere:

- ✓ Airline seats are now larger than they were 30 years ago.
- ✓ Baseball stadium seats are four inches wider on average than 25 years ago.
- ✓ Liposuction is the most common cosmetic procedure in the U.S.
- ✓ Diabetes rates have risen by 2/3 in the past decade.
- ✓ A woman's size 10 dress today was a size 14 in the 1940s.

- ✓ Doctors use needles that are longer today in order to penetrate thicker layers of fat.
- ✓ 1 in 4 women in their 50s are too large to have their body fat measured with a skin-fold caliper.
- ✓ The airline industry estimates that the additional fuel costs to fly people who exceed their normal weight is $600 million a year (based upon 2010 fuel costs)!

The costs of obesity to the American economy are enormous. According to the Robert Woods Johnson Foundation, in 2012 it cost $48 billion to treat obesity-related disease and $390 billion in obesity-related lost productivity.

GOOD NUTRITION IS THE FOUNDATION OF GOOD HEALTH

"Don't eat anything that comes in a can or has a label."
— Deepak Chopra, author of *The Seven Spiritual Laws of Success: A Practical Guide to the Fulfillment of Your Dreams* www.deepakchopra.com

You really are what you eat.

We value food primarily for how it tastes. But you also need to think of it as fuel. If you put poor grade fuel into a machine it will not operate as well. It may cause damage to the engine and moving parts. It might even stop working altogether.

In the same way, your body craves good fuel—food that delivers the amount of fluids, protein, carbohydrates, good fats, vitamins, and minerals it needs to operate properly. Give your body good fuel and all the parts will operate better and last longer (guys, that includes your favorite part).

FOOD STORES STOCK VERY FEW REAL FOODS

"Don't eat anything your great-great grandmother wouldn't recognize as food" — Michael Pollan, author of *Defense of Food, Food Rules, The Ominivore's Dilemma* www.michaelpollan.com

The average grocery store stocks a whopping 38,000 products, according to the Food Marketing Institute. Fewer than 5% of the items on grocery store shelves are living foods untainted by artificial additives, genetically modified ingredients, or unhealthy processing. About 80% include some form of sugar (there are 56 different ingredients that are essentially a form of sugar).

Foods that are "alive," that are unprocessed and unrefined—like organic fruits, vegetables, whole grains, lean meat, seafood, dairy, and fowl—will provide your body with high-grade, high-octane fuel. A good rule of thumb is if it doesn't occur naturally in nature, don't eat it. The only exceptions to this rule are minimally processed "natural" foods such as yogurt, cheese, olive oil, and butter.

Life Rule: To eat well you must be very vigilant. ALWAYS read labels.

THE "AMERICAN" DIET

Currently there are more than 80,000 food additives approved for use in the American food supply. Many food additives banned in other advanced countries are still in common use in the U.S.

More than 90% of the food in a typical grocery store did not exist just 50 years ago. "Foods" like Twizzlers and Ding Dongs and Red Bull are recent inventions. These "foods" are high in sodium, preservatives, and the ubiquitous high-fructose corn syrup (Americans eat an average of 13 teaspoons of the stuff every day).

Many ingredients in modern processed foods sound more like the ingredients in rocket fuel. Mono-diglicerides, Polysorbate 80, sodium aluminosilicate, dipotassium phosphate—and so on. The McDonald's McRib sandwich has more than 70 ingredients (other than meat), including one that is also used in making gym mats.

The chemical additives in your food, many derived from petroleum, can be mind-boggling. In *Fast Food Nation: The Dark Side of the American Meal*, investigative journalist Eric Schlosser details the artificial ingredients in a Burger King strawberry "milk" shake. These include amyl acetate, amyl butyrate, amyl valerate, anethol, anisyl formate, benzyl acetate, benzyl isobutyrate, butyric acid, cinnamyl isobutyrate, cinnamyl valerate, cognac essential oil, diacetyl, dipropyl keton, ethyl acetate, ethyl amylketone, ethyl butyrate, ethyl cinnamate, ethyl heptylate, ethyl lactate, ethyl methylphenylglycidate...well, you get the idea. There are an additional 27 artificial ingredients (including solvent).

The typical American diet includes hundreds of potentially dangerous chemicals. While food additive chemicals are in minute amounts, the long-term accumulation can be significant. Even worse, more than 90% of the chemicals and additives in our food have not been tested for safety. Add to these the hundreds of chemicals—bisphenol A, propylene glycol, 4-dioxin, and DMDM hydantoin—found in everyday products like shampoo, makeup, toothpaste, and hair sprays and, well, it's a wonder we all aren't growing a third eye.

The amount of oversight into the safety of these products is appalling. No one knows the long-term effects of food additives because most didn't exist in the human diet until recently. But the increasing incidence of hyper-tension, tooth decay, heart disease, diabetes, autism, and other maladies doesn't bode well for the future. Food should be sustaining us, not killing us.

THE KILLER CARBS

"Americans eat 75 acres of pizza every day." — *Harpers Index*

"Fake" foods are also usually high-carbohydrate foods. Highly refined carbohydrates have become the mainstay of the American diet. The USDA recommends that our diet consist of 45% to 65% carbohydrates. These recommendations were devised in the early 1970s, partially as a result of food industry lobbying. It's no coincidence that the explosion of obesity and diabetes began about that time.

Refined high-carbohydrate foods include donuts, wheat bread, cinnamon rolls, crackers, Vitamin water, Cheerios, French fries, pretzels, white rice, tortillas, ice cream, candy bars, pizza, cookies, soft drinks—most of the items our nation eats in enormous quantities every single day. According to a Harvard physician's article in the *Journal of the American Medical Association* (2010), "Carbohydrates are a nutrient for which humans have no absolute requirement." We get enough naturally occurring carbs (the good carbs) in foods like fruits, grains, and meat.

A high-carbohydrate diet seriously influences the functioning of your metabolism. When you take in carbs your body responds by secreting insulin. The refined carbs cause your blood sugar (sucrose) level to rise, which in turn causes your body to immediately stop burning fat.

Too much blood sugar triggers your body into storing excess energy as fat. Your liver, which normally controls blood sugar, becomes overwhelmed by the sheer enormity of insulin circulating throughout your body. Eventually you become resistant to insulin. So your body pumps out even more of the hormone. The result is you store more fat—and like an addict you crave even more carbs. This destructive cycle is one reason why people in America are fat and diabetes is at epidemic levels.

In his books *Good Calories, Bad Calories* and *Why We Get Fat*, author Gary Taubes makes a strong case for humans being able to live their entire lives without deliberately eating a single carbohydrate (your body makes carbohydrates naturally out of protein, leafy green vegetables, and the animal fat you're burning). The core of obesity isn't fat, but carbohydrates.

SUGAR ISN'T SWEET

"Sugar scares me."
— Craig Thompson, President, Memorial Sloan-Kettering Cancer Center

Another toxic ingredient in the modern American diet is the national addiction to sugar. According to a 2012 article in the *San Francisco Chronicle* by Robert H. Lustig, author of *Fat Chance: Beating the Odds Against Sugar, Processed Food, Obesity, and Disease*, "up to 40% of normal-weight people also manifest some aspect of the medical disorders associated with obesity—high blood pressure, high cholesterol, heart disease, diabetes—and will die of one of these diseases."

He goes on to describe how scientific consensus now points the finger at sugar as being a culprit. "Our daily median consumption of added sugars is 22 teaspoons (nearly 100 pounds annually), yet the American Heart Association recommends we cut back to 6 to 9 teaspoons." The average soft drink contains two or three times this much. A flavored yogurt, which you might assume is healthy, contains around 15 to 35 grams of sugar.

Sugar is difficult to avoid. Of the 600,000 items in the U.S. food supply, an estimated 80% contain added sugars in one form or another. Even baby formula contains high amounts of sugar; Similac formula is 43.2% cane syrup solids and 10.3% sucrose. It's like feeding your baby a milkshake.

THE DIABETES EPIDEMIC

1 in 3 Americans has Type 2 diabetes or pre–diabetes. You can have either even if you are young and at the correct weight for your age and body type. Nearly 1 in 4 don't know they have the disease, according to *Sugar Nation: The Hidden Truth Behind America's Deadliest Habit and the Simple Way to Beat It* by Jeff O'Connell.

The best way to prevent diabetes is to change your toxic lifestyle. That's right...toxic. In 2002 the Diabetes Prevention Program, a major research study, showed that making healthy revisions in diet, exercise, and weight loss resulted in reducing the incidence of diabetes by 58%. The most effective drug to prevent diabetes at that time only reduced the incidence by 31%. Other studies have confirmed these results. Diet, exercise and weight–reduction work in all but a few genetically caused cases.

Unfortunately, the message isn't getting through to the average person... or the medical industry. Instead, the medical community simply devises more (and more expensive) treatments. The pharmaceutical industry is in cahoots with them because they stand to make billions on diabetes drugs. And don't expect to get any serious nutritional or exercise advice from your physician; most are just as ignorant about these subjects as you are. Why? Because, appallingly, they don't teach it at most med schools.

HUMANS DIDN'T EVOLVE TO EAT SUGAR

Over the hundreds of thousands of years of human evolution, sugar was something that simply wasn't a part of the daily diet. Only rarely would ancient humans ingest sugar, and then it was in the form of honey, fruit or dates. As a result, our complex bodily systems have developed without sugar. But since its worldwide introduction during the past 500 years, sugar has become the source of about 1/3 of all our caloric intake. There simply hasn't been enough time for the human body to adjust to sugar, if it ever can.

SUGAR IS ADDICTIVE

Sugar travels many of the same neural pathways in the brain as heroin. The addictive results are similar, which is why it is so difficult to break the sugar habit. Reducing my own sugar habit was easy when I substituted "sweet" healthy foods, like carrots, nuts, fruit, and chocolate with high cocoa content for things like cookies, pie, cakes, and candy. Within a short time I lost my taste for high-sugar foods, even (amazingly) my wife's incredible chocolate chip cookies (OK, almost).

READ LABELS...CAREFULLY

Read the labels carefully. Many seemingly "healthy" foods really aren't. A San Pelligrino Limonata has 33 grams of sugar. A Waldorf chicken salad at California Pizza Kitchen looks healthy but packs 1,290 calories and 84 grams of fat! I advise picking up a copy of the *EAT THIS NOT THAT!* books by David Zinczenko and Matt Goulding. Their books provide extensive food swap information, including calories, fat, sodium, and sugar content of many popular food items.

FOODS WITH MORE SUGAR THAN A TWINKIE

You might be surprised at some foods that often have more sugar than the much reviled Twinkie.

- ✓ Flavored yogurt.
- ✓ Tomato sauce.
- ✓ Granola bars.
- ✓ Fat-free salad dressing
- ✓ Bran muffins.
- ✓ Canned fruit.
- ✓ Smoothies.
- ✓ Breakfast cereal.

Life Rule: Avoid sugar…in all its various forms.

LESS THAN 4% OF THE POPULATION EAT ENOUGH FRUITS OR VEGETABLES

Our food choices have become so distorted that a recent 2009 study by the Center for Disease Control and Prevention found that fewer than 1% of adolescents, about 2% of adult men, and just 3.5% of adult women consume the recommended 3 ½ to five cups of fruits and vegetables a day. Fully 96% or more of our population isn't eating enough of the very food that can have the most impact upon their health.

Here's what's even more unbelievable—the study included jam, jelly, orange juice, and French fries (even the ketchup on the fries) as fruits or vegetables! It's a very sad comment on the American diet that by age two 41% of the vegetables consumed on average by children are French fries!

MAKE THESE FOODS THE FOUNDATION OF YOUR DIET

Your body is like a computer in many ways—garbage in, garbage out. Feed your body right and it will treat you right. Think of everything you eat as either enhancing your health or detracting from it. Nutritionist and author Elisabeth Somer estimates that 50% to 70% of health ills—including heart disease, cancer, Type 2 diabetes, high blood pressure—could be eliminated by choosing the right foods and being more active.

A NEW WAY OF EATING FOR A NEW YOU— YOUR *NEW*TRITIONAL PLAN FOR LIFE

"You are what you eat." — Anonymous

Here's a shopping list of foods to build your *New*tritional Plan for Life—the foundation of a new healthy way of living—and a new you. There's no excuse for deviating from this diet—it's rich with delicious tasting nutritious foods. Discipline yourself to stay with the program for just 60 days and I assure you it will change (and maybe even save) your life.

DARK CHOCOLATE

"What you see before you, my friend, is the result of a lifetime of chocolate." — Katherine Hepburn

Let's begin the Newtritional Program for Life list with a user-friendly food—chocolate. Who knew it could be a health food? And aren't we glad. It proves there is a benevolent God after all.

The flavenoids in cocoa help prevent arteries from clogging up with fatty deposits that lead to heart disease. One study of 114,000 people found that those who ate more chocolate significantly reduced their risk for heart disease. Those who ate the most chocolate had a 37% lower risk of any heart disease compared to those who ate the least amount.

A study published in the *American Journal of Clinical Nutrition*, showed that dark chocolate decreased blood pressure and improved insulin sensitivity in healthy people. In another study released in 2011, the equivalent of two candy bars (45 grams) of chocolate a week reduced the risk of stroke by 20%. Cocoa also contains a healthy dose of magnesium, an important mineral that contributes to heart health.

Chocolate may also help prevent cancer. Preliminary studies indicate that people who ingest a high level of flavonoids (found in chocolate) are less susceptible to developing cancers than those who don't consume them.

A Harvard University study found that dark chocolate may even help you live longer. When compared with those poor souls who ate none, the chocolate eaters lived a year longer (and likely enjoyed their life a little more too).

And, of course, chocolate has long been associated with romance. It's anybody's guess how many marriages, babies, and other fun stuff started with a nice box of chocolates. With between 400 – 500 beneficial compounds, real chocolate could well be a true aphrodisiac. NOTE: Women love chocolate so much that a British survey found that half of all women prefer chocolate over sex.

The Aztec Montezuma, an early chocoholic, reportedly consumed more than 30 cups of cocoa a day, perhaps to better service his 600+ harem (I gotta find that chocolate recipe). Italian researchers found that women who often eat chocolate have a higher sex drive than those who don't.

Eat chocolate with at least 60% cocoa content if you want the benefit of the flavonoids. Typical commercial chocolate is high in fat, sugar, waxes, chemicals, and low in cocoa. Buy the darkest, tastiest, organic bars you can find. If pure dark chocolate is too bitter for you, find a bar that contains nuts and fruits. This will "sweeten" the taste and add antioxidants. Also, stick to about an ounce a day (regrettably about the size of two Hershey's kisses).

BLUEBERRIES

An entire chapter could be devoted to the beneficial effects of eating blueberries. Dr. Mehmet Oz thinks blueberries are so beneficial to good health that he eats them nearly every morning with Greek yogurt. One of the Super Foods, blueberries are packed with phytoflavinoids and contain compounds like anthocyanins that are both antioxidant and anti–inflammatory. Inflammation is to the human body like Kryptonite is to Superman and is a key component in all chronic diseases. Blueberries are your magic potion to help protect against inflammation.

Blueberries help ward off everything from Alzheimer's, Parkinson's, diabetes, heart disease, arthritis, macular degeneration, high blood pressure, urinary problems, glaucoma, and cataracts.

Blueberries are also a memory-protecting food that helps neurons in your brain communicate and connect with one another more effectively. Research by the Laboratory of Neuroscience on Aging at Tufts University has shown that blueberries actually help the brain grow new neurons (maybe we should start shipping them to Congress).

Blueberries are ranked as the highest-scoring healthy fruit, containing not just antioxidants and anti-inflammatory compounds but pterostilbene, a lipid-lowering compound that was found to be superior even to Reversatrol, the healthy-aging compound found in grapes. Pterostilbene in blueberries helps prevent the build-up of plaque in the arteries.

In studies conducted by the University of Illinois, blueberries had the greatest anti-cancer activity of any fruit. Cancer affects one in four Americans, so blueberries should be part of everyone's cancer prevention program. In another study, reported in the *Journal of Clinical Nutrition*, people who ate a cup or more of blueberries every week had a 23% lower risk of developing Type 2 diabetes.

RASPBERRIES

Besides being a superb source of fiber, raspberries are rich in calcium, magnesium, phosphorus, potassium, Vitamin C, Vitamin K, and ellagic acid. The American Cancer Society has studied ellagic acid as a natural supplement that causes cancer cells to die—without affecting normal, healthy cells. While these are only lab results at this time, ellagic acid does have proven antioxidant, antiviral, and antibacterial properties. Raspberries also contain anthocynanins, a natural arthritis treatment. Of all fruits and berries tested, raspberries have the second highest level of anthrocynanins (cherries are first).

NUTS

Nuts should be a part of your diet every day. In 2013, the *New England Journal of Medicine* reported on a study of 120,000 people over 30 years. Those who ate nuts every day were 20% less likely to die during the study.

In 2003, the Food and Drug Administration said scientific evidence suggests that eating 1.5 ounces of most nuts daily may reduce the risk of heart disease.

People who eat the most nuts also tend to have the lowest BMIs—body mass index—a measure of obesity. While high in fat, it's a good fat—and the main reason why nuts are so beneficial to your health. In one study of dieters eating the same number of calories, the group that ate nuts lost more weight.

Peanuts. Peanuts are the most widely consumed nuts in the world and rival other high anti-oxidant foods in their health benefits. One study of peanuts published in the *Journal of the American College of Nutrition* was titled *Eating Peanuts Improves Cardiovascular Risk Factors in Healthy Adults*. That about says it all. Peanuts also help improve the nervous and digestive systems, skin health, and blood sugar levels.

In a study of 64,000 Chinese women, those who ate peanuts every day cut their risk of diabetes by 21%. Even if you're not Chinese (or a woman), a finding this significant shouldn't be ignored if you want to cut your risk of developing diabetes.

WARNING: Obviously, if you have an allergy to nuts, you'll have to forgo this nutritious and delicious addition to your diet.

Almonds are the oldest cultivated nut in the world. They're also one of the most nutritious foods you can eat. Packed with heart-healthy ingredients, almonds can help you reduce "bad" cholesterol and even lose weight (despite their high fat content). Almonds are high in protein and fiber too.

Pecans are an all-American nut indigenous to the United States. Pecans are rich in monounsaturated fat, the same kind of heart-friendly fat found in olive oil. They're loaded with many other nutrients as well... Vitamin E, potassium, phytosterols, fiber, and beta-sitosterol. Pecans, like other nuts and seeds, promote healthy cell membranes. Since your body has about 100 billion cells, you really should give them more TLC.

Brazil nuts are high in selenium, which according to dozens of studies and the Physician's Desk Reference, are high in antioxidant, immunomodulatory, anticarcinogenic, and anti-atherrogenic properties—in layman's language this means it protects your cells, boosts the immune system, and helps ward off a host of nasty health problems like cancer, diabetes, and heart disease. Selenium has been shown to mitigate the negative effects of toxic metals such as mercury and cadmium. It also helps regulate thyroid function.

Cashews are probably the most popular nut due to their slightly sweet taste. Like most nuts they are rich in calcium, magnesium, phosphorus, potassium, copper, and selenium. Cashews are high in protective mono-saturated fats and anti-oxidants that help lower the risk of coronary heart disease.

Pistachios are a good source of fiber. A one-ounce serving (about 50 nuts) contains 3 grams of fiber...more than most fruits and about the same as a bowl of oatmeal. Pistachios are also an excellent source of vitamins B6, A and E as well as copper, manganese, phosphorus, thiamine, carotenoids, and phytosterols.

In one study, after consuming pistachios for three weeks as 20% of the calories in their diet, participants in a double-blind study saw their LDL (the bad cholesterol) drop by 14% and good cholesterol (HDL) rise by 26%. A 2008 study in the *American Journal of Clinical Nutrition* reported that pistachios were found to actively lower harmful cholesterol levels.

Pistachios are rich in antioxidants, which fight potentially harmful inflammation. A Penn State study showed that pistachios increase blood levels of lutein, a powerful antioxidant that can protect against heart disease.

Hazelnuts help reduce cholesterol and can lessen the symptoms of BPH—benign prostatic hyperplasia, the bane of most men over 45. They also contain a nice dose of potassium, magnesium, Vitamin E, and omega-3 fatty acids.

Some nuts, like **walnuts**, also provide a healthy dose of heart-healthy Omega -3s (found mostly in fish such as salmon and sardines). Omega-3s have been studied extensively; foods containing them are now routinely recommended without reservation as part of a healthy diet. In his book *The Omega-3 Connection*, Dr. Andrew Stoller, a Harvard Medical School professor, says current clinical and scientific evidence indicates that eating more Omega-3s appears to improve mood. Omega-3s also help improve brain function and memory.

NUTS ARE HIGH IN ANTIOXIDANTS

Most nuts are high in antioxidants. Here are the antioxidant ratings for the nuts eaten most often in the American diet:

• Pecans	5000	• Peanuts	1500
• Walnuts	4000	• Cashews	1000
• Hazelnuts	3000	• Brazil nuts	750
• Pistachios	2000	• Macadamia	750
• Almonds	1850	• Pine	500

Source: *Men's Health*, 2007

The best strategy is to eat a mixture of nuts—about an ounce a day. For good health, go nuts.

FRUIT

Want to stay very, very healthy your entire life? Eat mostly fruits and vegetables. As the sweeter of these two healthy food groups, fruit holds the most attraction to sugared-up Americans.

Cherries

A *Newsweek* magazine article about healthy foods said, "The day when doctors say 'take 10 cherries and call me in the morning' may not be far off." Cherries are packed with anti-oxidant, anti-inflammatory, anti-cancer healthy aging compounds. Does it get any more positively "anti" than that?

Cherries contain a good portion of both ellagic acid and quercetin. Ellagic acid is touted by the American Cancer Society as being a promising treatment to inhibit tumors caused by certain carcinogens. Even the prestigious Memorial Sloan-Kettering Cancer Center has found ellagic acid to have antiviral and antibacterial properties. Quercetin is also an anti-inflammatory and is especially effective against allergies and asthma.

Apples

I'm sure you've heard that eating "an apple a day keeps the doctor away." It turns out to be true. Dozens of scientific studies have demonstrated the healthy benefits of eating apples. Apples are excellent sources of antioxidants, perhaps exceeded only by cranberries and blueberries among commonly consumed fruits. Eating an apple a day has been shown to reduce the risk of heart attack by 32%. An apple a day lowers your risk of death from stroke by 36%, according to *The American Journal of Clinical Nutrition.*

Apples also reduce the risk of some cancers, lower the incidence of cardiovascular disease, alleviate asthma, and help prevent diabetes. A Mayo Clinic study in 2001 found that just one of the healthy ingredients in apples (quercetin) helped prevent the growth of prostate cancer cells. A Cornell University study of the phytochemicals in apples indicated that the reproduction of colon cancer cells was reduced by 43%. Apples help reduce the risk of lung cancer by as much as 50%.

Apricots

There are few fruits as tasty as a perfectly ripe apricot. Or as good for you. Apricots are packed with skin-nourishing Vitamin A, beta-carotene, potassium, and anti-oxidants. Dried apricots make an excellent snack food—one that even kids like because of their sweet taste.

Avocados

Avocados are one of the Superfoods—a nutrition-packed food that should be part of every diet. While high in fat, it is largely monounsaturated fat (the same as in olive oil). They're also high in beta-sitosterol, which prevents the absorption of cholesterol. Avocados contain Vitamin C, B vitamins, Vitamin K, folic acid, and copper. They are also a good source of potassium, a mineral that helps regulate blood pressure. Avocados rank high in lutein, which acts as an antioxidant.

Cantaloupe

Melons are great for people on diets. They are high in water content and fiber—so they make you feel full fast. They are also low in calories. An entire cantaloupe contains only 275 calories, equivalent to about three bites of New York cheesecake.

Cantaloupes are high in potassium and Vitamin A—both can help lower your risk of heart disease and stroke by lowering blood pressure. A single cup of cantaloupe contains more than 3,000 mcg of beta-carotene, a powerful anti-oxidant that protects against cellular damage and some forms of cancer.

Coconut

People often avoid eating coconuts because of its saturated fat content. But coconut (and coconut oil or coconut juice) is one of the healthiest foods you can eat. Contrary to the popular myth, fats (in moderation) are not evil. In fact, without fats humans would eventually die. In coconuts, about half the fat is lauric acid, which has antiviral and antibacterial properties and is also a heart-protective fatty acid. The only other major source is mother's milk (not yet available at your grocery store).

Virgin coconut oil is said to have an amazing ability to counter free-radical damage, due to its high content of ferulic and p-coumaric acids. In fact, in Indian Ayurvedic traditional medicine, coconut oil is a primary treatment for many skin conditions.

Oranges

Perhaps it's that oranges are so "familiar" to us that they often aren't recognized for the incredible health benefits they offer. Oranges contain more than 60 flavenoids, powerful anti-oxidant and anti-inflammatory compounds. They are an excellent source of Vitamin C, the primary water-soluble anti-oxidant. Oranges provide important nutrients—in a low-calorie (60 calories), easily portable package.

To get the most nutrient value from oranges, consider eating the peel and pulp. The best way to do this is by adding some of the peel (well washed) and pulp to your smoothie recipes. Phytonutrients that promote heart health and lower cholesterol are concentrated in this part of the orange.

Papaya

Papaya is the only natural source of papain, a digestive aid that breaks down protein. As a result, less food settles into the metabolism to become fat, so they are excellent for people trying to lose weight. Papayas are packed with nutrients including Vitamin C (33% more than oranges and 13 times more than apples), potassium, folate, Vitamin E, lycopene, and lutein.

If you haven't eaten a papaya recently (and you probably haven't), add it to your list of Newtritious foods.

Pomegrante and Pomegrante juice

Guys, you may want to begin making pomegranate juice a regular part of your daily diet. After just one month of drinking an 8-ounce glass daily, men reported firmer, longer lasting erections, according to a joint 2007 USC and UCLA study. Pomegranate has an extremely high antioxidant content that helps keep arteries free of plaque—which means increased blood flow to <u>all</u> parts of the body.

Another study found that pomegranate juice may help slow aging and reduce the risk of heart disease and cancer. The antioxidant power of pomegranate juice is due to its concentration of flavonoids—two to three times that of red wine or green tea. At least six credible studies have confirmed the beneficial effects of pomegranate juice on cardiovascular health.

Cranberries

Cranberries are one of those foods (like turkey and yams) that have somehow been relegated to dietary solitary confinement—in this case Thanksgiving. But cranberries are so nutritious they should be part of your diet all year long.

Low in calories and sugar, cranberries contain some of the most potent antioxidants of any fruit. You have probably heard that the antibacterial properties of cranberries aid in the prevention of urinary tract infections. But cranberries also help inhibit the growth of cancer tumor cells associated with lung, prostate, cervical, breast cancer, and leukemia. The *Journal of Agricultural and Food Chemistry* found that cranberries have a higher concentration of phenols than blueberries, strawberries, apples, and red grapes.

Bananas

Americans eat an average of 26.2 pounds of bananas a year—more than apples and oranges combined. Bananas are an excellent source of potassium and fiber and relatively low in calories—about 100. They've long been associated with promoting stomach health and proper elimination. Bananas also lower the risk of high blood pressure, heart attack, stroke and some cancers, according to the FDA.

Bananas can even cheer you up—it's the only fruit to contain the amino acid tryptophan and vitamin B-6. Together these two key ingredients in bananas produce serotonin, the natural brain chemical that alleviates mental depression and boosts mood.

Plums

Plums and prunes (the dried version of European plums) offer powerful antioxidant protection. Plums can help reduce your risk of age-related macular degeneration, a leading cause of vision loss. And, of course, prunes are famous for their high insoluble fiber content and resulting laxative effect. With plums as part of your diet you should be good to go!

Dates

Dates are little sweet–tooth bombs of nutrition. California dates are reasonably low in calories (about 25 calories each), fat–free, sodium–free, cholesterol–free and a good source of dietary fiber, both soluble and insoluble. They also contain respectable amounts of potassium and calcium. While a bit high in carbohydrates, they are natural carbs––not refined.

If you are on a diet or sugar–free program, you know how bad a craving for something sweet can be. Instead of chowing down on a fistful of Gummy Bears, try a few dates.

Watermelon

Watermelon is a nutritional heavyweight (bad pun intentional). A large slice (about 2 cups) provides a third of a day's worth of vitamins A, C, B1, and B6…as well as a good dose of potassium. Watermelon is a rich source of lycopene—even more than tomatoes. Lycopene has been shown to help reduce the risk of heart disease, stroke, and prostate cancer.

Since watermelon is low in calories (about 50 calories a cup) and fat–free, it makes a great "snack." Because watermelon is 92% water, it is extremely filling and a top choice for dieters.

Figs

There is nothing quite like a fresh, sweet fig. A rich source of dietary fiber and phytosterols (great for lowering cholesterol), figs also contain a good dose of potassium and manganese. Figs are low in calories…50 each. When not in season, dried figs are also a nutritious treat.

Persimmons

Persimmons are probably the most overlooked nutritious fruit. When was the last time you stocked up? Right, you've likely never even eaten one.

Low in calories, persimmons are packed with nutrients that help fight disease and regulate body processes. They're rich in phytochemicals such as polyphenolic antioxidants that are similar to the catechins in green tea, and cancer fighting betulinic acids. These ingredients are antibiotic, anti–inflammatory, anti–hemmorrhagic…which means they are very pro–health.

Mangos

More mangos are eaten fresh around the world than any other fruit. But you won't find many Americans eating them. Which is a shame, because mangos are an excellent source of Vitamins A and C, potassium, and beta carotene. Mangoes are low in fat (about 1 gram) and calories (about 110), rich in anti-oxidants, and high in fiber.

COFFEE

Surprisingly, coffee is the single biggest source of anti-oxidants in the American diet. Most people drink coffee because they develop a taste for it—and for the caffeine jolt to the nervous system that enables them to stay stimulated and alert for up to six hours. But coffee is also surprisingly healthy.

Drinking four or more 6-ounce cups of full-caffeine coffee a day reduces your risk of heart disease by 53%, according to researchers at Brooklyn College. In another study, people who drank four cups of coffee daily had a 30% lower risk of diabetes—caffeinated or decaf worked equally well.

Researchers studied nearly 48,000 men for 20 years in the Health Professionals Follow-up Study and found that those who drank one to five 8-ounce cups daily had a 30% lower risk of lethal prostate cancer than those who consumed no coffee. Men who drank at least six cups a day lowered their risk by 60%. Apparently it wasn't an effect of the caffeine in coffee since the results were the same for decaf or regular.

The journal *Hepatology* reports that you can reduce your risk of liver cancer by 41% if you drink coffee every day. There is even evidence that regular coffee drinking may reduce the risk of developing other forms of cancer, such as colon and liver cancer.

An exciting new study by the University of Washington and Rutgers University, published in the *Proceedings of the National Academy of Sciences*, found that caffeine can lower the chance of UV-associated skin cancer by inhibiting a DNA repair pathway, which helps cells die after exposure to sunlight. Other studies confirm these findings. In 2007 nearly 94,000 women took part in a study that found that those who drank caffeinated coffee daily had a 10% lower risk of non-melanoma skin cancer. Those who drank six or more cups of caffeinated coffee a day reduced their risk by almost 40%.

Few pharmaceuticals can make these claims for the diseases they treat. Why, Starbucks is practically a health food store.

SALMON

Salmon is loaded with high quality protein and Omega-3 fatty acids—while being relatively low in calories. Omega-3 fatty acids can help your heart, protect against skin-cell damage and boost your immune system. Eating foods rich in Omega-3s can result in a 37% decrease in the risk of colon cancer, according to the *Journal of Epidemiology.*

A 3-ounce serving of salmon contains just 155 calories, 16 grams of protein, and only 9 grams of fat. In fact, most seafood is high in protein and low in calories. So it makes an ideal addition to any weight-loss program.

Of all the beneficial seafood available, salmon should be at the top of your list. Try to incorporate it into your diet at least once a week. But stay away from farmed salmon. Unlike "wild" salmon, it contains fewer beneficial nutrients—and much higher amounts of contaminants.

MILK

Milk has gotten a bad rap in recent years. Milk, except for the lactose intolerant (50 million Americans), should be considered as a part of every healthy, well-balanced diet. Milk is a cheap form of excellent protein, a healthier form of hydration than soda, and contains vitamin D, magnesium, and calcium.

Drinking a glass or more of milk daily reduces the risk of diabetes by 40%. Milk has also been shown to be effective in reducing blood pressure, which is linked to dementia and stroke. In a study of 2,200 adults age 55+, those with the lowest blood pressure had the highest intake of milk.

Researchers at the Harvard School of Public Health tracked the diets of a half-million people in five countries for six to sixteen years. They concluded that people who drink at least one cup of milk daily had a 15% lower risk of being diagnosed with colorectal cancer than those who consumed less than two cups a week.

Look for organic milk from cows that are grass-fed or pasture-raised, if possible.

SPINACH

Spinach contains ample supplies of iron, Vitamins A, E, B1, B2, and C, selenium, niacin, calcium, phosphorus, fiber, protein, omega-3 fatty acids, and at least 13 different flavonoid compounds that function as antioxidants and anticancer agents...all with almost no fat and just 40 calories per cup.

FLAXSEED

Flaxseeds and flaxseed oil has been valued for its healthy properties for centuries. Flaxseeds are one of the best sources of valuable alpha-linolenic acid (ALA) omega-3 essential fatty acids in our diet. They also contain lignans, which provide protection against some forms of cancer (e.g. breast, uterine, and prostate cancer).

Flax seeds are found in an increasing number of food products. Whole flax seeds are indigestible—so buy ground flax seed or use flaxseed oil.

OATS

Oats are most often ingested by humans as oatmeal, one of the healthiest carbohydrate foods. It contains valuable vitamins and minerals such as selenium, potassium, manganese, zinc, copper, and magnesium. The Vitamin B1 (Thiamin) in oatmeal helps cells' enzyme systems convert oxygen into energy.

High in protein and low in calories, oatmeal is a delicious source of soluble fiber (a blood sugar stabilizer), which makes it an excellent choice for diabetics. Eating a bowl of oatmeal for breakfast can easily reduce cholesterol by 8% to 23% in just a couple months for most people.

EGGS

Eggs are often called the "perfect" food—a completely usable form of protein (6 grams each) providing a wide range of other nutritional benefits. Compared with other forms of protein (especially meat, poultry, fish, protein powders, or "energy" bars) an egg is nature's bargain food, costing about 40 cents for an organic egg from a pasture-raised chicken. Low in calories (about 70), eggs contain healthy levels of tryptophan, selenium, choline, Vitamin B-12 and Vitamin D. Eggs also contain all nine essential amino acids.

Don't avoid eating egg yolks because you are afraid of cholesterol. According to the *Harvard Medical School Guide to Healthy Eating,* no research has ever shown that people who eat more eggs have more heart attacks than those who eat less.

Select organic eggs from local, pasture-raised chickens whenever possible.

- Eggs can also help prevent breast cancer. In a well-reviewed study published in *Cancer Epidemiology Biomarkers and Prevention*, women who ate six eggs per week had a 44% lower risk of breast cancer compared to women who ate only two.

OLIVES/OLIVE OIL

Olives and olive oil play an important role in the Mediterranean Diet, shown to have disease-preventive and healthy-aging qualities. While olives are high in fat, it's the good fat—monounsaturated fats, especially oleic acid. Olives are also a good source of antioxidants and Vitamin E.

According to recent tests, 3 out of 4 foreign Extra Virgin olive oils actually are not extra virgin. I suppose lying about your virginity is an age-old practice. The good news is that American olive oil producers (almost exclusively in California) now produce exceptional olive oil—and all brands tested as Extra Virgin were shown to be accurately labeled.

MUSHROOMS

Mushrooms are low in calories and high in nutrients. Shiitake mushrooms contain powerful ingredients, like ACC, that helps boost your immune system and slows aging, and polysaccharides, which can help ease the pain and nausea associated with chemotherapy.

RED WINE

While all wine has some degree of antioxidant protection, red wine contains the most. Here are the top five (healthy) things drinking a glass of red wine each day can do for you.

1. Strengthens your heart muscle.
2. Helps prevent Alzheimer's disease.
3. Regular wine drinkers have a 34% lower incidence of stroke.
4. Helps elevate good cholesterol levels.
5. Helps protect against lung cancer.

Like chocolate, wine is a health food that proves that life is fair after all.

LEAN, ORGANIC, GRASS-FED BEEF

If you can make the switch to vegetarian you'll likely be healthier and live longer. But that isn't to say that meat is bad for you. It is an excellent source of protein and minerals.

The problem with meat (and poultry) in America is the way it's processed. Ground beef may come from a dozen different sources in the U.S. and, increasingly, from Mexico or New Zealand. The long distance to market, and the multiple opportunities for contamination, can result in a potentially harmful product.

- A recent study (2011) found that half the meat and poultry sold in U.S. supermarkets may be tainted with the staph germ. Salmonella and E.coli have also been detected in ground beef. Every year more than 3,000 people die from these and other food-borne illnesses, according to a 2011 Centers for Disease Control report.

If you choose to eat meat or poultry...

1. Cook your food thoroughly at a temperature high enough to kill most pathogens.
2. Buy local, organic, grass-fed beef or poultry.

GREEN TEA

Green tea is one of the healthiest beverages you can consume.

- A UCLA survey of nine different studies found that drinking three cups of green tea a day reduced the risk of stroke by 21%.
- Another study (of Chinese women) determined that green tea may cut the risk of breast cancer by12%.
- Still another study of overweight exercisers found they lost three more pounds on average when they drank green tea instead of another beverage with the same number of calories.

It seems there's no end to the health benefits of green tea. So, instead of grabbing a soda or beer from the fridge, do yourself a favor and brew some green tea.

MAKE THE SWITCH TO REAL FOOD

"Every day you do one of two things: build health or produce disease in yourself." — Adelle Davis, author of *Let's Get Well* and *Let's Eat Right to Keep Fit*

It may take a while to adjust to including only healthy foods in your diet if you are accustomed to eating fast food, processed snacks, and sweets, but when they stick with it most people eventually prefer the healthier foods.

For in-depth data on the best foods to eat, I recommend reading *The 150 Healthiest Foods on Earth* by Jonny Bowden, Ph.D. www.jonnybowden.com www.jonnybowdenblog.com and *The World's Healthiest Foods* by George Mateljan www.whfoods.com.

ONLY THE NUTRITIONALLY IGNORANT DRINK VITAMIN WATER

Millions of Americans believe "energy" drinks and "vitamin" waters are actually healthy—rather than a sugary and nutritionally-deficient waste of money.

- Since its inception in 1997, the energy drink industry has grown to more than $6 billion in sales—and continues to grow every year.
- Americans get 25% of their daily caloric intake from sugary liquids.

Vitamin-fortified drinks are simply flavored sugar water with a few vitamins of dubious quality added to assuage your guilt about drinking them. It's one of the most successful marketing scams ever.

➢ In 2009 the Johns Hopkins Bloomberg School of Public Health published a report in the *American Journal of Clinical Nutrition* in which it showed that the quickest way to lose weight **is** to decrease liquid calorie consumption—especially beverages that contain sizeable amounts of added sugar.

The leading brand is Vitamin Water from Coca-Cola, containing 26 grams of sugar per 16 ounces (almost as much as, well, a Coca-Cola) and a smattering of synthetic vitamins. How gullible do you have to be to think you can get your nutrition from a company that makes nutritionally bankrupt drinks? Stick to pure, filtered water.

START EATING RIGHT—RIGHT NOW.

Most heart attack sufferers begin to revise their diet and start exercising. And most regret not having done this much earlier in life. Don't wait until it's too late. Begin a *New*trition Program for Life today.

A few more nutrition tips to consider:

- 40% of meat eaters are overweight compared with 30% of vegetarians.
- You could gain 25% more weight eating artificially sweetened foods.
- Odds of being obese are 17% *less* if you drink 1 – 2 alcoholic beverages a day on average (I'll toast to that!).

➢ "Eating junk food regularly increases your chance of being depressed by 60%." *Men's Health* magazine, 2011.

As you can see, good nutrition takes both discipline and education to get right...but the payoff is so enormous in improved and lengthened life that you'd be foolish not to do it.

FAST FOOD IS A FAST WAY TO POOR HEALTH

Millions of people start their day with breakfast at a fast-food restaurant.

- 1 in 5 breakfasts is eaten at McDonalds.

While everyone should eat breakfast as part of a healthy diet, an omelet sandwich, hash browns, and orange juice at Burger King adds up to slightly more than 1,300 calories—and includes loads of fat and carbohydrates.

Have a bowl of whole grain cereal with a sprinkle of blueberries and a glass of juice (just 600 calories) or, even better, a couple of eggs (120 calories) and turkey bacon (200 calories) at home and you'll save money as well as your health.

The rise in obesity, diabetes, and heart disease over the past 50 years closely parallels the rise in the number of fast food chains.

- In 1900 only 2% of all meals were eaten outside the home—more than 50% are now. Most of these meals are eaten in fast food restaurants where healthy food choices are rare.
- An estimated 1 in 4 meals is eaten at a fast food restaurant.

- Every day 50 million Americans eat fast food.
- Fast food restaurants are one of the principal causes of obesity in America.

Any "restaurant" with food that has "Monster" or "manly" among its descriptive food terms is to be avoided—as is any restaurant that advertises an "all you can eat" menu. Need proof? The Wendy's Baconator burger is a "manly" 1,680 calories and 103 grams of fat. Too many of these and your "manhood" will take a nosedive. Literally.

Life Rule: Eliminating fast food restaurants from your life is one of the most beneficial actions you can take to improve your health.

Learn more about the dangers of fast food, read *Fast Food Nation* by Eric Schlosser...or see the film by the same name. You'll find out things about fast food that will definitely kill your appetite.

EAT YOUR WAY TO WEIGHT LOSS

There are several foods that use up more calories to digest than they contain. Not surprisingly these "negative calorie" foods are all fruits and vegetables.

- ✓ Celery.
- ✓ Oranges.
- ✓ Grapefruit.
- ✓ Carrots.
- ✓ Apricots.
- ✓ Lettuce.
- ✓ Tomatoes.
- ✓ Cucumbers.
- ✓ Watermelon.
- ✓ Cauliflower.
- ✓ Apples.
- ✓ Hot chilis.
- ✓ Zucchini.

Incorporate these nutritious and non-fattening foods into your diet—and watch the pounds melt away.

BUDGET NUTRITION

Barry Popkin, Ph.D., author of *The World is Fat,* writes that eating healthier foods actually costs less than processed, convenience, and fast food. His book provides comparisons of healthy foods versus unhealthy foods and shows the cost differential. Healthy foods almost always win out.

Below is a list of foods that are both healthy and inexpensive.

- ✓ Oatmeal.
- ✓ Potatoes.
- ✓ Apples.
- ✓ Bananas.
- ✓ Nuts.
- ✓ Coffee.
- ✓ Sardines.
- ✓ Spinach.
- ✓ Kale.
- ✓ Whole grain pasta.
- ✓ Milk.
- ✓ Beans.
- ✓ Broccoli.
- ✓ Yogurt.
- ✓ Eggs.
- ✓ Peanut butter.
- ✓ Whole grain bread.
- ✓ Chicken/turkey.
- ✓ Ground beef.
- ✓ Water.
- ✓ Soup.
- ✓ Salads.
- ✓ Tea.
- ✓ Chocolate.
- ✓ Popcorn.

For a comprehensive guide to eating good food on a tight budget, go to The Environmental Working Group's website http://www.ewg.org/goodfood/.

"HEALTH" FOOD THAT ISN'T HEALTHY.

Americans gobble hundreds of millions of "health" bars every year without realizing they are simply candy bars with some added artificial protein and vitamins. Millions also choose bottled tea drinks, some with as much as 60 grams of sugar, thinking that the meager tea ingredients are healthier than drinking soda pop (not). The SoBe Green Tea (20–ounce size) has 61 grams of sugar and 240 calories. Since most Americans can read, you have to assume they are somehow missing the nutrient labels on the side of the can or bottle.

- Here's a simple test. Buy just about any protein or health bar and compare it with a candy bar, say a Baby Ruth or Snickers. Very similar, aren't they? Take out a few synthetic vitamins and protein powder and they *are* the same. In fact, Snickers has rebranded a slightly modified version of their Snickers candy bar as an energy bar (with 21 grams of sugar).

Don't waste your money on protein bars that are just candy bars in sheep's clothing.

"FOODS" TO AVOID AT ALL COST

Americans are so ignorant of good nutrition that 9 in 10 surveyed think their diet is "healthy." But the proof is in the pudding (and ice cream and Jello and Ding Dongs)...America's diet is deadly. Keep these "porn foods" out of your diet.

1. **Margarine**. Butter is better.
2. **Cereals**. Nearly all processed cereals are merely stomach fillers with little or no nutritional value. Stick to all-natural oatmeal or organic, non-GMO whole grain cereals.
3. **Donuts**. The most nutritious part of a donut is the hole. Last year Americans ate an incredible 10 *billion* pounds of donuts. Keep all donut relatives out of your diet too—Twinkies, Ding Dongs, HoHo's, cupcakes, muffins, scones, cakes, and pies.
4. **High fructose corn syrup**. Found in a wide range of processed foods.
5. **Sugar**. Many recent scientific reports say that sugar is almost as addicting as opium. In fact, sugar triggers many of the same brain receptors as opium.

Ancient humans ate the equivalent of 20 teaspoons of sugar a year from natural sources like honey. Modern humans (in the U.S.) ingest the equivalent of 22 teaspoons of sugar and other sweeteners a day...about 150 pounds a year (2000). Americans consume about 1 ½ tons of sugar in an average lifetime...enough to fill an industrial-size dumpster. Our pre-agricultural era genes—farming began only about 10,000 years ago—are not equipped to adequately deal with this huge influx of sugar. It's why diabetes is at pandemic levels in America.

6. **Soft drinks**. Here's one area where America is still #1—soft drink

consumption. Americans drink more than 600 soft drinks a year on average—nearly 60 billion liters. That's about 10 times as much as the Japanese, French, and Italians. Soft drinks have NO nutritional value.

7. **Potato chips, crackers, pretzels.** Americans eat billions of dollars of these little time-bombs of bad nutrition.
8. **"Diet" foods.** Read the label carefully. Diet foods are often packed with sugar and additives. Diet soft drinks have been implicated in a number of health problems, including kidney disease. Avoid any food with Aspartame or other artificial sweeteners.
9. **"Nutrition" and "energy" bars.** Most are simply candy bars with a few grams of protein or a sprinkling of artificial vitamins. Here are the stats on a typical "nutrition" bar: 380 calories, 12 grams of fat, 12 grams of sugar PLUS honey and brown sugar syrup.
10. **French fries** are the primary "vegetable" in the American diet. Last year more than 4 billion pounds of fries were consumed in the U.S. Eat the real thing—baked potatoes or sweet potatoes.

WHY DIETS DON'T WORK—AND WHAT DOES

- According to a UCLA study, the majority of dieters regain all the weight they've lost within a year...and more. As reported in *American Psychologist*, 2007.

At any given time 1 in 6 Americans is "on a diet." Yet statistics show that fewer than 5% of dieters successfully reach their goals. With those kinds of stats, why put yourself through the agony of yet another fad diet?

New research shows there's better way. Low-fat diets are not the answer to getting slim and fit. A great deal of the fat most people contend with—belly fat—is the result of two factors: carbohydrates and stress. Eliminate these two diet-busters from your life and you will immediately begin losing the belly fat (called omentum fat).

DIETS DO MORE HARM THAN GOOD

Diets actually create psychological stress that counteracts the benefits of dieting by increasing the cortisol levels in the body. A study by the

University of California San Francisco found that women who counted calories and restricted their food intake were so stressed about it that their cortisol levels rose—just what you don't want when trying to lose weight.

Instead of dieting to lose weight, change your eating habits. In the computer industry there's a saying "garbage in, garbage out." It's the same with food. What goes into your mouth is what determines whether or not you are eating healthy. Change your eating habits and you'll change your life.

SCIENTIFICALLY PROVEN DIETING THAT WORKS

Diet programs that have proven relatively successful are Weight Watchers www.WeightWatchers.com and Jenny Craig www.JennyCraig.com. Both rely on proven scientific behavior modification techniques—first posited by the behavioral scientist B.F. Skinner—to keep their dieters on track.

The award-winning journalist David Freedman, author of *Wrong: Why Experts* Keep Failing Us—And How to Know When to Trust Them*, wrote about the use of Skinnerian behavior modification to change unhealthy habits in *The Atlantic* magazine in 2012.

- ✓ Set modest goals to encourage sustainable progress.
- ✓ Rigorously track food intake and weight...precise measurement is key to changing behavior, especially when it comes to eating, since a few bites a day can make the difference between weight loss and weight gain.
- ✓ Utilize counseling or coaching to diagnose what lifestyle factors are prompting or rewarding certain behaviors.
- ✓ Engage fellow participants for support and encouragement.
- ✓ Transition to less calorie-dense foods to avoid the powerful, immediate reinforcement provided by rich foods.
- ✓ Be more active—any way you can—to burn calories.

Freedman points out that study after study proves the effectiveness of this Skinnerian behavior modification formula, which is the basis of the great majority of well-regarded weight-loss programs.

HEALTHY-AGING EATING

As the 78 million Baby Boomers can attest, getting older is a bitch. And as the multi-billion dollar healthy-aging industry can attest, it's also quite profitable. While nothing can reverse aging, you can slow it down and "age well." The "fountain of youth" is exercise and good nutrition.

TOP 10 ANTI-AGING FOODS

1. Blueberries
2. Broccoli
3. Eggs (pasture-raised)
4. Leafy greens
5. Yogurt
6. Nuts
7. Dark chocolate
8. Red wine
9. Olive oil
10. Salmon, sardines, mackeral

TOP 10 BEAUTY FOODS

Foods that contribute to overall health and well-being will also help you look better. Here are the Top 10 "beauty foods" to stock in your pantry.

1. Blueberries
2. Wild Salmon
3. Low-fat yogurt
4. Oysters
5. Kiwi fruit
6. Sweet potatoes
7. Spinach
8. Tomatoes
9. Walnuts
10. Dark chocolate

Source: *AOL Health*, 2009

TOP 10 THINGS THAT AGE YOU

Getting older is inevitable, but here are some things that will "age" you even faster.

1. Lack of sleep
2. Sugar
3. Lack of exercise
4. Smoking
5. Drinking
6. Stress
7. Junk food/processed foods
8. Yo Yo Dieting
9. Dehydration
10. Sleeping face down

- Sleep "detoxes" the brain...mopping up waste products that are linked to dementia and Alzheimer's Disease, according to 2013 research from the University of Rochester Medical Center.

FOOD AS MEDICINE

"The food you eat can either be the safest and most powerful form of medicine—or the slowest form of poison." — Ann Wigmore, author of *The Healing Power Within: How to Tap the Infinite Potential Within Yourself*

Author Mark Hyman writes in *The Ultra Mind Solution* that "food is the fastest-acting and most powerful medicine you can take to change your life." In recent years the idea of food as medicine has become popular as researchers learn that you can use food to help avoid, and even treat, various physical ailments. Hundreds of studies have confirmed the single most important fact about why good nutrition should be the cornerstone of your Plan for Life...it works better than anything else to prevent disease.

The popularity of *Prescription for Nutritional Healing*, first published in 2000, proved that many people are hungry for information about how food can be used therapeutically. Also, the rising consciousness about the dangers of traditional medicine and pharmaceuticals encouraged people to find alternate solutions.

EAT TO YOUR HEART'S CONTENT

"American adults have a 1 in 2.7 chance of having cardiovascular disease." — The Milken Institute

- Heart disease is the #1 killer of both men and women in America, accounting for one in every four deaths.
- Heart disease, in most cases, is a result of poor nutrition, lack of exercise, and smoking.
- If you look at a map of the United States, the highest concentration of heart disease is in the South and Midwest...and correlates closely with areas of poor nutrition and lack of exercise.

Foods that help promote a healthy heart include:

- ✓ Nuts.
- ✓ Fish.
- ✓ Oats.
- ✓ Avocados.
- ✓ Black beans.
- ✓ Flaxseed.

Other top heart healthy foods with high levels of antioxidants are:

1. Blackberries
2. Walnuts
3. Strawberries
4. Artichokes
5. Cranberries
6. Coffee
7. Raspberries
8. Pecans
9. Blueberries
10. Ground cloves

Source: *American Journal of Clinical Nutrition*, 2008

On every list of foods that promote health you will find the same foods. Real foods. Foods that grow in the ground, fly, walk or swim in the sea.

Life rule: You are what you eat...so think about everything you put into your body before ingesting it.

INFLAMMATION

According to the University of California *Berkeley Wellness Letter*, "some researchers now believe that low-grade inflammation is associated with everything from heart disease and diabetes to Alzheimer's and arthritis, and may be the cause of most chronic diseases."

While the connection between inflammation and disease isn't thoroughly understood yet, to be safe it's important to consider how to counter inflammation in your overall health plan for life. Here are the stats on diseases exacerbated by inflammation:

- Auto-immune disease 24 million
- Allergies 50 million
- Asthma 30 million
- Cancer 10 million

- Arthritis 50 million
- Alzheimer's 5 million

Inflammation has many sources, including things such as Chlamydia bacterial infections (in some states as high as 40%), obesity, smoking, high blood pressure, and unhealthy cholesterol levels. You can check for inflammation by having a CRP (c-reactive protein test...about $50). If your level is high, your physician may want to take steps to decrease inflammation.

Some steps you can take to prevent or reduce inflammation are:

1. Eat fish and walnuts frequently...or take Omega-3 supplements (1 gram).
2. Don't smoke.
3. Talk to your doctor about taking a low-dose aspirin daily. Check out the Mayo Clinic's pro and con report on aspirin therapy. www.mayoclinic.com
4. Maintain a healthy weight with a nutritious diet and exercise.
5. Control your blood pressure.

MORE THAN HALF OF ALL CANCER CAN BE PREVENTED

"1 in 4 Americans will die of cancer." — The American Cancer Society

- According to the Harvard School of Public Health, poor diet, lack of exercise, and unhealthy lifestyle habits are responsible for 65% of cancer deaths.

Most people know by now that smoking is the biggest danger, accounting for nearly a third (30%) of cancer deaths. What isn't so well known is that poor nutrition and obesity account for just as many deaths (30%). Or that lack of exercise (5%) accounts for more cancer deaths than environmental pollution (2%) or carcinogens in the workplace (5%). Genetics account for only 10% of cancer deaths, so there is a lot you can do to help avoid this life-changing disease.

While there are dozens of books about cancer and how to prevent it, the best course of action you can incorporate into your life are the nutrition and exercise recommendations in this book—eat right and exercise regularly.

YOUR CHANCE OF GETTING FOOD POISONING IS ALMOST 100%

According to the Centers for Disease Control and Prevention, 1 in 6 Americans (48 million people) will get a food-borne illness each year...and 128,000 are hospitalized. More than 130,000 Americans, many of them children, are made sick by food-borne disease—every day! About 2,500 are sickened enough to be hospitalized every week and more than four dozen will die, according to the Centers for Disease Control and Prevention. These figures are most certainly conservative. In reality, nearly every American will experience at least one incident of food poisoning this year. Unfortunately, more than 3,000 people will die as a result.

Most food poisoning is mild and often mistaken for indigestion, the ubiquitous "upset stomach" or "stomach flu." Along with diarrhea, these are all signs of food poisoning. And it's why Pepto-Bismol and Imodium sales top $200 million a year in the U.S.

There are dozens of pathogens that cause food poisoning, including:

- Salmonella (1,000,000 cases)
- Campylobacter (850,000 cases)
- Streptococcus (240,000 cases)
- Norovirus (5.5 million cases)
- Shigella (130,000 cases)
- E. Coli (200,000 cases)
- And others such as Yersina Enteracolitica, Giarda, Listeria, and Cryptosporidium.

KEEPING FOOD SAFE AT HOME

"Barely 2% of imported food is inspected once it reaches the U.S."
—USDA (2013)

It's important to eat safely at home.

✓ Sanitize your kitchen surfaces frequently.

✓ Wear gloves.

✓ Handle carefully anything raw—ground beef, chicken, eggs (and even raw vegetables)—all can harbor e coli or salmonella.

Consider nearly every food a potential source of food poisoning. To reduce the chance of poisoning:

✓ Start by choosing organic foods. This will eliminate toxic pesticides, antibiotics, and other chemicals. Organic foods are generally grown and processed under stricter, more sanitary, conditions.

✓ Be careful about potential cross-contamination from other foods, such as chicken or ground beef. Sanitize cutting boards and preparation surfaces. Wash your hands after handling high-contamination foods such as ground turkey, chicken, beef, or seafood.

✓ Follow the handling directions on meat and foul.

✓ Sanitize surfaces often.

✓ Keep the temperature in your refrigerator below 40 degrees.

TOP TEN "DIRTY" FOODS

While most foods are potential carriers of pathogens, some are more dangerous than others.

1. **Chicken.** According to Consumers Union and the USDA, 42% of raw chickens tested were infected with Campylobaceri jejuni and 1 in 6 with Salmonella enterides. Look for organically raised, free-range chickens—they're less likely to be contaminated.

2. **Ground beef.** Ground beef can come from many sources—even many countries. If you've ever been to a slaughter house and meat-packing plant, you will likely become an instant vegetarian. It's hard to believe that every package of ground beef isn't seriously contaminated.

When the USDA tested samples of ground beef, they found that more than half (53%) were infected with Clostridium perfringens, 30% with Staphylococcus, and 12% with Listeria monocytogenes. Handle ground beef carefully and always cook thoroughly. For safer beef look for organic, pasture-raised beef that is raised locally.

3. **Ground turkey.** You might think that turkey is safer than ground beef,

but you would be wrong. According to the USDA, the odds are 1 in 4 that ground turkey is contaminated with one or more potentially deadly bugs, including Salmonella (24%). Organic, free-range turkey is safer.

4. **Raw oysters.** Eating raw oysters is like playing food Russian roulette. Oysters filter out waste from the sea. These little ocean garbage disposals pick up some nasty stuff along the way because, unfortunately, there's a lot of nasty stuff in the ocean now.

When the University of Arizona tested oysters from a "safe-certified" oyster bed, they discovered that nearly 1 in 10 (9%) were infected with Salmonella. In some tests of raw oysters, fully 100% tested positive for E. Coli. Recommendation? Eat them cooked.

5. **Eggs.** In 2011, the abominable conditions at the massive egg factories in Iowa showed graphically the direct link with food-borne illnesses. You are what you eat, and this is true for the animals we eat. If they are fed antibiotics, eat fecal matter and other dead animals, and consume diets high in adulterated feed, they produce eggs and meat of low quality.

Eggs can be one of the most nutritious foods…if they come from healthy chickens. 93% of eggs produced in the U.S. come from giant egg factories, some with as many as 5 million chickens in cages so cramped they can't turn around. As much as 23% of these eggs are contaminated with salmonella, according to one report.

Look for local, organic eggs. It's important that you buy pasture-raised chicken eggs—even "free range" chickens spend nearly their entire life inside large coops. You'll find pastured eggs at farmer's markets and stores like Whole Foods. Or consider raising your own backyard chickens; there's nothing like the taste of a truly fresh egg just minutes from the source.

6. **Cantaloupe.** The FDA found that 7% of cantaloupe tested positive for Salmonella or Shigella. Always wash cantaloupes thoroughly before cutting.

7. **Peaches.** Peaches are doused with up to nine different toxic chemicals, according to Consumers Union, and are among the most pesticide-laden produce. Wash thoroughly or peel before eating.

8. **Pre-packaged lettuce**. Unbelievably, lettuce accounts for 1 in 10 cases of food-poisoning outbreaks…and "salad mix" for 28%. Always buy organic lettuce and wash very thoroughly.

9. **Cold cuts.** In delis, the big contamination culprits are the food slicer and the length of time items are kept at improper temperatures. Cold cuts are frequently left out at unsafe temperatures. What's more, the ingredients in cold cuts are heavily doctored with chemicals and preservatives.

10. **Scallions.** These innocuous little flavor boosters are implicated in a surprisingly large number of deadly Salmonella and Shigella outbreaks. 3% of all scallions tested by the FDA harbored one or both of these two bugs.

Eating at home is one way to avoid getting sick, but only if you keep a clean kitchen, practice safe food handling, and have good personal hygiene. Otherwise, your own kitchen can be just as dangerous as the worst restaurant "dive."

The takeaway here is to always be aware of what you are eating, where it came from, and how it was prepared. For more information go to http://www.foodsafety.gov

Life Rule: Be wise…sanitize.

WHEN WAS THE LAST TIME YOU CHECKED THE KITCHEN IN A RESTAURANT?

Probably never. But you should.

As a former restaurant owner, I find it difficult sometimes to eat out, knowing the potential dangers in even the most responsible establishments. The high volume, multiple food prep surfaces, and poor sanitation practices among many low-paid restaurant workers, makes eating out a potentially deadly experience. Even at high-end restaurants few food preparers use protective gloves. I've never seen a restaurant kitchen that washed their fruit and produce thoroughly. Often it's not washed at all. The truth is that the food you eat at a restaurant is often contaminated…sometimes with bugs that have the potential to kill you. And sometimes, with real bugs.

While we did everything possible at our restaurants to keep the food and food preparation areas clean and sanitary, I know we were the exception. Most restaurants keep some "dirty" secrets that are so shocking you would likely never eat out again if you knew.

- If you don't eat all the rolls in your bread basket, there's a good chance the next diner will be seeing the ones you passed up...the rolls you just put your hands on...after catching a sneeze in your hand...because you are just getting over the flu.
- In a rush, many restaurants don't put all their dishes through the dishwasher...they just rinse them off and use them again. Haven't we all found a glass with a lipstick smudge on it?
- The "daily special" isn't so special after all...it usually consists of food that has reached its expiration date and is either served up "special" or thrown out in the garbage.
- Most restaurant workers don't use protective gloves when handling your food. Some of the finest chefs seem to enjoy getting their hands into their work. Cross-contamination from workers' hands is the top reason food becomes tainted.
- Of course, you've heard of the "three second (or ten second) rule?" Anything (including your filet mignon) that is dropped on the floor and picked up quickly is OK to serve at many establishments.
- Many of the workers in restaurants come from cultures where high cleanliness standards aren't practiced when handling food. Plus, few restaurant workers get paid sick leave. If an employee is already barely surviving on a minimum wage salary, do you think they'll stay at home when they're sick?
- The buffet is a breeding ground for bacteria. The food is often kept at unsafe temperatures for hours...even served again the next day after sitting out.
- If you think the salad bar is a healthy option, just the opposite is frequently true. The vegetables are seldom washed thoroughly, the length of time on the serving line is long, the temperature control often unsafe, and the items can be exposed to dozens of people.
- Lemons are frequently served with water...but they have been handled (usually unwashed) by the person who picked the citrus, the person who packed it, the person who unpacked it, the person who put it

on the plate...and so forth. Up to ten people may have touched the lemon that goes unwashed into your drink. Cheers!

- Restaurant kitchens are frequently closed by the Health Department for insect or vermin infestation. Unfortunately, a restaurant is also a dining destination for these disease-carrying visitors.
- Food preparation surfaces can easily become contaminated by human touch, raw meat or foul, and contaminated food. In a busy restaurant, sanitizing these surfaces is often overlooked.

As with most things in life, you usually get what you pay for...and this is true for restaurants too. Newer, higher-priced restaurants typically have newer kitchens, better trained staff, and a reputation that can be destroyed with one bad Health Department closure. Personally, I like to eat at restaurants with "open" kitchens that are visible to the diners. And more than once, I've asked to see the kitchen. If a restaurant refuses, you have to ask yourself why.

Life Rule: When in doubt, don't eat out.

1 IN 10 AMERICANS IS VITAMIN-DEFICIENT

Americans eat so poorly that nearly 1 in 10 is deficient in one or more vitamins, which is difficult to do with our modern, vitamin-enriched diet. But popping a synthetic vitamin isn't the best solution. Humans have evolved over hundreds of thousands of years to obtain their nutritional needs from food, not the lab. Natural vitamins are more complex, with phytonutrients that may have a synergistic affect that cannot be duplicated in a lab.

SUPPLEMENTS

To make up for their abysmal eating habits, Americans think that popping a pill will provide the nutritional "insurance" they need to stay healthy. Americans consume more vitamins and supplements than all other countries in the world combined, according to JAMA and industry estimates.

It's almost un-American to say anything negative about supplements, but...

- ➢ A 5-year study at Oxford University of more than 20,000 people showed absolutely no evidence that supplements have any effect on heart disease, cancer, cataracts, asthma or mental decline.

- Supplements could decrease your life span. In a study of 39,000 women in Iowa over 20 years by the University of Minnesota, 85% took supplements daily over the course of the study. Yet, the supplements didn't extend their life. Just the opposite. Those who took supplements died 3% to 10% earlier.
- Studies conducted or funded by organizations such as the American Medical Association and the National Institutes of Health have indicated that many synthetic supplements (e.g. vitamin E, beta carotine, calcium) are either ineffective or possibly harmful.
- In more than fifty scientific large–scale studies, not one has shown supplements prevent heart disease or cancer, despite the claims by vitamin manufacturers.

What's more, taking large doses of vitamins can upset the balance in your system and may be a cause of fatigue or suppressed immune function.

As a nation, we've been so indoctrinated with the hype on taking vitamins and supplements that even with substantial scientific evidence that supplements do little to improve health, we still pop them like candy every day.

SYNTHETIC VITAMINS ARE TO FOOD VITAMINS AS BABY FORMULA IS TO MOTHER'S MILK.

Natural vitamins derived from food are different from synthetic vitamins. Natural vitamins are more complex and are affected by trace minerals, phytonutrients, enzymes, coenzymes…as well as some interactions scientists haven't yet identified. This combination of ingredients, which are only derived from natural foods, are necessary to the full beneficial catalytic action of vitamins.

WHEN SHOULD YOU TAKE SYNTHETIC VITAMINS?

All that being said, since most Americans consume a diet that is based primarily upon highly processed manufactured foods, high–fat and nutritionally deficient fast food (one in four meals), and sugary drinks or desserts, adding a high quality multivitamin each day is good basic protection.

The Shaklee Corporation makes an excellent multivitamin called Vitalizer. www.Shaklee.com New Chapter makes an extensive line of quality whole food supplements that are organic and non-genetically modified. The daily multivitamin is sold under the Every Man and Every Woman label. www.NewChapter.com

Few people eat enough fish, walnuts, or flax seed—primary sources of Omega 3, 5, 6, 7, and 9. The Omegas have been shown to benefit cardiovascular, immune system, brain, and digestive health.

- A study of 2,700 people over age 65 by the Harvard School of Public Health and the University of Washington (published in 2013 in the *Annals of Internal Medicine*) found that Omega-3 fatty acids corresponded to a reduced risk of death in the elderly. Those with the highest blood levels of Omega-3s lived 2.2 years longer and had a 27% lower risk of mortality.

If you don't consume foods that provide Omega-3 fatty acids to your diet, try one of the minimally processed fish oils such as New Chapter Wholemega 1000mg sustainably caught wild Alaskan salmon oil. The better (and more effective) choice, of course, is to eat wild salmon or cold water fish twice a week.

Be sure to buy quality, whole food sourced vitamins. Keep in mind that these daily multivitamin and fish oil capsules alone will cost about $125 a month. Adding another supplement, such as Vitamin D and Potassium (both common deficiencies) can add another $50—or more than $2,000 a year total. That much money can buy a lot of wholesome food. As always, your best source of vitamins to meet your body's needs is fresh, organic, non-GMO food.

VITAMIN D GETS AN A+ FOR GOOD HEALTH

Recent research has put Vitamin D in the spotlight because of its many health advantages. It's vitally important to good health and disease prevention. Yet, about 3 in 4 Americans don't get the minimum amount of Vitamin D their body needs, especially during winter months. African Americans are at particular risk of deficiency...one study in 2004 found just 3% had the recommended levels. A deficiency negatively affects every cell of your body—including fat cells.

Research shows that people with larger intakes of Vitamin D have less belly fat. In fact, people who consumed larger amounts of the vitamin not only lost more weight and stored less fat, they also improved their cardiovascular health markers.

- Vitamin D is manufactured in the skin through exposure to the sun... about 15 - 20 minutes is all you need. The other way to get Vitamin D is through food or fortified dairy products.

The minimum recommended amount of Vitamin D is 400 iu daily. However recent research indicates that even the government recommended daily intake may not be adequate. If you live in northern states, work indoors or don't ingest dairy products you may need as much as 1,000 iu to 2,000 iu daily. The Indocrine Society recently recommended this amount for good health. If you're like 2/3 of Americans and are overweight or obese, you'll need more because fat traps Vitamin D and decreases its effectiveness.

Vitamin D isn't just a vitamin, it's also a hormone. Higher amounts of Vitamin D benefit the immune system, pancreas, muscles, heart, brain... nearly every key bodily function. It can help prevent heart disease, diabetes, high blood pressure, memory loss, and some cancers.

Good natural sources of Vitamin D include fatty fish such as salmon or mackerel, dairy products, fortified orange juice, liver, and eggs. However, it would be difficult to get enough Vitamin D from these sources alone if you don't get sun exposure daily for at least 20 minutes.

SUPPLEMENTS CAN BE DANGEROUS

Supplements—especially those sold for weight loss, sexual "enhancement," or bodybuilding—are often spiked with dangerous and untested drugs. They may contain steroids, chemically modified ingredients—or worse. There are dozens of deaths or serious health complications (such as liver disease) each year from supplements.

Many supplements are manufactured under production facilities in places like Pakistan, India, and China. According to the FDA, 99% of the supplements from overseas that are sold in America aren't tested for their composition or purity of their ingredients. *Nutrition Business Journal* estimates that more than 60% of the raw materials for supplements come from China, a country with a questionable history of adulterated products.

One way to protect yourself is to purchase supplements certified by the NSF (see the NSF website for a list) www.nsf.org. The NSF has been in the public health and safety business since 1944. Most health departments require NSF approved food–handling equipment for restaurants. The NSF maintains testing laboratories in the U.S. and China to evaluate both supplements/vitamins and the raw materials that go into them.

As always, the best vitamins are those that occur naturally in wholesome organic foods.

Life Rule: Get your vitamins from real food. If you take vitamin supplements, choose those derived from real food…a multivitamin and Vitamin D is all you need in most circumstances.

AMERICA IS WHERE SIT HAPPENS

For every hour an adult over age 25 spends sitting and watching TV, about 22 minutes are cut from longevity…smoking a cigarette reduces lifespan by just 11 minutes.

The new American lifestyle is essentially motionless. Nearly half of adults and children walk less than a mile a day. But Americans do sit a lot. We sit at our desks at work. We sit in front of the TV. We sit while we play video games. We sit while we surf the Internet. We sit in our cars. We sit in airplanes. We sit at the movies. We sit to watch baseball, hockey or football. We sit at NASCAR races. We sit while we eat. America's new national slogan should be "Sit Happens." On average we sit 9.3 hours a day. We sleep an average of just 7.7 hours.

- Fifty years ago Americans burned 50,000 calories more each year on average. Today more than 250 million Americans don't get the minimum level of exercise required to be fit.
- The number of jobs that require physical activity has declined by 30% since 1960.
- According to a 40–year study by the University of South Carolina, men who reported sitting more than 23 hours a week had a 64% greater risk of dying than those who sit 11 hours or less a week.
- Sitting for 6 or more hours a day increases your risk of death within 15 years up to 40% more than someone who sits less than 3 hours a day.

Men and women who sit the <u>least</u> had:

- ✓ Better cardiovascular health.
- ✓ Lower blood pressure.
- ✓ Improved metabolism.
- ✓ Lower cholesterol.
- ✓ Reduced risk of diabetes.
- ✓ Reduced risk of some forms of cancer.
- ✓ Lower weight.
- ✓ Smaller waist.
- ✓ More active sex lives.

Our bodies are the products of thousands of years of hereditary development. And for thousands of years human beings moved almost constantly and rarely sat. Homes, such as they were, were largely devoid of chairs as recently as 500 years ago. Work actually involved work, not sitting in front of a computer screen. People walked to where they wanted to go.

Even worse, when not sitting Americans aren't moving all that much. Of our time awake each day, less than 1 hour is spent in medium to vigorous activity (0.7 hours). This is an average...for millions of people there is virtually no vigorous activity in the day. 1 in 5 (22%) of American adults (and a rising number of children too) gets no exercise at all. None. Ever. In some states, like Mississippi and Kentucky, almost a third of the population gets no exercise, according to the Centers for Disease Control and Prevention.

Too much sit can even cause cancer. In an analysis presented to the annual conference of the American Institute for Cancer Research in Washington D.C., lack of physical activity was directly attributed to more than 90,000 cases of cancer each year. A mind–boggling 49,000 cases of breast cancer and 43,000 of colon cancer may be prevented by simply getting more Americans off their butts and using their legs.

In one major study by the American Cancer Society, women who sat a lot were nearly 40% more likely to die during the study than women who did less sitting. Men who sat a lot were 18% more likely to die. In a review of more than 200 cancer studies worldwide, researchers found convincing evidence that regular physical activity reduces the risk of breast cancer, colon cancer, and endometrial cancer by 25% to 30%. There's also evidence that exercise reduces the risk of lung, prostate, and ovarian cancer.

THE MORE YOU SIT, THE FATTER YOU GET

It's no surprise that sitting makes people fat. Obese people sit for 2 ½ hours more each day on average than thin people.

Sitting expends almost NO energy. Even standing expends about 10% more calories than sitting. For comparison sake, chewing gum uses up 15% more calories than sitting. Only sleeping uses up fewer calories. If you sit doing your job, or spend inordinate amounts of time sitting in front of the TV, chances are you're fat.

THE IMMEDIATE EFFECTS OF SITTING

Sitting takes an immediate toll upon your body. As soon as you sit down...

- Calories burned drops to just 1 per minute.
- Electrical activity in the leg muscles shuts off.
- Blood flow to the legs slows dramatically, a common cause of potentially deadly DVT (deep vein thrombosis).
- Enzymes that aid in breaking down fat in the body drop by 90%.

The longer you sit the worse it gets. After two hours...

- Good cholesterol levels drop by 20%.
- People who sit 3 hours or more a day watching TV are 64% more likely to die of heart disease (and even those who exercise are just as fat as those who don't).

Since sitting is inevitable in modern life, take proactive measures to decrease the amount of time you sit.

- ✓ Bike or walk to work or the store.
- ✓ Limit TV and computer time, especially video games.
- ✓ Take frequent breaks—walk around, stretch or stand for a while.
- ✓ Make walking or running an integral part of your exercise program.

✓ Consider using, if you can, a standup desk.

Sources: www.MedicalBillingandCoding.org, American Cancer Society.

Life Rule: Avoid sitting. Buy a standup desk. Take frequent breaks to walk or stretch.

USE IT OR LOSE IT

Exercise needs to be a part of your lifestyle for life. There are 168 hours in a week. Just six hours a week (less than 4% of the week) will be enough to stay fit if you take part in an aerobic exercise for four hours—walking, running, swimming, basketball or cycling—and two hours of resistance exercise—weight training.

This isn't much…less than 4% of your week…to feel great, look great, have more energy, and live longer. Seems like a pretty good return on investment.

Combine these activities with a healthy diet, stress reduction techniques, regular checkups, avoidance of drugs, and overuse of alcohol and you'll greatly increase your odds of living a vibrant, long, and disease-free life. It's that simple. But remember, it takes both a good nutritional program and exercise…you can't out-exercise a bad diet.

Despite the dozens of fitness programs hawked on late-night infomercials, the hundreds of books on fitness, and the hundreds of millions of dollars Americans spend on health club memberships, you don't need much to stay fit.

THE 20-MINUTE FIT FOR LIFE HOME WORKOUT

"Weight training is the 'miracle cure' for having great fitting clothing, an erect posture, and for stress relief." — Carolyn Phillips, Founder, Fit Behavior www.fitbehavior.com

You can stay fit with an investment of just 20 minutes a day.

Run in place for 5 minutes to warm up. Then begin your exercise routine by strengthening your core muscles.

Situps: Bring one leg up toward the opposite shoulder and elbow into it from a lying position. Then do the other leg. Do two sets of 25 each.

Leg Raises: Sit on the edge of a chair and raise both legs back toward your chest. Do two sets of 25 each.

Strengthens your upper torso muscles.

Pushups: Start with 10 pushups and work up to as many as you feel uncomfortable doing. Try some with your feet elevated on a chair or sofa to work your upper chest muscles.

Strengthens your bicep arm muscles.

Dumbbell Curls: Start with 10 at the heaviest weight you can lift comfortably. Two sets of curls is enough.

Strengthens your legs and back.

Dumbell Lifts: Standing with one leg slightly forward and both legs spread apart about two feet. Begin with 10 dumbbell lifts up to chest level. Start with 10 at the heaviest weight you can lift and work up from there to as many as you feel comfortable doing. Break your lifts into sets of 10 if you like. Two sets is enough.

Strengthens legs.

Leg Squats: Holding a dumbbell in each hand, squat until your upper thighs are horizontal to the floor. Slowly stand up. Start with light weights and 10 reps. Again, two sets is enough.

Strengthens side oblique back muscles.

Dumbbell Rows: Holding one dumbbell, bend over and lift in a rowing fashion. Keep your other hand on the back of a chair for balance. Start with 15 and work up to as many as you feel comfortable doing in each set.

Strengthens chest (pectoral), arm and back muscles.

Dumbbell Flys: If you have an ottoman or other narrow flat surface, lie down with your back and head on it and your legs bent with your feet on the floor. Bring the dumbbells into a perpendicular position above your chest. Slowly lower them until they are horizontal with your chest. Then raise them up to a perpendicular position again. Start with 10 reps and build up to 15. Then do as many sets as you feel comfortable doing.

Strengthens shoulder, arm and back muscles.

Dumbbell Presses: From chest level, alternately lift each dumbbell straight up. You can do this from a standing or sitting position. Start with 10 reps for one set. Build up to two or three sets of 15 reps.

Strengthens shoulder and arm muscles

Pullups: Using a wide grip with your hands on the bar with palms forward, pull your body up until you can touch the bar with your chin. Keep you legs crossed at the ankles. You may only be able to do a few of these at first but eventually should be able to do 10 or more easily. Then do another set gripping the bar with your palms facing toward you.

Abdominal Leg Raises: Sit with your legs outstretched. Bring them up toward your chest in a bicycle riding motion. Do two sets of 25 each to strengthen your core muscles.

If you join a health club, there are many other options to exercise specific muscles or muscle groups. However, the key to improvement is consistency. Often it's too much hassle to drive to the health club, so people tend to exercise sporadically. Exercising at home for 20 minutes with the ten exercises listed above is far better than an hour or two at the club two or three times a month. Plus, it's a whole lot cheaper.

NOTE: Too much exercise can be unhealthy. Extreme endurance cardio, such as marathon running, sets in motion inflammatory mechanisms that can actually harm your heart...so much so that veteran endurance athletes have five times the risk of atrial fibrillation. Extreme marathoners have 62% more plaque in their heart tissue.

The ideal distance to run is just 10 – 15 miles a week at a moderate pace over two or three runs. A 2012 study of 52,000 runners and non–runners found that the benefits of running disappear when the distance topped 25 miles...the non–runners and extreme runners had almost exactly the same mortality rate.

The benefits of weight lifting top out after about a half hour, with two or three workouts a week. Despite the American penchant for "more is always better," this doesn't apply to exercise...no matter what the fitness fanatics tell you.

JUST 4% OF YOUR WEEK WILL ADD YEARS OF GOOD HEALTH

Now in addition to your 20–minute workout five times a week, mix in some walking, jogging or running a couple days—or an hour of your favorite sport: swimming, tennis, cycling, volleyball, skiing, baseball, basketball—anything you enjoy that also gets your heart rate up 25% or more beyond its resting level.

WALKING

"An early morning walk is a blessing for the whole day."
— Henry David Thoreau

Perhaps the easiest and most convenient way to exercise is walking. There is an inverse correlation between walking and heart disease, high blood pressure, obesity, and a host of other common ailments. But despite how easy it is to do, Americans walk less than any other industrialized nation in the world.

➢ Healthcare and exercise professionals agree that everyone who is able should walk a minimum of 10,000 steps a day...or about five miles.

✓ Australians average 9,695 steps.

✓ The Swiss walk 9,650 steps.

✓ The Japanese walk 7,168 steps.

And Americans? We walk a pathetic 5,117 steps on average, barely more than half of the minimum necessary for good health.

Unfortunately, over the years America has successfully engineered walking out of our lives, replaced by automobiles. Many streets were built in the latter half of the 20th century that didn't include sidewalks, making walking inconvenient...even dangerous. In some cities, like Houston, pedestrians almost seem out of place.

There are strategies you can use to increase the amount of walking you do.

✓ First, substitute walking with a friend for the long lunch or lattes at the local coffeehouse. People tend to walk more when they do it with a friend.

✓ Second, wear a pedometer. Perhaps because it makes you aware of how much (or little) you walk, a pedometer seems to be a spur to activity.

✓ Finally, keep track of your progress. This seems to ignite the competitive spirit in most people, who will then try to do more miles every month.

RUNNING AND JOGGING

➢ According to a 2012 Danish study, joggers live 6 years longer and have a 44% lower mortality risk from all causes.

If you really want to lose weight fast and get in shape, there's hardly a better way than to take up jogging or running. Combined with good nutrition, the pounds will melt off fast.

And, of course, meet with your physician to be sure you're healthy enough to begin running.

FITNESS ON A BUDGET

What's the best way to stay physically fit and stay financially fit? These exercises give you the most burn for the buck.

Exercise	Calories per dollar
• Running/walking	1,100
• Rollerblading	625
• Kayaking	350
• Swimming	240
• Cycling	175

Life Rule: Exercise and good nutrition are the true "fountains of youth."

SEE YOURSELF AS YOU WANT YOURSELF TO BE

"Although your body is very intelligent, it cannot tell the difference between an actual situation and a thought. It reacts to every thought as if it were a reality."

— *A New Earth: Awakening Your Life's Purpose* by Ekhart Tolle

Dr. Robert Arnot writes in his book *Dr. Bob Arnot's Guide to Turning Back the Clock* that it's important to picture yourself as a dynamic person full of energy and youthful exuberance. He suggests creating a brilliant, guided vision of who you hope to become to "program" your brain for success. Deepak Chopra writes in "*Ageless Body, Timeless Mind*" that we program our consciousness to a set span of aging, and out biology responds to that programming.

"Your health is bound to be affected if, day after day, you say the opposite of what you feel, if you grovel before what you dislike and rejoice at what brings you nothing but misfortune. Our nervous system isn't just a fiction,

it's part of our physical body, and our soul exists in space and is inside us, like teeth in our mouth. It can't be forever violated with immunity."
— Boris Pasternak, from his book *Dr. Zhivago*

There's something to this philosophy. "You're only as young as you think" is equally as true when you decide to "act your age" and lead a sedentary, "mature" lifestyle as you age. It's important to understand that your mind and body are intricately connected.

THE MIND/BODY CONNECTION

"Health is not valued till sickness comes."
— Dr. Thomas Fuller, 16th-century British physician

In "*The Mind Body Prescription*" Dr. John E. Sarno claims that 90% of his patients (which include celebrities like John Stoessel, the former ABC News reporter) are cured of chronic back pain, migraines, and fibromyalgia using mind control techniques.

There's obviously some truth to this—physicians have used placeboes for centuries to treat physical ailments that are unresponsive to traditional medical intervention.

- It's estimated that 90% of all illness is partially or wholly psychosomatic—a result of repressed emotions or entrenched beliefs.

Dr. Sarno points out that anger and rage are especially manifested with physical problems—a condition called TMS (Tension Myositis Syndrome). Besides pain, emotionally exacerbated physical manifestations include premature aging, skin diseases, heart problems, diabetes—even early death. Stories of people getting sick after losing a job, home or a loved one are so frequent that emotions cannot be ruled out as a key component of health.

Another overlooked causative reason for psychosomatic illness is the billions of dollars spent by pharmaceutical companies advertising treatments for everything from jumpy leg syndrome to social unease. In studies, there is a direct correlation between the popular awareness of a physical problem and the number of people suffering from it.

Our minds are a powerful factor in how healthy we are—or believe we are. In a recent study, people who visualized doing bicep exercises with a dumbbell for 30 minutes a day actually increased the strength in their arms by 15% compared to a control group. Athletes routinely perform these mental exercises to improve their performance.

When test subjects are given a sugar pill they believe to be a powerful medicine to treat chronic pain, a sizeable percentage experience real relief. This is called the "placebo effect." The opposite is also true, a "nocebo affect" where people feel worse if they believe something (e.g. a particular food) will make them sick. Your mind, as in all things, has much more influence over your body than you realize.

There are a number of ways to combat mind-induced illness.

- ✓ Exercise produces hormones that help people relax and feel good.
- ✓ Yoga and meditation are proven techniques to quiet the mind.
- ✓ The teachings of people like Eckhart Tolle, author of "*The Power of Now,*" and the Dalai Lama, author of *The Art of Happiness* and *How to See Yourself as You Really Are*, have helped millions keep their mind demons at bay.
- ✓ A nutritious diet correlates highly with emotional well-being.

I suggest trying several to see which method works best for you. Just don't put it off...emotional health impacts too many other areas of your life.

AMERICANS ARE STRESSING THEMSELVES TO DEATH

"It's not stress that kills us, it's our reaction to it."
— Hans Selye, author of *The Stress of Life*

STRESS LESS

America holds the crown as the most stressed-out nation in the world. We live in a society that is constantly "on." Hardly a day goes by when some form of intrusive media—TV, radio, iPods, cell phones, computers—is not bombarding us with messages demanding our attention and response.

Many people spend their lives with their nervous systems operating at full capacity. Personal conflicts, commuting, loneliness, loss of a loved one, world events, high-pressure jobs—even "good" stress like weddings or exercise—combine to create a perfect storm of stress in 21st Century life that manifests itself in physical symptoms.

THE HARMFUL EFFECTS OF STRESS

- In several studies, including one by the Centers for Disease Control and another by Stanford University, it is estimated that between 80 – 90% of all illness is stress related.

This is a HUGE percentage. You wouldn't fly an airline if 90% of their planes crashed. You wouldn't logically do anything with a 90% negative return. But people endure stress that is so harmful it can cause disease—even death.

- In one study, 78% of those surveyed said they were "on the verge of complete burnout."
- American businesses lose an estimated $300 billion annually due to stress-related absence, turnover, medical expense, and lost productivity, according to the American Psychological Association.

It's instructive to look at the photos of presidents when they enter office and when they leave a few years later. In almost every case, the effects of stress are clearly visible.

Stress…

- ✓ Raises blood sugar.
- ✓ Promotes high blood pressure.
- ✓ Causes insomnia.
- ✓ Is a major factor in premature aging.
- ✓ Causes the majority of headaches, back pain, and skin problems.
- ✓ People under stress suffer more from colds, asthma, and digestive disorders.
- ✓ Major stress actually reduces the amount of brain tissue in regions of the brain that regulate emotions and self-control. It's one reason why so many people are having emotional "meltdowns," panic attacks, and difficulty controlling their impulses.
- ✓ Stress reduces job performance and productivity by as much as 25%.
- ✓ In one study of 200,000 employees with stressful jobs, stress increased the likelihood of heart attack by 23%.

✓ In another study, men under stress were found to be much less sexually attractive to females. Considering how negatively stress affects looks and sex drive, this isn't surprising.

FINANCIAL STRESS

Finances are the #1 cause of stress for most people, including:

1.	Living beyond your means	70%
2.	Saving for retirement	51%
3.	Child's education	48%
4.	Paying off debts	45%
5.	Unexpected fees	41%
6.	Affording girlfriend, wife, family	39%
7.	Losing a job	36%
8.	Picking right insurance	34%
9.	Poor purchase decision	25%
10.	Confusion about investment	21%

Source: *Generation Debt: Take Control of Your Money*, by Carmen Wong Ulrich.

Taking control of your financial life will reduce stress levels significantly.

In CHAPTER 2: *WEALTH*, you'll find guidance and resources to help you get your financial plan for life underway.

RELATIONSHIP STRESS

Conflicts in the major personal relationships in your life are a major source of stress. An unhappy marriage or divorce, misbehaving children, a boss from hell—all can create havoc in your life. Choosing these relationships more carefully, and managing them successfully, will have a major impact on your stress level in life.

In CHAPTER 4: *LOVE* and CHAPTER 7: *YOU*, we will discuss methods to find and create better personal relationships—and how to make the most of your #1 asset...you.

THE HOLMES AND RAHE SCALE OF STRESS

In 1967, psychiatrists Thomas Holmes and Richard Rahe studied the medical records of 5,000 patients to determine what stressful life events might cause disease. A 1 to 100 scale was developed to indicate the degree of stress of typical life events.

If you are like me you've experienced at least a half dozen of these in the past few years.

- 100 Death of a spouse
- 73 Divorce
- 65 Marital separation, end of an intimate relationship
- 63 Detention in jail or prison
- 53 Major injury or illness
- 50 Marriage
- 47 Dismissal from work
- 45 Marital reconciliation
- 45 Retirement
- 44 Major change in health or behavior of a family member
- 40 Pregnancy
- 39 Sexual difficulties
- 39 Gain a new family member
- 39 Business readjustment
- 38 Major change in financial status
- 37 Death of a close friend
- 36 Change to different line of work
- 35 Change in frequency of arguments
- 32 Major mortgage
- 30 Foreclosure of mortgage or loan
- 29 Change in responsibilities at work

- 29 Trouble with in-laws
- 28 Outstanding personal achievement
- 26 Spouse starts or stops work
- 26 Begin or end school
- 25 Change in living conditions

DRIVING YOURSELF TO DISTACTION

Another major cause of stress in the 21st Century is commuting. A study reported on ABC-TV in 2012 told of the harmful effects of commuting to work. If you commute, you are much more likely to be overweight... even if you exercise the same amount as a non-commuter.

Commuting typically is done sitting down. The dangers of sitting for long periods include increased risk of cardiovascular disease, diabetes, cancer, and early death. If you combine the negative health effects of a one or two-hour commute and a sedentary desk job, the risk of developing serious problems increases exponentially. Numerous studies tracking the stress of commuting show elevated stress levels, even for short commutes. Yet 28.5 million Americans commute 30 minutes or more to work, according to 2010 U.S. Census data.

Daily elevated stress levels can result in chronic stress, with all its negative consequences.

When choosing a career or place to live, a major factor to consider is the level of physical activity involved. Although in 21st Century America it is increasingly difficult to avoid sitting and inactivity, you should remember that a sedentary career choice will likely cost you more in health care costs...and a shorter life. This is something almost no one thinks about when deciding what to do in life or where to live.

If inactivity is unavoidable in your job, make sure to stay involved outside of work in an ongoing fitness program. And while at work, take frequent breaks, go on a walk during lunch, and take advantage of any company fitness programs. Exercise—along with adequate rest, meditation, music, good nutrition, vacations, and a successful life—is the key to decreasing stress.

R&R

Rest and relaxation are as important to your health as vigorous exercise. Yet most Americans are woefully clueless about how to relax.

- As a nation we work an entire day (8.6 hours) more each week than the Germans, a nation known for its industriousness.
- Fully 28% of Americans who are employed are on the job by 7 AM and 15% are still on the job at 7 PM. Four in ten American workers don't take lunch. Another 56% take a half hour or less.

Americans are an incredibly hard-working and productive workforce—about the best in the world. But America's work ethic takes an enormous toll on its workers' health. Hank Cox of the National Association of Manufacturers points out "We're a workaholic society. The world is much more competitive than it used to be. These days, you have to run faster and harder just to stay in the same place." As a result, Americans are stressed out by their career, something that ideally should provide a sense of satisfaction and comfort.

VACATION TIME/TIME OFF/SABBATICALS

"Every now and then go away, take a little relaxation, because when you come back to your work, your judgment will be surer."
— Leonardo da Vinci

No other major industrialized country gives its workers so little vacation time, and no other country's workers use so little vacation time, as the United States. Americans average just 13 vacation days annually compared to 38 in France and 27 in Germany. Even the super-industrious Japanese take more time off than we do.

In 2013 American workers left unused 577 million earned vacation days—an average of four days per person, according to Expedia.com...100 million more days than in 2010. The annual total adds up to nearly 1.6 million years. More than 1 in 3 workers don't take all the vacation time they've earned. The French, perhaps wiser about these things, take 94% of their vacation days.

Apparently Americans love their corporations so much they want to present them with a tax-free $67 billion gift every year. That's the collective value of unused vacation time.

IT'S HARD TO GET AHEAD IF YOU'RE DEAD

So why is it important to take your vacation days? Isn't hard work and dedication to the job what made America great? Isn't this the sure way to get ahead? Aren't vacations for wimps?

- In a study of 12,000 middle–aged men, those who took their vacation time reduced their risk of death from heart disease by 30%.
- The Framingham Heart Study found that those who took vacations every six years or less were 8 times more likely to develop heart disease or have a heart attack than those who vacation 2 times a year.

Literally working yourself to death is not the way to get ahead in your career.

Source: *Via magazine*, May/June, 2008, "One nation in need of a vacation." Steve Rushin

Your time to relax, recharge, and de–stress is just as important to your health as exercise and good nutrition.

50 WAYS TO REDUCE STRESS

Here are 50 ways to reduce stress in your life:

1. Take all vacation time you are entitled to receive.
2. If you are married, schedule a date night with your spouse at least once a week.
3. Listen to music.
4. Incorporate silence into your life.
5. Get up 15 minutes earlier and avoid the morning rush.
6. Make love.
7. Play with your kids or someone else's kids. Children live "in the moment" and will take you there with them.
8. Don't lie.
9. Get 7 hours of sleep each night.
10. Take 10 minutes a day and meditate or just be still and breathe deeply.

11. Get organized. It's good feng shui.
12. Losing things is stressful. Keep your wallet/purse and keys in one place. Install the Find My iPhone app on your cellphone. Tag important items with a Tile tracking device www.thetileapp.com.
13. Make it a point to meet with friends at least once a week—particularly friends you can talk to about what's on your mind—good or bad.
14. Keep a journal.
15. Exercise every day.
16. Don't procrastinate.
17. Simplify.
18. Arrive at appointments 15 minutes early.
19. Take a book, magazine or ereader when you know you will be waiting.
20. Plan ahead.
21. Practice preventative maintenance on everything from your car to your relationships.
22. Bless and "love" everything you do—even taking out the trash.
23. Live in the moment.
24. Take a hot bath, shower or immerse yourself in a hot tub.
25. Don't bottle up your problems. Talk them out with a friend.
26. Count to 50 when you feel angry.
27. Don't be a perfectionist. Good is good enough.
28. Say "no" to activities or projects that take up time but provide little positive return.
29. Focus on others rather than yourself.
30. Focus on understanding rather than being understood.
31. Focus on giving rather than getting.
32. Focus on listening rather than speaking.
33. Focus on what you love and want in your life.

34. Banish negative thoughts as soon as they occur. Replace them with positive thoughts. Instead of "I'm fat" say "I'm exercising and watching what I eat." Then do it. Negative self-talk is one of the most damaging things you can do to yourself. It's emotional suicide.
35. Take care of yourself. Looking good makes you feel better. Get in shape. Dress well even when you don't need to. Get plenty of sleep. Relax.
36. Learn to be flexible. Life requires it.
37. Do one thing at a time and do it well.
38. Be grateful for something every day. Keep a gratitude journal. Count your blessings. Say Thank You often. Appreciate what you have.
39. Delegate.
40. Take your lunch break—and don't eat at your desk.
41. Remember that beyond Maslow's hierarchy of "needs" such as food, clothing, and shelter everything else is a higher order "preference." Don't treat preferences as needs. Don't get attached to "wants."
42. Forgive.
43. Avoid people who don't add to your life experience. Negative people abound, naysayers are everywhere, and toxic personalities are all too prevalent.
44. Cultivate optimism. Optimistic people are healthier, wealthier, and happier in life.
45. Reduce or eliminate sugar, artificial ingredients, and caffeine in your diet.
46. Give back. Volunteer.
47. Visualize. Use the power of your mind to imagine success in everything you do. Think positive thoughts before going to sleep.
48. Write it down. Don't rely on your memory. Keep a notebook handy.
49. Get massages. Massage decreases stress, lowers cortisol levels, and boosts the immune system.
50. Own a pet. The companionship and unconditional love of a dog or cat or horse is good for your health—and soul.

Life Rule: Reduce stress and anxiety by taking control of your life (isn't that why you're reading this book?). Make time to play and relax.

ADDICTIONS

"Watch your thoughts, they become words. Watch your words, they become actions. Watch your actions, they become habits. Watch your habits, they become character. Watch your character, it becomes you."
— Attributed to Frank Outlaw

Addictions are deal killers in life. It doesn't matter what you have going for you—you can be rich, talented, great looking, have a killer body, a 150 IQ, and a super personality—it's still possible to fail miserably in life due to a bad habit.

In her book *Addict Nation*, author Jane Velez–Mitchell writes that the motive for any addictive behavior is always the same—to escape painful feelings and unpleasant truths by altering one's mental and emotional state with the addictive substance/behavior. Humans are capable of becoming addicted to nearly anything, from coffee to texting. By this broader definition of addictive behavior, fully 90% of Americans are addicted.

The major addictions that derail people today are:

✓ Smoking.

✓ Gambling.

✓ Drugs.

✓ Alcohol.

✓ Porn/sex.

✓ Unhealthy eating.

The best way to avoid the damage caused by addiction is to not start one. This isn't as easy as it sounds for some people who may have a genetic predisposition to addictive, risky behavior. In *Beyond Addiction: How Science and Kindness Help People Change*, by Jeffrey Foote Ph.D., Carrie Wilkens Ph.D., and and Nicole Kisanke Ph.D., the authors point out that substance abuse problems in particular are often driven by underlying psychiatric disorders such as depression, anxiety, bipolar disorder or attention deficit disorder that require specialized treatment beyond the addiction or abuse problem itself. If you sense you have an attraction to addictive or abusive behavior, get help fast. Once an addiction has taken hold it is often a lifetime struggle to escape.

DO A BAD HABIT PURGE

"What it lies in our power to do, it lies in our power not to do."
— Aristotle

While it may seem logical that you should tackle one bad habit at a time, new research from Baylor College published in the June 2007 *Archives of Internal Medicine* suggests that tackling multiple bad habits may be more effective in ending them permanently. People with a bad habit tend to have others, and they often reinforce each other. Do a clean sweep and purge them all at the same time.

"We first make our habits, then our habits make us."
— John Dryden, British playwright 1631 - 1700

If you smoke and overeat and take drugs you may want to approach your addictions as related problems both psychologically and physically.

- Multiple bad habits are going to require professional help and a lot of personal discipline.
- You'll have to rewire how you think about these habits and learn coping mechanisms.
- You'll have to find new behaviors that replace the harmful ones.
- Overcoming multiple bad habits requires significant social and psychological reinforcement.
- In many cases you will be battling your own body's genetic predisposition toward addiction.

"The chains of habit are generally too small to be felt until they are too strong to be broken."
— Dr. Samuel Johnson, author of *A Dictionary of the English Language*

Enlist someone who cares about you deeply to be your cheerleader, help monitor your progress accurately, and even participate with you in treatment programs, if necessary. It's a fact that people who diet with a friend or spouse have greater success. A support group, like Alcoholics Anonymous, can provide assistance and motivation from others who are experiencing the same addiction. An online resource to help you modify your habits in just 21 days is www.magicfuture.com.

"Each year, one vicious habit rooted out in time ought to make the worst man good." — Benjamin Franklin

Life is full of challenges and transitions. It's often difficult to find the time and motivation to break a bad habit or begin a good one. Giving up cigarettes when you've just lost your job is difficult. Sticking to a diet when you've been dumped by your boyfriend (and need some comfort food) will be a challenge. But for some people tough times can provide extra motivation to make a significant life change. Frequently when a marriage or relationship ends, it provides the "kick in the pants" needed to lose weight or begin an exercise program.

BAD HABITS COST AMERICANS BILLIONS EVERY YEAR

Bad habits cost the U.S. hundreds of billions of dollars every year…money that is often passed on to everyone in higher costs for healthcare, security, law enforcement, and increased taxes. Some bad habits are worse than others. Here are the hard facts about the worst bad habits.

SMOKING

Despite decades of incontrovertible proof about the harmful effects of smoking, nearly 1 in 5 American adults (20.6% of men and 15.3% of women) continue to do so. (2013) Centers for Disease Control

- Tobacco smoke contains 7,000 chemical compounds, including 250 that are known to cause harm and 69 that are known to cause cancer.

As a child I watched in horror as my grandfather died of cancer, a result of decades of smoking. It was a long, painful, humiliating death that seemed to go on for years. I watched as his lung cancer spread to his throat, requiring the surgical removal of his voicebox. Although he couldn't speak, he continued to smoke, exhaling smoke through the tracheotomy hole in his throat.

The cancer spread quickly to his face, requiring the removal of his left jawbone. Then he lost his tongue. The cancer was literally eating him alive. Disfigured and in constant pain, the cancer finally spread to his brain. That was when Grandpa "went crazy," as I remember it.

We visited him in the hospital ward of the institution for the insane where he spent the last days of his life. The memory of it, and the toll it took on my father, has been etched on my mind ever since.

My other grandfather, my mother, and my father all died of smoking related ailments. Although my parents had given up smoking by their early 40's, the damage done by unfiltered Chesterfields smoked daily from the age of 17 couldn't be totally reversed. My relatives joined the 440,000 Americans who die every year simply because they smoked.

No one is immune from the harmful effects of smoking. Movie star John Wayne died from lung cancer. Johnny Carson died of emphysema. Humphrey Bogart died of cancer. And ironically, the original Marlboro Man, died of lung cancer. Few people who smoke throughout their life escape without some serious physical damage.

Nearly a third of all cancer deaths are directly caused by smoking. Lung cancer is the leading cause of cancer death in the U.S. for both men and women. It's also the most preventable cause of cancer related death in America.

THE DANGERS OF SECOND-HAND SMOKE

It's now known that second-hand smoke is much more dangerous than previously thought. The number of Americans who die from second-hand smoke is alarming. As a child, with two parents who smoked, I often suffered from bronchial infections. At one point it became so serious that I was nearly misdiagnosed as having tuberculosis. I remember preparing myself to leave home for treatment. Luckily, a sharp physician saw that I had serious bronchitis and not tuberculosis. My brother developed asthma. When my parents finally gave up smoking, our lung problems disappeared.

- ➢ According to the EPA (Environmental Protection Agency), hundreds of thousands of children suffer from lung infections such as bronchitis, asthma, and pneumonia due to second-hand smoke.
- ➢ Hundreds of thousands of children experience ear infections as a

result of second-hand smoke.

- ➢ Second-hand smoke causes at least 3,000 deaths from lung cancer each year.
- ➢ An estimated 35,000 deaths from heart disease in non-smokers is caused by second-hand smoke.
- Smoking causes more than $157 billion in health-related economic costs every year—more than $1.6 trillion dollars every decade.

The damaging effects of smoking are considerable:

- 1 in 2 lifetime smokers will die from smoking, with half occurring during middle age.
- 87% of lung cancer deaths are due to smoking.
- More than 100,000 men and 100,000 women will develop lung cancer this year.
- Male smokers will lose an average of 13.2 years of life and female smokers 14.5 years of life, according to the American Cancer Society.
- Smoking destroys the cardiovascular system. The ability of blood to flow throughout your body is severely restricted. If you smoke, your risk of vascular disease is 16 times greater than a non-smoker—greater than any other cause, including obesity, high blood pressure or diabetes.
- 1 in 5 deaths from heart disease are caused by smoking.
- Smoking increases periodontal (gum) disease and loss of teeth.
- Smoking weakens the immune system, causing you to be more susceptible to disease.
- Smokers have a higher rate of asthma and allergies than non-smokers.
- Smoking reduces the number and quality of a man's sperm, resulting in increased risk of miscarriage and birth defects, even if the mother doesn't smoke.
- Smoking is directly linked to higher levels of osteoporosis and loss of bone mass.

- Smoking reduces blood flow to the brain. It affects memory and the ability to think clearly.
- Smoking is the cause of 1 in 4 strokes.
- Smoking is linked to macular degeneration, an eye disease that can cause blindness.
- Smokers experience hearing loss about 16 years earlier than non-smokers.
- Women who smoke during pregnancy have higher rates of miscarriage, stillbirths, premature births, cleft pallet, autism and most other birth defects.
- Children born to smokers have a higher incidence of dying during the first year (especially crib death—about 700 babies annually), lower IQ, and impaired emotional development.
- Men who smoke experience erectile dysfunction earlier and more often than non-smokers.
- Smokers have facial wrinkling in their 40's comparable to people in their 60's.
- Smokers have higher rates of diabetes.
- Smokers have higher rates of colon cancer and polyps.
- Smoking is a leading cause of oral cancer.
- Smoking is a major cause of cancer of the cervix.
- Smokers have higher rates of bladder cancer.
- Smoking is a leading cause of stomach cancer.
- Smokers heal more slowly from injury than non-smokers.

Sources: Center for Disease Control, American Cancer Society, the EPA, QuitSmoking.com, Cancer Facts and Figures (2008), the American Council on Science and Health book *Cigarettes: What the Warning Label Doesn't Tell You* referencing more than 450 articles from respected medical journals and reviewed by over 40 medical experts.

- ✓ Smokers are twice as likely to quit when they get texts encouraging them to stick with it. The National Cancer Institute offers this service. To sign up, text QUIT to 47848.

For more help with quitting, go to www.smokefree.gov or call 1-800-QUIT-NOW.

GAMBLING

As I'm writing about the harm a gambling addiction can cause, a story appeared on the nightly news about a young man who gambled away more than $90,000—money his parents had worked years to accumulate for his college education. Obviously, this rash act will affect the rest of his life. But his story isn't unusual.

An estimated 1% of the population (about 3 million people) are pathological gambling addicts. Another 2% – 3% (6 – 9 million people) are "problem" gamblers.

Gambling has gone from a practice that was frowned upon by most Americans to a national pastime.

- ➢ According to the National Council on Problem Gambling, 85% of Americans have gambled at least once in their life, 60% within the past year.
- ➢ The National Research Council estimates that Americans spend more than half a trillion dollars annually gambling.

Gambling has other, insidious, affects upon people. Those who gamble are significantly less likely to feel happy and in control of their lives. This loss of control and feeling of well-being leads to depression. And depression leads to....well, you see where this is going. It's a downward spiral. In fact, on average gamblers account for more suicides, crime, and child abuse than non-gamblers...by a wide margin.

If you have a gambling addiction, get help. Call Gamblers Anonymous at 888-GA-HELPS and go to www.gamblersanonymous.org for more information. Another resource is the National Council on Problem Gambling at 800-522-4700.

WE LIVE IN A DRUGGED SOCIETY

➢ "47.9% of Americans used at least one prescription drug during the past month." Centers for Disease Control, 2012

Federal and State governments, as well as hundreds of private organizations, have spent billions on fighting the massive drug invasion of America. Yet, in 2007 there were 19.9 million people who took illegal drugs—about 8% of the population. This is a war we're not winning. Millions more take…and more than 100,000 each year die from…misuse of prescription drugs.

Americans are the most medicated population on the planet, despite having one of the highest standards of living and the most expensive health care system. Fully a third of the population takes one or two over-the-counter drugs. Another 28% take between 3 – 6 OTC drugs. 32% take that many prescription drugs. Most frightening of all, about 1 in 10 people take more than seven OTC or prescription drugs. As a result, thousands die or are permanently injured every year. No one is immune to the power of drugs and alcohol.

✓ 1 in 4 deaths in America is attributable to alcohol, tobacco or drug abuse.

Drug and alcohol abuse seems to be the preferred way of inducing early death among celebrities:

- Heath Ledger (prescription drugs)
- John Belushi (heroin and cocaine)
- Lenny Bruce (morphine)
- Truman Capote (multiple drug intoxication)
- Billie Holliday (drugs, alcohol)
- Montgomery Clift (drug and alcohol abuse)
- Judy Garland (barbiturates)
- Jim Morrison (heroin)
- Tommy Dorsey (sleeping pills)
- Michael Jackson (propofol, lorazepam, diazepam, midazolam)

- Bruce Lee (prescription pain killers)
- Philip Seymour Hoffman (heroin)
- Brian Epstein (sleeping pills)
- Chris Farley (cocaine and morphine)
- Hank Williams (morphine, alcohol)
- Jimmy Hendrix, (barbiturates)
- Janice Joplin (heroin and alcohol)
- Richard Burton (alcohol)
- Margaux Hemingway (phenobarbital)
- Marilyn Monroe (sleeping pills)
- Elvis Presley (drugs and alcohol)
- Keith Moon (prescription medication/alcoholism)
- River Phoenix (cocaine and heroin)
- Anna Nicole Smith (chloral hydrate and benzodiazapines)
- Ike Turner (cocaine)
- Jeanine Deckers—the Singing Nun (barbiturates, alcohol)

And so on.

Nearly 21 million people (9.4% of the U.S. population aged 12 or older) needed treatment for a drug or alcohol problem, according to the National Survey on Drug Use and Health (2007). Yet, only 1 in 10 actually received treatment.

DRUGS AND ALCOHOL KILL IN OTHER WAYS TOO

Crime, HIV, traffic deaths, domestic abuse, divorce, and billions in healthcare treatment are the most obvious consequences of drug and alcohol addiction.

➢ The National Survey on Drug Use and Health reported in 2009 that 1 in 25 people (10.5 million) age 12+ drove while under the influence of illegal drugs. For younger drivers 18 – 25 the figure was about 1 in 6. It's not surprising that 1 in 5 fatally injured drivers tested positive for at least one drug, according to the National

Transportation and Safety Administration.

- A survey by MADD (Mothers Against Drunk Driving) put the figure even higher...they report that 1 in 3 drivers who were killed in motor vehicle crashes in 2009 tested positive for drugs. Roughly 1 in 8 weekend nighttime drivers tested positive for illicit drugs. 1 in 10 high school seniors reported driving a car in the past two weeks after using marijuana.

Drug addiction is pervasive in our society. Every day a child gets on a bus driven by someone under the influence of drugs. Drug addicted doctors treat patients. A surprising number of police officers are high on the job. On any given day you will likely encounter someone under the influence of drugs.

Drug addiction has serious health risks, including increases in:

- ✓ HIV/AIDS.
- ✓ Hepatitis.
- ✓ Kidney disease.
- ✓ Liver disease.
- ✓ Cancer.
- ✓ Prenatal problems.
- ✓ Lung disease.

Drug addiction is extremely difficult to treat successfully. Many people are genetically predisposed to addictive behavior that makes successful treatment problematic. Drugs can cause significant changes in brain structure that exacerbate the difficulty of escaping addiction.

Many who turn to drugs and alcohol are "self-medicating" as a way to deaden the pain of abusive childhoods, mental disorders, trauma, and desperate life circumstances. There is a high incidence of addiction in returning war veterans, the poor, minorities, and those suffering an enormous loss. While the number of hard-core addicts is huge, most drug users are just like you and me. They hold jobs, care for children at home, drive cars, and say Mass (well, I don't say Mass).

Consider this...if you are an illegal drug user, you are an accomplice to murder—there have been more than 50,000 murders in Mexico alone in the past ten years by the drug cartel. Consider that the next time you snort cocaine or shoot up heroin.

The best choice in life is never to try illegal drugs at all. With some drugs just one exposure can trigger the brain changes that lead to addiction.

If you or a loved one is an addict, get help. You can begin by visiting the National Institute on Drug Abuse website at www.drugabuse.org and the Partnership for a Drug-Free America at www.drugfree.org. Or email findatreatment.samhsa.org. For immediate help call 800-662-HELP.

ALCOHOL

"Nothing is stronger than habit." — Ovid

More than 30% of all American adults (42% of men, 19.5% of women) have abused alcohol or suffered from alcoholism at some point in their life, according to a study by the National Institute on Alcohol Abuse and Alcoholism.

- Americans spend more than $1 billion a week on alcoholic beverages.
- The average length of time it took to seek treatment for alcoholism was eight years.
- More than 10,000 deaths each year are the result of drunk driving... one every 48 minutes...accounting for 1/3 of all traffic-related fatalities, according to the Centers for Disease Control.
- Alcohol is a factor in:

✓ 60% of fatal burns.

✓ 83% of all homicides.

✓ 41% of all rapes.

✓ 81% of all wife battering cases.

✓ 50% of sexual abuse.

✓ 40% of fatal car crashes, suicides and falls.

Over-consumption of alcoholic beverages is linked to crime, disease, sexual infidelity, lost worker productivity, heart disease, liver damage, and early aging.

- ➢ There are more than 12 million Americans who are alcoholics, according to Learn-About-Alcoholism.com. More than 1 in 4 people are considered "heavy drinkers." And by some estimates 1 in 15 people are "alcohol dependent."
- ➢ Recent studies from the *Journal of the American Medical Association* show that you are 97% more likely to live to be 85 if you have fewer than three alcoholic beverages a day.

Americans spent $155 billion on alcohol in 2006. Yet 35.5 million Americans couldn't afford to buy enough food to eat.

Thousands of lives have been changed forever by drunk drivers.

- Arissa Garcia was riding in a car struck by a drunk driver. She survived with minor injuries. But her father, mother, and three sisters all died—as did the drunk driver.
- Steven Boyce, a 20-year old Virginia man, killed an entire family while driving drunk. Mark and Amanda Roe and their two young children, Caleb and Tyler, were waiting at a stoplight when Boyce plowed into their vehicle…and destroyed a family.

Every year there are tens of thousands of stories like these. Lives are cut short, families destroyed, careers ruined, hundreds left maimed, and billions of dollars in destruction, lost wages, and lawsuits…just because someone couldn't control their drinking.

Alcoholism is a disease with many complex causes, often the result of a genetic "addictive" personality. It can be extremely difficult to overcome. As the author Stephen King, himself a former alcoholic and drug addict, once said, "Telling an alcohol or drug addict to just stop is like telling someone with diarrhea not to shit."

The discussion of the causes and cures of these two terrible addictions has filled thousands of pages in hundreds of books. There isn't room in this book to give it the attention it deserves. The best advice is to not start. Then you won't need the 12-step programs, detox facilities, interventions, or any of the dozens of methods designed to help alcoholics.

If you are an addict, one place to get help is ALANON. Go online to find a chapter near you. Alcoholics Anonymous is another support organization. www.aa.org

The U.S. Department of Health and Human Services Substance Abuse and Mental Health Services Administration offers a toll-free number for alcohol or drug information and a referral routing service: 1-800-622-HELP (4357). They can help you find local substance abuse treatment and support programs.

To break a harmful addictive behavior, read *Recover to Live: Kick Any Habit, Manage Any Addiction*, by Christopher Kennedy Lawford. It includes a self-treatment program for addiction to alcohol, drugs, gambling, eating disorders, hoarding, smoking, sex, and porn.

The good news is that more than 1 in 5 women and about 1 in 10 men never drink alcohol. While there's nothing harmful about an occasional drink (and there may even be some health benefits), for many people even one drink is one too many.

Life Rule: 90% of what Americans do is rooted in habit. You ARE your habits. So make them good ones. Get rid of the bad ones.

GOOD HEALTH MAKES YOU SMARTER

There are numerous studies showing that a good diet and exercise program can make you smarter.

- Students who eat breakfast consistently score higher than those who skip. Skipping breakfast resulted in a 7% to 10% decline in cognitive tasks, according a report in the *The Wall Street Journal* (2012)
- A study by the University of Pittsburgh School of Medicine, as reported in the journal *Neuroscience* in 2010, also showed that exercise improves cognitive function.
- One study reported in the British *Journal of Sports Medicine* found that aerobic exercise improves both creativity *and* mood.
- A 2011 study by the National Academy of Sciences found that aerobic exercise increases the size of the brain, especially the hippocampus, with new brain cells and enhanced connections which led to better learning and memory.

Creative people often attribute their best ideas to the oxygenation their brain receives during a good run or bike ride. Good blood flow to the brain is essential to its optimal functioning. When there is good blood flow the synapses are firing more efficiently.

In 2005, researchers at the Harvard University Medical School examined data from more than 15,000 women aged 70 and older. Women who ate a diet with plenty of vegetables—especially broccoli, brussel sprouts, leafy greens, and spinach—showed the slowest rate of cognitive decline compared to women who did not.

Neurologist Paul E. Bendheim says, "If you think of the brain as an engine, it's going to run better on high-grade fuel. That's what a brain-healthy diet provides."

Eating the right foods can boost your IQ by as much as 15 points. By providing antioxidants, increasing blood flow to the brain, and promoting the growth of neural connections, these foods are a smart choice.

The Top 10 "Brain" Foods

1. Oysters
2. Whole grains
3. Eggs
4. Curry
5. Berries
6. Nuts/seeds
7. Leafy green vegetables
8. Tea (green or black)
9. Seafood
10. Dark chocolate

WANT GOOD HEALTH? SLEEP ON IT

Sleep may be the secret ingredient to a successful life—one that is within nearly everyone's reach. Yet many Americans are sleep deprived. "The average adult in our society is getting six or seven hours sleep if they're lucky, and many people routinely get by on five hours or less," said David Neubauer, Associate Director of the Johns Hopkins Sleep Disorders Center. "They may not even remember what it's like to feel fully refreshed and awake."

Lack of sleep is very hard on your body. It can increase the risk of many serious and expensive health problems such as heart disease, diabetes, obesity, and high blood pressure. As the number of hours of sleep goes down, the number of physical problems (and hospital visits) goes up.

"Inadequate sleep reduces innovative thinking by 60 percent and flexibility in decision making by 39 percent." — From *Simple Secrets for Becoming Healthy, Wealthy & Wise,* David Niven, Ph.D.

The people who often sleep the least are the ones who need it the most—executives, creative types, and entrepreneurs. Numerous research studies show conclusively that sleepy people make more mistakes, think less clearly, anger more easily, and experience more accidents. The 1989 Exxon-Valdez oil spill off Alaska, the Challenger Space Shuttle disaster, and the catastrophic nuclear meltdown at Chernobyl have all been attributed to human error caused by lack of sleep.

➢ According to the National Sleep Foundation and *Journal of Clinical Sleep Medicine* (2005), 43% of people with sleep problems report being confused in their thinking.

- Sleep-deprived employees have nearly three times as many absentee days as their well-rested colleagues and significantly lower productivity.
- There are nearly as many sleep deprived Americans—50 million—as there are people in France.
- A third of all adults are chronic or occasional insomniacs.
- Americans spend as much as $20 billion a year on sleep products and prescription medications.
- People who are poor sleepers have medical expenses that run $4,220 a year more than people who sleep well.

THE BENEFITS OF A GOOD NIGHT'S SLEEP

"The best cure for insomnia is to get a lot of sleep." — WC Fields

A good night of sleep has many benefits.

✓ Sleep helps you live longer and healthier.

✓ You'll look better. Your skin will have fewer wrinkles and sags—lack of sleep is a major cause of premature aging. The stress hormone cortisol breaks down skin collagen, the protein that keeps skin smooth and elastic.

- ➢ Sleep affects your metabolism. Growth hormones increase with sleep, according to Dr. Mehmet Oz, author of the *YOU* books. Higher growth hormone levels translates to more muscle mass.
- ✓ You will feel better after a good sleep. Your attitude will be better. And you will think more clearly.
- ✓ Sleep is good for your brain. Tests show that people perform better when rested. Students who get adequate sleep score higher than when sleep-deprived.
- ➢ You are less likely to be injured or killed in an accident... lack of sleep is a cause in more than 100,000 auto accidents every year, according to the National Highway Traffic Safety Administration.
- ✓ Sleep improves sexual performance. Lack of sleep kills sex drive...and lowers the testosterone level in men.
- ✓ Sleep improves your mood. Insomniacs are five times more likely to suffer from depression.
- ✓ Adequate sleep will help you lose weight. People who sleep less than six hours a night are nearly 30% more likely to become obese than those who sleep seven to nine hours.
- ➢ More than half of all people experience insomnia at least a few nights a week, according to the National Sleep Foundation (2005).
- ➢ A study of 7,000 northern California residents in Alameda County found that people who slept less than six hours a night had a 70% higher risk of dying than those who slept seven or eight hours a night. If you're dying to get a good night's sleep you may just be right.

ADAPTING CAVEMAN SLEEPING PATTERNS TO A MODERN 24/7 WORLD

Humans have historically (going back to caveman days) begun their days with the first light of day and went to sleep when it got dark. Ancient man slept so much that they often had two sleep cycles during the dark hours, waking in the middle of the night after six or seven hours sleep to have sex or a bite to eat, then back to sleep for another four or five hours.

Modern humans send conflicting signals to their body by staying up late, watching TV, working on the computer, working night shifts, getting up too early or sleeping in a room that is too light or too warm. All these things disrupt the natural circadian rhythm that a good night's sleep is dependent upon.

MELATONIN...THE MAGIC SLEEP HORMONE

Melatonin is a natural hormone (and antioxidant) created by your brain during sleep that is intimately tied to your circadian rhythm. Melatonin suppresses potentially harmful free radicals, slows the production of estrogen, and may even prevent cancerous tumor development.

Melatonin can be switched off simply by exposing yourself to bright light at night. The bluish light that emits from laptops or iPads is particularly disruptive. Even a brief trip to the bathroom, a night light or the light from an alarm clock can halt the production of melatonin. Avoid light at night. And consider taking 1 – 2 mg of melatonin supplement several hours before retiring.

SLEEP MEDICATIONS ARE LARGELY INEFFECTIVE

Sleep medication is a multi–billion dollar business in the U.S. But these drugs are ineffective at best and dangerous at worst. A 2007 review of sleeping pill studies conducted by the National Institutes of Health, found that drugs like Ambien, Lunesta, and Sonata reduce the average time to go to sleep by just 13 minutes, hardly more than a sugar pill placebo.

HOW TO SLEEP WELL

So how do you get a good night's sleep? Here are a few suggestions. Follow them and they can have an enormous impact upon the quality of your life.

1. **Sleep in complete darkness**. Even a small amount of light can disrupt your pineal gland's production of melatonin and serotonin. An Ohio State University study sponsored by the National Science Foundation found that exposure to light while sleeping can cause you to gain weight.
2. **Go to bed at the same time every night**. Just as you can program your internal "time clock" to help you wake up at the same time every day,

you can also do the same to fall asleep more easily.

3. **Avoid watching TV or using your computer at night.** This may require an overhaul of your lifestyle. However, the impact of light and stimulation at night can have a serious detrimental impact on your sleep. Light makes your brain think it's still daytime and shuts off melatonin production, which under normal circumstances begins around 8 – 9 pm for most people.

4. **Take a hot bath two hours before bedtime.** Besides washing off allergens you've picked up during the day that may be clinging to your body (and causing you to be congested at night), the heat increases your core body temperature and signals your body that you are ready for sleep.

5. **Soft music may help turn off your mind to sleep–killing thoughts**. Use music only for as long as it takes to relax, then keep your bedroom quiet and noise–free. Studies have shown that people who live next to busy streets or noisy factories suffer from poor sleep and have more health problems. Even a ticking clock can be too stimulating to your brain and disrupt the secretion of melatonin. Also, a loud alarm clock can be very stressful to your body and set off a chain reaction of physiological effects that can start your day off poorly.

6. **Sleep in a cool room**. Too many people mistakenly believe that it's important to sleep in a warm room. Just the opposite is true. During natural sleep, your internal core temperature drops to its lowest level about four hours after you fall asleep. A warm room disrupts this natural sleep pattern, causing restlessness and distorted circadian rhythms. The optimal room temperature for good sleep is between 60 – 68 degrees. If you use a heated blanket, make sure it is used just to warm the bed prior to sleep. Don't use it throughout the night.

7. **Consider sleeping in separate bedrooms**. More and more couples sleep in separate bedrooms. If one person snores or is a restless sleeper, it affects the sleep quality of their partner.

8. **Go to bed earlier**. If you typically stay up until 11pm or later, try going to bed an hour earlier. People who make this change in their routine report that it makes an enormous impact upon the quality of their life.

9. **Use your bed for sleep (and sex) only**. Using your bed as a

workstation or to watch TV has been shown to be harmful to getting a good night's sleep.

10. **Get regular exercise**. Daily exercise is one of the best sleep aids (just don't exercise immediately prior to sleep).
11. **Meditation or journaling can help declutter your mind**. Worrisome thoughts racing through your mind can be a sleep killer. Try meditating or journaling to clear your mind and induce a relaxed state.
12. **Read**. Many people find that reading is an excellent way to promote sleep... although stay away from "page turners" that can keep you up all night.
13. **Sleep-inducing snacks**. The right kind of snack can help you go to sleep faster. Oatmeal, almonds, honey, whole grain bread, bananas, hummus, cherries, non-fat popcorn, herbal tea...even dark chocolate...all have ingredients that help you sleep. Avoid caffeinated drinks, spicy foods, processed meats, alcohol, tomato sauces, ginseng tea, or soy products.
14. **Exercise**. Regular exercise is one of the top methods of insuring a good night's sleep...just don't exercise during the hours before bedtime.
15. **Lavender**. Essential oil of lavender, or a sachet of lavender flowers, has been shown to help promote sleep. Lavender slows heart rate, blood pressure and induces a relaxed, parasympathetic state, according to University of Miami researchers.
16. **Stretch, massage, deep breathing**. The benefit of relaxation techniques has been proven to help people get to sleep more easily. Plus, massaging your partner can often lead to sex, which can induce sleep for many people.
17. **Lose weight**. People who are overweight often find it difficult to get to sleep at night...and when they do it is frequently interrupted by obesity-related sleep apnea, a dangerous condition that can be deadly.
18. **Quiet**. If possible, keep your sleeping area as quiet as possible. If you live in a noisy environment, try ear plugs. Being awakened by noise is one of the top causes of poor sleep and insomnia.
19. **Melatonin and Valerian root**. Melatonin (a hormone) and Valerian root (an herb) have been used successfully by many people for

generations to induce sleep. Research by the U.S. Health & Human Service Department validates their effectiveness. Just be sure not to take too much melatonin, as recent research indicates it can be harmful...and even cause sleeplessness.

20. **Soothing colors**. Paint your bedroom in soothing colors to help you relax and get to sleep faster. Several research studies indicate that the optimal colors to help you fall asleep are light green, blue, light yellow, and peach.

INVEST IN A GOOD NIGHT'S SLEEP

Since you spend 1/3 of your life in the bedroom doesn't it make sense to invest in making it a sanctuary of comfort and soothing aesthetics?

First, get a big enough bed and furnish it with good linens, a comfortable mattress and pillows, a mattress topper, and a light comforter. Furnish your bedroom so that it is relaxing and inviting, using soothing colors and soft lighting. According to the National Sleep Foundation, the quality of your pillows, sheets, and mattress have a greater impact upon the quality of your sleep than any other factor. If you choose goose down for your pillows and comforter, be sure you aren't allergic to it. Studies indicate that latex pillows work better for most people.

Many people report mattresses made with viscoelastic foam (which molds to your body), such as the Tempur–Pedic brand, to be the most comfortable they have ever slept on. www.temperpedic.com This kind of mattress, or one with pocket coils, has what the mattress industry calls "low motion transfer." That means when any other people in bed with you moves around the mattress doesn't transfer their movement to you (1 in 4 report that "partner movement" is a factor in the quality of their sleep). Also, encase all your bedding, including the mattress, with zip tight cases to keep dust mites from living in your bed with you...to control allergens.

- Keep kids and pets out of your bed. Nearly 1 in 3 said their sleep was negatively affected by these factors.

Whatever choice you make, invest in top quality. Good bedding will make 1/3 of your life much more rewarding. For more information, read *Power Sleep*, by James Maas, Psychology Professor at Cornell University.

For proven strategies on how to get a good night's sleep, go to the National Institute of Health website at www.nih.gov or The National Sleep Foundation www.sleepfoundation.org.

Life Rule: Sleep deprivation can affect everything you do…even how long you live. Make it a priority.

WATER

Two of the most overlooked healthy decisions you can make involve the very elements of life: water and air. Deprive the body of either and life as you know it will end rather quickly.

- ➢ 48% of Americans drink soft drinks every day, according to a study by Yale University's Rudd Center for Food Policy and Obesity (2012)

An amazing array of beverages have been created to replace the best one of them all—water. Americans drink an average of more than 600 soft drinks a year, according to the National Soft Drink Association, each containing as much as 26 teaspoons of sugar or a potentially deadly array of diet chemicals.

It isn't a coincidence that soft drink sales correspond neatly with the rise in diabetes in America, which is now at epidemic levels.

So called "healthy" drinks like Gatorade, Vitamin Water, sweetened tea, and Sobe fruit drinks are a multi-billion dollar business. "Energy" drinks (soft drinks with a few manufactured vitamins and a shot of caffeine) are the 20-somethings' coffee without the antioxidants of coffee. Yet, the healthiest and least expensive drink of all—water—is something we aren't consuming in adequate quantities.

Americans chug prodigious amounts of coffee and tea, both drinks that have many health benefits when not adulterated with other ingredients. In a large study of 400,000 healthy men and women between the ages of 50 and 71 for 13 years by the AARP and National Institutes of Health, those who drank six or more cups of coffee a day were 10% and 15% less likely to die during the study than non-drinkers.

Coffee has been shown to lower the risk of:

- ✓ Diabetes.
- ✓ Alzheimer's disease.
- ✓ Cirrhosis of the liver.
- ✓ Parkinson's disease.

Tea drinking also has many health benefits:

- ✓ It supports the immune system.
- ✓ Lowers the risk of heart disease.
- ✓ Lowers blood pressure.
- ✓ Reduces the risk of Parkinson's disease.
- ✓ Decreases cancer rates.

MOST AMERICANS ARE DEHYDRATED

Americans drink 4.6 glasses of water a day on average....78% of Americans drink less than 8 cups of water daily, according to the National Cancer Institute's Food Attitude & Behavior Survey (2007). It's estimated that 75% of Americans are chronically dehydrated.

Your body is 75% water and your brain is 85% water. Both are highly sensitive to dehydration. When dehydrated, 2/3 of the water loss comes from the interior of the 160 trillion cells in the human body. Virtually every function of the human body depends upon proper hydration to operate properly. That's why it is important to drink enough water—and make sure the water you drink is pure. Hydration has a direct, and often substantial, impact upon your health. In a study by Loma Linda University scientists reported in *Men's Health* magazine, men who drank five glasses of water a day had a 54% decreased risk of having a fatal heart attack compared with those who drank two glasses a day or less.

According to Dr. F. Batmanghelidj, author of *Water: For Health, For Healing, For Life: You're Not Sick, You're Thirsty!* common symptoms of dehydration include:

- ✓ Feeling tired.
- ✓ Anxiety.
- ✓ Irritability.
- ✓ Poor sleep.
- ✓ Irresistible cravings.
- ✓ Lower back pain.
- ✓ Colitis pain.
- ✓ Heartburn.
- ✓ Fibromyalgia.

Chronic dehydration, says Batmanghelidj, can eventually cause irreversible tissue and organ damage.

Even mild dehydration can have serious consequences. According to research published in the *Journal of Nutrition*, dehydration can affect everything from your performance in sports and on the job to your mood and how old you look. At the 1% dehydration level researchers found there were significant adverse effects in test subjects. Their mood changed (for the worse), concentration was hampered, it was difficult completing tasks successfully, and many experienced headaches. In separate studies, physical performance declined among test subjects as dehydration increased. Clearly, it is important to constantly replenish your body with pure water.

WATER CAN HELP YOU LOSE WEIGHT

Water can help you lose weight. *The Journal of Clinical Endocrinology and Metabolism* reported that drinking two cups of chilled water after waking increases metabolic rate by 30%. In a 2011 report in *Obesity* magazine, researchers found that dieters who drank two cups of water before meals lost nearly a third more weight than those who didn't drink water. Lexi Burke Alexander points out in her book *Drinking Water to Lose Weight* that swapping out water for some of the most common drinks in America can help you lose more than 50 pounds a year.

"DIET" DRINKS CAN MAKE YOU FAT

If you think diet drinks can give you a hall pass on sweet drinks, think again. According to the American Diabetes Association, diet soda drinkers have larger waistlines than non–diet drinkers…up to 70% larger. Diet drinks have proven to have no effect upon weight loss. And the chemicals in diet drinks have been implicated in a host of physical problems from cancer to heart disease. Your best bet is to stay away from them. Water is better.

THE MANY BENEFITS OF DRINKING WATER

✓ Hydrates and moisturizes the skin for healthier, more youthful looking skin.

- ✓ Boosts energy and metabolism, especially if you drink chilled water first thing in the morning.
- ✓ Aids in digestion.
- ✓ Regulates body temperature.
- ✓ Helps prevent kidney stones, keeps the bladder bacteria–free, relieves leg cramps.
- ✓ Increases physical and mental performance.
- ✓ Lubricates internal organs.
- ✓ Lessens stress.

Life Rule: For adequate hydration divide your body weight in half and drink that many ounces of water daily (e.g. 140 pounds = 70 ounces of water).

For more information, go to www.epa.gov.

SAFE WATER

The New York Times ran a series of articles in 2009 about toxic water in the United States. The Times discovered that 40% of U.S. community water systems are in violation of the Safe Water Drinking Act.

As a result, 19.5 million Americans fall ill each year from drinking water contaminated with parasites, bacteria, and viruses.

According to the USDA Pesticides Data Program, 54% of tap water in America tests positive for pesticides and other endocrine disrupting chemicals known as "obesegens. These toxic chemicals have been linked to weight gain...as well as birth defects and fertility problems.

There are hundreds of pollutants spoiling our water systems.

- Farmers spread 110 *billion* pounds of commercial fertilizer over 1/8 of America each year.
- The waste from cows in Wisconsin is so bad that the state's water is ranked as the second worst in the U.S.
- Chemicals from industrial plants are routinely dumped into our waterways, despite EPA rules. 45% of U.S. lakes and 39% of rivers are considered "impaired" and unsafe for drinking, fishing or swimming because of pollutant levels in the water.

Filtration and purification plants do not eliminate all potentially harmful substances from our drinking water. Each year there are thousands of safety violations at water purification and treatment facilities. Here are the states with the most violations.

TOP 10 DIRTIEST WATER STATES

1. California
2. Wisconsin
3. North Carolina
4. Florida
5. Texas
6. New York
7. Nevada
8. Pennsylvannia
9. Ohio
10. New Mexico

Despite California's healthy image, New York City's famous pure tap water, and Wisconsin's wholesome Midwest image, the water supplies in these states are frequently polluted. America isn't Bangladesh or Sudan (where millions die from impure water every year), but you should assume the worst anyway just to be safe. Check out your local water supplier. And filter your water.

The best choice is a reverse osmosis filtration system installed where water enters your home. If this isn't possible, install a filter on your tap and use a pitcher filter. Two that are highly recommended are from Brita and Clear 2O. Clear 20 claims to filter out 53 potential contaminants. The cost is only $20 – $30 and it will filter out 99% of the most harmful contaminants.

More than 300 potentially harmful pollutants have been found in America's drinking water supplies—half unregulated. Here are the cities with the cleanest drinking water, according to The Environmental Working Group's analysis since 2004 of cities with populations of 250,000+.

TOP 10 CITIES WITH THE CLEANEST DRINKING WATER

1. Arlington, TX
2. Providence, RI
3. Fort Worth, TX
4. Charleston, SC
5. Boston, MA
6. Honolulu, HI

7. Austin, TX
8. Fairfax County, VA
9. St. Louis, MO
10. Minneapolis, MN

TOP 10 CITIES WITH THE DIRTIEST DRINKING WATER

1. Pensacola, FL
2. Riverside, CA
3. Las Vegas, NV
4. Riverside County, CA
5. Reno, NV
6. Houston, TX
7. Omaha, NE
8. N. Las Vegas, NV
9. San Diego, CA
10. Jacksonville, FL

1 IN 5 PUBLIC WATER SYSTEMS HAVE VIOLATED SAFE DRINKING STANDARDS

In 2009, 20% of the water providers in America were cited for at least one serious safety violation. It's important to keep this in mind before you take your next drink of water. It's up to you to make certain your water is beneficial to your health…not harmful to it.

- To find out more, and to see how your municipal water system scored, go to www.ewg.org, the Environmental Working Group website. You'll find a wealth of other health and safety data on their site from produce safety to pet health.
- Each year by July 1 you should receive in the mail a report—the Consumer Confidence Report—from your water supplier that tells where your water comes from and what's in it. Or you can go to www.epa.gov to see if your annual drinking water quality report is posted online. The EPA (Environmental Protection Agency) has a wealth of information about water at this site.

You can also test your own water. Testing kits are available (fees range from $25 for bacteriological sampling to as much as $300 to test for a range of potentially harmful substances). Be sure to use a certified lab or ask your local water company or health department for a referral.

Life Rule: You are mostly water...so be sure to drink enough to avoid dehydration. Make sure your water is pure. Avoid ALL sugary, toxin–laden drinks...make water your drink of choice.

AIR

"127 million Americans live in areas receiving an 'F' for air quality."
— American Lung Association

Every day of your life you breathe in about 30,000 times...more than 10 million times a year. The quality of this air is important to your health and longevity. Yet, 60% of Americans live in areas where the air is considered at unhealthy pollution levels, according to the Environmental Protection Agency (2009).

The EPA ranks cities and counties each year based upon the air quality measurements reported by state and local agencies. The findings are shocking. Unhealthy air quality can be found in virtually every major city in America, affecting 186 million Americans. The health effects of polluted air, especially over time, can be serious and include:

- ✓ Impaired lung function.
- ✓ Chronic coughing.
- ✓ Nasal congestion.
- ✓ Heart disease.
- ✓ Chronic obstructive pulmonary disorder (COPD).
- ✓ Lung cancer.

In its 2009 "*State of the Air Report*," the American Lung association included rankings of the cleanest and most polluted cities in the U.S. For ozone air pollution, only nine cities made the grade as cleanest in America—where no ozone was found in the unhealthy range.

TOP 9 CITIES WITH THE LEAST OZONE IN THE AIR

1. Billings, MT
2. Carson City, NV
3. Coeur d'Alene, ID
4. Fargo, ND

5. Honolulu, HI
6. Laredo, TX
7. Lincoln, NE
8. Port St. Lucie/Sebastian/Vero Beach, FL
9. Sioux Falls, SD

TOP 10 CLEANIEST CITIES FOR LONG-TERM PARTICULATE POLLUTION

1. Cheyenne, WY
2. Santa Fe, NM
3. Honolulu , HI
4. Farmington, NM
5. Great Falls, MT
6. Anchorage, AK
7. Tucson, AZ
8. Bismarck, ND
9. Flagstaff, AZ
10. Salinas, CA

TOP 10 MOST POLLUTED CITIES BY YEAR-ROUND PARTICULATES

1. Bakersfield, CA
2. Pittsburgh, PA
3. Los Angeles/Long Beach/Riverside, CA
4. Visalia, CA
5. Birmingham, AL
6. Hanford/Corcoran, CA
7. Fresno/Madera, CA
8. Cincinnati, OH
9. Detroit, MI
10. Cleveland/Akron, OH

If the quality of the air you breathe is important to you (and it should be), be sure to check before you move. Some places, like Hilo, Hawaii, and Fairbanks, Alaska, would "logically" seem to have good air quality. Yet these two cities are listed by the World Health Organization as among the most polluted in America. Air quality isn't something most people consider when choosing a place to live or a job. But considering that every breath you take can either help or hurt your health, maybe it should be.

It may also help to purchase a HEPA air filter for your home (portable or installed in your heating system) and at your office. Indoor air is often more polluted than the air outside. Many people report fewer allergic reactions, better sleep, and more energy. You may also want to make sure the car you drive includes an air filter. Check out the *Consumer Reports* rankings of air purifiers. www.consumerreports.org. Or go to www.air-purifiers-america.com for reviews of popular brands.

Life Rule: When you choose a place to live, think about how the air you breathe will affect your health.

SEX...EVERYONE'S FAVORITE WORKOUT

Sex is as important to your health as water, air, food, and sleep. Having sex prompts your brain to release oxytocin, which helps you sleep better. More sleep correlates with better health, weight–loss, and less stress. Sex gets your heart–rate and circulation pumping, which improves your cardiovascular system, lifts mood, and can help you have better skin. People who have sex at least three times a week have 30% more immunoglobulin A proteins, which boosts your immune system. People who have sex at least three times a week cut their risk of heart attack in half, according to recent studies. The increased heart rate and blood flow keeps your heart and circulatory system in top condition.

Frequent sex has a high correlation with feeling optimistic, energized, focused, creative, and less stressed, which can help you perform better and achieve more of your goals. Sex makes people look younger. The hormones produced by sexual activity help refresh skin and lower body fat. Scientists at the Royal Edinburgh Hospital found that couples who have lots of sex look 4 – 7 years younger than less randy test subjects.

Women who have frequent sex have more regular periods, according to endocrinologists as Columbia University and Stanford University. Sex also strengthens the pelvic floor muscles. And did you ladies know that semen contains zinc, calcium and other minerals that can help prevent tooth decay? Just sayin'.

For men there is hardly a better way to increase testosterone and prevent erectile dysfunction than frequent sex. Also, the more frequently a man ejaculates, the more his chance of getting prostate cancer is reduced, according to the *Journal of the American Medical Association.*

Having sex will make you feel more confident, according to sex therapist Sandor Gardos Ph.D., founder of www.mypleasure.com. People also report that sex makes them happier than money, according to the National Bureau of Economic Research.

Life Rule: Don't let outmoded thinking keep you from leading a robust sex life.

ADDING (OR SUBTRACTING) YEARS FROM YOUR LIFE

Trisha Macnair M.D., and Olga Calof M.D., authors of *The Long Life Equation: 100 Factors that Determine How Long You'll Live* list 100 factors that can either add or subtract years from your life, along with the substantiating support data. Here are a few of their findings:

- **+9 years.** Low levels of life satisfaction correlate with higher mortality. Happy people have stronger immune systems and live longer.
- **+8 years.** The Mayo Clinic found that optimistic people live nearly a decade longer than pessimists...and are 50% less likely to die prematurely.
- **+7 years.** Married people live an average of seven years longer than singles, according to a UCLA research study.
- **+2 years.** A Harvard study of 71,000 men found that regular exercise extended life more than two years compared to sedentary men.
- **+9 years.** Long–living parents translates to good genes and a long life for you too.
- **+6 years.** Good dental hygiene correlates with good health.
- **+4 years.** Good safe sex...and lots of it...supports physical and mental health.
- **+7 years.** Have faith. Hundreds of studies show a longevity and health link between religion or spiritual belief and how long you will live.
- **+10 years.** Place of birth. Living in a safe, comfortable climate, adds years to your life.
- **+2 years.** Washing your hands frequently can add years to your life.

Also, ask your doctor if he/she has washed up before examining you... only 40% do, according to a World Health Organization study.

- **+3 years.** Getting all the vitamins your body needs...ideally from real food...correlates with a longer life.
- **+10 years.** Being female.

Now for the bad news.

- **–8 years.** Smoking.
- **–8 years.** Risky sex.
- **–2 years.** Stress. Death of a spouse or family member, divorce, illness or injury, marriage or losing a job are among the top stressors...and could shorten your life.
- **–10 years.** Bad genes.
- **–3 years.** Obesity.
- **–1 year.** Too much sugar.
- **–4 years.** Fast food.
- **–8 years.** A sedentary lifestyle or sitting too much.
- **–4 years.** Side effects from prescription drugs. Every year an estimated 7,000 people die from hospital medication errors and 106,000 (about the same as the population of Santa Barbara) die from the side effects of prescription drugs.
- **–5 years.** Extreme sports. Every year there are millions of injuries and hundreds of deaths caused by engaging in sports. And if you think being an athlete will help you live longer consider this, the average age at death of an NFL pro is 55 years.
- **–4 years.** Recreational drugs.
- **–2 years.** Binge drinking.
- **–3 years.** Divorce. Divorced people have higher rates of stress, emotional problems, accidental and intentional deaths, heart disease, cancer, drug abuse, depression, anxiety, and alcoholism.

So, if you're a divorced, obese, alcoholic, drug-taking, skydiver who likes to eat Big Macs, sit in front of the TV all day, has sex with prostitutes, once played in the NFL, and have parents who died at a young age...well, start shopping for your burial plot NOW.

Life Rule: The way you choose to live will likely determine how long... and how well... you live.

IF YOU DO NOTHING ELSE, DO THESE FOUR THINGS

In a long-term study of more than 23,000 Germans between age 35 - 65 by the European Prospective Investigation into Cancer and Nutrition (EPI) Potsdam study (2009), four lifestyle choices resulted in a reduction in the probability of developing a chronic disease by as much as 80%. The four factors are:

1. Never smoked.
2. Body mass index (BMI) of less than 30%.
3. A minimum of 3 ½ hours of physical activity every week.
4. A nutritious diet with a high intake of vegetables, fruits, whole grains... and low red meat consumption.

HEALTHY LIFE RULES to incorporate into your Plan for Life:

- Eat from the Plan for Life list of healthy foods only, mostly fruits and vegetables. Choose organic, non-GMO food.
- Add an ounce of nuts to your diet every day.
- Eat lean meat and fowl from organic pasture-raised animals on occasion.
- Eat organic eggs from free-range chickens 2 - 4 times a week.
- Cut overall caloric intake by 1/3.
- Eliminate soda, energy drinks, vitamin waters, sugary coffee concoctions, and ice cream shakes from your diet.
- Increase Omega 3's in your diet by eating seafood or taking fish oil three times a week.
- Take Vitamin D (or get 20 minutes of sun exposure daily).

- Drink water, at least 5 glasses a day. Buy a water filter and drink tap water rather than bottled water.
- Keep your kitchen sanitized. Wash your hands frequently...especially after touching high risk surfaces such as shopping cart handles and gas pumps.
- Wash fruits and vegetables. Consider purchasing a Tersano Lotus Sanitizing System (available on Amazon.com for about $200) to thoroughly remove both bacteria and pesticide residue.
- Avoid processed foods.
- Don't eat at fast-food restaurants.
- Don't drink alcohol in excess...or at all. If you do drink, keep it to a glass of wine or beer once or twice a week. If you are an alcoholic, get help.
- Exercise at least five times a week, doing both aerobic and resistance exercises. Join a health club...or check out your local YMCA or community center for less expensive exercise alternatives. Or purchase one of the exercise-at-home courses, such as Jillian Michaels Body Revolution (about $140) www.jillianmichaelsbodyrevolution.com, Tony Horton's PX-90 program www.beachbody.com or the popular Zumba dance exercise classes www.zumba.com.
- Don't smoke. If you do, give it up.
- Don't take illegal drugs. Join a drug rehab program to kick the habit. Be careful about prescription drugs—more than 100,000 people die from prescription drug misuse every year.
- Brush your teeth at least twice a day. Use dental floss. See your dentist once a year.
- Get a physical exam every other year (every year if you are older). If you have an illness or disease, stay involved in managing it with your doctors. Always get a second opinion. Consider getting a DNA profile to uncover genetic predispositions to certain diseases.
- Sleep at least 7 hours every night. Invest in good bedding. Keep your room cool, dark, and quiet. Avoid late-night stimulation.
- Meditate for 15 minutes a day or more to lower stress. Consider adding

yoga to your fitness regime.

- Take vacations. Have some fun. Laugh.
- Live where the air and water are clean.
- Avoid toxins in your home.
- Have lots of (safe) sex with someone you love.
- Spend time with friends.
- Get massages.

Resources:

- Fitbit Force. This tiny clip–on device tracks how far you've walked, how many calories you've burned (and you can input how many you've consumed), how you've slept and how long, and several other things that will help you stay on top of your overall physical fitness. Plus, it downloads automatically to your computer or smartphone, where you can track your progress every day and over time. $130 www.fitbit.com
- Up by Jawbone. The UP system includes a high–tech wristband that tracks your movement and sleep to give you an instant snapshot of your health. The accompanying app displays data, lets you add food items and calories…even your mood. Up tracks the number of calories you've expended, the number of steps you've taken, and alerts you when you sit too long. It can even wake you up at the perfect point in your sleep cycle with its built–in alarm. $130 for the UP and $150 for the UP24. https://jawbone.com/up
- Basis www.mybasis.com is a wristband monitor that tracks all phases of sleep, walking, running, cycling, and heart rate. The tracking reports are impressive. $179 – $199.
- Vitamix ($350 – $450) www.vitamix.com or Blendtec ($350 – $1,000) www.blendtec.com blenders are highly recommended for juicing.

1 in 5 smartphone users has at least one health–related app (as of 2012). Here are a few to check out:

- **Lose It!** www.loseit.com (85% report losing weight with this app based upon scientific, Skinnerian research)

- **MapMyRide** www.mapmyride.com
- **MapMyFitness** www.mapmyfitness.com
- **MapMyRun** www.mapmyrun.com
- **MapMyWalk** www.mapmywalk.com
- **RunKeeper** www.runkeeper.com
- **Nike Training Club** (part of a comprehensive fitness program from Nike) www.nike.com **Endomondo** (sports tracking) www.endomondo.com
- **Hundred Pushups** www.hundredpushups.com
- **Fooducate** www.fooducate.com
- **My Food Diary** www.MyFoodDiary.com (75,000 foods and 700+ activities)
- **The Daily Plate** www.TheDailyPlate.com

Online resources:

- www.medline.com
- www.webMD.com
- The New York Times Well Blog www.well.blogs.nytimes.com
- Time Healthland https://www.facebook.com/TIMEHealthland
- YogaMint www.yogamint.com
- www.weandMe.com

Further reading:

Eat This, Not That! by David Zinczenko and Matt Goulding
This series of books takes a look at similar foods from different sources and shows which one is the healthiest choice. A few easy food swaps can make a huge difference in the amount of calories and fat you ingest. The *Eat This Not That!* books cover almost every food and dining out choice you can imagine. Plus, the authors provide plenty of nutrition and food preparation tips to help you eat a healthier diet.

There are (at last count) ten other books in the series, including *Drink This, Not That!* and *Cook This Not That!*. http://eatthis.menshealth.com/home .

The Real Age Makeover by Michael F. Roizen M.D.
Your birthday may say 30 but your "real" age could be 50, depending upon the kind of lifestyle you lead. Dr. Oz's pal Dr. Michael Roizen examines a wide range of choices that will either help you stay young or prematurely age you. Start by taking the Real Age Makeover test at www.realage.com to determine your "real age."

This is a big book—almost 500 pages. But you'll find something on nearly every page that can help you live longer, feel and look younger, be happier, and stay disease-free.

YOU The Owner's Manual by Dr. Michael Roizen and Dr. Mehmet Oz
Few health advocates have captured the attention of America as well as Dr. Mehmet Oz and Dr. Michael Roizen. Their books have sold millions. The Dr. Oz program is a favorite on cable TV. Both doctors "walk the walk" by living productive, healthy lives. They've produced nearly a dozen books, hundreds of articles, CDs/DVDs, and television programs. Yet, Dr. Oz still performs several heart surgeries every week (more than 5,000 total). In other words, these guys have major credibility. There are several books in the YOU series, covering a wide range of health issues. Each contains many facts and resources that can help you live a healthier and longer life.

Also by Dr. Oz and Dr. Roizen:

- ✓ ***You. Staying Younger.***
- ✓ ***You. Being Beautiful.***
- ✓ ***You. On a Diet.***
- ✓ ***You. The Smart Patient.***
- ✓ ***You. On a Walk.***
- ✓ ***You. Breathing Easy.***
- ✓ ***You. Having a Baby.***
- ✓ ***The Real Age Makeover.***
- ✓ ***The Real Age Diet.***

Additional recommended reading:

- ✓ ***Disease Proof*** by Dr. David Katz www.diseaseproof.com.
- ✓ ***The Most Effective Way to Live Longer*** by Johnny Bowden, Ph.D. www.jonnybowden.com.
- ✓ ***The Seven Pillars of Longevity*** by Johnny Bowden, Ph.D.

- ✓ ***The 150 Most Effective Ways to Boost Your Energy*** by Johnny Bowden, Ph.D.
- ✓ ***Food Rules: An Eaters Manual*** by Michael Pollan.
- ✓ ***You Are What You Eat: The Plan That Will Change Your Life*** by Dr. Gillian McKeith.
- ✓ ***Anti Cancer: A New Way of Life*** by David Servan–Schreiber, MD, Ph.D.
- ✓ ***The Power of Habit: Why We Do What We Do In Life And Business*** by Charles Duhigg.
- ✓ ***Yoga Cures: Over 50 Simple Routines for Radiant Health*** by Tara Stiles.
- ✓ ***The Omega 3 Connection*** by Andrew Stoll MD.
- ✓ ***The Blood Sugar Solution*** by Dr. Mark Hyman.
- ✓ ***Why We Get Fat: And What To Do About It*** by Gary Taubes.
- ✓ ***Mindless Eating: Why We Eat More Than We Think*** by Brian Wansink Ph.D.
- ✓ ***Maximum Strength: Get Your Strongest Body in 16 Weeks with the Ultimate Weight–Training Program*** by Eric Cressey.
- ✓ ***The First 20 Minutes: Surprising Science Reveals How We Can Exercise Better, Train Smarter, and Live Longer*** by Gretchen Reynolds.

Life Rule: Your health is intimately connected to the success of every other area of your life. Make it a daily priority in your life.

NOTE: If you have a health or fitness resource you've found valuable that could be helpful to my readers, send it to eric@APlanForLife.com

CHAPTER 2
WEALTH

MONEY MATTERS

"Money is better than poverty, if only for financial reasons."
— Woody Allen

Money matters. A lot. You'll likely live longer, better, and more happily with money than without it. Next to your health, money may be the most important part of your life you'll need to manage well. In fact, both are intimately connected. As a person's financial health improves, so does their real health. People making more than $100,000 a year can expect to live a decade longer than their less well–off neighbors.

If you are financially secure you'll have access to first–class healthcare. With enough money you can afford vacations, yoga retreats, a health club membership, a personal trainer, and healthy organic food. Money can buy you a safer car and a safer neighborhood. Or more education that often translates into even more money. Money allows you to purchase the "little things" that add up to greater well–being…like high quality bedding that enables you to sleep better, feel more refreshed, and be more productive. Money problems are at the root of much of the high levels of stress and anxiety in America. Stress and anxiety are at the root of most health problems.

- Money is the cause of more divorces than cheating or sex…57% of divorced couples said money fights were the primary reason they didn't get along, according to a 2010 Citibank study.

Most important, money can buy a future of hope, promise, and fulfillment. As the poet Carl Sandburg said, "Money is power, freedom, a cushion, the root of all evil, the sum of all blessings."

MONEY FUELS PROGRESS

"Money alone sets all the world in motion." — Publilius Syrus

Money can change the world. Money funds entrepreneurs...and the businesses they start up...driving innovation that helps our economy grow, creates jobs, and makes the world a better place. Money funds advances in science and medicine, supports schools and charities, and advances in healthcare. Money is the lifeblood of the 21st Century.

MAKING IT (MONEY) IS HARDER THAN EVER

In the past 30 years, 96% of the growth in average income in the U.S. has gone to the richest 10% while the other 90% have seen average income decline.

In 1998 the percentage of Americans who said they considered themselves among the "have nots" was 17%. While this figure seems extraordinary in the world's richest nation, consider this—the percentage of Americans in 2006 who said they are among the "have nots" was 34%. In less than a decade the number of people who consider themselves "have nots" doubled.

A 2012 survey by CashNetUSA.com found that 25% of Americans report being "flat broke." A 2013 survey from the Associated Press found that 4 out of 5 Americans face joblessness, poverty or near poverty, or a reliance on welfare for at least part of their lives.

According to the U.S. Census Bureau, 46 million Americans live in poverty (defined in 2010 as a family of four earning $22,314 or less). The U.S. Department of Education reported in January, 2015, that 51% of public school students now live in poverty. The Middle Class is fast becoming a thing of the past as technology replaces jobs people once held, millions of jobs are sent overseas, and companies do more with fewer workers.

Nearly 1 in 4 (23%) of retired married couples and almost 1 in 2 (46%) of retired single people receive at least 90% of their income from Social Security. Most seniors are heavily, if not entirely, dependent upon Social

Security benefits—averaging about $1,234 a month (2012). According to the Congressional Budget Office, a significant percentage of Baby Boomers will be financially destitute at retirement age.

The future looks even worse for recent college grads. Many are burdened with high debt loads from student loans averaging nearly $29,400 (2013). Job prospects remain dim, with millions of college grads working at or near minimum wage in jobs that don't make use of their education. In fact, 46% of college grads are working at jobs that require only a high school education.

Yet prices are skyrocketing on everything from food to transportation to healthcare. The result is an ever tightening financial noose. The only way people have been able to survive at all is to stop buying things they want or need—or drain their hard-earned savings.

REAL WAGES HAVEN'T INCREASED SINCE 1979

"Money isn't everything...as long as you have enough."
— Malcom Forbes

Although worker productivity has increased about 80% since 1979, adjusted for inflation, real wages haven't increased at all. The result is the largest inequality in income since the 1920's. The top 1% of Americans now has a higher aggregate income than the bottom 50%. The richest 85 people in the world have more wealth than the bottom 50%...3.5 billion people. Sometimes the wealth disparity is dramatic. Ted Turner, for instance, owns 5% of the state of New Mexico. His total land holdings are nearly the size of three Rhode Islands, about 2 million acres. His pal John Malone is the largest private land owner in America at 2.2 million acres, including 1.2 million acres of Maine...5% of the state.

Former presidential candidate Mitt Romney is worth hundreds of millions and owns four palatial homes. When asked, presidential candidate John McCain famously couldn't remember how many homes he owned. Secretary of State John Kerry is married to the heir to the Heinz ketchup fortune, Teresa Heinz, whose net worth is more than $1 billion (compared to her husband's $200 million). There are dozens of millionaires in the U.S. Senate and House of Representatives. And big money interests now have more influence over our government than at any time in recent history.

Celebrities get paid millions every year.

- ✓ The often incoherent Glenn Beck pulls down more than $30 million annually.
- ✓ Kim Kardashian makes tens of millions every year for...being Kim Kardashian.
- ✓ Mariah Carey has a net worth of half a billion dollars.
- ✓ Sports stars routinely are offered contracts totaling more than $100 million.
- ✓ Aaron Spelling's home is valued at $147 million.

Obscene amounts of wealth are concentrated at the top with an ever-decreasing amount to be shared by everyone else. It has never been as important to create a plan for your life that will help you survive—even thrive—during these challenging times.

A NATION OF FINANCIAL ILLITERATES

"A fool and his money are soon separated." — Anonymous

According to the Jump$tart Coalition for Personal Financial Literacy www.jumpstart.org, most Americans have abysmally low levels of financial literacy. They get little or no usable financial training at school. And few people have parents who are financially literate enough to teach them about wealth generation and management. Most Americans learn about finances the hard way...by trial and error. A lot of error.

- ✓ 6 out of 10 Americans miss taking legal deductions on their taxes.
- ✓ 22 million overpay on their taxes.
- ✓ 56% don't have a personal or family budget.
- ✓ 4 in 10 carry credit card balances from month to month.
- ✓ 23% of American adults have never reviewed their credit report.
- ✓ Millions pay for their credit report when they could get it free from www.annualcreditreport.com.
- ✓ 40% of Americans never balance their checkbook.

- ✓ 50% of Americans with children haven't created a will.
- ➢ More than 40% of Americans have less than $1,000 in liquid non-retirement savings, according the US Census Bureau.

Americans do almost no financial management during their lives: They...

- Have no clue what they spend their money on.
- Don't save regularly.
- Invest foolishly on "tips" from friends or strangers.
- Are easily scammed.
- Gamble away billions of dollars.
- Blow billions on tobacco, alcohol, and illegal drugs.
- Make buying decisions based upon astrology. Or some loud-mouthed money guru on TV.
- Buy homes they have no way of ever affording.
- Pay too much for the things they buy.
- Engage in "retail therapy," shopping for stuff they don't need to feel good temporarily.
- Have no plans for retirement. Fewer than 25% know how much they will need to retire—and only 2 in 10 have enough saved.
- Only 1 in 10 people have any idea what an annuity is or how it works. The same is true for insurance investments and the stock market. And forget about REITs, ETF's, derivatives or other moderately complicated investments.
- 4 in 5 mismanage their 401k plans.

BE SMART ABOUT MONEY

Incredibly, Americans think they know about personal finance. A 2006 survey by *Entrepreneur* magazine revealed that 70% feel they are good or excellent at managing their finances.

So the how do you explain that 43% of Americans spend more than they earn? Or that there have been nearly a million personal bankruptcies every year since 2000? Or that half of retirees have less than $10,000 in savings and investments? Or that most college grads don't know how to properly balance their checkbook. What Americans think they know about finance…and what they actually know…are worlds apart.

30 REASONS WHY YOU SUCK AT FINANCE

It's the Kruger–Dunning Effect…the cognitive bias that you think you know more than you really know. In reality, you don't know enough to know you don't know. Here's why you suck at finance.

1. When you make more money you automatically spend more money. After all, isn't that why you made it?
2. You buy stuff, like expensive cars, to impress The Jones…when The Jones could care less about you.
3. When the government runs a deficit, you think they're fools…but when you run a deficit, well, that's OK.
4. You run up a huge student loan debt to get a nearly worthless degree and join the ranks of MBA baristas so you earn enough to pay off the loan in 90 years.
5. It hasn't dawned on you that you need to be a "millionaire" just to live a moderately nice retirement.
6. You've made a little money and now think you're smart enough to trade stocks online, not realizing you're competing against computers making thousands of trades a second and that a simple low-fee index fund will surely do better.
7. Your company offers matching 401k contributions…but you're too lazy to fill out the forms.
8. When the market goes up you believe you're a brilliant investor without knowing that you played almost no part in your success…but when it goes down you blame it on Obamacare, the crooks on Wall Street or "bad karma."
9. You invest based on a stock top your barber said he got from a "big shot on Wall Street."

10. You subscribe to every investment magazine printed, read the *Wall Street Journal*, have The Motley Fool bookmarked on your computer, and watch live stock market TV 24/7...and think that it makes you a smart investor by osmosis.
11. You allow cognitive bias...the delusional propensity to selectively choose to believe what reinforces your ingrained prejudices...to rule your decisions.
12. You spend endless hours on your "investments" when putting that same time and energy into your career would pay off much better.
13. You pay $12,000 more to buy a hybrid car in order to save money on gas...not realizing you will have to own the car for 8 years to make up the difference in cost-savings.
14. You believe that renting a home is "just throwing good money down the toilet" when in many situations it's smarter than buying.
15. You retire at 62, thinking that the $300,000 you've saved will last for the next 20-odd years (your life expectancy) and wonder why so many others who retired with even more are living in trailer parks.
16. You never factor inflation into any of your savings goals.
17. You make decisions based upon popular financial experts and economists...the same ones—30,000 of them—who didn't see the Great Recession coming.
18. You think of the stock market as a doppelganger of Las Vegas and "invest" in your home instead...not realizing that home values trail the average 10% return the market has realized in the past 70 years...or figuring out where you'll live when you cash in that "investment."
19. You succumb to the "Madoff Phenomena"...the "I'll just bury my head in the sand, put my life savings in the hands of a poorly understood investment, because the returns have been 'too good to be true.'" Yes, too good to be true.
20. You "invest" in rubber plantations in Costa Rica and are surprised when the checks bounce.
21. You make all your investments based upon past returns, not realizing there is almost no correlation with future performance.

22. You invest in funds with high fees…so the fund manager can live in the Hamptons, own a private jet, keep a 100–foot yacht, and send his offspring to Ivy League schools with the money he makes selling you mediocre investments that don't outperform the market.
23. You have no idea what you spend your money on. None.
24. Investing in commodities seems like a sexy idea.
25. You send that nice Nigerian priest a few thousand to help the poor. After all, he said his grateful congregation will pay it back with 25% interest.
26. You start collecting Hummel figurines…they are sure to increase in value.
27. You decide to take a chance without insurance. Nothing bad has ever happened to you.
28. You love those shoes…even more than the other 60 pairs you own.
29. Your tarot card reader said you are going to be very rich someday. So you buy some lottery tickets.
30. You're like the majority of Americans who don't bother balancing their checkbooks.

If you're like most Americans, you probably don't know even the basics of investing, finance, and creating real wealth. Which is why so few Americans have any wealth.

A DIZZYING ARRAY OF FINANCIAL CHOICES

In our grandparents day the typical family had a checking account and a savings account at the local bank. Mortgage documents were usually just three or four pages long—not the dozens of pages home buyers and sellers have to review now. You couldn't trade stocks online. Visa, Mastercard, and American Express didn't exist. Cars weren't leased back in those simpler days. There was no 401k. Or IRA. No 529 plan for college. No student loans. There wasn't much your grandma needed to know about personal financial management.

In the 21st Century you have to make decisions about dozens of options that impact your financial well-being. In our increasingly busy and distracted lives, it is more difficult than ever to keep up with the complex financial options available.

Making matters worse, these options change with dizzying frequency. Just when you understand an IRA, there's a Roth IRA to integrate into your financial knowledge. When you think you know what to do about your health insurance, that all changes. Meanwhile, it seems that everyone from your bank to your friendly insurance agent is trying to make a buck off of you with endless offers, hidden fees, and downright subterfuge.

IT TAKES STUDY, WORK, AND EFFORT TO BECOME MONEY-SMART

Finances will play a large role in how successful and happy you are in life. So it pays (literally) to educate yourself in the basics—budgeting, saving, real estate, IRAs, stocks, 401ks, bonds.

For those who haven't already grabbed the brass ring, foreclosures, record job losses, bankrupt companies, budget deficits, government ineptitude, and a global financial crisis are about to make life more difficult than they could have ever imagined. Macro forces are in play that will disrupt everything in the next decade.

- ✓ The continued outsourcing of labor.
- ✓ Globalization and the rise of previously Third-world economies.
- ✓ The increased use of tech-driven automation and robotics by nearly all industries.
- ✓ The disruption of established industries by startups and the internet.
- ✓ The rise in population.
- ✓ The increased expense of basic resources, including food, housing, and fuel.
- ✓ The rise in the percentage of educated Americans.

All these major disruptive forces will make it more important than ever to plan a path to success for the future. It's important...indeed, it's your DUTY...to learn everything you can about how to manage your money well.

Make an effort to educate yourself about financial matters. It will be well worth it over a lifetime. One place to begin is Bank of America's online personal finance course (in partnership with Khan Academy), Better Money Habits www.bettermoneyhabits.com.

Life Rule: Become financially literate...or pay the consequences.

SAVE

Most financial advisors recommend saving 10% or more of your after-tax income. This will usually require two things:

1. Living below your means.
2. Creating a personal budget.

Assuming you have a job (the key ingredient in saving), there are many ways, big and small, to save.

HOW ANYONE CAN SAVE $5,000 A YEAR—OR MORE

"Beware of little expenses; a small leak will sink a great ship."
— Benjamin Franklin

Assuming you earn at least $40,000 a year, it's easy to save a minimum of $5,000 a year with very little effort. It's even possible on a lot less income. If you're like millions of Americans who are either unemployed or under-employed, saving $5,000 or more a year can make the difference between survival and disaster.

I took my own advice and used the savings tips listed below, tracking the savings over two years. The first year our family saved more than $11,000 and the next year our savings topped $14,000. While I can't promise you'll do as well, you should be able to save $5,000 easily.

Each savings tip includes a range of possible annual savings. Guess-timate how much you actually spend on each of the activities or items below. Be conservative. You'll still be surprised at how it adds up. Once you've decided where to save, begin tracking your actual savings. Here are 56 ways to save:

1. Find the least expensive gas stations in your area and buy only from these stations. To find the least expensive stations, go to

www.gasbuddy.com Download the app. Gasbuddy monitors prices by crowdsourcing the latest data sent in by its users. Gas is cheapest on average on Tuesdays, so make that your day to fill up every week.

Also, Americans waste $2 billion a year buying gasoline with a higher octane rating than what is specified for their car. Only about 5% of cars need premium gasoline, yet 20% of all gas sold is premium. Premium gas will not improve your car's performance. In fact, in some cases it can damage your vehicle's engine. Check your owner's manual for the recommended fuel grade. *Annual Savings: $100 – $200*

2. Unplug. When you leave appliances and electronics (microwave, coffeemaker, TV, VCR, computers, game consoles, cell phone chargers) with standby power plugged in 24/7, it's draining electricity continually even when not in use. The power these "vampire" appliances use can add up to as much as 10% of the total electrical usage in your home. If you plug these devices into a power strip you can easily turn it off and disconnect the power completely. Add a timer to shut everything off at night. *Annual Savings: $100 – $250*

3. Switch your standard light bulbs to compact fluorescent or LED bulbs. They use up to 90% less electricity and last as much as 50 times longer. Once installed throughout your home you can save $150 – $250 a year and hundreds more over their lifetime in both energy and replacement costs. The new compact fluorescent bulbs fit most lamps and replicate the "warm" lighting of incandescent bulbs. *Annual Savings: $150 – $250*

4. Drink tap water. Americans spend $20 billion on bottled water every year. If you rely on bottled water, you'll spend about $3 a day...$1,096 a year. Often this water is no better than tap water... sometimes worse. If you want to be sure your water is safe, install a water filter. Water filters are inexpensive, often less than $25. www.brita.com Spend less than 3 cents a gallon for purified tap water versus $4.50 a gallon or more for bottled water. For the best results, install a reverse osmosis whole house filtration system. *Annual Savings: $500 – $3,000*

5. Buy fewer clothes. People seldom plan their wardrobe for maximum

effectiveness, cost–savings, and quality. As a result, you likely have more than enough clothing in your closet now—a lot of it of questionable value. The average person spends about $1,750 a year on clothing and wardrobe upkeep, according to the Bureau of Labor Statistics. Go on a clothes diet and you can save at least half this amount or more. *Annual Savings: $500 – $5,000 +*

6. Find free entertainment. Americans spend about $1,800 a year on various types of entertainment. You can easily save most of this by taking advantage of the many free forms of entertainment available. Visit a museum—most have monthly free days. Or go to an art gallery opening. Get some friends together and watch a movie on TV. Attend a street fair. Or go with friends for a hike in the local park. There are hundreds of fun free activities. With average movie ticket prices at $8.38 (2013)...and live concert tickets five or ten times that much, it pays to get creative about entertainment.

   Watch current movies for free on Hulu www.hulu.com. Join Amazon's Prime ($99 a year) www.amazon.com to stream 41,000 movies and TV shows to your devices. Or check out the On Demand section from your cable or satellite TV provider. And don't forget the local library. When I last looked at the movies available to check out (for free) from our small town's library there were more than 500 titles, many recently released on DVD.

   If you have a smartphone or tablet there are apps that enable you to listen to any of 50,000 radio stations worldwide. Try the TuneInRadio app www.tunein.com.

   Pandora is another popular way to access free music online. You create "stations" by entering the name or a song that represents a style of music you enjoy. Then Pandora delivers songs of that type. For example, enter Ricky Nelson and you will get 60's songs. Enter Lady Gaga and you'll receive songs that are in the same genre. You then either decide you like or dislike the song. Pandora's algorithm will modify the selection of songs it sends you based upon your preferences so that you receive more of what you like. www.Pandora.com.

   Another popular online service is Spotify www.spotify.com. With Spotify you have access to millions of songs on your home computer, tablet, smartphone or streamed to your home entertainment system. You can even download music for offline use.

Or do what families did decades ago—play board games or cards or build puzzles together. It may seem quaint and old-fashioned, but it's a great way to connect with your family—and save money. *Annual Savings: $1.000 – $2,500*

7. To save money on gas cots, think twice about driving. Combine trips. Or shop online. By cutting fuel costs in half, most people can save more than $500 a year. Besides reducing the amount of driving you do, you can save money on gas by following these suggestions.

- **Maintain your vehicle.** A vehicle that runs smoothly uses less gas than one that is poorly maintained.
- **Keep your tires inflated.** Although the savings on gas isn't huge (about 3%), it does make a small difference to keep your tires inflated to the recommended pressure. And more importantly, it's safer and your tires will last longer.
- **Don't drive during rush hour.** Avoid the rush hour. Getting stuck in a traffic jam, and stop-and-go driving, wastes gas.
- **Telecommute.** Working from home can save in gas, not to mention giving you more time, productivity, and happiness.
- **Minimize idling.** One of the worst offenders in lowering your gas mileage is engine idling. If you are going to idle for a minute or less, leave your car on, but if it's any longer than a minute, turn off your car.
- **Accelerate and brake gently.** Driving too aggressively, starting fast and braking fast, is bad for fuel economy. Accelerate gently, and try to minimize use of your brakes.
- **Buy a fuel-efficient car.** Consider a hybrid or electric vehicle. If you downsize from a gas guzzler, *Consumer Reports* estimates you'll save about $1,581 a year in fuel costs.
- **Roll up windows.** While many people think they're saving money by turning off the air-conditioner, it actually creates a strong drag if you are driving fast with the windows down, and decreases fuel economy.
- **Avoid adding auto "bling"** such as roof racks, brush guards, and other items that create wind resistance that can decrease gas mileage.

- **Use cruise control.** A steady driving speed will improve fuel economy.
- **Easing up on your driving** (saves about $400 in fuel costs), taking all the junk out of your trunk (every 100 pounds costs $100 a year in fuel costs), and adhering to regular maintenance ($348 a year savings in fuel on average) can save you hundreds each year.

Annual Savings: $500 – $2,000

8. Here's a savings millions can see immediately—buy your contact lenses online. Monthly disposable lenses can cost as much as $200. But you can cut this cost in half (a savings of $1,200 a year) by buying from an online discount provider. International Vision Direct www.visiondirect.com, 1-800- CONTACTS, and Costco sell contact lens for about $100 a month.

   There are big savings on eyewear online too. Fashionable frames for as little as $7 can be found at online retailers like Zenni Optical www.zennioptical.com.

   Annual Savings: $700 – $1,500

9. A few simple moves can save up to $1,500 a year on your automobile insurance. The amount insurers charge for the same coverage can vary by hundreds of dollars. Start your comparison shopping online at www.InsWeb.com.

Consider the following:

- Raise the deductible to $1,000 and save between 12% – 18%.
- Install a car alarm.
- Insure all cars in your family with the same company.
- Ask for the safe drivers' discount, if applicable.
- Ask for discounts if you don't smoke.
- If you have a student driver, ask for discounts for taking a safe driving course, attending school out of town, and being a good student.

Annual Savings: $200 – $1,500

10. According to *Consumer Reports*, the average family spends 40% of their food budget dining out. Eating one less casual or fast food meal a week and one less dinner or lunch at a moderate to expensive restaurant each month can save a family of four from $1,000 to $1,500 a year. For people

who eat out frequently, eating at home can save as much as $15,000 a year.

Brown–bag it to work too. The average lunch costs about $6.50. But if you bring your lunch from home the cost will be somewhere between $1.35 and $1.80 on average. You can easily save more than $1,000 a year. *Annual Savings: $1,000 – $15,000*

11. When traveling, spend a little time online at the major travel sites such as Orbitz and Expedia, as well as lesser known sites such as Kayak www.kayak.com and CheapTickets www.cheaptickets.com. Check airlines that aren't listed with the major travel sites, such as Southwest Airlines or the smaller regional airlines, to see if they have better deals.

    Airbnb www.Airbnb.com lists private homes and apartments all over the world available for rent. Costs are usually less expensive than at regular hotels and B&Bs. Photos and ratings make it easy to decide if you like a place or not. You can also earn money yourself this way. According to Collaborative Consumption, the average New Yorker listed with Airbnb makes $21,000 a year renting out space to travelers.

    Home exchange is another popular way to both decrease your personal travel costs and earn some extra income. Swapping homes has been around for some time and has only become more professional and sophisticated. Homeexchange.com www.homeexchange.com is one of the biggest and best (40,000 listings in 135 countries) but there are several other sites you should research before making a decision. Visit www.knowyourtrade.com to check out dozens of home exchange companies. Here are some other online resources for inexpensive travel deals:

    www.cheapoair.com
    www.airbnb.com,
    www.hotwire.com
    www.travelocity.com
    www.kayak.com
    www.priceline.com
    www.cheaptickets.com
    www.travelzoo.com
    www.budgettravel.com
    www.homeexchange.com
    www.homeforexchange.com

www.cheapcruises.com
www.discountcruises.com
www.homeaway.com
Annual Savings: $200 – $2,000

12. Prices are often 10% – 20% less at wholesale clubs like Sam's and Costco. Save as much as $1,200 a year.

    Annual Savings: $300 – $2,000

13. Get rid of your landline telephone. Using only your cell phone will save about $300 a year. If you make a lot of international calls, sign up for Skype www.skype.com, which offers extremely low-cost voice-over-Internet-protocol (VOIP) services.

    Check out Magic Jack, a device that costs just $40 (and includes a full year of local and long-distance phone calls) www.magicjack.com It connects to your computer and uses the internet to process calls. *Consumer Reports* evaluated the device and gave it a good review. The sound quality was rated almost as high as a regular land line.
    Annual Savings: $300 – $3000

14. Celebrate Christmas with unique gift ideas. The average American spent $854 on Christmas gifts in 2012, according to the American Research Group. There are ways to cut spending to near zero—and keep the spirit of Christmas.

- Give the gift of your time or skill.
- Give a certificate good for ten car washes or oil changes.
- Buy a block of ten movie tickets at a discount through a movie chain or mass retailer like Costco or Walmart and give them to your kids—and offer to accompany them to any movie they want to see (even if you have to sit through Scooby Doo).
- Buy your wife flowers, a card and include a coupon good for ten massages (from you).
- Give a bag of books picked up at a library book sale.
- Give gift cards and save on packaging and mailing costs.

  Annual Savings: $200 – $1,000

15. You don't need an expensive gym membership to get the workout you need to stay healthy. When UC Berkeley and Stanford University studied the habits of gym members, they found that the average number of times a person visits their health club is once a week. That's not enough time to make an appreciable difference. Instead, get your exercise inexpensively—go for a walk, play tennis, run or ride your bike. If you want to add resistance exercise to your fitness regimen, buy a pair of dumbbells for about $50 and use them at home three or four times a week. *Annual Savings: $700 – $3,000*

16. Save between 10% and 15% on your annual grocery costs by using store coupons. In a year-long test, our family saved 14% overall on our grocery costs. 140 million Americans saved $3.7 billion (2012) at the grocery store using coupons—or an average of $954 a year for the typical family.

    In a survey by the Harrison Group, 81% of consumers say value-conscious shopping is "fun." 93% said they will continue to do it when the economy improves. If your annual food costs are close to the national average of around $10,000 a year for a family of four, it's like giving yourself a luxurious vacation or a new flat-screen TV for doing nothing more than spending a few minutes a week clipping coupons.

    Check out these websites to get started: www.retailmenot.com, www.dealio.com, www.couponmom.com, www.groupon.com, www.coupons.com, www.smartsource.com,www.livingsocial.com,www.dailygrocerycoupon.com, www.redplum.com, www.livingsocial.com. The Roximity www.roximity.com app even finds coupons for businesses you pass as you drive around in your car. At eBates www.ebates.com you get paid cash for shopping at your favorite stores. *Clip and save $1000 – $4,000 a year.*

17. Buy pre-owned cars. Americans spend more than $380 billion a year on new cars. As soon as you drive off the dealer's lot your new car loses about half its value. Here's how to save money and drive in style.

    For the price of a Toyota Corolla or Kia sedan, you can drive an older model Mercedes-Benz or BMW. They are well built and luxurious. Most people who purchase luxury cars are wealthy enough to also care for them. A recent check of AutoTrader listed several late model BMW 740i 4–door sedans for just $12,000 – $18,000. A sporty 1989 Mercedes–Benz 560sl with just 72,000 miles listed for $9,200. You'll save money and ride in style. While maintenance may be more expensive, you'll save thousands on insurance and the purchase price.

Forbes.com listed several used cars that have been recognized as good, reliable values. They include:

- Honda Accord/Civic.
- Toyota 4Runner.
- Acura TL.
- Subaru Impreza.
- Lexus GS.

To research and find used cars, check out these websites: www.kbb.com, (Kelly Blue Book) www.autotrader.com, www.edmunds.com, www.cars.com, www.carsdirect.com, www.craigslist.com, www.NADA.com, and eBay Motors.
Annual savings: $1,000 – $15,000

18. More than $25 billion is spent on book purchases annually. While it's commendable that people are reading and supporting bookstores, you can save hundreds of dollars by visiting the local library. If you haven't been to your library recently, you'll be in for a surprise.

    Most libraries now offer recent bestsellers for a small fee, extensive free video selections, Internet access, audio books, ereaders, downloadable digital content, and a large range of periodicals from around the world. The amount of information can be staggering. The Harvard University and Boston Public Libraries each have more than 15 million volumes. If you are an avid reader, save money by using one of America's 122,000 free libraries.
    Annual savings: $50 – $300

19. Grow your own food. During World War II Americans grew 40% of their own fruits and vegetables in what were called Victory Gardens. Immediately after the attack on Pearl Harbor the U.S. National Defense Gardening Conference set a goal of 10 million urban gardens and 5 million farm gardens by 1942. That goal was reached… and exceeded in the years thereafter as Americans discovered the

economic benefits (and enjoyment) of growing their own food.

Entire communities grew joint "Victory Gardens." It became a popular way to socialize, meet new people, and trade gossip about the war effort. In San Francisco the city provided water, seeds, tools, and land in Golden Gate Park and on the lawn of the Civic Center Plaza.

If you have a home with a yard, use part of it for a garden. If not, there are public gardens in most cities where you can, often at no cost, grow your own food.

Savings vary but can easily exceed $1,000 annually.

20. Install a smart thermostat in your home. The latest and greatest is the Nest thermostat. It "learns" the temperatures you prefer throughout the house, turns itself down when you aren't home, and has remote control via wi–fi. It can control heating, air conditioning, and humidifier/dehumidifiers. While expensive ($250), the Nest can pay for itself in less than a year...and save money every year afterward. www.nest.com.
    Annual savings: $100 – $250

21. Hold a yard sale. If you don't have a garage or yard, list the stuff you never use and is cluttering up your life on eBay, CraigsList or Amazon. Your "trash" is someone else's treasure. Check out the ebook *Garage Sale Tips and Treasures* by Sherrie Le Masurier for advice on how to run a successful yard sale.
    Annual savings: $100 – $1,500

22. Use a grocery list and don't take kids shopping. You'll save a bundle—at least 5% of your total shopping bill. If you're grocery bill is $500 a month the savings adds up to $300 a year.
    There are several excellent grocery shopping apps: Grocery IQ www.groceryiq.com, ZipList www.ziplist.com, Locavore www.getlocavore.com Green Egg Shopper www.greeneggshopper.com, BigOven www.bigoven.com, and ZipList www.ziplist.com.
    Annual savings: $300 – $600

23. Buy store brands and save as much as 10%. Often store brands are manufactured by the same companies as national brands. The quality of store brands has increased dramatically in recent years, frequently equaling or surpassing the big brand names.

Annual savings: $600 – $1,200

24. Brew your own coffee. At $4 a cup, if you have just one a day on average it adds up to $120 a month or $1,400 a year. Even if you only spend $2 for a medium coffee three times a week, it adds up to nearly $300 annually. That's a latte bucks. Purchase a good coffee brewer with a gold mesh filter (or a $20 French Press) and make your own coffee. *Annual savings: $200 – $1,400*

25. Check unit prices. Buying the larger size often isn't the most economical choice. Take a calculator to compare prices. Or use a unit price comparison shopping app, like Apples2Oranges available for the iPhone, iPod, and iPad. *Annual savings: $25 – $200*

26. A timer on lights and other appliances can save $50 annually on your electric bill. See www.homecontrols.com for more resources. *Annual savings: $40 – $60*

27. Low–flow shower heads, aerated faucet heads, and a brick in the toilet (or new low–flow toilet) can save more than $100 annually on your water bill. *Annual savings: $50 – $120*

28. Only put full loads in the dishwasher and clothes washer—the two appliances in your home that are energy suckers. Optimize loads and use major appliances during off–peak hours to save on electricity. Most items can be washed in cold water, saving you as much as $200 a year. *Annual savings: $50 – $200*

29. Buy clothing that can be washed at home rather than dry–cleaned. There are now very high quality, fashionable clothes—suitable for office wear—that don't require professional cleaning. Try TravelSmith www.travelsmith.com, Orvis www.orvis.com, Lands End www.landsend.com, and LL Bean www.llbean.com. *Annual savings: $50 – $500*

30. If you are replacing an electrically powered item, check the power efficiency rating before buying. Look for the Energy Star symbol. Buying energy–efficient items can save as much as $3,000 a year. Many utility companies will perform an energy audit at no

cost. Or you can do it yourself by going to www.energysavers.gov.
Annual savings: $100 – $3,000

31. Vacation near home. The "staycation" is a popular alternative now to more expensive trips. It's surprising how many local attractions the tourists visit that we just never seem to get around to doing ourselves.
Annual savings: $500 – $5,000

32. Check out the B&Bs or small boutique hotels before committing to a luxury hotel. You'll often find more charming accommodations, personal service, and significantly reduced room costs. The granddaddy of all online resources for bed and breakfasts is www.bedandbreakfast.com. Other resources include: www.bbonline.com, www.bnbfinder.com, www.iloveinns.com, www.boutiquehotelsandresorts.com, www.preferredhotels.com, www.slh.com, www.greatsmallhotels.com.

33. Wait until the last–minute to travel. If you can leave at the drop of a hat there are great deals on last minute cruises. Recent deals included a five–day Caribbean cruise on Norwegian Cruise Lines for less than $600 and an Alaskan cruise on Caribbean Cruise Line for less than $500. Check out www.lastminutetravel.com, www.priceline.com, and www.cheaptickets.com.

34. Before you purchase anything, check Amazon www.amazon.com and eBay www.ebay.com first. You'll often find what you are looking for at one of these sites for less. Both have apps that enable you to shop anywhere.
Annual savings: $50 – $1,000

35. Watch movies during matinees and save 30%. Use Senior Discounts. And check out the pre–purchased tickets available from Costco, Sam's Club, and other big box retailers. You'll save at least 10%. Most of the movie chains offer discounts if you purchase blocks of tickets. Go to www.fandango.com for AMC theatres, www.cinemark.com. You can also save if you show your AAA www.AAA.com or AARP www.AARP.com card. Buy your treats in advance to save on outlandishly marked–up movie theatre snacks.
Annual Savings: $50 – $300

36. Work out at the YMCA or community center. Rather than joining a pricey health club, check out your local YMCA or

community center. Go to www.YMCA.net to find one near where you live.
Annual Savings: $500 – $3,000

37. Use your AAA or AARP cards for discounts on everything from hotels to car rentals. On a week–long trip from Los Angeles to San Francisco one family saved nearly $800 by using their AAA card at hotels, restaurants, and attractions. Most auto club memberships cost less than $75 a year. It's only $16 a year to join AARP (you must be over 50). www.aarp.org
Annual Savings: $200 – $2,000

38. Pay off credit card balances. 43.2% of Americans carry credit card debt averaging $15,257, according to the Federal Reserve. By carrying an average credit card balance you'll be paying hundreds of dollars a year in interest. In order to pay off this balance, according to Bankrate.com, you'll need to pay $551 a month for three years at 18% interest.

    To pay down your credit card balance as fast as possible, use this "snowball" calculator to determine how much additional to add to your minimum monthly payment. It will tell you how much and how long it will take to get the monkey off your back. www.whatsthecost.com
Annual savings: Hundreds or thousands of dollars.

39. Most large metro areas offer discounted tickets if you buy them at the last minute or from a ticket club. Live plays, museum events, concerts, and the ballet all offer last–minute discount tickets. I have friends who regularly score good seats at the San Francisco ballet for just $10. You can also get good deals at www.stubhub.com, where people resell tickets they can't use.

    You'll find savings up to 60% at several other online ticket sites. Scorebig www.scorebig.com offers tickets to sporting events at this discount with 100% guarantee and no fees. Other discount ticket resources include www.seatgeek.com, www.crowdseats.com, www.goldstar.com, and www.ticketsnow.com.

40. Check your bills. Credit card firms and banks have made hidden fees and frivolous charges an art form, but other companies require your scrutiny too. Little nagging fees that add up over a year are common. One common practice is known as "cramming." Your phone company, for example, will add charges to your bill that are vague, misleading or unauthorized. They

are often small charges that you may not notice easily. By carefully checking our phone bill we saved more than $300 in unauthorized charges.

Check receipts for discrepancies. In 2010, as reported in *U.S. News & World Report* magazine, 6% of shoppers were overcharged because of checkout errors. Almost no one was undercharged. According to Billing Advocates of America, 80% of all medical bills contain mistakes. And guess what? 90% of the errors are overcharges. How surprising. *Annual savings: $100 – $3,000*

41. Don't pay for 411. Dial 800–GOOG–411 to find a number for free. This handy service isn't just for finding phone numbers either. You can tell the computer that answers that you are looking for a good Italian restaurant and it will name several spots for you. It will even send a text message containing the address and phone number and connect you to the restaurant to make a reservation. Apple iPhone users can ask "Siri" to get numbers. *Annual savings: Not much, but hey, a dollar saved is a dollar earned.*

42. Unused gift card balances in the United States total billions of dollars. You can sell or swap gift cards at sites such as www.abcgiftcards.com, www.plasticjungle.com, www.raise.com, www.GiftCards.com, and www.cardpool.com. The redemption amount varies depending upon the retailer (most don't take Visa, Amex or MasterCard gift cards), ranging from around 80% to as high as 96% of the value. Most gift card sites will pay by check, Amazon credit or PayPal. There's usually a $25 minimum, although one or two sites will let you combine cards with smaller balances to reach that amount. Gift cards can also be purchased for an average 15% discount at most of these sites. *Annual savings: $25 – $500*

43. There are dozens of online resources to download ebooks for free to your computer, smartphone or eReader. Here are a few to get you started.

- The Gutenberg Project offers more than 45,000 free ebooks.
- The Library of Congress digital collection.
- The Online Books Page. Lists more than 1,000,000 free ebooks.
- Many Books. 20,000+ ebooks.

- Hundred Zeros. Free Kindle books.

Annual savings: $50 – $500

44. Finding the best price is now easy with sites like Become, www.become.com Tech Bargains www.techbargains.com, and Shopzilla www.shopzilla.com. If you own a smartphone, there are several apps that enable you to run a comparative price check instantly.

- Price Grabber www.pricegrabber.com.
- RedLaser www.redlaser.com.
- Shop Savvy www.shopsavvy.com.
- Google Shopper.
- Price Check by Amazon.
- Smoopa www.smoopa.com.
- Consumer Reports Mobile Shopper www.consumerreports.org

Annual savings: $50 – $500

45. Many Federal, State, and local programs encourage the purchase of energy–efficient products—from cars to clothes dryers—by offering discounts, rebates, and tax savings. A list of incentives organized by state can be found at www.dsireusa.org. Tax rebates on the electric Tesla are as high as $13,000 in some states. *Annual savings: $50 – $500*

46. Eat before shopping. According to a Cornell University study, if you are hungry when shopping you'll spend 23% more on everything, including big ticket items like flat screen TVs, cars, and appliances. *Annual savings: $200 – $500*

47. Pay in cash. Shoppers spend as much as 50% more when using credit cards. *Annual savings: $100 – $3,000*

48. Shopping carts have more than doubled in size during the past few years. Shoppers buy considerably more when carts are oversize. Skip the cart and take a bag with just enough space for what you need. A reusable shopping bag is good for the environment and your wallet. *Annual savings: $50 – $200*

49. Many products—from cars to blueberries—are significantly less expensive during certain times of the year. For a guided to the best time to buy almost anything, go to www.lifehacker.com and search for "Best Time to Buy."
Annual savings: $100 – 3,000

50. Consider getting expensive dental work done in Costa Rica. There are hundreds of competent, America-trained dentists in Costa Rica and other countries where the level of professionalism is high and the rates are low—typically 50% less than in the United States. One company that specializes in dental procedures in Costa Rica is Medical Tourism Corporation www.medicaltourismco.com, accredited by the Better Business Bureau. You'll need to so some extra planning to have work done outside the U.S., and aftercare is sometimes problematic, but thousands have reported excellent outcomes.
Savings: $2,000 – $30,000

51. Get medical procedures done overseas. American healthcare costs are the most expensive in the world, yet typical outcomes are no better (and often worse) than the same procedure done by doctors in other countries. According to a 2013 *Time* magazine report, a coronary bypass costs an average of $67,583 in the U.S. (enough to *give* you a heart attack) but the identical procedure is only $16,578 in Germany, $16,140 in France, and $4,525 in India.

    Why the difference? The U.S. medical industry spent $5.36 billion lobbying Congress between 1998 – 2012...more than all corporations, the defense industry, and the oil companies *combined.*

    Healthcare facilities in countries such as India and Singapore are equipped as well as any American hospital and staffed with highly trained doctors and nurses. Rates can be as much as 80% off U.S. prices, according to the American Medical Association. In 2012, consulting firm McKinsey & Company reported that 85,000 Americans chose to have medical care in other countries. "Medical tourism" has become big business with many support organizations.

    To learn more about the AMA guidelines for having medical care done overseas, go to tinyurl.comcpklcw. Check out the

Medical Tourism Association website for information on accreditation www.medicaltourismassociation.com and also the Joint Commission International www.jointcommissioninternational.org before making any decision.
Savings: $5,000 – $75,000

52. Printer ink cost more than Chanel No 5 perfume ounce by ounce... so it pays to economize. Costco and other stores now refill ink cartridges at half the cost of a new one. You can also save ink (as much as 20%) by using a smaller typeface, Fast Draft, Fast Draft in greyscale or EcoFont www.ecofont.com
Annual savings: $50 – $300

53. Sell your old cellphone for as much as $150 (I sold an old iPhone for $117 recently). Check out these sites to see what you might get for your used phone: www.gazelle.com, www.usell.com, www.cashforsmartphones.com, www.sellcell.com, www.sellmycellphones.com, www.nextworth.com, Amazon Trade–in and www.maxback.com. Be sure to scrub the data on your phone and ask the company if they do the same. Make sure the phone is deactivated by your service provider. Always remove the sim card before selling your phone.
Annual savings: $25 – $270

54. More than $58 billion in unclaimed money and property is sitting in holding accounts all over America waiting for the rightful owners to come get it. Some people have been shocked to find tens of thousands of dollars...and as much as $700,000. I found $190 in old bank accounts and utility deposits that had not been returned. Start by going to www.missingmoney.com and www.usa.gov (missing money).
Annual savings: $0 – $15,000

55. Americans have so much stuff that 1 in 10 rents a storage space to hold all the excess. You can sell what you don't want on Craigslist, www.craigslist.com eBay www.ebay.com Amazon, www.amazon.com or at consignment shops and auction houses. On Amazon, just click the "Have one to sell" link.
Annual savings: $50 – $5,000

56. The average cost of a new wedding dress is $1,211, according to a 2012 survey by TheKnot.com www.theknot.com. Buy a used dress at www.craigslist.org, www.swap.com, or www.half.ebay.com and save hundreds of dollars (after all, you'll only wear it one time… hopefully). Or rent a wedding gown at www.renttherunway.com. *Estimated savings: $500 – $700*

For more savings tips, check out Clark Howard's website at www.clarkhoward.com, The Frugal Shopper www.frugalshopper.com, and The Simple Dollar www.thesimpledollar.com.

Life Rule: Make saving a part of your life.

THE EMERGENCY FUND

➢ "46% of American households have less than $800 saved for the unexpected…20% have less than $100." 2012 survey by CashNetUSA.

A quarter of Americans report being "flat broke." Millions more are living paycheck–to–paycheck. It's like skydiving without a parachute. Before you do anything else with the money you save, establish an emergency fund. Experts recommend putting away enough readily accessible funds to cover six months of expenses. It's your "security blanket" that enables you to face the future with confidence if you lose your job, get sick or suffer from a natural disaster…something tens of millions of Americans experienced in 2013.

Life Rule: do what you can to put aside an emergency fund. The peace–of–mind will enable you to make better, more reasoned decisions when an emergency happens.

THE IMPORTANCE OF FINANCIAL CONTROLS

Control over your finances contributes as much to your financial happiness as how much money you have. Studies show that people who are organized, educated about money, and know exactly what they earn and spend (and on what) keep more money as a result.

Most people know the frustration of not being able to find an important financial document, like an auto registration, and being fined or paying late fees as a result. Fully 1 in 3 Americans forgets to pay a bill now and then—mostly because of their poorly organized personal finances. Banks charged $32 billion in overdraft fees in 2012, averaging $34 each (86% of overdraft fees are profit to the bank). Get rid of the financial "clutter" in your life and gain control of your wealth.

A SIMPLE BUDGET PLAN

This simple budget plan is about all the average person needs to stay on top of their finances. The goal of the plan is to live within a budget that equals about 2/3 of your gross income—the amount remaining after taxes. In the list below write down your monthly fixed expenses and total them up. Subtract the total of your fixed recurring expenses from your monthly net income. This is your disposable income, money you can use to buy things or save.

Here is a sample budget for a typical household of three people earning a gross income of $100,000.

Expenses	**Annual**
• Taxes	$25,000
• Mortgage/Rent ($2,500 a month)	$30,000
• Property taxes, maintenance	$6,000
• Auto payment (Two cars purchased used)	$7,000
• Auto insurance (Two cars, $1,000 deductible)	$2,000
• Gas/maintenance (Based upon average 15,000 miles annually)	$6,000
• Health insurance ($5,000 deductible)	$6,300
• Food/dining out ($700 for groceries, $100 dining out)	$9,600
• Phone/cell/internet ($120 for two phones)	$1,440
• Utilities ($250 for cable TV, gas, electric, trash, water)	$3,000
• Clothing/cleaning ($100 for new clothes and dry-cleaning)	$1,200
• Charitable giving ($100 per month in various donations)	$600
Total Expenses	**$98,140**

This budget is not unusual for a family earning $100,000 a year. In fact, many families will think it is too low. Spending $100 a month for clothing would be difficult for anyone with a professional job and a growing child. $120 a month for two (or three) cellphones would restrict the users to basic phone plans. A food budget of $800 (including dining out) doesn't allow much for anything but the basics. The costs for home ownership may be unrealistic as well; homes in California are hard to find at this price and property taxes can run thousands every year.

Nor is there anything budgeted for miscellaneous expenses that fall outside these categories, such as a new laptop or TV, gifts, books or a vacation. Nothing is allocated for retirement, long-term disability insurance, dental costs, tickets to a rock concert, school costs or a pet. If an unexpected emergency comes up—a death in the family, a $400 speeding ticket, a dishwasher that breaks down—the money will have to come from an already tight budget.

And this budget leaves little room for saving or investing, which most financial advisors say should be at least 10% of after-tax earnings (about $7,000 in this example). Even if you can save $7,000 a year it will take decades to save just $500,000...about 1/3 of what financial experts say you will need at retirement to live on about 70% of your pre-retirement earnings.

It's obvious why millions of Americans are in dire financial trouble.

TRACK YOUR INCOME AND EXPENSES

The foundation for controlling your financial destiny is tracking every penny of income and expenditure. Yet millions of people have no clue where they spend their money, how much they earn, what taxes they pay, or how much they've saved.

For those who are moderately savvy with a computer, I recommend using Quicken Premier software to track and control your budget. www.Quicken.com. With Quicken you can set up a comprehensive budget with goals and a tracking system. It's easy to learn, easy to use, and produces wonderfully instructive charts and graphs. You can also pay your bills online. And Quicken helps at tax time by exporting your data to tax preparation software such as TurboTax. www.TurboTax.com

Also recommended is Mint.com www.mint.com. Here you'll find a wealth of resources and financial advice. There are easy–to–use personal finance tools and calculators. You can track spending and income. And Mint allows you to monitor your banking accounts.

If you want to **create an income/expenditure tracking system manually**, here's a simple method:

1. Using manila folders, divide the front into six columns.
2. On the top tab indicate the month and year. For example: December/2012 Finances
3. Create a column listing all major categories such as Groceries, Clothing, Gas, Cable, Auto Expenses, Entertainment, Utilities, and so on—anything you spend money on.
4. Allocate enough space to list every expenditure you make in each category. Obviously, groceries will take more room than a one–time payment, usually an entire column. One–time expenses like Life Insurance or Telephone may only need a half–inch of space.
5. List every expenditure, the source, and the date. For example: $28.75 Gas/Arco 12/21/12. $26.90 Dinner/Domino's Pizza 12/23/12.
6. Put the receipt in the file folder.
7. Add these up at the end of the month and transfer to an Excel or Quicken file for each month.

On the reverse side of the folder list your dollar limits for each category to remind you where you have to be to stay within your budget for the month. For example: Groceries $800, Entertainment $200. And so on.

Next to the items put two columns, one titled Estimated Budget, the other titled Actual Expenses. This will tell you how close you are to staying within your budget. You may also want to make a list of your financial goals to remind you of them.

Knowing where every penny goes in your budget will provide a sense of control over your financial destiny. Just being able to get your hands on a receipt when you need it can be a money–saver.

Chart your expenditures month to month. Track trends in your expenditures to enable you to make course–corrections if necessary.

Next, buy a 3–inch spiral binder and tab dividers to list every major expenditure subject:

- **Income:** Put your paycheck stubs or copies of invoices/receipts here.
- **Banking:** Copies of monthly checking and savings account recaps.
- **Mortgage/Rent:** Copies of statements.
- **Home insurance:** Statements.
- **Home repairs/maintenance:** Receipts.
- **Home Misc:** Tax receipts.
- **Auto:** Payments.
- **Auto Insurance:** Statements.
- **Auto General:** Copies of repairs, service, registration.
- **Gas/Electric:** monthly statements.
- **Life insurance:** Statements.
- **Health insurance:** Statements.
- **Stock market funds:** Monthly statements.

And so on.

In this binder also include:

✓ Credit card information (interest rates, contact numbers, balance/payoff schedule).

✓ Recaps of all investments (stocks, CDs, real estate, annuities, etc.).

✓ Investment items you want to clip and save.

✓ A list of the top financial advice websites.

✓ Account numbers and passwords.

I recommend a tab or two with pages that include all that information that seems to always get lost:

✓ Social security numbers for your family.

✓ Social media and website passwords.

- ✓ Serial numbers of electronic devices.
- ✓ Warranties.
- ✓ Important dates to remember.
- ✓ A backup of your phone's numbers.
- ✓ A completed personal information form, like the kind you fill out on a job application.
- ✓ Contact information for key people like the local police, hospital, plumber, and congressperson.

Having all this information at your fingertips will provide a sense of comfort, control, and peace of mind that will make your life richer...both monetarily and psychically.

Life Rules: Get control of your personal financial life. Track every penny of earnings and spending. Incorporate saving into your lifestyle. Avoid buying on credit. Save a six-month emergency fund. Be a money "student" for life.

HOW THE RICH GOT RICH—AND KEEP GETTING RICHER

While millions are suffering, we're also living in a second "gilded age" of wealth almost beyond comprehension. America (as of 2012) counts 8.6 million households with a net worth of $1 million (minus the value of their principal residence), according to the Spectrum Group as reported in the *Wall Street Journal Wealth Report.*

And the rich keep getting richer.

- ➢ The top 1% of American households now control 64% of all business income, 70% of all bonds, and receive 43% of all tax benefits from retirement savings programs.
- ➢ Just 15,000 Americans (about 1/100 of 1%) received almost 4% of all the income in our country in 2008.

Even after the $145 trillion global financial meltdown, almost all the rich will still be rich. On Wall Street these days a million dollars is considered chump change. Corporate executives at companies you may never have heard of are structuring annual compensation packages that total tens of millions, even hundreds of millions of dollars.

One hedge fund manager received more than $6 billion dollars in compensation (that's for one year). Silicon Valley churns out millionaires and billionaires by the hundreds every year. In 2007 the top 25 hedge fund managers made more than the S&P 500 CEOs...combined, according to Tyler Cowen, author of *Average is Over: Powering America Beyond the Age of the Great Stagnation*. If you are in the top 5% of Americans you are likely richer than ever, no matter what is happening with the economy.

The disruption and chaos caused by the economic upheaval will (if history is any indicator) spawn thousands of new businesses and innovations—resulting in a whole new crop of millionaires. It's never been an easier time to become a millionaire than it is today. And it's never been harder to make ends meet for the majority of Americans than it is today.

THE RICH ARE DIFFERENT

Yes, as author F. Scott Fitzgerald famously said, the rich are different. First of all, they're rich—and most Americans are not. But the rich got that way by doing things differently than most other people. Sure, a few people inherited their wealth...or stole it. But these are anomalies and not the standard. In reviewing the available literature and scientific studies of wealthy people, remarkable similarities emerged about how rich people not only became rich but then stayed rich.

"I always knew I was going to be rich. I don't think I ever doubted it for a minute." — Warren Buffett

Three of the best popular books about how the rich got that way are:

- *The Millionaire Next Door* by Thomas J Stanley and William Danko.
- *Rich Like Them: My Door-to-Door Search for The Secrets Of Wealth In America's Richest Neighborhoods* by Ryan D'Agostino.
- *The Secrets of the Millionaire Mind* by T. Harv Eker.

These authors, along with several empirical studies, have found that there is a roadmap to wealth. Here's what they discovered:

- **Be focused**—do one thing and do it well.
- **Be passionate**—love what you do.
- **Be obsessed**—love what you do to the point of living it nearly every waking moment.
- **Don't plan a career**—plan a life.
- **Stick to your plan**—don't stray from your path.
- **Calculate every risk**—even the risk of doing nothing.
- **Be in business for yourself**—the majority of the richest Americans own their own business or have a unique and salable talent.
- **Take calculated risks**—sometimes the biggest risk is doing nothing at all.
- **Persevere**—don't give up when the going gets tough…keep going.
- **Understand your limitations**—focus on your strengths, delegate your weaknesses.
- **Never stop being a student**—to stagnate is to die.
- **Have a Plan B**—be persistent but have a fallback plan...know when to fold your cards and pivot in a new direction.
- **Inherit your wealth**—do it the old-fashioned way…inherit your wealth or marry it (not that easy to do either way).
- **True success is measured by satisfaction**—not money.
- **Never retire**—stay involved to stay alive.
- **Be generous**—despite the popular lower/middle class preconception, wealthy people are very generous (although the upper 1% are frequently quite stingy).
- **Spend on appreciating assets**—be frugal on everything else.
- **Delay gratification**—living for today will guarantee there's little for tomorrow.
- **Learn to sell**—a life of success requires constant selling in one form

or another.

- **Don't be afraid of hard work**—most wealthy people have worked hard to get where they are.
- **Marry well and stay married**—divorce can be financially devastating.
- **Live below your means**—the trappings of the "rich" life aren't what make people rich.
- **Don't worry about what others think**—all that matters is what you think.

THE RICH THINK DIFFERENT

Author Steve Siebold studied the habits of rich people around the world for more than three decades. His book "*How Rich People Think*" illuminates what separates them from everyone else. Surprisingly, it's less about money than mentality. Siebold found the Middle Class feels it should be "happy with what they have." They live in fear of money. The rich feel just the opposite. To the wealthy money is simply a tool to be used, like a hammer is to a carpenter.

But there are other ways the rich are different.

1. The rich think selfishness is a virtue, while others think it is a vice.
2. Most people have a lottery mentality. Rich people have an action mentality.
3. The un-rich think that formal education is their road to riches. They believe that master's degrees and doctorates are the way to wealth. Rich people believe that the acquisition...and eventual sale...of specific knowledge is the path to wealth creation.
4. Siebold found that people who believe their best days are behind them rarely get rich. They often struggle with unhappiness and depression. Self-made millionaires are willing to bet on themselves and project their dreams, goals, and ideas into an unknown future. They are optimistic about the future.
5. Average income people see money emotionally. Rich people are logical about money. The rich "see money for what it is...a critical tool that

represents options and opportunities."

6. Rich people make money following their passion. Average people earn money doing things they don't love.
7. Average income people have been trained to live in a linear thinking world that equates earning money with physical or mental effort.
8. Most people who aren't rich set low expectations of themselves. So, they are never disappointed. Rich people set high expectations for themselves and accept disappointment as part of the process of becoming successful.
9. The majority of Americans believe you have to do something to get rich. But rich people understand that you have to BE something to become rich. Siebold found the great ones are learning and growing from every experience, whether it's success or a failure.
10. The common belief is that you need to have money in order to make money. But wealthy people use the OPM (other people's money) rule. Rich people know that not being solvent enough to personally afford something is irrelevant. The question they ask is "Is it worth buying, investing in or pursuing?" Then they convince someone to finance their dream.
11. Most stock market investors think the markets are driven by logic. But savvy investors know the stock market is driven more by emotion and greed. This gives them an advantage over most other investors.
12. Most Americans (although fewer after the Great Recession) live beyond their means. The rich live below their means while they are getting rich so they never have to worry about living below their means in the future.
13. Rich people teach their children how to thrive…not simply survive. They don't preach tired platitudes about money that are standard fare with the "have–nots," but solid rules on wealth creation.
14. For most people, money is the biggest cause of stress in their life. But money provides peace of mind for the wealthy. To the Middle Class money is the "root of all evil," but to the rich it is liberating and provides peace of mind.

15. Average people read novels and entertainment magazines. But wealthy people read books that teach them something valuable.
16. Most people think the rich are snobs, but the rich simply want to surround themselves with like-minded people who are empowering.
17. The Middle Class focuses primarily on saving, the rich on earning. Even in the midst of a cash flow crisis, the rich reject the limiting "nickel and dime" thinking of the masses.
18. Most people play it safe with money, or take risks based upon emotion or poor information. The rich know when (and how) to take risks. They use solid knowledge from trusted sources, leverage, and a logical approach to taking risks.
19. Average people love to be comfortable. "Physical, psychological, and emotional comfort is the primary goal of the Middle Class mindset," says Siebold. Rich people learn to live with discomfort, uncertainty, and change while pursuing their goals.
20. Most people don't make the connection between money and health. Rich people, who live longer, know the value of staying healthy and having access to the best healthcare. Rich people also engage in more active pursuits and eat healthier food.
21. People who aren't rich believe that you can't have wealth and a happy family. The rich know you can have anything you want if you adopt the philosophy of love and abundance.

Other research uncovered these interesting differences between the rich and everyone else. Wealth expert Tom Corley www.richhabitsinstitute.com found that…

1. The rich eat correctly. 7 in 10 wealthy people eat less than 300 calories a day from junk food while 97% of poor people eat more than 300 junk food calories daily.
2. Wealthy people stay fit. More than 3 in 4 exercise aerobically a minimum of four times a week. Fewer than 1 in 4 poor people do.
3. The rich find time to read. 88% read material that enhances their education or career goals for at least 30 minutes daily. A mere 2% of

poor people do the same.

4. 8 in 10 rich people have a primary goal in life, compared to just 12% of poor people.
5. More than 8 in 10 wealthy people make daily "to do" lists while only 19% of poor people organize their day.
6. Rich people are more self-controlled and less likely to say something stupid...fewer than 12% say what's on their mind, compared to 69% of poor people.
7. More than half (52%) of poor people gamble (which is why they often win, despite astronomical odds) while just 23% of rich people gamble.
8. Rich people don't watch TV much...67% watch less than an hour a day. Only 6% watch "reality" TV, compared with 78% of the poor.
9. 63% of the rich listen to audiobooks during their commute versus 23% of the poor.
10. 79% of the rich network 5 hours or more a month. The non-rich? Just 16%.
11. 84% of rich people believe that good habits create opportunities and luck. Only 1% of the poor believe good habits translate to good fortune.
12. 86% of the rich believe in life-long education. Only 26% of the poor engage in ongoing education.
13. 44% of the rich wake up 3 hours before work begins. Only 3% of the poor are early risers.
14. 74% of rich people teach their children success habits daily, while only 4% of the poor do (most likely because they have none to teach).
15. 63% of rich people make sure their kids read two or more non-fiction books a month. Only 3% of poor people do this with their children.

While Corley's sample size is small, my own observations working with both rich and poor people is that his conclusions are correct. The primary findings of his survey are also supported by other researchers.

If you have some of these "poor" habits, you'll either be defensive about them...or want to change. Wealth expert Dave Ramsey says, "If you are broke or poor in the U.S. or a first-world economy, the only variable you can personally control is YOU." This may sound blunt, but it's true.

By showcasing these findings I'm not denigrating poor people. It takes extraordinary resolve to break out of the cycle of poverty. Contrary to popular belief, poor Americans often hold down two jobs. They pay a larger percentage of their income in taxes than the upper 5% of Americans. The poor usually have few positive role models to guide them as children. Their community and home environments offer little to support their ambitions. Crime is often a daily experience. Schools are third-rate...their chance of a good education is slim. Jobs are few and pay poorly.

Upward mobility in 21st Century America is largely a myth...41% of the Middle Class moves downward, not up, according to Pew Research data. The poor simply stay poor. Which is why it's vitally important for you to break free and create a successful Plan for Life.

THE RICH ARE DIFFERENT...AND NOT

While the flagrantly ostentatious lifestyles of a few rich people are how many people judge all rich people, research shows that most wealthy folks are quite ordinary. What makes the wealthy different are their values, attitude, work ethic, ambition, love of learning, social skills, networking savvy, and emotional intelligence. They understand money, live below their means, and are consistent in working toward their goals.

TO GET RICH, MAKE SOMETHING LOTS OF PEOPLE WANT

In most cases, wealth is the byproduct of worthy activity. Wealthy people frequently have made a contribution to the world—one the world is willing to pay for by the millions. Bill Gates, Dr. Mehmet Oz, Jack Canfield, Oprah Winfrey, Steven Spielberg, Steve Jobs, Lady Gaga, Warren Buffett, Jeff Bezos, Sergey Brin, Mark Zuckerberg, Ralph Lauren—all produce something the world wants or needs. And they are compensated handsomely for it.

The people who will ride the new wave of opportunity created by the disruption of society, work, technology, and globalization in the first few years of the 21st Century will be those who create value that others want to buy. Elon Musk helps create PayPal, goes on to successfully launch the all-electric Tesla, and then creates SpaceX to fill the void in space travel that NASA has largely abandoned. Or you create a chain of coffeehouses, as Howard Shultz did with Starbucks. Or you fashion the world's largest networking site for business professionals, as Reid Hoffman did with LinkedIn. That's how you become a billionaire.

Jan Koum and Brian Acton were former Yahoo! employees who were out of work (Jan was on welfare), had been rejected for jobs by Facebook and Twitter, but rebounded by designing a new texting app that attracted millions of users…and a $16 billion buyout in 2014 by Facebook. They went from rags to riches in four years.

On a smaller scale, it's important for you to develop a talent, hone a skill, create a product, or start a business that the world is willing to pay for…now and into the future. That is how you will get wealthy.

IT'S GOOD TO BE RICH

It's important to acquire wealth. Money can buy happiness—no matter what anyone tells you. If sailing a boat makes you happy, you need money to be able to buy the boat. If skiing the Alps makes you happy, it cost money to buy the plane tickets, rent the skis, pay for lift tickets, and book a hotel room. If good health makes you happy, you need money to buy nutritious food, belong to a health club, and afford the best professional healthcare.

Money is not the root of all evil, it's the root of all good. As people earn more money they report being more satisfied with nearly every area of their life: family, health, spiritual, even sex. For example, when asked if their sex life was extremely satisfying, wealthy people said "yes" 37% of the time. Only 21% of those surveyed who were living from paycheck to paycheck were extremely satisfied. And just 16% of those who reported being in debt said their sex life was extremely satisfying.

With wealth you can acquire more education, take exotic vacations, have romantic dates with your significant other, listen to music on the best sound system, live in a safe and beautiful neighborhood, own a gorgeous home filled with soul satisfying art and furnishings, drive a safer car—and many other things that make life an exciting grand adventure rather than a daily drudgery. Thoreau said that "most men lead lives of quiet desperation and go to the grave with the song still in them." But not if you're wealthy.

Wealthy people are:

- More than twice as satisfied with their family life.
- Three times as happy with their social life.
- And almost four times as satisfied with their health.

Overall, 55% of wealthy people say they are happy versus just 32% who are in debt. So while money doesn't guarantee happiness, it provides the means to more of it than being poor.

WEALTH STYLE

Often you can tell if someone is wealthy simply by their personal style. This isn't to say that you need to wear a Rolex watch, a $2,000 Brioni suit or a Harry Winston diamond necklace to have a "wealthy" style (not that these things will hurt). Wealthy style is more about attitude and choices.

I've spent a lot of time around wealthy people. They are fascinating. About half the time you can sense they are wealthy by subtle personality clues. Wealth often instills a confidence and self-assuredness that is palpable. The way a person of wealth speaks or moves projects a certain attitude of calm, focus, and expectation that needs will be met. It's the security and power that comes with wealth that makes this so.

A WEALTHY MINDSET

In order to become wealthy it's important to adopt a wealthy mindset. Watch wealthy people carefully and you will see they not only act differently, they often look different than most other people. They have the confidence and ease that money provides. The security. And the ability to make things happen.

The opposite is also true. You know instinctively that it's difficult, if not impossible, to project a confident aura, walk with a swagger, and speak with authority when you are insecure, worried, or depressed about your life. Financial difficulties are to confidence what oil is to water.

ADVICE FROM ARISTOTLE ONASSIS

The Greek shipping tycoon Aristotle Onassis once advised living in the best possible neighborhood, "even if it's in the attic." To become successful he believed it is vitally important to surround yourself in success, beauty, and ambition. Being in this milieu preconditions your mind for success. You can envision the possibilities of success and wealth every day because they are evident in all your surroundings. And the opportunity to meet other successful people (who can affect your success) is also increased.

Start creating your wealth mindset by participating, even in a small way, in the world that wealthy, successful people enjoy. As a money-challenged young man I often would pack a picnic basket and spend the day at the polo matches in Santa Barbara (usually for free). Other times I spent the day touring beautiful wineries, honing my taste and knowledge of fine wines. I'd look for discount tickets to plays or the opera and go dressed up as if it were opening night. I attended art gallery openings or spent the day at a museum developing a taste for fine art. Cars were a love of mine, so I would attend the Concours d'Elegance in Pebble Beach. I frequented the famous Polo Lounge bar at the Beverly Hills Hotel (where I met celebs such as Martin Scorsese and Dolly Parton). None of these activities cost much (I could nurse a drink for hours). It was fun. And two of these interests… cars and art…eventually led directly to creating successful businesses.

I invested in fashionable, high-quality clothes…not much, only what I could afford (and purchased during sales). I bought a used Rolex watch for $350. I only had three pairs of shoes, but they were by Ferragamo. I invested in a pair of classic Ray Ban Wayfarer sunglasses. I found a beautiful cashmere sweater at a consignment store in Beverly Hills that I still own today. I made sure to look the best I could whenever I went out by investing in quality.

The car I drove was a Mercedes-Benz…not a new Mercedes, a used classic 380sl sports car that I bought from a wealthy architect in Bel Air for just $15,000. I had more fun with it (and got more admiring attention) than a new car costing about the same (like a new Kia). I worked out at the same gym that Arnold Schwarzenegger worked out at. Over the years I've lived in the best neighborhoods (even if it was in a studio apartment)…Chicago's Gold Coast, Manhattan Beach, Montecito, Pacific Heights, Sausalito, and Tiburon.

The point I'm making is that with a little creativity you can lead a very classy lifestyle. I know that doing this has shaped my mindset, created new possibilities, and introduced me to life experiences that I would never have enjoyed by taking an ordinary path. Eventually I did make a lot of money, lived in a three-story home on a lake next to celebrities (the Lone Ranger was my neighbor), traveled to Europe frequently, collected art, and owned several vintage automobiles. You can do this too...if you want.

- ✓ Get dressed up and go to the most luxurious hotel in town and have a drink at the bar. For about $20 you can spend an uplifting half hour or so.
- ✓ Attend an art gallery event. They are almost always free (as is the wine).
- ✓ Save up to buy at least one great pair of shoes or watch. It will make you feel like a million bucks every time you wear it.
- ✓ Stop going to places that detract from a wealthy mindset (like Walmart).
- ✓ Shop at consignment or thrift stores in wealthy neighborhoods, where you will often find slightly used (and sometimes new) high-quality items preowned by the super-rich.

It's important in our society to provide the visual cues that indicate you are a person of substance now...or moving in that direction. You'll be judged quickly by:

- ✓ The people with whom you associate.
- ✓ The organizations you belong to.
- ✓ The clothes you wear...especially your shoes and watch.
- ✓ The style of jewelry you choose.
- ✓ How you style your hair.
- ✓ The schools you attended.
- ✓ The charities you support.
- ✓ What you have achieved.
- ✓ Where you live.
- ✓ Your personality...is it confident, engaging, self-assured, and "classy."

In an ideal world these things shouldn't matter...but they do because they are all indications of who and what you are. You'll also be judged negatively if you show any signs of déclassé behavior such as tattoos and piercings, stupid behavior on Facebook, and poor hygiene...unless you're a rock star, famous artist or movie star. If you want to lead an ordinary life...fine. Many people (most?) are happy with an average life. But if you want to lead an extraordinary life, you'll need to change your mindset and behavior. Then get down to the basics of what it takes to create wealth.

Life Rule: Change your mindset and your habits if you want to someday live as the rich do.

ADVICE FROM DAVE RAMSEY

Dave Ramsey is a financial expert whose common sense advice should be part of anyone's Plan for Life strategy. Check out his website at www.DaveRamsey.com for loads of terrific financial resources. Millions of people have benefited from his books, videos, seminars, syndicated radio show, and online financial management courses. If you're serious about getting your finances in order, Dave is one of a select group of advisors who can put you on the right track.

DAVE RAMSEY DO'S.

✓ Write down goals to maximize your chance of success.

✓ Visualize it happening.

✓ Live substantially below your means.

✓ Be focused and intense in your efforts.

✓ Sacrifice now for financial peace-of-mind in the future.

✓ Think long-term.

✓ Be patient.

✓ Keep accurate financial records.

✓ Start your own business.

✓ Give to worthy causes.

✓ Learn basic negotiating skills.

✓ Save with pre-tax dollars.

✓ Listen to your spouse.

- ✓ Use a health savings account.
- ✓ Make a will.
- ✓ Teach your children how to handle money responsibly.
- ✓ Get control over your #1 most powerful wealth-building tool—your income.

DAVE RAMSEY DON'TS.

- ✓ Don't have a car payment.
- ✓ Don't buy property with adjustable rate or balloon loans.
- ✓ Don't take out equity loans against your property.
- ✓ Don't buy whole life insurance.
- ✓ Don't lease a car.
- ✓ Don't lend money to friends or relatives.
- ✓ Don't co-sign for a loan.

One more "do" is to include Dave's book *The Total Money Makeover* in your personal finance library. It could save you tens of thousands of dollars. Other valuable resources are listed at the end of this chapter.

YOUR CREDIT REPORT IS YOUR FRIEND—UNLESS YOU MAKE IT YOUR ENEMY

With credit hard to come by even for people lucky enough to have unblemished credit records, it's more important than ever to do everything possible to maintain a spotless credit history. Here just a few of the consequences of a poor credit record:

- ✓ You'll pay 20% to 50% more for car insurance.
- ✓ Most prospective employers now check credit histories before hiring (although eight states have laws restricting it).
- ✓ You may be rejected when you apply to rent an apartment.
- ✓ Utilities may require a cash deposit, often as much as $500.

- ✓ Your phone company may require a cash deposit.
- ✓ School loans can be denied.
- ✓ Loans for everything from cars to homes may denied or will cost thousands more because of higher interest rates.
- In the United States it is rare for anyone to have a completely unblemished credit history...and 1 in 4 have "poor" credit scores.

Everyone should have a copy of their credit report. It's the foundation of your entire financial life. Its care and feeding is important because a healthy credit report will save you hundreds of thousands of dollars over a lifetime.

Since the passage of the 2003 Fair and Accurate Credit Transaction Act (FACTA), all Americans are entitled to one free credit report from each of the three major credit reporting agencies every 12 months. The three agencies are Equifax, Experian, and TransUnion. You can get your free credit report in less than five minutes by requesting it online at www.annualcreditreport.com.

Credit reports can also be obtained by calling 877–322–8228 or writing to Annual Credit Report Request Service, P.O. Box 105281, Atlanta, GA 30348–5281.

You are also entitled by law to a free credit report if you meet any of these conditions:

- If you've applied for a loan and been denied, you can request a free credit report by writing to the credit bureau that turned you down within 30 days of the rejection. You also must be informed in writing by the company that denied the loan request.
- If you are unemployed and looking for a job within the next 60 days.
- You are receiving public assistance.
- If you think there may be a mistake on your credit file.

You can contact each credit agency directly:

- **Equifax**
  800–685–1111
  P.O. Box 740256
  Atlanta, GA 30374

- **Experian**
  888-397-3742
  P.O. Box 2002
  Allen, TX 75013
- **TransUnion**
  800-916-8800
  P.O. Box 2000
  Chester, PA 19022

1/3 OF CREDIT REPORTS CONTAIN ERRORS OR OMMISSIONS

By some estimates 1/3 of credit reports contain errors. If you've had any kind of medical procedures done in the past you are particularly susceptible to having an error on your report. Petition in writing to have errors corrected, don't allow disputes to go into collection, and correct any omissions/additions that shouldn't be in your report. Keep in mind though that this is easier said than done...the credit bureaus have an abysmal record of responding to consumer requests.

KNOW YOUR FICO SCORE

MyFico—the Fair Isaac Company—is a public company that works with the credit bureaus to compute your FICO score, a creditworthiness number that many lenders use to determine what rate to offer you...or whether to lend to you at all.

FICO scores range from 300 to 850—the average American's was 681 in 2013, according to Experian's *State of Credit* report. A good score is in the mid-700s and 720 is considered the minimum score needed to qualify for the best rates. Good scores can save you thousands of dollars in interest by providing access to lower interest loans. If you score 700 points rather than 750, the difference could cost you $15,000 – $20,000 over the life of a $300,000 loan.

VantageScore, a credit rating product offered by all the reporting bureaus, is an alternative to the FICO score methodology. It uses a slightly different process to determine credit-worthiness, with less emphasis on payment history (28% vs 35%) and several other factors. VantageScore still uses numerical ranges but also applies a letter grade to them. A credit score less than 700 (a "D" grade is 601 to 700) is considered sub–prime territory.

Some other credit reporting sources, like FreeCreditReport.com, aren't really free and have been sued by the FTC for misleading marketing methods (they spend $75 million annually on advertising). *MSNBC* called the company a "scam." Ironically FreeCreditReport.com is owned by Experian, one of the credit bureaus. There are dozens of other "free" credit reporting companies and FAKO (as the FICO scams are called) companies. Avoid them. They will all try to up–sell you into a monthly "monitoring" contract.

The current cost at MyFico to obtain your FICO score is $19.95. Be warned that even MyFico will attempt to "up–sell" you to other financial management products, including a program with money guru Suze Orman. Despite being a "for profit" business, the FICO website is a good source of free financial information.

Here's how to raise your credit score.

- The most important way to raise your score is to pay your bills on time.
- Lower your debt to available credit ratio. If you are using 90% of your credit and pay off all your debts, it could raise your FICO score by as much as 100 points. However, don't cancel your cards or it could throw your ratio out of whack.
- Have more than one credit card. Otherwise lenders have no way of knowing whether you are capable of handling the payments on multiple debts. However, too many credit cards can be a detriment to your score.
- Apply for new credit carefully. It could lower your score if you open too many new credit accounts too quickly. You may want to keep your older accounts—even if you don't use them anymore because this will reduce your overall credit limit. People often make this mistake when consolidating high rate cards with one lower rate card.
- Correct any mistakes on your credit report. FICO scores are based upon the information in your credit report files. A mistake in your file could have expensive consequences. Keep a paper–trail of your correspondence with the bureaus.

Knowing your FICO score is one of the personal financial tools you will need throughout life. Work to get it reduced and check on it frequently. www.myfico.com

Insurance companies may use a proprietary scoring system or a LexisNexis Attract score, based upon credit reports, to determine whether or not you'll be a good loss risk.

Life Rule: Monitor and guard your credit score carefully.

DID YOUR RETIREMENT DREAMS INCLUDE POVERTY?

In one study of more than 4,000 workers, almost a third (32%) admitted they hardly ever thought about retirement. Another 38% said they thought about it a "little" or "some." 1 in 5 have tried but failed to develop a retirement plan. And perhaps scariest of all is this survey finding—a third of people age 50+ have never given a thought to retirement planning.

The sobering facts:

1. Americans now live an average of 18.7 years after age 65—roughly half will live longer. Your retirement years represent about 20% of your entire life.
2. Inflation averages about 3.21% a year, which means prices double every 22 years. Your retirement savings are cut in half by inflation during this time.
3. The average Social Security retirement payment is $1,220 a month, less than the poverty level.
4. Medical costs increase substantially after age 70. Even with Medicare, your entire Social Security income could be consumed by medical costs. Fidelity Investments estimates (as of 2012) that you will need an average of $240,000 just to pay for your medical expenses after age 65. According to the National Center for Policy Analysis, the average annual out-of-pocket medical expenses paid by seniors 65 to 74 years old is $3,851, $5,066 for 75 to 85 year olds, and a whopping $8,304 for those over 85 (2004). The average annual cost for an assisted living facility is nearly $40,000 a year.
5. Most income-producing investments return less than they have in the past. A short-term $100,000 CD would pay just $1,900 in annual income

at 2013 rates.

Sources: *MSN Money,* 2013; Fidelity Investments (2012), *Money CNN* (2012)

- A Congressional study estimates that half of all Baby Boomers will need to adjust their standard of living downward in retirement—and that figure was arrived at before the Great Recession.
- According to retirement security expert Teresa Ghilarducci at the New School of Social Research, as reported in MSN Money in 2012, half (49%) of Americans ages 44 to 55 are at risk for poverty by age 65.

Planning for the last 1/3 of your life is something you cannot ignore. It's one of your most important financial decisions.

Life Rule: Invest early and consistently to save enough for your retirement.

INVESTING IN STOCKS

"October is one of the peculiarly dangerous months to speculate in stocks. The others are July, January, September, April, November, May, March, June and December." — Mark Twain

Most individual investors do not have the skills or inclination to manage their own investments, according to Daniel Goldie and Gordon Murray, authors of *The Investment Answer*. As a result, the average person usually ends up on the losing end of the stock investment game.

In a 20-year study by research firm Dalbar Financial Services, the average active stock fund investor earned about 3.2% annually vs. 8.2% for the S&P 500 Index. Most active stock fund managers fail to meet their benchmarks or outperform the market (although they still take home millions in compensation).

WALL STREET CAN MAKE A MONKEY OUT OF YOU

Economist Burton Malkiel, author of *A Random Walk Down Wall Street*, claimed that a blindfolded monkey throwing darts at a newspaper's financial pages could select a portfolio that would do just as well as one carefully selected by experts. *The Wall Street Journal* decided to put Malkiel's claim to the test, and created the Dartboard Contest.

Wall Street Journal staffers (pretending to be monkeys), threw darts at a stock market page, while investment "experts" picked their own stocks. Six months later, after 100 dartboard selections, they compared results. The pros won 61 of the 100 contests versus the dart method. Investment experts performed better than the random dart method, but not much better than random chance. What's more, compared to the average performance of the Dow Jones Industrials, the pros were in a statistical dead heat by a slight margin of 51 to 49 picks.

During the booming 90's the average professionally managed stock mutual fund earned an annual return of 13.9%, while the stock market average went up 16.3% per year. So, if you want to pay 2.4% per year for the privilege of underperforming the market, well, go ahead. After all, those fund managers have kids to send to Ivy League schools and huge mansions, yachts, and Gulfstream jets to support.

Despite the hundreds of books by Wall Street gurus, the Bloomberg Channel with its sexy rolling ticker tape at the bottom of the screen, the always entertaining (but seldom accurate) antics of Jim Cramer, many financial experts think your best bet (and that is what you are doing in the stock market) is to buy the market index stock fund with the lowest fees you can find and then go do something productive with your life.

The S&P 500 Index performance from 1/1/70 to 12/31/09 was 9.87% (it's even better as of the time of this writing). In fact, over the past 70 years the market increased about 10% a year on average. Be satisfied with this return and don't get greedy trying to "beat" the market for a few extra dollars.

MUTUAL FUNDS

"The evidence powerfully confirms that, at least in the mutual fund industry, the Holy Grail doesn't exist. But investors seem hell-bent on carrying out the search for winning funds of the future. No matter how futile the search has proven to be."

— John C. Bogle, author of *The Little Book of Common Sense Investing* and *Common Sense on Mutual Funds,* Founder of Vanguard Group, President of Bogle Financial Markets Research Center

Mutual funds may be the biggest investment scam on Americans (among many scams) perpetrated by Wall Street. As Yale's legendary investment guru, David Swenson, effectively analyzed in a 2011 essay in *The New York*

Times, the mutual fund industry costs investors billions in lost returns while practically printing money for itself, its employees and its distributors across the country. In other words, the average American gets sold a lousy investment while Wall Street lines its pockets with billions of dollars. Sound familiar?

As David Swenson points out in *The New York Times*, "If every American who owns a high-cost actively managed mutual fund sold it and bought a low-cost index fund, the average returns of America's investors would rise considerably—in part because American investors wouldn't be paying billions of dollars of fees each year to mutual fund companies to lose money for them."

Ben Stein, who writes a weekly economics column for *The New York Times*, also advises buying index funds. "Trying to pick individual stocks is a trap," says Stein. "I can't do it. Warren Buffett can, but hardly anyone else can beat the indexes over a long period of time."

DO YOU REALLY WANT TO MAKE WALL STREET RICHER?

"Give a man a fish and you can feed him for a day. Give a man a hedge fund and you can feed him for 600,000 years." — Eric Wentworth

The only people who really have a chance of making big money from investing in most stock funds, hedge funds, and commodity pools are the managers of the investments. Investors paid more than $40 billion in fees to the brokers of the nearly 23,000 funds in 2003. Is it any wonder why million dollar bonuses are just chump change on Wall Street? Several hedge fund managers are billionaires, yet they produce nothing tangible. Incredibly, one hedge fund manager, John Paul, took home $5 billion in 2010. That's $2,400,000 an hour. Where does this enormous income come from? You. In fees, commissions, and other management costs.

"Performance comes and goes, but costs roll on forever."
— John C. Bogle

These obscenely large salaries would be partially justified if the hedge funds produced extraordinary returns for their investors. However, the opposite is true. As reported in *The Economist* (2013), from March 2009 to March 2013, the stock market rose 140% but hedge funds didn't even beat the market itself. If you had invested in 2003 in a 60/40 equity/bond index fund it would have returned about 200% over the next ten years... compared to just 120% for hedge funds. Yet in 2012, big-name hedge fund managers Ray Dalio and Steve Cohen took home $1.7 billion and $1.4 billion in compensation. Most people get fired for doing a lousy job. Hedge fund managers make billions. Nice work, if you can get it.

Two of the most influential financial titans in America—Warren Buffett and Peter Lynch—are ardent supporters of passive investing. If they recommend it, you can bank on it (sorry for the pun). Lynch has said of fund managers, "If you're good, you are right six times out of ten. You're never going to be right nine times out of ten." With odds that are just slightly better than even, and erosive fees, speculative mutual funds are a fool's game.

Richard Ferri author of *The Power of Passive Investing*, believes that a passive investing strategy allows you to focus on more important things in life." Things like performing better in your career, pursuing your hobbies, or spending time with your family and friends (the best long-term investment of all).

Index fund investing has grown increasingly affordable...nearly free in some cases (e.g. as low as 0.04% of assets per year and frequently with no broker commission) for an exchange-traded fund (ETF) that mirrors the stock market closely and delivers the same return. Add an international stock index fund and a bond fund, keep some readily available cash, and most people are good to go.

Remember this...you will never be good enough or smart enough to "beat" the stock market. The majority of stock trading is done by incredibly sophisticated computer algorithms making millions of trades...often in less than a second. You can't trade better or faster. You also don't have the advantages of insider knowledge or the power of being a wealthy investor to help turn the market to your advantage. If you want to lose your money gambling, Las Vegas is a lot more fun.

Of course, your experience may be different. I'll be the first to admit I am not a financial expert or advisor of any kind. I'm only reporting what I've learned and find useful. As with any important decision in your life it is crucial that you consult with your attorney and financial experts, learn as much as you can about investments, and be ready to accept the possibility that even a carefully considered investment may not perform as you hope.

STUDY AND UNDERSTAND THE BASICS OF INVESTING

"We have two classes of forecasters: Those who don't know and those who don't know they don't know." — John Kenneth Galbraith

Before you decide you can be another Master of the Universe, take a "trial run" by investing in stocks, CDs, etc. without really using any real money. With $100,000 in imaginary funds, take a year or two to invest in the market, real estate, art, CDs, mutual funds, etc. Track how well your investments perform. Without risking any real money, this experience will provide you with a solid basic education in investing. It may also show you just how good (or not) you are at investing. Better to lose imaginary money than real hard-earned cash.

- If you want to have some fun with this, go to www.updown.com to compete against others with "Monopoly" money. The players get a chance to win real money. Plus, you'll learn a lot about the capricious nature of the stock market.

There are dozens of good financial books you should read before relying on your Uncle Bernie's hot stock tip or your minimally competent financial advisor's recommendation to invest in pork belly futures. A good place to start is Andrew Tobias' classic *The Only Investment Guide You'll Ever Need*. When you stray beyond the tried and true basic investments it gets very complex, so you really need to know what you're doing. My advice—don't try to compete with Wall Street. After all, look at what a mess they've made of things.

Life Rule: Don't try to beat the market with fancy investments.

THE GREAT CREDIT CARD ROBBERY

The mostly unregulated and unrestrained credit card industry and its greedy top management are like pigs at the trough—dining on the American consumer.

➢ In 2012, **consumers paid nearly $32 billion in overdraft charges** alone, according to the Center for Responsible Lending.

- In 1990, financial banks and credit card companies made 3% of their income from fees and penalties. By 2007 the figure had surpassed 50%.
- **Consumers paid an average of $225 in overdraft charges** in 2012, according to the Consumer Financial Protection Bureau.

The banks and credit card companies in America have gotten away with robbery for years. Their accomplices, our elected officials, have aided and abetted this rip-off of Americans. You need to protect yourself at all costs—because not doing so could cost you plenty.

Whenever the greed of the financial institutions has become egregious, taxpayers have bailed them out. Although the economic meltdown of 2008 is still fresh in our minds, many have forgotten the multi-billion dollar Savings and Loan debacle of the mid-1980s. It's always the taxpayer who pays for their mistakes. But like a sociopath who shows no remorse or conscience, instead of thanking taxpayers the banks and Wall Street are busy figuring out new schemes to defraud Americans.

Senator Bernie Sanders of Vermont received thousands of emails from irate consumers when he asked how credit card companies are treating Americans. Here's a typical response:

"I don't know why consumers are not protected in any way from these predatory lenders who were bailed out with my taxpayer dollars and then turn around and raise my interest rate from 7% to 27% because of "difficult economic times" for the credit industry. This is outrageous! I have never missed a payment and my credit rating is in the high 800's. How can they keep getting away with this?"
— Donna, Neptune, NJ

Another taxpayer writes, *"I owned a summer business for 43 years. My business credit card was with Advanta at 7.9% for years. Last year my payment jumped about $400 per month. I thought there was fraud involved. Upon checking I found my interest had been raised from 7.9 % to 28.8 %. I always paid more than the minimum and always on time. When Advanta was contacted and asked why, I was told it's a floating interest. I was advised that's the way it was and they could do nothing to lower it. I shut down my business. After 43 years it took usury to shut me down. I am 75 years old and a vet. It's time we had honesty in the banking system."* — Walter, Poultney, VT

Few people are old enough to remember when credit company

charges like those in place now were considered usury...and against the law. Usury is condemned in both the Bible and the Qur'an...but is apparently OK on Wall Street.

CREDIT CARD COMPANIES ARE LIKE DRUG DEALERS

Credit card companies begin early by bombarding kids just out of high school with offers they are ill–equipped to handle responsibly. With the full collusion of the colleges and universities and their alumni groups, students are hustled by the credit card companies before they have any financial worth to warrant getting credit at all.

Little known is the fact that schools are paid big bucks by the credit card companies to be allowed to fleece their students. Florida State University was paid $10.7 million over seven years and the University of Michigan $25.5 million over eleven years. The University of South Florida (paid $4.1 million over seven years) even provided the bank with addresses, email, and phone numbers for 35,000 students.

Students these days often graduate with enormous debt loads to pay off (the average is $29,400 in 2013). Besides student loans, credit card debt makes it unlikely they will dig their way out of their mountain of debt for years, even decades—especially with payrolls actually shrinking in real dollars. Like drug pushers, the credit card companies are pushing our youth into harmful habits that will haunt them for years, perhaps a lifetime.

Resources: www.cardratings.com www.bankrate.com www.rewards.com www.creditcards.com

Consumer debt (excluding mortgages) has risen to astronomical levels. In 2013 it topped $11.2 trillion dollars, according to the Federal Reserve Bank of New York. Of the various forms of credit debt, credit card debt is perhaps the most insidious–or perhaps second to student debt. It deprives people of their freedom. It ruins marriages. It's a major cause of personal bankruptcy. Yet fewer than 1 in 50 people read all the fine print in the credit agreement document they sign. And those who do seldom understand what the agreement says.

Senator Elizabeth Warren, former Harvard law professor and head of the Federal Consumer Protection Agency, asked the students in one of her classes to decipher the fine print on a typical credit card offer. Virtually none of the students could accurately determine what it said. If Harvard law students can't figure it out, what are the average consumer's chance of getting it right?

Credit cards are the source of much angst, confusion, and stress in America. Here are a few findings that indicate how conflicted Americans are about their plastic.

- In a 2008 study by www.CreditCards.com, 58% of respondents said they "somewhat" or "strongly" agree with the statement "I don't trust credit card companies."
- According to a www.compete.com survey, 54% of those polled were not aware that some credit card companies will increase your annual percentage rate if you are late or miss a payment with any of your other creditors. Likewise, insurance companies may increase your rate for the same reason.
- 78% agreed with the statement that "nobody really reads the terms and conditions when signing up for a credit card." Why? Because the fine print is so hard to decipher. Later, people are stunned by the extent and severity of the fees and penalties.
- In 2013, Americans held $857 billion in credit card debt, according to the Federal Reserve.
- The average household credit card debt was $15,270 in 2014, according to the Federal Reserve.
- About 1 in 3 cardholders incurred a late fee in 2011, averaging about $25 (it's lower now due to the Federal Credit Card Act).

Here are a few tips to help you manage your credit cards more effectively:

- To avoid late payment fees, pay online. Payments made before 3pm EST are credited the same day.
- If you receive unsolicited mail from credit card issuers, be sure to shred them so no one else applies in your name.
- If you usually carry a balance, find and use cards with the lowest interest rate (APR) you can to minimize finance charges.
- To avoid high fees, pay on time, stay within your credit limit, and

never take cash advances.

- Rewards cards are generally more expensive. You typically get just 1% of what you charge as your "reward" and a high annual fee can easily wipe that out. Reward cards that make sense include cards that offer rebates at stores where you already shop. For example, an Executive Card Member at Costco often shops for a small business, large family or organization. The cash back reward can accrue to a maximum of $500 every six months. If you fly frequently you may want to check out loyalty cards that help you accumulate mileage toward future travel.
- Debit cards draw funds directly from your checking account. It's like writing a check. Banks often provide "courtesy" overdraft on debit cards—but you'll usually pay a hefty fee for each "courtesy." Some smaller community banks waive these fees.
- When you use your debit card at some establishments—many gas stations and rental car agencies—additional funds may be "held" or "blocked" in your account. This can range from a few dollars to hundreds of dollars. The result? Your next purchase may trigger an overdraft fee.

While Americans are paying down credit card balances, and generally being more responsible about their use, just having a credit card is dangerous.

- Shoppers using credit or debit cards spent 70% more on junk food than cash customers at the grocery store, according to a study by the *Journal of Consumer Research.*
- A Sloan School of Management study found people were often willing to spend twice as much when using credit cards instead of cash.

The best advice? Get the best credit card you can find and use it only for emergencies. Pay the balance in full and on time every month. Anything else will cost you money. To compare current credit card offers, go to www.creditcards.com, www.nerdwallet.com or www.creditkarma.com.

Life Rule: Pay cash whenever possible. Choose a credit card carefully.

HOME SWEET FINANCIAL DISASTER

Shelter is one of Maslow's basic needs that human beings require to survive.

It's also one of life's most important and complex decisions. Choosing the right neighborhood. Buy or rent? City, suburbs or country? Condo or house? Big or small? Complex financial contracts. Huge financial commitments. Few things in life are more difficult to get right. Yet here again people mess it up with alarming regularity.

- Millions buy homes they can't afford—often without even reading the fine print in the mortgage documents they sign.
- They pay thousands in junk fees that boost the real estate industry's profits on an already expensive purchase.
- They buy in dicey neighborhoods because they are so focused on attaining the "American Dream" that they don't consider their locations' possible nightmarish consequences.
- They get ripped off by contractors because they don't check them out or create a work plan.
- They pay too much for home insurance because they don't comparison shop.
- They even use their homes as banks—a third of all home equity borrowing was used to pay debts: credit cards, car loans, even the home mortgage.

Where once people purchased a home as a place to live, now a home is considered an "investment." And yes, homes usually do appreciate over time. But as an investment, homes generally perform poorly. Unlike the stock market, bonds, gold or other investments, a home requires constant upkeep and maintenance, insurance, property taxes, and is difficult to unload when things go south…as we've seen in recent years. It's better to think of your home as a home, and not an investment. And if it is your only "investment," you're not a very savvy investor.

REAL ESTATE VS THE STOCK MARKET

Your home is part of a market, like the stock market, which is not under your control. Some massive fortunes have been made in real estate. And lost. Many who bought into the American Dream in the past ten years have found it to be a nightmare instead. Millions of homes have been lost to foreclosure. Many others have learned the hard way that the "investment" they convinced themselves real estate would be is anything but.

- Residential real estate provided an annualized return of 8.6% during the period 1978 – 2004, compared with 13.4% for the S&P 500 Index. Source: Jack Clark Francis, Bernard Baruch College, Roger G. Ibbotson, Yale School of Management; Contrasting Real Estate with Comparable Investments, 1978 – 2004, April 2007.
- If you buy a $300,000 home with a 30–year loan, your interest payments could exceed the home's original cost if you stay in it for the life of the loan. After you pay three decades of insurance premiums, maintenance, repair costs, and property taxes, you could end up paying upwards of $1 million. Even the financially illiterate can see that this isn't a good investment. Source: David Crook, *Your Home Isn't the Investment You may Think It Is, Wall Street Journal Online*, March 12, 2007.

According to Nobel Prize–winning Yale University finance professor Robert Schiller, author of *Irrational Exuberance*, real estate's historic real returns are closer to zero after adjusting for inflation. Because of temporary dramatic increases in the value of real estate (which happen regularly) it is easy to begin thinking of a home as an investment. But in real estate it is smarter to look at the long–term trend–lines and ignore the peaks and valleys. The trend is always upward, just not as much as in the stock market (which also experiences the same dramatic ups and downs).

"Housing is not viewed as a great investment," Schiller says. "It takes maintenance, it depreciates, it goes out of style. All of these are problems. And there's technical progress in housing. So, new ones are better." He goes on to say that housing as an investment was an idea that took hold only within the past 20 years. Putting money in investments with higher, more reliable returns instead of a house may be the better choice. Renting seems to be a very sensible choice for many people.

Find out about renting vs buying, how to buy a home, remodeling… and more real–estate tips at www.APlanForLife.com.

HEALTH CARE INSURANCE

Health care insurance is one of the biggest challenges most people face when developing a financial plan. Which plan is best? How much coverage and what type do you need? Do you need it at all? Like eating junk food, you can get away without health insurance when you're young—if you are lucky. But it's rare for anyone to reach their middle-age years without at least a few health expenses.

- Nearly 1/3 of all 19 to 29 year-olds have no health insurance.
- More than 40 million Americans either can't afford or choose to go without insurance.
- Even with health insurance, 25 million Americans spent at least 10% of their income on out-of-pocket medical expenses (2007).

Health care expenses in the U.S. are astronomical and only heading higher. For example, a typical pregnancy can easily cost $10,000 - $12,000. A diagnosis of diabetes (21 million Americans have the disease) can be financially devastating, costing tens of thousands of dollars. If you are injured in an auto accident (2.2 million people this year) it could ruin your life. Remember, the biggest cause of bankruptcy isn't that people are deadbeats...its divorce or medical expenses.

Many Americans, through choice or necessity, go without health insurance. But the peace of mind that goes with having a safety net is immeasurable. With the passing of The Affordable Care Act, more options may be open to you than ever before.

Significant changes are underway. The U.S. has been nearly the only advanced country in the world that doesn't provide universal healthcare coverage for its citizens. Canada, Brazil, New Zealand, Australia, France, Germany, Spain, Sweden...and many more have offered healthcare for years. Even third-world countries like Costa Rica and Kyrgyzstan have healthcare coverage for their citizens.

The Affordable Care Act will have a far-reaching, and mostly positive, impact upon healthcare in America. It will also affect the financial health of the nation. Healthcare costs (now the highest in the world, despite the U.S. being #27 in longevity) will come down, allowing cash-strapped people to live better. To make it work best for you, be sure to become informed. You can find more information online at www.healthcare.gov.

Life Rule: Most people will need health insurance at some point in their life. Do your research and find a plan that's right for your circumstances.

MAKE MORE MONEY

Ultimately, the only real way to combat the rising cost of living is a bigger paycheck, says Loral Langemeier, author of "*The Millionaire Maker's Guide to Creating a Cash Machine for Life.*" Once you've chosen a career that you'll be happy doing (and, hopefully, can provide the kind of compensation you need to live well), determine what it takes to become invaluable. It might be a special skill that you do better than anyone else. It could be your record of dependability and attention to details. Perhaps it's your reputation for coming up with money-making creative ideas. Being outstanding in your core profession is, and always will be, the single best way to earn a lot of money. Check out CHAPTER 3: *CAREER* for guidance and resources.

MONEY MOMENTUM

Many people I've spoken to have related a phenomena so common that it deserves a few words, despite being unproven by science. It's the "momentum" or "flow" of money. I've personally experienced this phenomena myself, and while I don't understand the process, it seems valid.

Money momentum is a form of the old saying "Nothing succeeds like success." The more success you experience, the more success you experience. The same seems to apply to money, the more that comes in… the more that comes in. If your money momentum stops for some reason—usually due to a job loss or business reversal—it's important to find a way to keep the money flowing, even if it's just a trickle compared to your former income. At least your money momentum is moving forward and not stagnant or moving backward.

For some unexplained reason, this forward money momentum fuels a continuation of income in most cases. The same principal can be applied to life in general, as long as you are moving forward, building, creating, connecting, and growing, your chances of maintaining forward momentum are good.

The key to making this process work for you is to keep the flow going as strongly as possible despite setbacks. If your momentum becomes stalled, it will be doubly hard to restart and get your life back on track.

ADDITIONAL INCOME STREAMS

You may need to augment your income immediately due to a job loss or some other setback.

Here are a few ideas to keep the money flowing in:

- ✓ Sign up to do jobs at TaskRabbit. www.taskrabbit.com.
- ✓ Sign up with Fivvr www.fiverr.com to make extra cash.
- ✓ Take headshot photographs for social media sites.
- ✓ Sign up with a temp agency.
- ✓ Help people organize their closets, garage or office.
- ✓ Clean someone's house (or a local business at night).
- ✓ Donate sperm…most sperm banks pay $40 to $200 per, uh, shot.
- ✓ Sign up with Sidecar, Lyft or UberX and earn money using your car as a rideshare taxi (available in a limited number of major cities).
- ✓ If you have a truck, haul away unwanted items for recycling/dumping.
- ✓ Do handyman work on the weekends.
- ✓ Learn to create Wordpress blogs and websites.
- ✓ Start a blog and sign up for affiliate and Google Adsense advertising programs.
- ✓ Register with Scoopshot.com and take photos for cash.

"It's not always sexy—these are often service-based jobs that you can do in addition to your full-time job," says Lorel Langemeier, noting it only takes an extra $50 a day (Monday -- Friday) to earn another $1,000 per month. But for anyone having a tough time living on a single income source (or none at all), it's one way to pay the bills and keep the money momentum flowing.

In the challenging economic times we are now in there is a great need for part-time workers, freelancers, and consultants. Why? Because bringing on full-time employees is a major, costly commitment for any business. Also, during uncertain times businesses have to run lean and mean. They can't extend themselves when everything is changing and economic projections are just guesses at best. But businesses still need help. So if you can be the one to save the day for them you'll always have work.

Nearly anyone can develop a successful part–time, freelance or consulting business of some kind. Often this will evolve into a full–fledged business or full–time job. Here are a few ideas from Ramit Sethi, author of the New York Times bestseller *I Will Teach You to be Rich.* www.iwillteachyoutoberich.com

Business

- ✓ Technical writing.
- ✓ Copywriting and editing.
- ✓ Project management.
- ✓ Business writing (business plans, grants, proposals).
- ✓ Sales.
- ✓ Public relations.
- ✓ Research.
- ✓ Transcription services.
- ✓ Human resources.
- ✓ Payroll services.
- ✓ Event planning/coordination.

Creative

- ✓ Design (brochures, logos, newsletters).
- ✓ Web design.
- ✓ Photography.
- ✓ Presentation design (PowerPoint).

Marketing/Technology

- ✓ Internet marketing consultation.
- ✓ Search engine optimization.
- ✓ Pay–per–click advertising consultant.
- ✓ Google analytics.
- ✓ Ecommerce consulting.
- ✓ Lead generation.
- ✓ Database creation/management.
- ✓ Blogging.
- ✓ Small business marketing.
- ✓ IT security.
- ✓ Social media consultant.

Tutoring/Coaching

- ✓ Education (SAT and LSAT prep, tutoring).
- ✓ Life coaching.
- ✓ Business training.
- ✓ Presentation coach.
- ✓ Martial arts instruction.
- ✓ Dance instructor.
- ✓ Image consultant.
- ✓ Music instruction.

Financial

- ✓ Accounting/bookkeeping.
- ✓ Tax preparation.
- ✓ Financial planning.
- ✓ Personal/virtual assistant.
- ✓ Cook/barista.
- ✓ Pet walking/grooming.
- ✓ Home maintenance.
- ✓ Physical therapy.
- ✓ Child care.
- ✓ Auto/motorcycle repair.

Those fortunate enough to have jobs today are working harder than ever. This creates opportunities for those without jobs for part-time or temp support work assisting with childcare, grocery shopping, deliveries, yard and house work, car care, and the dozens of time-consuming, mundane errands of over-scheduled and overworked families.

TASKRABBIT

When you are out of work or need to supplement your income, it pays (literally) to be resourceful. Fortunately, there are a number of new services that provide potential sources of revenue, like TaskRabbit.

Once you register with TaskRabbit, and go through a multiple-step application process that includes an essay, video interview, and background check, you can begin bidding for jobs in your interest area. Some dedicated, established Task Rabbits earn more than $50,000 a year. At the beginning of 2014 Task Rabbit was available in Boston, San Francisco, Portland, New York City, Atlanta, Austin, Seattle, Dallas, Washington DC, Denver, San Antonio, San Diego, Phoenix, Chicago, Miami, Los Angeles and Orange County, California. More cities will be added soon. Go to www.taskrabbit.com for more information.

Another similar service is Zaarly www.zaarly.com. As of early 2014, Zaarly operates in the San Francisco Bay area and Kansas City.

FREELANCING

Another way to earn income is by freelancing. For many people it has become a full-time career. The most widely used services include:

www.elance.com
Two million freelancers from around the world: writers, web developers, programmers, marketing pros, graphic designers, data entry, translators, PR...and dozens more job descriptions.

www.oDesk.com
The top freelance site with 4.5 million freelancers and more than a million jobs available.

www.99designs.com
Designers compete to win business in graphic design, mobile apps, business cards, website development, logos, banner ads, and book covers. You get to choose from dozens of designs.

www.freelancer.com
Claims to be the "world's largest outsourcing marketplace" with nearly 10 million freelance workers and more than 5 million jobs in design, mobile apps, website development, marketing, data entry, SEO, coding, copywriting...and many more.

www.guru.com
More than 400,000 freelancers in technology, creative arts, and business.

www.thewealthyfreelancer.com
Training and strategies to develop your freelance career. They also publish a helpful book, *The Wealthy Freelancer*, available on Amazon.

https://helpouts.google.com
Helpouts is a little-known feature of Google with a wide variety of jobs. You can post or hire. Some are free, presumably to build a customer base or advertise a business. It seems the average rate for expertise is about $15 an hour.

SIGN UP FOR RESEARCH STUDIES

As marketing becomes more consumer–driven, companies want to get to know you and hear your thoughts about their products, competitors, and the marketplace. An industry of consumer research providers has emerged that presents an opportunity for you to earn extra cash. For an hour or two of your time (in most cases), you can earn from $75 to as much as $400. The "work" is fun too…I've participated in several focus research groups in the past couple of years, earning more than $2,500 in extra "pocket change."

Here are a few of the companies you can sign up with to be considered for upcoming research projects:

- www.schlesingerassociates.com Schlesinger Associates
- www.FocusPointeGlobal.com Focus Pointe Global
- www.focusroom.com Focus Room
- www.fieldwork.com Fieldwork
- www.ffrsf.com Fleischman Field Research
- www.NicholsResearch.com Nichols Research
- www.virtualjury.com Virtual Jury
- www.asksocal.com Ask Southern California
- www.focuscope.com Focuscope (Chicago)
- www.WatchLab.com WatchLab
- www.TruePanel.com True Panel
- www.FocusGroup.com FocusGroup.com (10 markets + nationwide)
- www.HarrisPanel.com Harris Panel
- www.HarrisPollOnline.com Harris Poll Online
- www.murrayhillcenter.com The Murray Hill Center (New York, Dallas, Chicago, Atlanta)

Life Rule: Don't break the money flow.

LEAKING MONEY

"Money isn't the most important thing in life, but it's reasonably close to oxygen on the 'gotta have' scale." — Zig Ziglar

Just as people "leak" time, they also spend money on an endless number of non-essential "wants" that do little to further their progress toward key financial goals. They "leak" money. As any retailer will tell you, the number of credit card purchases goes up as the traditional payday dates loom near. The simple reason is that people run out of cash. But they don't stop spending. Especially on the little impulse buys and "treats" that seem so insignificant but add up over time.

SAVE A WHOLE LATTE MONEY

Consider the morning or afternoon latte at Starbucks that cost $4. Over the course of a month this adds up to about $120—or $1,440 a year. Sure it's a treat. But wouldn't a weekend in Cabo San Lucas be an ever better treat? Or a new Armani dress? Or (best choice of all) a contribution to your 401k, IRA or 529 college fund?

Wouldn't the smarter decision be to buy a pound of coffee and make your own? Even Kenya AA or a nice Kona blend will only set you back about $15 and you should be able to get a few dozen cups from it. That's quite a savings—not to mention the time spent going to Starbucks and standing in line (10 minutes a day X 365 = 3,650 minutes or the equivalent of 7 ½ eight-hour work days). How much could you accomplish in a week? What could you do with an extra week of time?

Other money "leaks" are the little impulse buys that are a mini version of retail therapy, a tiny lift during the day from just buying something, anything. It could be a candy bar (over $30 billion is spent on candy each year) or a soft drink ($61 billion is spent on soft drinks annually) that doesn't contribute anything to your health. Or an amusing trinket that adds to the clutter of your home or office.

Use the Rule of 752 to put small recurring weekly costs into perspective. Multiply the cost (for example, $20 for coffee) by 752 to get the 10-year cost of an expense ($10,040 in this case).

Life Rule: Stop the money leaks before you sink your financial ship.

WANTS VS NEEDS

To eliminate needless expenditures, always ask yourself if what you are about to buy is a "need" or a "want." If it's a "want" resist the urge to purchase the item immediately. Tell yourself you will come back tomorrow to decide. Nine times out of ten the urge to buy will pass.

By some estimates as much as half of all purchases are impulse buys. Infomercial marketers are masters at taking advantage of impulse buying weaknesses. It's why Suzanne Somers can sell $100 million worth of Thighmasters and George Foreman can sell $200 million worth of grills. Yes, that is hundreds of millions of dollars.

Life Rule: Always ask yourself if a purchase is a need or a want.

TAX RETURNS

"The avoidance of taxes is the only intellectual pursuit that carries any reward." — John Maynard Keynes, economist

The difference between one tax preparer and another can be significant. The Tax Code is 80,000 pages long and constantly changing. It's nearly impossible for anyone to understand it all. In a study conducted in 2004, fifty tax preparers were given the same return. The difference between the highest and lowest return was more than $10,000! Even more shocking, only one tax preparer actually completed the return correctly.

In another study conducted by the Government Accountability Office to test the accuracy of work done by large chain tax-preparation firms, 100% of the returns were incorrect. Many of the errors amounted to more than $1,000 in incorrect refunds and overpayments. Only two were close to being correct. Source: Washington Post, 4/5/06

According to *U.S. News*, there are 1.2 million tax preparers in the U.S. More than 70 million tax returns are done by paid preparers—but only a small percentage are Federally-licensed enrolled agents. In most states anyone can go into the tax preparation business without special training or a license.

According to the *National Tax Journal* (Dec. 2000), a study of 1994 tax returns claiming the Earned Income Tax Credit had a 26% error rate. Most errors were by the chain tax preparers and "other" preparers. The least number of errors (still 14.8%) were by CPAs, EAs, and tax attorneys.

Many returns contain costly mistakes that could result in penalties by the IRS. So choose your tax preparer wisely. The IRS website www.irs.gov includes tips for choosing a tax preparer. The IRS also has a help line to answer any questions you may have about your taxes: 1-800-829-1040.

If you have someone prepare your taxes, how much should you pay? According to the National Society of Accountants 2011 Income & Fees Survey, the national average cost is $246 for an itemized 1040 Federal return with a Schedule A and state tax return. Complex returns can cost as much as $1,500 to $2,500.

If you prefer to prepare your own taxes, there are numerous excellent software programs to help. Filing your tax return online is also now simple. Popular tax preparation software to consider are TurboTax by Intuit, https://turbotax.intuit.com from H&R Block Home, www.hrblock.com and TaxACT, www.taxact.com. Most cost between $35 and $100. For tax preparers and accountants, the ProSeries by Intuit (about $800) is highly recommended www.accountants.intuit.com/tax/proseries/. Tax software is regularly updated to adjust to the ongoing revisions in the Tax Code. These can be downloaded for free from the software company website.

The IRS has contracted with tax-software companies, including these three, to offer free online federal tax preparation and e-filing for filers whose adjusted gross income is less than $54,000. The IRS Free File option is available only through the IRS website.

- The IRS reports that just 1% of individual tax returns are audited each year.

One final tip, stay away from early tax refund loan sharks. These loans are a rip-off and can cost you plenty. Ask if your company has a tax refund loan program in place; many of the more enlightened firms offer this service to reduce the potential harm and stress to their employees.

BUYING QUALITY FOR LESS

According to *Money Magazine* (as reported by Clark Howard on his website), you can save $180,000 over a lifetime by buying "average" cars rather than fancy or luxury cars. For example, if you buy a Honda Accord LS (a top-rated car) rather than the more expensive Acura TSX you'll save thousands of dollars without sacrificing much in the way of features and quality.

While it pays to buy quality, don't confuse quality with luxury. Luxury items may or may not also be quality items. And quality often isn't expensive. Top quality automobiles, as named by J.D. Power & Associates, have included the Honda Civic, Chevrolet Malibu, and the Mini—all at the lower range of affordability. Autos we associate with quality and luxury, like the Mercedes-Benz or Range Rover, may not even make the top ten list any longer.

You'll often be surprised by the product comparisons in *Consumer Reports*. More often than not, the top-rated products are also less expensive. Take dishwashers. In 2011 the $620 Kenmore brand was rated more highly (79) than the $1,300 LG brand (62). *Consumer Reports* should be your first stop whenever you decide to make a purchase for anything you'll own more than three months. It's fair, unbiased (they have never accepted advertising) and accurate. www.consumerreports.org

Buying quality (at a decent price) is another reason to buy intelligently—not impulsively or emotionally. Ask yourself why you want and need a Porsche Carrera. If you take the time to examine your purchasing rationale, you'll often see the wisdom of another, less expensive, choice.

Life Rule: Buy quality. Always.

IT'S A SCAM SHAME

Nearly everyone will be the victim of a scam at some point in their life.

- Last year (2013) an estimated 12 million people fell for a scam.

Often, it's something small that does little lasting damage. But far too often a scam can be devastating...and life-changing. The now infamous $50 billion Bernie Madoff scam ruined the lives of many people who trusted him with their money.

Don't think it can't happen to you. Even smart, successful people get scammed. In the Madoff scandal, among the hardest hit was director Steven Spielberg and actors Kevin Bacon and Kyra Sedgwick.

One couple who lived in my hometown, Bruce Engel and Karen Wold, were scammed out of $1.6 million—virtually their entire life savings—by

Blessed Marvelous Herve, a convicted scammer who claimed his father was the Republic of Congo's president. Bruce had founded First Marin Realty 30 years earlier and Karen was a retired school teacher. Blessed Marvelous Herve claimed he wanted to purchase several properties in cash for his father. Just one small problem he said…the U.S. government had seized $43 million of his money after he had transferred it from Switzerland to San Francisco. After six years and many more wild stories (always requiring more cash from Engel and Wold), the smooth–talking Herve was finally arrested by the FBI in 2013.

Unfortunately, Engel and Wold lost everything, including a $100,000 inheritance from his mother and money they borrowed from friends and family to help Blessed Marvelous Herve. Their previously cushy lifestyle of yachting, European vacations, and a comfortable retirement is gone forever. The couple is destitute and $200,000 in debt. Engle is 69 years old and sells cars in a small town in Florida to survive. Wold is 71 years old and is looking for a job. "I am totally, totally ruined," she said. Even her teacher's pension is being garnished to pay debts. "We absolutely believed this guy," said Engle. "I just can't believe I was so stupid."

Dishonesty in America is rampant. As I am writing this more than 100 frauds are being prosecuted and the FBI is investigating another 100 Ponzi type financial scams.

- 4 in 10 Americans cannot recognize the signs of a scam, according to research by the FINRA Investor Education Foundation.

Here are the current top 10 scams defrauding millions of people out of <u>billions</u> of dollars.

TOP SCAMS

The Nigerian 419 Scam

A ubiquitous and costly scam is the 419 Scam. It's primarily an online fraud. Scammers in Nigeria (or some other country, including the U.S.) write and ask for money to help a dying Nigerian widow, a preacher who is helping starving children or to free a political prisoner. Once the money is sent, it's never seen again. Various versions of this scam have been around for centuries. Usually you're asked to send money to a lawyer or priest or government official.

Now it's hard to imagine someone being so gullible they would fall for the 419 Scam, but $9.3 billion was lost in 2009 alone to this fraud, according to the investigative firm Ultrascan. It's estimated that $45 billion has been scammed altogether, although some estimates go much higher. In Nigeria these scammers are considered "rock stars."

Travel and Vacation Scams

Victims are lured to high-pressure sales pitches for timeshares or vacation travel with the promise of expensive "free" gifts, such as a car or cruise package. To receive the "gift" the victim must pay a "fee" for delivery and processing. After investing in what seems to be an attractive timeshare package, the victim learns it doesn't exist or the timeshare company "has gone out of business."

Always do your due diligence and check out the company with the Better Business Bureau and the American Society of Travel Agents. **NEVER send money in advance.**

Rental Scams

In these scams the victim is searching for an apartment or home for rent and finds one at a low price in a desirable location. The victim contacts the landlord (scammer) who requests a deposit be sent immediately by wire or online to hold the apartment. Scammers often use photos of real properties to make the offer seem legitimate. The victim arrives to find that no such rental exists. This is often one of the first scams gullible young recent grads experience, especially in rental-scarce cities like New York or San Francisco.

Ebay, Craigslist, and Auction Scams

A potential "buyer" emails you and indicates he/she wants to buy the item you have for sale...but will be out of town. If you will be so kind (gullible) to just pay his/her assistant/sister/etc. with your credit card they will add an extra $40 or $50 for the "inconvenience" and reimburse you when the item is picked up. Which, of course, is never. So you end up paying for your own item (plus the extra money) and never hear from the scammer again...except when they use your credit card number.

Free Trial Scam

The problem starts when you give your banking information to pay for "shipping and handling." In the fine print the company now can begin charging you each month for not canceling the free trial. Even if you are successful canceling the charges, the company may have sold your bank information to another company.

Work from Home Scam

Who wouldn't like to work from home? Turn your computer "into a money making machine." Stay away from them all...and certainly don't give them your banking information. You'll just end up with identity fraud and rogue software on your computer.

The Charity/Disaster Scam

The terrorist attacks on the Twin Towers gave birth to a rash of scams, including one that defrauded the widow of a 9–11 victim out of a quarter million dollars. It hardly gets any lower than that. Other scams included fake insurance claims, enormously inflated prices by contractors, and faked deaths. A former Naval officer who was at the Pentagon when it was attacked faked a leg injury and collected $300,000 from a victim's fund. He was even awarded a Purple Heart for his "heroic" actions that day.

Every disaster seems to bring out the scammers, cheats, and criminals in droves. People are vulnerable and the crooks take advantage of this weakness. It happened after Hurricane Katrina, the Gulf Oil Spill, the tsunami in Southeast Asia, and the earthquake in Haiti. Nearly 5,000 websites popped up after these events claiming to be legitimate relief agencies. Be especially vigilant during disasters and in times of crisis.

Whenever you are aware of a scam, report it immediately to www.econsumer.gov and www.onguardonline.gov to help stop this epidemic of dishonesty. Also report it to your local police department. They probably won't do anything about it but you have a police report on record in case you need to bolster your case with insurers.

IDENTITY THEFT

As dramatically demonstrated on *Dateline NBC* on September 7, 2008, identity theft is a serious and growing problem. Approximately 1 in 10 Americans has been the victim of identity theft—more than 30 million people.

Identity theft costs are staggering—more than $5 billion annually. With the proliferation of credit cards and the Internet the perfect environment exists for grand theft on a global scale. And don't expect the thieves to be apprehended and prosecuted. Less that 1% of identity theft ever results in criminal charges.

If you have ever had your identity stolen, it essentially is compromised forever. Once your Social Security number, credit card information, name, and other personal data are in the hands of international Internet thieves, it can (and will) be bought and sold all over the planet. Your bank and investment accounts can be drained, your credit ruined, and hundreds of hours of your valuable time used to deal with the consequences of identity theft. I know, because it has happened to my family.

Here are the steps the experts recommend to keep yourself safe from identity theft.

1. Don't open more than one credit card and don't use a debit card. This may fly in the face of most financial recommendations but if you only have one card to steal your financial exposure is limited to the credit available on that card. Fortunately, most credit card companies will reimburse you for your losses.

   You will need at least one card for emergencies, to rent a car, and to help establish a credit history. But carrying and using a dozen or more cards to pay for everything from a $3 latte to a flat-screen TV doesn't make sense.

   As for debit cards, they are just like checks tied directly to your bank checking account. If yours is stolen you can likely kiss whatever balance you have goodbye. In recent years, millions of people have had unauthorized deductions from their checking accounts after their debit card data was stolen…usually online, or at ATM machines, retail stores, gas stations, coffeehouses, and restaurants. In late 2013 more than 70 million people had their credit compromised when hackers accessed credit card information stored by Target and Neiman-Marcus.

"Online is the #1 place where consumers should not use their debit cards." — Bankrate.com

2. Be careful online. The Internet is the happy hunting grounds for identity theft and scam artists.

- **Never provide personal data online**—especially your social security number.
- **Don't post personal information in your social media profiles**—not

even your birthdate. Thieves troll social media and are especially adept at figuring out enough about you to steal your identity. Always use privacy settings.

- **Never announce to the world that you are on vacation** in France for the next two weeks. It's like sending an invitation to burglars.
- **Don't reply to unknown emails.**
- **Be careful about online banking.** There have been dozens of thefts from supposedly secure institutions.
- **Avoid porn sites**—they are particularly vulnerable to viruses.
- **Never use unsecured wi-fi**—at home or in public. Thieves can literally steal your private information out of the air.
- **Avoid free software.** It is usually laden with special codes (i.e. viruses) that infect your computer and cull private information.
- **Change your password every 90 days**—and don't use your spouse's name or other personal information to create a password. Even the U.S. military can screw this one up…for 15 years the Strategic Air Command's "secret" code to authorize launching nuclear missiles (and potentially starting World War III) was 00000000. Really.

HOW HACKERS STEAL FROM YOU

Reported cyber security incidents increased 660% from 2006 to 2010, according to the Government Accountability Office.

The "hacks" into major financial and other corporations costs Americans hundreds of millions of dollars and has resulted in millions of people having their important financial information stolen. One incident in 2011 cost Sony $173 million when their popular Playstation Network was taken down and put out of commission for a month. If you are concerned about using the internet for privacy or financial reasons, you should be.

It's not just Nigerian scammers or Russian mobsters who are in the hacking game. More than 30% of the hacking incidents originated in the U.S., according to IT security company AVG. No company is invulnerable. Amazon, MasterCard, CitiBank, and PayPal have all been subjected to hacks, as have dozens of other well know companies. Even the U.S. government has come under attack.

Here's how a hacker "phishes" for your data.

1. You get an email claiming to be from a familiar and legitimate source.
2. The email contains a question or a threat and you are urged to go to the company website.
3. You click on the link and are taken to a site that looks real, exactly like your bank, for instance. But the site is a fake.
4. You're asked for private, sensitive data such as your account number and password into the site.
5. The "phisher" uses the data you provide to steal your money, identity or access a corporate network.

PASSWORD PROTECTION

Companies steal your private information every day. Just viewing a Home Depot online ad sends your name and email address to 13 different companies. Open the *NBC–TV* website and your username is shared with seven other companies. Stanford University found that supposedly anonymous data collected on personal web browsers is gathered and sold. It's called Big Data, and the practice will only become more pervasive in the future.

Consider your online information under constant attack and protect yourself with a strong password.

- About a third of all passwords are connected in some way to personal information, and 1 in 5 people use the same password for five or more accounts.
- ➢ 23% keep a written list of their passwords in an insecure place, according to a 2011 Survey by *Consumer Reports* National Research Center.

Since 8,000,000+ people fell victim to identity theft last year, and more than 1.5 million had their bank accounts compromised, you are likely to become a victim eventually unless you take action to prevent it. Your password is the first step to protecting your online assets.

CYBER-THEFT IS OFTEN AS SIMPLE AS 1, 2, 3, 4, 5, 6

The most popular password is 1 2 3 4 5 6, which is like having no password at all. The other most used password is PASSWORD. Really. Professional hackers keep lists of all the more popular passwords, many based upon common words, phrases, names, birth dates, or facts from your own life. If your wife's name is Mabel and she is 47 years old, it probably isn't a good idea to have as your password mabel47.

CREATING A HACK-RESISTANT PASSWORD

It's much harder for crooks to steal your password if you:

1. Make it long, at least 10 letters and numbers.
2. Use a mix of upper and lower case letters.
3. Use numbers.
4. Use special characters.
5. Change your password regularly.

Use the first letters of a sentence you can easily recall, such as "One Really Hot Chick From Baltimore For You Too" 1rhcfB4u2 or "The Only Thing Better Than One Of Me Is Two!" Totbt1omi2! or "Oh my god I am a total idiot too!" Omgiaati2!

"It takes just 2 hours to hack a password containing eight lower-case letters...but 200 years if it contains just one capital letter."
— Lawyers.com

PASSWORD RESOURCES

There are a number of excellent password managers available. Most are free or inexpensive.

- www.ShouldIChangeMyPassword.com You can check your password on this secure site to see if it has been compromised.
- LastPass (cross platform) www.lastpass.com Stores your data in encrypted format. Free.
- 1Password (cross platform now but originally MAC)

https://agilebits.com/onepassword Some different features than Last-Pass. Free for up to 20 items. $39.95 for a single user license.

- Sxippper (Firefox) Although Firefox has a password manager, you can up the anty with Sxipper, an add-on that manages all the usernames and passwords you enter on different websites on a daily basis. Then next time you visit the site you won't have to type the same information again—including complete forms.
- KeePass www.keepass.info Free open-source password manager.
- Clipperz www.clipperz.com Free password protection, form entering, one-click services and personal online "vault" for sensitive data.

All it takes is one hacker to steal your data and really disrupt your life. Take the time and make the effort to protect yourself.

HOME SECURITY

➢ "43% of people surveyed by *Consumer Reports* (2011) who have an alarm in their home say they occasionally don't turn it on when they're not at home."

About half of all home break-ins are actually walk-ins. Burglars know that people are often hurried in the morning, are late for work or an appointment—and forget to lock up. A surprising number of homes with expensive security systems are left unprotected, at least some of the time. All a good burglar needs to do is be patient until he finds one (often quickly).

Here are a few more ways people make it easy for burglars:

✓ Leaving the garage door open.

✓ Telling all your Facebook and other social media friends of your travel plans (wait until you get back).

✓ Not leaving a light or two on and taking other measures (like having mail and newspaper delivery held) while away from home for an extended period.

✓ 19% in one survey admitted to occasionally leaving a door unlocked while away.

- ✓ More than 1 in 4 people say they sometimes leave a window unlocked when not at home.
- ✓ More than half of people in non–metro areas (city folks know better) say they have left their car unlocked outside their home.
- ✓ Obscuring your home with high hedges, tall fences, or thick foliage—giving thieves the cover they need to take your things.
- ✓ Hiding your house key under the welcome mat...nice of you to welcome burglars to your home.

According to the FBI, there were:

- ➢ More than 2 million burglaries in 2012.
- ➢ 1 in every 36 homes was burglarized.
- ➢ A burglary took place every 15 seconds.
- ➢ The average value stolen was $1,675.

Yet, only 17% of homes have a security system installed.

Worse than the loss of valuables is the loss of life…dozens of people are murdered by thieves every year.

Take action:

- ✓ Report suspicious activity…unknown people collecting for "charity" or handing out business cards.
- ✓ Trim hedges and plants.
- ✓ Install deadbolt locks.
- ✓ Install a peep hole…and never open your door to a stranger.
- ✓ Have someone pick up your mail and newspapers while you are away.
- ✓ Put timers on lights so they turn on/off randomly when you aren't at home.
- ✓ Ask to see identification from police, delivery men, and municipal workers.
- ✓ Do background checks on everyone who works at your home: maids, gardeners, handymen.

- ✓ Install a video monitoring system.
- ✓ Never post vacation photos when you are on vacation…it's an open invitation to burglars.

There are many excellent video monitoring systems available. The cost is generally $400 – $1,000. Most require wiring but some are now wireless. Many systems download to your electronic devices, so you can check on them when you're away. Some cable companies offer excellent home monitoring systems (e.g. Comcast Xfinity total home security).

A new system I like is the DropCam encrypted, cloud–based, wi–fi video monitoring service www.dropcam.com. The cameras are simple to install and provide live streaming to your smartphone, tablet or computer. The system also features two–way talk, night vision, email and text alerts, zoom, excellent color resolution, and a wide field of view. Cameras cost either $149 or $199 each. The optional cloud recording and storage service allows you to review your video later. For seven days of storage the cost is $9.95 a month, $99 a year. For 30 days of storage the cost is $29.95 a month, $299 a year. There's 2–day delivery and a 30–day money–back guarantee.

Life Rule: Very few people escape being the victim of a scam, fraud, identity theft, burglary or robbery. Take precautions now to avoid a devastating loss.

Further reading: *A License to Steal* by Walter T. Shaw (a former burglar).

A FEW WORDS ABOUT THE HOLY 401K.

401k plans are the primary retirement investment for many people. But in many cases they've simply (yet again) been sold a bad bill of goods by the financial system. The typical 401k plan charges excessive, indefensible fees, and consists of poor, under–performing investment options.

"The 401k will turn out to be the greatest hoax ever perpetrated on an unsuspecting public."
— William Wollman, author of *The Great 401k Hoax.*

The primary beneficiaries of these plans are employers (who offload the cost and responsibility for securing the retirement of their employees) and the mutual fund industry (which gouges the $6 *trillion* in assets in these plans with unconscionable fees and expenses).

FOR 401K MANAGERS IT'S A FEE-FOR-ALL

Here are just ten 401k plan fees that can eat away at your retirement savings:

1. Account termination fees.
2. Account maintenance fees.
3. Account transfer fees.
4. Roth conversion fee.
5. Federal fund wire fee.
6. Special investment fee.
7. Special investment setup fee.
8. Form 990-R filing fee.
9. Loan processing fee.
10. Record-keeping fee…and more.

But you get the idea. It's the financial system looting your investments again. The IRS lists 17 different fees altogether. Revenue-sharing agreements between employers, 401k administrators, and mutual funds eats up even more. Then there are legal services, record-keeping charges, and even telephone and delivery charges. Of course, these are all buried in the plan's fine print…if at all.

Here's how fees can affect your 401k plan, according to a 2013 article in *The New York Times*, "Consider a worker with a 401k balance of $25,000 who earns 7 percent over the next 35 years. If this person paid 0.5 percent in fees, even if she stopped making new contributions, her account would grow to $227,000 at retirement. But if she paid fees totaling 1.5 percent, hers savings would rise to only $163,000, 28 percent less."

- ➢ In a 2011 survey, 76% of 401k holders either thought they paid no fees or simply didn't know.
- ✓ The investment options in many 401k plans are restricted, relatively poor choices. Do you really want your retirement dependent upon mediocre stocks?
- ✓ Investing a sizeable portion of your funds in the stock of the company

you work for is often the worst choice of all. Yet, 20% of all 401k assets are comprised of stock from the company the holder works at.

- ✓ Employers frequently (usually?) offer plans that benefit themselves the most. Gee, an employer who has their own best interests in mind and not yours? I'm shocked.
- ✓ 403b plans are the worst of all, left to greedy investment houses offering third–rate investment options. They're usually provided by employers who just don't give a damn about their employees.
- ✓ Don't forget that you will still need to pay taxes when withdrawing from your account. Tax–deferred does not mean tax–free. So, are you really sure (a) your 401k portfolio of stocks will appreciate at such a high rate that they will (b) overcome the laundry list of hidden fees, (c) inflation, and (d) taxes? If a 401k is your only retirement investment I wouldn't be planning any trips to Paris just yet.

NOTE: As of 2012, a new Department of Labor rule requires 401k managers to provide participants with a simple explanation of each fund's average annual returns over one, five, and 10–year periods; the comparable returns of a benchmark fund; and the average annual operating costs as a dollar figure per $1,000 invested as well as a percentage of assets...ostensibly so you can make "apples to apples" comparisons. I'm sure the attorneys are already brainstorming how to obfuscate this information so the average investor will simply ignore it.

DISCLAIMER: the author is NOT an investment advisor. I am simply the messenger of advice from others. You will need to find a competent investment advisor to help you understand the complex investments and most useful strategies for your particular financial plan.

To see how your company plan stacks up, go to www.brightscope.com. For more information on 401k plans, go to www.dol.gov. If you need help with your investment portfolio, consider hiring a fee–only planner who charges by the hour. You can get referrals from the www.garrettplanningnetwork.com.

Find out everything you need to know about 401k plans by reading Daniel Solin's highly informative book "*The Smartest 401(k) Book You'll Ever Read.*" I also advise reading his highly acclaimed book "*The Smartest Investment Plan You'll Ever Need.*"

RETIREMENT

"Many people take no care of their money till they come nearly to the end of it." — Johann Wolfgang von Goethe

Retirement in America has become a potential nightmare. More than 38 million Americans are classified as "senior citizens." That figure will mushroom to 72 million by 2030. 10,000 Baby Boomers retire every day. Source: *US News & World Report*, May 12, 2008.

- 1 in 6 Americans age 45 – 64 have postponed plans to retire, according to a 2013 AARP survey.

Baby Boomers, on the cusp of retiring, are quickly revising their plans. Challenging economic times are forcing many to curtail their "golf and travel" plans, cut back on expenses, or even continue working. More than 1 in 4 report having made a withdrawal from their retirement fund to survive—not a good sign.

In just one year—from 2007 to 2008—the percentage of retirees who reported feeling "very comfortable" about having enough money for their retirement dropped from 41% to just 29%. Only 1 in 3 (34%) feel they will have enough for basic expenses, according to a study by the Employee Benefit Research Institute and Mathew Greenwald & Associates. These worrisome percentages were how retirees felt *before* the Great Recession.

Fewer than 1 in 8 retirees have savings totaling more than $100,000. 18% have between $10,000 and $50,000. More than half, a whopping 51%, have under $10,000 in retirement savings. Very few retirees are prepared to support themselves adequately for the long and increasingly expensive life ahead.

Here are some retirement mistakes you don't want to make.

1. **CUTTING BACK ON CONTRIBUTIONS TO A 401K.**

Despite what we said about 401k's as mediocre investments, if you have one it's usually not a good idea to cut back on it. For most people, the 401k, even with all its flaws, is their only retirement investment. The value of the 401k for most people is that it siphons off money from their paycheck that "forces" them to save. It's invisible and painless. Money you don't see is the best way to save.

Many companies match 401k contributions, which is like getting free money. Many funds are set up so the company contributes 50 cents for each dollar the worker puts into their account—up to 6% of your total pay. It's the same as getting 50% return on your investment—not bad these days.

- Nearly 1 in 4 Americans don't contribute to their 401k, according to the Profit Sharing 401k Council of America. And many more don't add enough to get the full matching company funds. If you are 50 or older you can also make "catch up" contributions to your 401k, IRA, SAR–SEP IRA, 457 plan or 403b plan. Since 2008 you can put an additional $5,000 in your account and many companies will still match it. And, if you are like many over–50 Americans you will need to do a lot of catching up in order to have a decent retirement nest egg.

2. **DON'T USE YOUR RETIREMENT SAVINGS AS A BANK.**

When times are tough it's tempting to dip into your 401k, IRA or other retirement account. Do whatever you can to avoid it. If you can't pay it back within the allotted time period it is treated as an early withdrawal subject to income taxes and a 10% penalty.

3. **DON'T PANIC WHEN YOUR RETIREMENT ACCOUNT BALANCES FALL.**

Financial advisors say it almost never pays to move funds around trying to find a better or safer investment. Remember, if the fund managers can't predict what the market will do, you won't have any better luck. Moving from stocks to CDs or money market funds may cause you to miss out when the market moves upward again. Stocks, more than any other long-term investment, still deliver the most dependable returns over time... about 10% for the past 70 years (before taxes, fees, and inflation).

When the market drops, that's when you should think about buying, not selling. The oldest maxim in the investment game is "Buy low, sell high." When the market dropped by almost half in 2009 those investors who purchased stocks could easily have doubled their investment by the time the market rebounded to its former level in 2013.

4. **NOT HAVING A RETIREMENT PLAN**

If you are fortunate enough to retire with any appreciable assets (the average retiree has less than $10,000 in net worth), think about how you will use these to fund your "golden" years. Consider all your assets, including your home equity, insurance, and total investment holdings as your pool of available money. Then compute how much you may need, factoring in inflation and possible new expenses for healthcare, more travel or helping raise grandkids (there are more than 2.4 million households with children with grandparents as the primary caretakers...up 19% since 1990 and representing 7% of all households with children under 18).

Many financial advisors suggest that you live off of 5% of your retirement nest egg. Again, they assume you have a million dollars saved for retirement...and most Americans aren't remotely close to this figure. Even if you have a million dollars saved, living off 5% ($50,000) won't be luxurious, especially considering healthcare costs. The truth is that unless you find some form of passive, recurring income to support you from age 70 to 90+, you're going to be in trouble. With cuts looming in social security and Medicare, you may be wise to start shopping for a double-wide trailer to live in during your "golden years."

Many retirees get bored after a lifetime of steady work. So consider working beyond age 65. After all, today's 65 is the new 45. You still have a lot of life in your life if you've taken care of yourself.

- Retirees born in 1943 and after will see Social Security benefits increase by about 7% each year you delay taking them from age 62 – 66 and about 8% from 66 – 70. Factor in inflation of just 3% and the benefit you receive will increase at 10% – 11% each year you delay. This is a pretty good return on investment.
- You'll need to plan for healthcare. Approximately 25% of Americans over 65 are in fair or poor health. Estimates are that 70% of 65-year olds will need long-term healthcare at some point. That correlates with the 7 in 10 people who are 90 and are disabled in some way.

Source: *US News & World Report*, "5 Mistakes That Will Sink Your Retirement" by Kerry Hannon.

MAKE MONEY AN IMPORTANT PART OF YOUR LIFE

The management of money...making it, keeping it, growing it, investing it...is crucial to your lifetime happiness and success. So it makes sense that money management should be a key part of your ongoing education in life.

Wealth Life Rules to incorporate into your Plan for Life.

- Save/invest 10% or more of your earnings.
- Keep a budget.
- Balance your checkbook.
- Check your bills for errors.
- Use A Plan for Life savings tips to save at least $5,000 a year.
- Save 4 – 6 months of emergency living expenses.
- Track every expenditure every day by category…and keep all receipts in a manila folder.
- Learn the basics of money management and investing.
- Start investing early in life and reinvest earnings when possible.
- Take advantage of IRA/Roth IRA/SepIRA, low–fee stock index funds, and 401k (when matched by employer).
- Hire a good CPA/tax advisor.
- Avoid scams. If it sounds too good to be true…it usually is.
- Avoid traffic tickets, drive carefully and within the speed limit.
- Invest in security…purchase insurance, install a security system, use passwords that can't be easily hacked…and change them regularly.
- Be a smart shopper. You need less than you think to lead a good life. Is it a need or a want?
- Develop a second source of income.
- Draw up a will.
- Ditch the bad habits: smoking, drinking, drugs, gambling.

RESOURCES:

In the 21st Century we've seen the emergence of a plethora of new online tools and services that help consumers save money and manage it wisely. Most are free. Whether you're looking to track your credit score, find a better savings rate, set up an online checking account, or balance your budget, start your financial management program with these sites.

www.Bankrate.com

www.Mint.com

www.ClearCheckbook.com

www.MoneyStrands.com

http://finance.yahoo.com

http://money.cnn.com

www.CreditKarma.com

www.Credit.com

www.WiseBread.com

www.TheSimpleDollar.com

www.GetRichSlowly.com

www.Billshrink.com

www.creditcardinsider.com

Top personal finance management software includes:

AceMoney (Windows)

Quicken Starter Edition (Windows)

MoneyWell (MAC)

iBank (MAC)

Additional reading:

- ✓ ***The Difference: How Anyone Can Prosper In Even The Toughest Times*** by Jean Chatzky.
- ✓ ***Money Made Simple: How to Flawlessly Control Your Finances in Minutes a Year*** ***and Life*** and ***Debt 2010: A New Path to Financial Freedom*** by Stacy Johnson.
- ✓ ***The Real Cost of Living: Making the Best Choices for You, Your Life, and Your Money*** by Carmen Wong Ulrich.

- ✓ ***Marketing Shortcuts for the Self–Employed: Leverage Resources, Establish Online Credibility, and Crush Your Competition*** by Patrick Schwerdtfeger.
- ✓ ***The Money Diet: Reaping the Rewards of Financial Fitness*** by Ginger Applegarth.
- ✓ ***The Only Investment Guide You'll Ever Need*** by Andrew Tobias.
- ✓ ***Clark Howard's Living Large for the Long Haul: Consumer–tested Ways to Overhaul Your Finances, Increase Your Savings, and Get Your Life Back On Track*** by Clark Howard, Mark Meltzer, and Theo Thimou.
- ✓ ***The Millionaire Next Door: The Surprising Secrets of America's Wealthy* and *The Millonaire Mind*** by Thomas J. Stanley Ph.D.
- ✓ ***Think and Grow Rich*** by Napoleon Hill.
- ✓ ***Your Money or Your Life: 9 Steps to Transforming Your Relationship with Money and Achieving Financial Independence*** by Vicki Robin, Joe Dominguez, and Monique Tilford.
- ✓ ***The Top 10 Distinctions Between Millionaires and the Middle Class*** by Keith Cameron Smith.
- ✓ ***Index Mutual Funds: How to Simplify Your Life and Beat the Pros*** by Dale C. Maley.
- ✓ ***The Bogleheads Guide to Investing*** by Taylor Larimore, Mel Lindauer, and Michael LeBoeuf.
- ✓ ***The Bogleheads Guide to Retirement Planning*** by Taylor Larimore, Mel Lindauer, and Richard Ferri.
- ✓ ***The Coffeehouse Investor: How to Build Wealth, Ignore Wall Street, and Get on with Your Life*** by Bill Schultheis.

CHAPTER 3
CAREER

"Find out what it is in life you don't do well—and then don't do that thing." — Dos Equis beer commercial, career advice from "The World's Most Interesting Man."

IS THE AMERICAN DREAM TURNING INTO A NIGHTMARE?

"The most basic requirement of the American Dream is a job."
— *Time* magazine, 2012

Upward mobility in the U.S. is taken as a birthright…one of the best things about being American. Yet, the truth today is that America lags behind many other nations in economic upward mobility. France, Germany, Sweden, Canada, Finland, Norway and Denmark all provide the "American Dream" of upward mobility better than the United States.

In recent years more Americans are experiencing downward mobility instead. Household incomes on average are falling. Younger Americans may not achieve a lifestyle as affluent as their parents.

THE GREATEST UPHEAVAL IN WORK SINCE THE INDUSTRIAL REVOLUTION

➢ **A new McKinsey Global Institute study found that 230 million white collar jobs, representing some $9 trillion in income, will be transformed or even eliminated by computers in the next decade. (*Time*, 2014)**

What Americans are only just beginning to realize is that the way things were will never be again. We've entered a period of change not seen since the Industrial Revolution, when much of the world transitioned from a rural, agrarian society to an urban, industrial society. The Industrial Revolution created unprecedented disruption in the lives of millions…as well as widespread poverty. It also created massive amounts of wealth for those who adapted and took advantage of the creative chaos.

The revolution we are now experiencing will have similar affects. Already there are tens of millions of people who have been reduced to poverty by transition from a manufacturing–based society to a working world dominated by service industries and technology. Conversely, there have been scores of billionaires created by these same changes. And it's all happening at lightning speed.

The next 20 years will be a state of continued creative chaos throughout the world as technology, global interdependence, increased social interaction, massive information access, and disrupted industries make life uncertain and unpredictable.

THE NEW WORLD OF WORK

The new world of work has changed dramatically too.

- The average job length is down to just 4.4 years.
- The typical man will hold 11.4 jobs during his career.
- For women, the average is 10.7 jobs.

The length of time workers have to "make it" in their career has shortened drastically. According to www.payscale.com, earnings "top out" for men around age 45 and for women about age 38. Given that many young people are unable to get their career started until they are in their late 20s, there isn't a large window of opportunity to build a successful life.

Forty years ago it was unusual for an American job to be outsourced to a worker in another country. Now 42% of American jobs…more than 50 million…are vulnerable to being sent overseas, according to a Harvard Business Review study (2012). Millions of Americans are standing in unemployment lines while someone in China, India or Mexico is gainfully employed doing "their" job.

Overseas competition has put pressure on American salaries. As a result, millions of Americans work at jobs that pay poorly and provide little opportunity for growth. It's understandable that in 2013 more than 4 out of 5 Americans report being stressed out at work, according to *Time* magazine.

THE CURRENT RECESSION MAY BE A FOREVER RECESSION

"We can never really be prepared for that which is wholly new. We have to adjust ourselves, and every radical adjustment is a crisis in self-esteem." — Eric Hoffer

Author and social observer Seth Godin perceptively writes, "For 80 years, you got a job, you did what you were told and you retired. People are raised on this idea that if they pay their taxes and do what they're told, there's some kind of safety net, or pension plan that's waiting for them. But the days when people were able to get above average pay for average work are over." Godin believes that the current recession will be a "forever recession." www.sethgodin.com.

THE HARSH TRUTHS ABOUT THE JOB MARKET

"50% of all jobs will be replaced by automation by 2024."
— *Harper's* magazine

The job market has changed drastically in the past ten years. If you haven't kept up with the changes, you'll find it especially hard to find a job.

1. Employers know how to do more with less. New systems, outsourcing, contract labor, robots, and weeding out the "dead wood" has made modern American business more efficient. And while corporate profits are soaring, workers are making the same real wages as in 1975.
2. People don't know how to look for a job.

✓ They don't know which job boards to use.

✓ Their resume is badly written, reflects poorly upon their abilities, and is not searchable easily by applicant tracking system software.

- ✓ Job searchers seldom know how to interview well.
- ✓ Few people network effectively...even though it is still the #1 path to a good job. Not enough people are on LinkedIn who should be—and many of those who are don't know how to use it. Even fewer know how to use Twitter to find a job (it's the #2 online source of jobs).
- ✓ Recruiters are swamped and can't spend much time with you unless you're a stellar candidate. The typical resume receives six seconds of their attention.
- ✓ HR departments are understaffed. The HR Directors are often young and inexperienced.
- ✓ The hiring process has become ridiculously complicated. Companies are looking for perfect candidates, making decisions more slowly, conduct multiple interviews with several people, make the job-seeker take personality tests, grill past employers, and then tender offers that typically pay less than expected.
- ✓ The skills and knowledge needed in 21st Century America are not the same as you probably learned. Huge swaths of people will be out of work until they get the necessary skills to compete. Even then they will be playing catch-up with recent grads who already have the needed skills.

82% OF AMERICANS ARE DISSATISFIED WITH THEIR CAREER

Far too often people abdicate the responsibility for the direction their life takes by following the dictates of others. They live a linear trajectory—go to school, get a job, work hard, get married, have children, buy a home, work harder, acquire the trappings of the "good life," then retire so they can finally start "living." The irony is that by that time the life has been wrung out of them. They've forgotten how to live (if they ever really knew how). Or they are simply so exhausted getting to this point that there is no life left. It's why so many people retire and then die shortly thereafter.

The compromises people make along their career path often trap them in a job they hate, a career they don't know how they ever selected, ongoing frustration, and anger. According to a *Harvard Business Review* study released in 2011, fully 82% of Americans are dissatisfied with their career. A *Yahoo Finance* survey found that 60% would choose an entirely new career if they could start all over again.

Considering the high unemployment rate, it would seem that anyone with a job should be happy. Yet, in one survey 40% said they "hated" their job and 1 in 3 "hated" their boss. That's a lot of hate doing something that takes up more time than any other daily activity.

In another study, 7 out of 10 people said they disliked their job so much that they would change to any job that paid as much or more...sight unseen. Think about this for a moment. If you were no longer in love with your husband would you take another man sight unseen just to be away from him? Well, maybe some would!

IT'S EVERY MAN OR WOMAN FOR THEMSELVES

"If you board the wrong train, it is no use running along the corridor in the other direction." — Dietrich Bonhoffer

Workers today are impatient to capitalize on their skills to gain more money, benefits, challenging work, more responsibility, and the freedom to work when and where they want. But the increasingly competitive workplace is making that difficult. Never in modern history has the job hunt been more competitive than it is now.

- According to *World of Work*, in a 2012 survey by international employment matchmaker Randstad, more than half of today's employed people are actively searching for a new job.

A WELL CHOSEN CAREER IS THE BEST INVESTMENT IN YOUR FUTURE

"The best prize that life offers is the chance to work hard at work worth doing." — Theodore Roosevelt

Mike Hogan wrote in *Barron's* that "our career choices are among the most important investment decisions we'll ever make—because that paycheck underwrites so many other bets, like housing, education, and retirement." No matter what you decide to do in life, the financial prospects of your career will affect everything else you do. You need to factor that in and plan your life accordingly.

The key is to find work you love that also provides a living. If the work you love doesn't pay well, accept that you may have to adjust your lifestyle in order to continue doing it. Chances are that doing what you love will eventually reward you well. But there are no guarantees.

Life Rule: Life is too short to spend most of it doing something you don't like doing.

YOUR FOUNDATION FOR CAREER SUCCESS

For those who have put in the thought and due diligence required to determine what their purpose is in life (or who are fortunate enough to know it intuitively), there is always the danger of straying from your chosen path—especially when serious financial needs arise. In turn, this can lead you down a path that isn't of your choosing but of someone else's—not a recipe for lasting happiness and fulfillment.

That's why it is vitally important to do the following as early in life as possible:

1. Live below your means.
2. Save 10% minimum of everything you earn.

This will enable you to have the capital to take advantage of opportunities that arise to expand your personal, career, and financial future. It will also help you weather the inevitable setbacks in life: job loss, recession, illness, bad investments, divorce.

PLAN YOUR LIFE, THEN YOUR CAREER

"Nothing is really work, unless you would rather be doing something else."
— J.M. Barrie

You've heard it dozens of times—do what you love and the money will come. It's mostly good advice, as long as doing what you love is also something others love to pay you for doing. Most people who have successful careers are obsessed with their work, whether it is writing novels or painting or building a chain of coffee shops. They love going to work—unlike the hordes of Americans you see every night on the freeways literally fleeing from their jobs.

Fact: More people commit suicide and suffer heart attacks on Monday morning than any other time of the week. For most Americans, the work week begins at 9 a.m. on Monday.

Successful people have a passion for their work that often began at an early age. The pop singers Justin Bieber and Britney Spears knew from the time they were children that they wanted to become singers. Many actors started out in television commercials as kids. Most successful authors have been writing stories from the time they first learned to spell.

Others try out several different things before they settle on a career path. Dr. Ruth Westheimer, the famed TV sex therapist, once trained as a sniper in the Israeli military. Former Secretary of State Madeline Albright worked at Jocelyn's department store selling bras. Ralph Lauren was a glove salesman. And Brad Pitt once dressed up as a chicken for El Pollo Loco restaurants. Some people need to "try on" a few career paths before discovering their passion. Or take a job to simply earn some money.

DOING WHAT YOU LOVE

"A man is a success in life if he gets up in the morning and goes to bed at night and in between does what he wants to do." — Bob Dylan

Your career path should begin by doing what you love. Otherwise, there's always the danger your "temporary" job could become permanent. Millions are "stuck" in jobs they hate simply because they took the job initially to make some money and life events conspired to keep them shackled to it.

Here are a few comments about doing what you love from the 2005 Commencement address at Stanford University by the late Steve Jobs, CEO of Apple Computer:

"You've got to find what you love. And that is as true for your work as it is for your lovers. Your work is going to fill a large part of your life, and the only way to be truly satisfied is to do what you believe is great work. And the only way to do great work is to love what you do. If you haven't found it yet, keep looking. Don't settle. As with all matters of the heart, you'll know when you find it. And, like any great relationship, it just gets better and better as the years roll on. So keep looking until you find it. Don't settle.

Your time is limited, so don't waste it living someone else's life. Don't be trapped by dogma—which is living with the results of other people's thinking. Don't let the noise of others' opinions drown out your own inner voice. And most important—have the courage to follow your heart and intuition. They somehow already know what you truly want to become. Everything else is secondary."

THE ROAD LESS TRAVELED

"The secret of success is making your vocation your vacation."
— Mark Twain

Life isn't good for people who are unable to shape their own destiny. There's always an inner dissatisfaction reminding them of their failure to create the life they really want to live.

Embracing life is far too frightening for most people. It means risk. It means being willing to accept failure from time to time. It's hard work. And it requires the personal strength to face who we are and what we believe—and then play our hand in life with the cards we were dealt. It's just too much for most people.

"There is no scarcity of opportunity to make a living at what you love. There's only a scarcity of resolve to make it happen." — Dr. Wayne Dyer

Many people say they "don't know" what they want to do. They "have no idea" what they're good at. This is sheer intellectual laziness. They simply haven't made the effort to examine their life or engage in self-reflection. They have already adopted a lazy attitude toward life, seldom being curious or adventurous or involved. Our society makes it easy to become observers rather than participants in life. They probably have some passions, some interests, but these are buried so deeply they never emerge into the light of day. As a result, many people just drift into a career, taking what comes along or what requires the least amount of effort.

It's important to be curious about life, to engage in adventures, to learn, discover, and create. The more a person seeks, the more they will find—and eventually discover their "passion" in life. It's also why life-long learning and "adventuring" are so important. Without continual involvement in life, you may not recognize a new "passion" when it comes along.

On his deathbed an insurance executive reminisced about his life and its emptiness. "I always thought God had a greater plan for me, something that would give my life meaning, something special. But I never discovered what that was. I never figured out who I wanted to be when I grew up. Now I realize it was because I didn't really look for it." As the old man neared death he said, "Tell my children—tell everyone—to resist going with the flow. Make a difference. Don't let them off the hook. Tell them to do the work necessary to discover their purpose in life—and then follow it without looking back."

FINDING WHAT YOU LOVE

"Your work is to discover your work and then, with all your heart, to give yourself to it." — Buddha

It's a genuinely happy person who makes a living at something they can't wait to wake up to do every day. And if you plan correctly, this is the kind of career you can have. The key is doing something you love that others will pay you to do.

I love to relax and sleep late and travel and make love and eat at fine restaurants and read and play with the dog and hit baseballs with my son. But it would be difficult, if not impossible, to earn income from any of these things I love to do (although I did start a travel company once, a job that didn't even seem like a job). If you can find a way to make money by doing something you value and enjoy every day, you've taken a huge step toward lifetime happiness...because it's important to earn enough to live well and provide a degree of personal security.

HOW TO FIND OUT WHAT YOU MAY BE GOOD AT DOING

"The things that you love control your life." — Richard Bolles

If you don't have a career passion, one way to discover what you may be good at is to take a skills and personality assessment. I recommend the procedure that Richard Bolles outlines in his book *What Color is Your Parachute?: A Practical Manual for Job-hunters and Career-Changers.* It is both comprehensive and enlightening. *Time* magazine called this book "one of the 100 best and most influential (non-fiction) books written in English since 1923." It should be your career management "bible." Bolles thoroughly updates the book every year, so it still remains the best single source of job search information.

I attended a week-long intensive training with Bolles at his home outside San Francisco. One of the most valuable lessons he teaches is discovering who you are and what you are good at doing…your "passion." The process begins by taking inventory of your skills, a careful evaluation of your personality type, and an examination of your interests. He likens your quest for self-discovery to a flower with seven petals, because there are seven sides to You.

1. What you know.
2. The kinds of people you like to work with…and serve.
3. What can you do.
4. Your ideal working conditions.
5. Your preferred salary level and level of responsibility.
6. Geographic location.
7. Your goals or mission and purpose.

In the current (and likely future) job market, your transferrable skills are also important. Bolles demonstrates just how expansive your job-search can be if you recognize all that you are potentially capable of doing. By identifying transferrable skills, a new world of potential opportunities will emerge. Find out more by visiting www.JobHuntersBible.com and www.eParachute.com.

Other useful tools to evaluate your personality and skills include the C. Jung and Briggs Myers personality tests. www.MyersBriggs.org HumanMetrics has a brief version you can take to get started. www.HumanMetrics.com. Other job aptitude tests can be found at Career Path www.careerpath.com (the Job Discovery Wizard) and Mind Tools www.MindTools.com.

EVERYONE HAS TALENT

"The secret of business is to know something that nobody else knows."
— Aristotle Onassis

We all come into this world with some combination of talents that can set us apart, something we enjoy more than anything else. The lucky ones are those who "know" it from an early age. My former teacher, the late Roger Ebert, knew from the time he was a small child that he loved movies. He also liked to write. Combining these two "loves" led him to a successful Pulitzer Prize-winning career as a film critic. Donald Trump loves making deals and he loves real estate (and making money). Combining these "loves" has made him a billionaire (a couple of times).

"What is it that you like doing? If you don't like it, get out of it, because you'll be lousy at it." — Lee Iacocca

In "Do *What You Love, The Money Will Follow*," author Marsha Sinetar says this about people who know what they love to do in life, "It is as if they instinctively know what they must do with their time and energy and then determine only to do that." Helen and Scott Nearing, in their book "*Living the Good Life*," write "the objective of economic effort is not money, but livelihood." Some of the most satisfied people are those who are engaged every day in a passion...whether it is carpentry or computer coding or as a river rafting guide...and earn enough to live well.

"Pleasure in the job puts perfection in the work." — Aristotle

If the money never comes to any great degree, the person who is doing what they love is rewarded by the sheer joy of doing something every day that provides happiness and soulful compensation.

MOST CAREERS ARE JUST JOBS

"Life is too short—and too long— to spend it being miserable."
— Jill Lonnen Brewer

Ernie Zielenski writes in *Career Success Without a Real Job: The Career Book for People Too Smart to Work in Corporations,* that most work is "characterized by stifling boredom, grinding tedium, poverty, sexual harassment, loneliness, deranged co-workers, petty jealousies, bullying bosses, seething resentment, illness, exploitation, stress, helplessness, hellish commutes, humiliation, depression, appalling ethics, physical fatigue and mental exhaustion." Yikes!

I've been fortunate in my career to have enjoyed interesting work at mostly enlightened companies. However, like most people, I have experienced at least one of these conditions at one time or another (well, eight to be exact). How many have you experienced? Enough said.

Life is simply too short and too full of possibilities to spend at least 25% of it doing something that has no meaning to you. Think back to when you were a child. Did you dream of having the career you now have? Are you working as an accountant? Short-order cook? Insurance claims adjuster? House painter? There's nothing wrong with these jobs. They are honorable professions. And necessary. But are they the jobs of dreams? Most likely no. These are jobs people have settled for because they didn't pursue their dreams.

One of the biggest fears most people have is living a life that proves to be meaningless. A well-chosen career can give meaning to your life. So, do whatever you can to make your life meaningful with a worthwhile career.

"One of the huge mistakes people make is that they try to force an interest on themselves. You don't choose your passions, your passions choose you." — Jeff Bezos, Founder, Amazon

Find something to do that has the potential to generate an obsession within you. Try several things out for size. Get past the awkward early learning stages. You never know where an interest will lead to if you follow it with passion. Anthony Bourdain loved travel, food, and writing. These interests led to a highly successful career as a chef, author of several best-selling books about the restaurant business (*Kitchen Confidential: Adventures in the Culinary Underbelly, A Cook's Tour*), and a popular TV show (No Reservations).

My friend Mary Beth Bond has always had a passion for travel. That passion has taken her to more than 100 countries around the world, a career as a *National Geographic* magazine author of twelve books (*Gutsy Women: Advice, Inspiration, Stories*), a radio program about travel, a popular website www.gutsytraveler.com, and more adventures than most people could have in five lifetimes.

If you haven't discovered your passion in life, here's a tip that will make it easier. Be passionate about doing great work…no matter what you're doing. If you are only half engaged in what you do, waiting for your passion to magically appear someday, you'll never learn the primary secret of passionate people...is doing great work.

YOU DON'T HAVE TO BE GOOD AT SOMETHING TO BE GOOD AT SOMETHING

My friend Daniel runs a youth center for disadvantaged kids. He is passionate about what he does but it didn't require a "talent" to do. The work he does every day requires a range of skills from fundraising to coaching. These are tasks that are within the ability range of most intelligent people. The point is you don't have to be naturally good at something to be good at something.

Babson College president Leonard A. Schlesinger, Innovation Associates president Charles F. Kiefer, and New York Times contributor Paul B. Brown, authors of *Just Start: Take Action, Embrace Uncertainty, Create the Future*, www.JustStartTheBook.com say that if job fulfillment is not possible, for whatever reason, and it looks as if things won't change soon, accept the fact and find fulfillment elsewhere.

They point out that many famous people have held ordinary jobs while pursuing their dreams in their free time. Writer Wallace Stevens, winner of a Pulitzer Prize and two National Book Awards, worked as an insurance lawyer his whole life. Albert Einstein worked in a patent office. Actor Harrison Ford was a carpenter. All eventually found a path to success and fulfillment.

They advise that you:

1. Continue to do excellent work at your primary job.
2. Don't moonlight on company time.
3. Don't talk about your outside activities.
4. Schedule time in the evenings or on weekends to develop the skills you will need to succeed in what you are passionate about doing.

FINDING WHAT TO DO IN A CHANGED WORLD

The truth is that most people, even those who pursue a passion, will work for someone other than themselves. Which means they must find a job.

Job hunting, whether or not you like your job, is now a constant subtext in 21st Century career management. Nearly everyone will be "between jobs" at some time during their career. You must be prepared to go job-hunting for the rest of your life—to constantly be "in the game." Staying current with the tools, resources, and the personal support network required to maintain a healthy career is job number one.

Deep structural changes in the U.S. and global economy has resulted in the permanent elimination of many jobs. Internet and digital technologies, as well as competition from foreign economies, has changed American business forever. For example, 90% of music is downloaded digitally. Which means CD sales are down drastically. Which means record stores are closing. Which means fewer record store employees are hired. That's how it works.

Technology has created many new jobs, requiring new expertise from those who work in these jobs. But what most people haven't yet realized is that technology will eventually be a net job destroyer. As more things become automated by technology, fewer people will be required to do these jobs. Keep this in mind when choosing a career path. Can your job be done by a machine someday?

Many of our manufacturing industries are dying, beaten into submission by high-quality goods produced by lower paid workers overseas. America is becoming primarily a service economy. And service economies are highly vulnerable to the whims of the marketplace.

- It's estimated that nearly 30% more jobs and companies will leave the U.S. in the coming decade.

Off-shoring is accelerating at a fever pitch. Hummer is owned by the Chinese. Anheuser-Busch (the Great American Beer) is owned by the Belgians. Our automobile industry employs more than a half million fewer people than just twenty years ago. It's difficult to buy anything Made in the USA any longer. The U.S. is now like an unemployed person who must resort to selling possessions and running up credit card debt just to survive.

When *ABC-TV* News emptied out a typical American home of all the foreign-made products as part of their series *Made in America*, the entire home was left bare—except for the kitchen sink. While some products can still be found that are made in America, most Americans aren't buying them.

The impact of this historic change in the economy upon jobs is that we are fast becoming a nation of haves and have-nots. Future jobs will be concentrated at the low end and high end. Obviously, your goal is to be in the high end. That will require specialized skills and advanced education in careers suited for the 21st century...or a career based upon a unique creative skill.

Life Rule: Work at what you are passionate about...or be passionate about the work you do.

IT'S IMPORTANT TO STAY FOCUSED—AND WORK WHILE YOU LOOK FOR WORK

"Unemployed Americans spend an average of just 18 minutes a day looking for a job." — *Harper's* magazine, December 2009

The job market is so competitive that it's easy to become discouraged...especially after sending out hundreds of resumes, going on dozens of interviews, and always coming up short. It's not easy to be strong enough to withstand disappointment after disappointment. After months or years of unsuccessful job search many people simply put in the minimum amount of effort required.

Recruiters and HR professionals can see the defeated look of long-time jobseekers as soon as they meet them. If you allow this to happen to you then it will be doubly hard to get back in the game.

Dream Job University www.DreamJobUniversity.com Founder Ron Nash provides insightful advice in his book *Leveraging LinkedIn: The Essential Guide to Building Your Career Network* when he says, "when the sky is dark and filled with clouds, it's your best opportunity to find the silver lining. It just depends on what you focus on." He goes on to say, "If you keep your dreams close to you (in focus) and you work while you're waiting for the opportunity to present itself, you will always be prepared when the moment arises—and it will arise if you stay focused on your dreams and *expect* that the moment will come. While this sounds magical, which it is, it's also deeply rooted in science."

THE RECENT GRADUATE

"You may delay, but time will not." — Benjamin Franklin

Olympic high-divers say the approach is the most important part of completing a successful dive. So too a graduates' first job has an inordinate influence on their career path and lifetime earnings, according to Austan Goolskee, former Chairman of the Council of Economic Advisors. Don Peck, author of *Pinched: How the Great Recession has Narrowed Our Futures and What We Can Do About It* writes that fully "2/3 of real lifetime wage growth typically occurs in the first ten years of a career."

In this recession–battered job market, getting your career off to a good start is especially important. If you don't know what to do with your fresh college degree, then you are already behind the loop. This is one of the critical junctures in your life...you can drift and let yourself be carried along to wherever life happens to lead you or you can take the first step along the road to career fulfillment.

Despite what your friends and family may have told you, a college diploma is no longer a guaranteed ticket to the good life. At best it's your entry ticket. You are still responsible for creating your career. And that takes intellectual examination, hard work, exploration, courage, and creating a plan. You'll need to build a network, find mentors, continue your education, and develop your "street smarts."

EVEN RECENT GRADS NEED EXPERIENCE

In the 21st Century even recent college grads need experience. Employers don't want to take the time or spend the money to train employees, especially when they know most people in their 20s will find another job within three years. A 2013 Chronicle of Education Survey of Employers listed these qualifications as most desirable in college grads.

- 23% Internship
- 21% Employed during college
- 13% College major
- 12% Volunteer experience
- 10% Extracurricular activities
- 8% Relevance of coursework
- 8% GPA
- 5% College reputation

These findings are the opposite of popular belief. Perhaps instead of spending big bucks on that Ivy League education and burying yourself in the library to make good grades, you should be working summers or volunteering for Habitat for Humanity.

MANAGE YOUR CAREER ONLINE

Like everything else in our life, the Internet has changed the world of work. If you aren't using the Internet to manage your career you are already at a disadvantage. But with this powerful career tool comes some potential hazards that can derail your career.

Social media can affect your job prospects even before you are in the job market. One quarter of colleges use web searches to evaluate candidates for special programs. 1 in 10 college admissions professionals say they visit prospective students' online pages…and 38% reported they were negatively impacted by what they found (everything from inappropriate behavior and language to nude photos). Conversely, students who show mature and sophisticated use of social media were viewed more positively.

A 2011 study of randomly selected hiring authorities by Reppler and Lab42 found 91% now use social networking sites and Google search to help them screen job candidates (Facebook 76%, Twitter 53%, and LinkedIn 48%). A quarter said they made a hire after reviewing a social media profile. Here are some other findings:

✓ 69% have rejected a candidate based upon what was found online.

The reasons?

✓ 13% of candidates lied about their qualifications.

✓ 11% posted lewd or inappropriate photos.

✓ 11% posted inappropriate comments.

✓ 11% said negative things about their previous employer.

✓ 10% posted content that indicated they used illegal drugs.

On the positive side, 68% said they hired a candidate based upon what they found online. Here's why.

✓ 39% projected a positive attitude.

- ✓ 36% had a profile that supported their professional qualifications for a job.
- ✓ 36% showed creativity.
- ✓ 34% had good references.

A surprising number of college students, who are spending four or five years and tens of thousands of dollars for an education, blithely destroy their chance of getting a job by being stupid online. Those hilarious photos of you throwing up on your date when you got drunk at the college frat party may come back to haunt you someday. Worse, estimates are that as many as 1/3 of 20 year olds have posted a naked or revealing photo of themselves online, or "sexted" a revealing photo on their smartphone (on in this case, dumbphone). That oh-so-cute naked photo of you having revenge sex that you emailed to your ex-boyfriend is lingering out there in cyberspace just waiting to go viral and mess with you.

Since it's estimated that 70% of all resumes contain inaccurate information—and 43% include downright lies—designed to enhance a job prospect's work, personal or educational history, what appears online is often a reality check for employers. Most HR Directors say that even one lie or distortion is enough to disqualify a candidate. So, resumes are cross-checked against other available data—including social media, criminal records, credit score, and past employment dates. In many cases, discrepancies are found that can disqualify a candidate. Again, what company would want an employee who is dishonest?

YOUR LIFE IS AN OPEN BOOK AND THE INTERNET IS THE LIBRARY

If a company really wants to drill down to find out personal and professional information about you, well, it's easier than ever in the era of Big Data. Several companies and websites provide information that was only available to private investigators in the recent past. Whether or not you are on the internet, you're personal privacy is, for all intents and purposes, gone.

HOW EMPLOYERS JUDGE YOU IN THE NEW WORLD OF WORK

The new world of work isn't anything like your father's workplace. Here are the Work 2.0 ingredients employers now judge potential employees on:

1. Google presence and ranking.
2. Online reputation.
3. Business social media presences.
4. Personal website.
5. Blog.
6. Facebook presence.
7. Linkedin profile, connections, recommendations.
8. Twitter followers and Tweets.
9. You Tube presence.
10. Knowledge of social media.

Not only has the job market become more competitive, managing a career effectively today is significantly more complex.

JOB SEARCH 2.0

The days of sending a typed cover letter and resume to answer a job posted in the newspaper or a trade magazine are long gone. Job search is now conducted online. Data compiled by Jobvite in 2011 shows graphically the amazing change in where job-seekers find their jobs today.

- ✓ 1 in 6 workers use social media to get hired now.
- ✓ 9 in 10 job-seekers have a profile on a social media site.
- ✓ 54% of job-searchers used Facebook, Twitter or LinkedIn to search for jobs.
- ✓ Half of all job-hunters used Facebook, 26% LinkedIn, and 25% Twitter to look for a job in the last 12 months.

A decade ago few people could conceive of the importance social media now plays in career management. The fact is…if you're not online, you're probably in the unemployment line. With a job market as challenging as the current one, with several job–seekers for every available position, learning to use social media is imperative.

THAT WAS THEN, THIS IS NOW

Career management expert Josh Waldman, author of *Job Searching with Social Media for Dummies* and the popular blog Career Enlightment www.careerenlightenment.com points out several key ways today's job search is different.

1. Google has replaced the resume. Sure, you still need to have a 2.0 resume on steroids, but recruiters today are using Google and LinkedIn searches to find talent.
2. Your resume Summary is important to getting noticed…it's the open or closed door to your qualifications. The average time spent reviewing a resume is less than 10 seconds. If you don't grab the attention of the recruiter or hiring manager in the space of a TV commercial, you've probably wasted your time applying. Make sure your Summary includes the right keywords and appeals to the self–interest of the company.
3. "Social proof, testimonials or recommendations seriously reduce the perceived risk of you as a candidate," says Waldman. Consider including a real testimonial statement or two in your resume.
4. Relationships outweigh resumes in importance. Personal networking is still the top path to getting a job, and probably always will be.
5. Employers only care about what they want. Keep the focus of your resume and job search on what you can do for the employer.
6. Keywords are king. Study up on how to select and use keywords to find a job. Applicant tracking software and keyword searches on LinkedIn have changed how resumes (and profiles) need to be structured. It's important to develop several resumes—each with a different focus, customized for every job application to match as closely as possible with the advertised position. Incorporate words from the

job description as keywords in your custom resume.

7. You are your brand in 21st century career management. Carefully decide what personal image you want to create that supports your goals, is based upon core truths about you and your capabilities, and then apply it consistently in every area of your life…online and offline.

A good introduction to using online resources to support your career goals is *Social Networking for Career Success: Using Online Tools to Create a Personal Brand* by Miriam Salpeter www.keppiecareers.com. Whether you are a beginner or advanced social media user, you'll find a lot of useful information here.

Career expert Dick Bolles adds these key points:

1. Resumes have an atrocious success record…only 1 in 270 lands a job. Your new "resume" is online.
2. There are more jobs available than you think. At any given time there are about 3 million openings.
3. Small companies with 100 employees or less are the best ones for job-hunters to approach…especially for older workers, those with handicaps or returning vets.
4. At the end of an interview, ask for the job.

LINKEDIN IS YOUR LINK TO PROFESSIONAL SUCCESS

"If you want to be found, be where people are looking."
— Eric Wentworth

Linkedin has more than 330 million members (January, 2015)—with two new members joining every second. Fully 90% of Fortune 100 companies use LinkedIn Talent Solutions to augment their HR capabilities. LinkedIn, according to the 2012 Bullhorn Reach Social Recruiting Activity report, is the most important networking tool for career management.

If you're not on LinkedIn, you should be. With LinkedIn you can easily expand your reach to hundreds of thousands—even millions—of contacts. LinkedIn uses the power of the Internet to supercharge your networking capabilities. Use it to find employees, job opportunities, share information, increase your knowledge, and make contacts that can enhance both your professional and personal life.

- A 2012 survey by Jobvite found that 93% of recruiters use LinkedIn to find qualified job candidates, compared to 66% for Facebook and 54% for Twitter.

Neither Facebook or Twitter alone come close to matching the career tools available on LinkedIn. As a result, LinkedIn gets 5.7 times more job views than Facebook and three times more than Twitter.

YOUR LINKEDIN PROFILE

The "hub" around which everything else on LinkedIn depends is your personal profile. Your profile must stand out and be search (keyword) friendly. To find out which keywords are most powerful and will be tagged by search engines most often, look at what keywords others in your field are using, scan job descriptions, and check out industry websites.

TEN TIPS TO BUILD A STRONG PROFILE

The key to building a strong profile on LinkedIn is to think of yourself as a brand. Brands build trust by using an authentic voice and telling a believable story that connects with the target audience. Here are ten tips to help you do the same:

1. **Don't cut and paste your resume to build your profile**. Describe your experience and abilities as you would to someone you just met, not in formal "resume" speak. Write for the screen with short punchy blocks of copy and visual or textural support.
2. **Learn from the best advertising copywriters**. Lighten up your profile with your unique voice, as you would if you were excited about telling a friend about your career and skills. Introduce yourself much as you would at a conference or meeting with a client. Use your authentic voice.
3. **Write a personal tagline or slogan**. The best marketers "tag" their marketing messages with a memorable line that stays with the consumer. Budweiser, the King of Beers; BMW, the Ultimate Driving

Machine; and Things Go Better With Coke, are just a few. In the line of text that goes just under your name—the first thing people see on your Profile—write a branding statement, a slogan, for yourself. Note: in some cases your company's brand may be so strong that it and your title are all you need.

4. **Use your "elevator pitch,"** the 30-second description that is the essence of who you are and what you can deliver, in the Summary section to engage readers.
5. **Talk about your skills**. LinkedIn recommends thinking about your Specialties field as your own personal search engine optimizer, a way to refine and target how people find you. This is also where you list your particular abilities and interests that may make you stand out from the crowd. You can include the personal values you bring to your professional experience...and even include a note of humor or passion.
6. **Describe your experience**. Help the person reviewing your Profile with key points that say what your company does and what you did for them. Use bullet points to point out specific and measureable achievements.
7. **Distinguish yourself from your competition**. Use the Additional information section to round out your Profile with a few key interests—especially those that enhance your overall professional description. Add a website connection or Slideshare presentation that showcases your abilities. Edit the default "My Website" label to promote click-throughs to increase your Google page rankings. Add awards received, trade associations you belong to, and interest groups you have joined to show your professional engagement.
8. **Join groups that reach the target groups you want to connect with most.** Belonging to a group in an industry or interest area that can further your career goals is one of the best ways to reach people with similar interests. It's also an excellent method to expand your list of contacts since you can directly invite other group members to be part of your network.
9. **Improve your Google page rank**. Request recommendations from colleagues, clients, and former employers who can attest to your abilities.

Ask them to focus on a specific skill or personality trait that supports your overall professional brand. Be sure to give back by doing the same for your contacts.

10. **Build your LinkedIn connections**. Connections are at the heart of using LinkedIn successfully. People are naturally judged by the people they associate with professionally and personally. It reflects the quality of your brand. When someone scans your profile and notices that you are both connected to the same contact, your stock soars. If people reviewing your Profile see that you are connected to many others in your field, or your contacts show you associate with influencers in your industry, your value increases.

NETWORKING WITH LINKEDIN

The next step is to begin networking. You can import the names of people you already know and are in your browser contact list or from Facebook and Google+ "friends." Whenever you meet someone at a conference or while on the job, get their business card and follow up with a note and invitation to connect on LinkedIn.

Signing up for and participating in groups (as many as 50) is another great way to build your list of contacts. Thousands of LinkedIn groups cover every career and interest subject imaginable. Participating in these groups enables you to get exposure and even demonstrate your knowledge in front of peers and potential employers. The groups are also a great way to stay on top of new developments and differing opinions.

Check the connections of your connections to see if there are people you would like to reach out to and include in your circle of contacts. Over time these people will often transition from being "cold" contacts into lifelong personal or professional friendships as you become known to each other, much like if you had actually met the person. In many markets there are frequent networking events to meet your connections and make new ones.

Do these things diligently and consistently and soon you'll have a list of contacts numbering in the hundreds. These contacts will put you just one or two degrees from tens of thousands of other potential contacts.

While many LinkedIn members prefer to connect only with people they've met or done business with, there are others who connect with anyone. "Top linked" members may have thousands of contacts, although they will actually know only a fraction of these connections. There are pros and cons to either linking strategy. My own linking strategy is a hybrid… about 80% of my connections are people I know and the others are people I'd like to know or who want to connect with me for professional reasons.

YOUR LINKEDIN HEADSHOT

Unlike on your resume, where including a photo is discouraged, the opposite is true of LinkedIn. Profiles without a headshot are reviewed far fewer times than those with a good photo. It's important that your photo is professional. Why people continue to use snapshots taken by their cousin or on a smartphone for their "professional" online image is hard to understand. If your photo says "geek" or "unprofessional" then perhaps it's time to consider putting your best face forward.

I don't recommend getting a Photoshopped "studio" photo that bears only a faint resemblance to the real you, or one that was taken 15 years (and 30 pounds) ago. You don't want people to hardly recognize you when you finally meet. But using a bad snapshot to promote your career is just naïve. LinkedIn recommends, when appropriate, having a professional photo taken in your working environment. Your headshot is a key ingredient in the success of using LinkedIn.

MANAGING YOUR CAREER ON LINKEDIN

➢ If LinkedIn was a country, it would have the fifth largest population in the world.

First, and most importantly, make a commitment NOW to using LinkedIn to help manage your career…on a consistent basis, even when you aren't in the market for a new job. Too many people turn to LinkedIn only when they are out of work and realize they have a poor professional network, realize that HR Directors and recruiters almost all use LinkedIn to screen or find job candidates, and discover their career management is non–existent at a time when competition for good jobs is more intense than ever before.

Once you sign up with LinkedIn, make the investment in time and energy to learn how to use it. LinkedIn is a phenomenal professional career management tool...and relatively easy to use (even for the technically deficient). But don't stop using it once you've landed a new job.

LINKEDIN TOOLS

There are several valuable career management tools on LinkedIn.

- You can tell LinkedIn what types of jobs you are interested in and receive notifications when they become available. Then you can apply for those jobs through LinkedIn. There are several search parameters that enable you to drill down to exactly what you are looking for in a job.
- It's possible to "follow" companies that interest you. There are nearly 3 million company pages on LinkedIn (2013). Each includes information about the company and shows how you are connected to its employees and former employees. You can find out the address of the company, how many people work there, and when it was founded. You can see how many other LinkedIn members are following the company. Often there are links to websites, blogs, updates on company activities, and listings of products or services. By reviewing the profiles of people who work at the company you can gain valuable insights into what they are looking for in an employee. LinkedIn lists other similar companies, as well as the companies people who viewed the page have also searched, to provide you with a wider search field.
- Every day you are alerted to who has viewed your profile. If a hiring manager has looked at your profile you will know. LinkedIn provides a cool graph showing the total views and the last three months activity. Below this graph is the number of times you have appeared in LinkedIn Search and the percentage you are trending (up 3%, for example).

If you want to become a LinkedIn pro you can't go wrong with three LinkedIn trainers who have been in the game for years: Mike O'Neil and Lori Ruff at Integrated Alliance www.integratedalliances.com, authors of *Rock the World with Your Online Presence: Your Ticket to a Multi-Platinum Online Profile*, or Ron Nash, creator of TheInAcademy program (highly recommended for every job-seeker) www.TheInAcademy.com, www.TheInAcademy.com and author of *How to Find Your Dream Job... Even in a Recession* and *Leveraging LinkedIn: The Essential Guide to Building Your Career Network.* Ron can also be found at www.ed2go.com, an exciting online education resource.

Lori and Mike have both been named a Forbes Top 50 Social Media Power Influencer and are among LinkedIn's top 50 Most Connected Individuals www.rocklinkedin.com Follow them on Twitter @linkedintrainer @linkedindiva. Ron Nash is a LinkedIn expert, motivational speaker, and former executive recruiter. Connecting with these pros on LinkedIn is like networking on steroids.

Linkedin co-founder Reid Hoffman has written a valuable guide to using social media to further your career titled *The Startup of You: Adapt to the Future, Invest in Yourself, and Transform Your Career.*

PROMOTE YOURSELF ON LINKEDIN

As LinkedIn has evolved during the past ten years, they have stepped up their game in enabling self-promotion to enhance your career or job search. Now you can post presentations, videos, awards and certificates, and links to your website. In 2014 LinkedIn launched a publishing platform that will be a game-changer, enabling you to showcase your best work, including posts from your blog.

USE FACEBOOK AND TWITTER IN YOUR JOB SEARCH

Twitter

Twitter is becoming a popular job search tool as more recruiters, employers, and human resources departments use it to post job opportunities. To search for jobs, use hashtags, the little # that precede words and enables pinpointed search on Twitter.

You can search for tweets using hashtags (with or without the #) in the search box of your Twitter profile, and Twitter will generate a list of all the recent tweets posted with that specific hashtag.

As with all Internet search, the more specific you are the better your results. Some popular hashtags are #jobs, #hiring, #hotjobs, #greenjobs, #NewYorkJobs, #advertisingjobs, and so on. Check out TweetMyJobs and sign up for the free services. You can list the job titles you're interested in pursuing, and the locations where you are willing to work, and these will be tweeted to you as they become available.

Twitter is also an effective networking tool. You can join in the discussions at #jobhuntchat and #careerchat, just two of many career–related Twitter locales. Follow leaders in your field and executives at the companies you are interested in. You can often create a relationship via Twitter that can lead to a job opportunity. You can use Twitter to help become known as a leader or expert in your field. Companies often seek out these individuals first for key positions.

Twitter is evolving rapidly (especially since going public), and related support apps and sites are being added almost every week, so it's important to spend some time researching how best to use this important job search tool. For a good introduction to using Twitter for your job search, check out *The Twitter Job Search Guide: Find a Job and Advance Your Career in Just 15 Minutes a Day* by Susan Britton Whitcomb and Chandless Bryan.

Facebook

Employers and recruiters are using Facebook to help evaluate potential hires. This can work for or against you. Many people have lost (or gained) a job opportunity based upon what was on their Facebook page. It's hard to believe, but every day thousands of people post stupid, embarrassing, or damaging comments and photos on their page. Conversely, Facebook posts can also validate, or even improve, your stature. So decide upon a strategy and goals for your Facebook presence...then stick to it.

Many companies now have their own Facebook page. Here's a wonderful opportunity to find out the latest info on the company by "liking" and following them. With both Facebook and Twitter you can learn a lot about the company culture. Also, jobs are frequently posted on these sites before other venues.

In Facebook groups you can discuss and post news about a particular subject, industry or interest. Connect with people who may be in a position to facilitate a job opportunity.

Facebook as a career management tool can be a bit dicey. It's hard to control what your friends post, and often you'll be judged by the company you keep. It also enables companies to have a much closer look into your personal life than ever before. You'll need to decide if you want your Facebook presence to remain social among friends and family or let potential employers into your private life. My advice is to keep it strictly social and add the necessary privacy controls to keep the outside world outside.

THE BRAND CALLED YOU

"Personal branding is how we define ourselves in the workspace while at the same time incorporating the personal elements that makes us who we are." — Dawn Rasmussen

Film stars and politicians have long understood the importance of managing and directing their personal image to support their career goals. For example, there is only one known photograph of Franklin D. Roosevelt in a wheelchair during his Presidency. Celebrities know the value of personal branding. Now it's just as important for you to do the same.

In the 21st Century, your personal brand image is important to your success. Dan Schwabel, www.danschwabel.com personal branding expert and author of *Me 2.0: Build a Powerful Brand for Career Success*, makes the case that every person must create a unique, memorable, value–driven identity.

Competition is fierce in the marketplace. Sometimes there are hundreds, even thousands, of people who want what you want. So how do you stand out from the crowd? By developing a unique set of valuable skills, a memorable persona, and a public presence.

Business scientist Edward Deming advised people to do as corporations do—write a Mission Statement. Make your mission statement broad enough to encompass your general life goals and branding, but specific enough (with action steps) to create a path to achieving your goals.

To build a personal "brand" you must consistently do things that lead steadily toward your Mission. While people are willing to overlook the occasional misstep, if you make too many then that becomes your reputation. You are what you do consistently.

For more on how developing a distinctive personal brand can impact your personal life, go to CHAPTER 7: *YOU*.

PERCEPTION IS REALITY

"Be your message." — Mahatma Ghandi

Perception often becomes reality. Once you've decided how you want to be perceived by others, you've got to do what is necessary to promote that brand. Perhaps it's with a blog or a book. Maybe it's with specialized training or a degree. It could be through volunteer or extra-curricular activities. Some people engage in public speaking. Others do special projects at work that are highly visible. Perhaps a personal "makeover" will set you apart or reinforce the kind of image you want to present. The key is to find things that support your "branding" and to be consistent with it.

YOUR RESUME

"The primary purpose of a resume is to get yourself invited for an interview." — Richard Bolles, author of the 10 million copy bestseller *What Color is Your Parachute?*

With all the attention given to resumes—and resources available to help write one—it is surprising how often they are poorly conceived. By some estimates, three out of four resumes are considered poorly written. So right from the start most job-hunters are at a disadvantage. A well-crafted resume will propel you ahead of the majority of your competitors.

While a resume is seldom the only reason you will get a job, it is often your first impression. It's your calling card, and it sets in motion the cascading perceptions potential employers will have of you. And if you don't make a good first impression you likely won't get a second chance.

NOTE: Don't rely on your resume alone to get a job. In the age of social media, resumes are becoming less important. Networking online (and in person) is how most jobs are found.

Your resume is also, first and foremost, a sales document. And you are the product. Keep this in mind as you craft and refine your resume… is it just reciting accomplishments or is it selling those accomplishments. Employers don't care all that much about what you've done unless it can show them what you are capable of doing for them. This is the biggest mistake that most people make on their resumes, but there are many others.

Here are five common mistakes HR Directors and recruiters find on resumes.

1. **Typos.** If you don't kare enuff to make make sure your rezume is acurate how can a potential employer beleive you'll be any diferent on the job? One recent survey indicated that 84% of hiring professionals toss a resume in the trash can after spotting one or two typographical errors. Typos simply show a lack of conscientiousness and professionalism.

2. **Inappropriate email address.** OneHotSlut@gmail.com will always be viewed less favorably than EmilyAnnCandidate@gmail.com (unless, of course, you are applying for Chief Slut at XXX Productions). C'mon, if you show this much lack of common–sense do you really expect to get hired?

3. **Including non–job related or irrelevant information.** Most hiring executives aren't interested in your hobbies, love of kitties, abilities as a magician (although this might help in the financial services sector) or the last book you read. After reading thousands of resumes (and that's just for the job *you* applied for) HR pros learn to skim resumes and pick out only the information of interest to the job they are filling. Make sure that's what is in your resume.

4. **Poor structure.** You're lucky if your resume gets read—at least every word of it. Most HR Directors only read the first few lines or, at best, skim resumes. They know what to look for quickly. Some resumes aren't even looked at by humans (and yes, HR Directors are human, at least in theory). A computer programmed with a specific algorithm will review your resume for keywords pertinent to the job. The best thing you can do is make your resume easy to read and scannable. Stay away from neon colored paper, resumes carved in wood or pheromone scented cover letters designed to excite the HR Director (unless you want a date with one).

5. **There's no "I" in resume.** Keep your resume in the accepted formal style eschewing personal pronouns. Don't say "I created a new widget that boosted sales 1,500% in one year." Instead say "Created new widget that boosted sales 15,000% in one year."

6. **Boasting.** Statements like "You will never meet a widget genius like me,"

or "It would be impossible to find a better qualified widget designer!" seem obnoxiously arrogant and amateurish. It's better to list honors and awards separately as simple statements. "Won 2013 Cannes Lion Gold Award for Acme Widget TV commercial," for example.

7. **Not customizing each resume you send out.** Include the same keywords that are in the job description. Limit your resume to only the accomplishments that pertain to the job you are seeking. Lead with your strengths. If you have several awards and commendations, consider listing them separately.

8. **Weird typefaces.** Use a typeface that is easy to read—a standard type (e.g. Times Roman or Microsoft sans serif) and large enough to read (usually 10 – 12 point).

9. **Not focusing on your achievements—and how you monetized them.** Many resumes focus incorrectly on responsibilities instead of achievements. Always write your resume to appeal to the company's selfish interests—what you can do for them. Achieving sales growth, increasing efficiency, cutting costs or retaining a higher number of customers is much more impressive than the fact that you were a VP. Tell how your actions resulted in increased sales and then put a number to it. "Created new CAD–based widget design program that resulted in 190% more production and $240 million in annual sales."

10. **Hiding your skills.** Put your skills up front where they will attract the attention of the HR professional. And always lead with the skills that are most relevant to the job you are seeking.

11. **Listing references on your resume**. In fact, don't put the common "Excellent references on request" line in your resume either. It's assumed that you will provide references, if asked.

12. **Trying to put everything in your resume.** You may have more experience than any other person in your field of work, but don't feel obligated to put it all in your resume. While it may seem contradictory, less is more—even in resumes. Research shows that longer resumes are read less than shorter ones. Zero in on only the golden nuggets from your career and leave out everything else. You can always talk about what else you've done during your interview.

13. **Keep emotion out of your resume.** Some job-hunters have been fired from previous jobs, had conflicts with their boss or co-workers or have simply been out of work so long they've become resentful. You may desperately need this job to prevent being evicted and your car repossessed. You may actually feel suicidal because the last time you had a job George Bush was president. Don't show it. Stay professional at all times. Emotion (except enthusiasm) is a "red flag" to a trained HR professional.
14. **Avoid using resume creators.** These are difficult to work with if reformatting is needed. Make it easy at all times to view your resume.
15. **Use bullet points** instead of long paragraphs to describe your accomplishments.
16. **Use "white space"** to make your resume more attractive and easier to read.

APPLICANT TRACKING SYSTEMS

While there's a good chance your resume will be looked at by a human being at small and mid-sized companies, most (90%) larger firms now use applicant tracking software systems to analyze the thousands of resumes they receive. Often costing millions of dollars, these sophisticated software programs search for keywords and phrases to match up applicants with individual job requirements. If your resume doesn't get tagged by the ATS parameters, it will be automatically discarded. It doesn't matter if you're the next Steve Jobs, if the all-knowing (and slightly Orwellian) ATS doesn't select you as worthy, you are nothing. Your carefully crafted resume will disappear into a computerized black hole.

It's ironic but ATS systems often work against companies finding the best people. According to headhunter Nick Corcodilos www.asktheheadhunter.com, the out-of-the-box creative thinking employers claim they want is weeded out automatically. If you don't fill out a "required box," your creative thinking is rejected.

Employers shoot themselves in the foot with ATS systems. ATS systems don't account for personal and social skills…the "soft skills" that are the most important ingredient in job success. What companies (and you) need to do is meet face to face, usually in a non–interview setting, to really determine if the potential employee (or employer) is right.

Since HR departments are overwhelmed by resumes from desperate job–seekers, they use these systems to help them cope with the deluge. Or at least that's what they say. If you ran a business the way most HR departments are run, you'd be out of business in no time. The fact is… many HR departments are staffed with people who have little or no actual business experience who like to say "no" a lot.

If you suspect your resume will be scanned by ATS software, you'll need to dial back on the creativity in your resume and match the requirements of the software. Do everything in your power to circumvent the archaic hiring system by making a personal contact.

Your potential value to a company must be communicated quickly by your resume's keywords in order to distinguish you from all the other applicants. The ATS software will rank your resume, and depending upon how well you fare against the other job–seekers, you'll either get a call or not. If the company you applied at has decided to only see the top five candidates, and you are number six in the ranking, you lose. Besides keywords, there are other factors that can affect your resume's ranking, so it's important to apply them all if you want to come out on top.

1. **Resume formats**

Most ATS software is programmed to read only the reverse chronological resume.

2. **One page or two?**

There are trends in job–seeking. One recent trend that seems counter–intuitive is the single–page resume. In recent years, job–hunters struggled to put their entire career onto one page. While this worked well for recent grads with no experience, it didn't work for people with twenty or thirty years of work history. A one–page resume is like reading only the headlines of a newspaper. While shorter is generally preferred, two and even three–page resumes are acceptable now because companies want to see the details of your career…to help them find the ideal candidate for the job.

3. **If your objective is to get noticed, don't use the heading "Objective"**

Many ATS systems don't pick up resumes that start with "Objective."

Always remember, when searching for a job, it's not about you...it's about the needs of the company. Your resume should start with "Summary" or "Profile Summary" and include the exact title of the position you seek.

4. **Opening statement**

The opening statement is the most important part of your resume. It's much like the headline in an ad; if it doesn't get noticed, the rest of your resume won't be read. Your opening statement must begin with a strong, attention–getting value proposition. In advertising, this is called the USP, the unique selling proposition. It summarizes what you can do for the employer, and why you are the most qualified to do it.

The Opening Statement is also the place where you can add a personal branding description that highlights what makes you unique among the job applicants.

5. **Qualifications, skills, and competencies**

Skills statements are picked up by ATS software keywords and demonstrate that you have the qualifications needed by the employer. Highlight the key skills in the job description and include them on your resume. These will be picked up by the ATS. Assuming you have grabbed their attention with your Opening Statement, this is where you back up your claims with specific skills.

6. **Backup proof statements**

Linking each skill to a successful outcome completes the value proposition. Show specific examples of how your skills translated to a clear benefit to your past employers.

7. **Experience**

Potential employers are interested in your experience only as it relates to their needs. So, keep this in mind as you describe your experience and accomplishments at each job you've held.

Also, in order for ATS software to pick up this section of your resume, it must be headed with the word EXPERIENCE. Be sure to provide an accurate description of each company. For example, instead of saying Sony, you'll need to say Sony Corporation of America. Always include the Inc., Corporation, or LLC as it applies to each company you've worked at in order for the ATS software to recognize the name of your former employer.

Use what's called the Harvard Format...a brief paragraph describing your roles and responsibilities, followed by bullet point statements of results and achievements. This is an easily scannable and readable format.

Use the CAR method to format each section...the Challenge, your Actions and, in bullet points, the Results of your actions. The CAR method will drive home (pun intended) your accomplishments.

8. **Education**

You don't need to go into great detail in the Education section of your resume. Simply state the name of the educational institution, location, your major, and degree. If you are an older worker, you may want to leave off the dates of your education to avoid age discrimination.

9. **Affiliations**

Include only affiliations that pertain to the job you are seeking. The Acme Widget Corporation isn't impressed that you belong to the Indiana Beekeepers Association. Avoid listing political or religious organizations.

10. **Testimonials**

A third-party endorsement...testimonial...from someone who you've previously worked with is a powerful statement. Consider including one or two in your resume, perhaps in the Opening Statement. The ideal testimonial is, of course, one from a former supervisor or client. Next best is from co-workers and direct reports.

11. **Address, phone number**

Today your address is more than where you physically live, you also have "addresses" online. Besides your name, street address, city, state, zip code, and telephone number, include your email address and your customized LinkedIn address. In some cases, you may want to leave out your physical address (e.g. if you have to commute a long distance or are applying for a job in another city).

12. **Mimic the job description keywords**

Customize your resume for every job application. The best way to do this is to highlight the key words, phrases, and qualification requirements of the job description as created by the company itself, then mimic these as closely as possible as they apply to your own experience, skills, and expertise.

Analyze every word of your resume to determine if it supports your value proposition. Make sure it is keyword intensive. Check your grammar, spelling, and punctuation. I know one highly qualified person who lost out on a job because she spelled 2013 as 3013. Not a big deal? Well, it was to the financial services firm, where numbers are important (a simple typo could cost millions).

WHAT RESUMES AREN'T

Resumes are only a "foot in the door." It's the jobseeker's calling card. A first impression. But a resume alone will seldom land a job. To do that you need to get personal. Don't be afraid to show initiative. Find out who works at the company you want to work at and contact one or two key people (on LinkedIn it's easy, you can "follow" companies and see many of their employees). I can guarantee that 90% of the people you contact, whether you know them or not, will help you. It's a great way to find out insider information about the company and the job—which will give you an advantage over other candidates.

If this is uncomfortable for you, at least you can check out the backgrounds of the people you may be working with so that you can find some common ground when meeting them.

FOLLOWUP INTELLIGENTLY

Follow–up on your resume submission to insure it gets seen. Make sure you contact the person with the authority to hire or direct the hire. Personally, I've had the most luck contacting the CEO directly. Doing this shows you are comfortable dealing with C–level executives and immediately sets you apart from many other applicants.

Have a contact plan. Know what you are going to say in advance, even if you have to write out a rough script. Offer new information about yourself that's not included in your resume and cover letter that adds more value to your qualifications. Stand up when making the call. It will help you project more enthusiasm and energy into your voice.

SEND A HARD COPY TOO

Consider sending a hard copy of your resume as a backup to your online submission. These days you'll stand out just for doing that. And even HR Directors are human—a beautiful resume on a fine quality paper is impressive. In places like Silicon Valley this might be considered déclassé or very "last century," so choose your target company wisely.

Also, an electronic resume can print out poorly—or not at all if there's a glitch. Always email your resume and other attachments first to a secondary email address, or the address of a friend with a different brand computer, to see how it will look to others.

WHAT NOT TO DO WHEN JOB HUNTING

Like buying a home or getting married, job-hunting is something most people do just a few times in their life. As a result, they aren't very good at it. Here are some things to watch out for when you find yourself looking for a new job.

- ✓ **Don't lie on your resume**. A national survey found several, uh, "discrepancies" when doing background checks on applicants.
- ✓ **31% lied about their job or educational qualifications**. Many even made up Ivy League degrees or claimed they worked at companies where they were never hired. Harvard University said that about half of the resumes listing Harvard degrees they are asked to verify are false.
- ✓ **24% were linked in some way to criminal behavior**, including time spent behind bars for offences as serious as rape, child molestation, and robbery.

It got worse when they checked online.

- ✓ 19% bad-mouthed their former employer—many on social networking sites like Facebook.
- ✓ 19% boasted about drinking or doing drugs in social networking sites or in their blogs.
- ✓ 15% shared confidential information about former employers.
- ✓ 11% actually posted provocative photos of themselves online.

- ✓ 8% used an unprofessional screen name.

Many recruiters and HR pros use a service called Checkster to thoroughly vet all your former jobs, references, education credentials, and other claims. They can find people you've worked with previously that you might rather they not contact. Checkster's CEO, Yves Lermusi, literally wrote the book on this subject, *Reference Check 2.0: How Digital Social Networking is Transforming the Selection Process.*

With so much lying and "enhancing" the truth going on in the competitive workplace, it's no wonder employers are taking their time hiring these days. Their potential liability from a dishonest or criminal employee is enormous—in dollar losses, employee morale, legal costs, and reputation.

Life Rule: Never lie about your credentials or background.

THE JOB INTERVIEW

The job interview is where you will either be voted off the island or selected to stay. In *Fearless Resumes: The Proven Method for Getting a Great Job Fast*, author Marky Stein points out that the interview is not just important to getting the job but getting the job *well.* First impressions and the salary you negotiate follow you long after the interview.

PREPARING FOR THE INTERVIEW

Preparing for the interview will increase your confidence and performance. Remember to:

- ✓ Prepare your wardrobe.
- ✓ Practice your first impression.
- ✓ Know your resume.
- ✓ Practice questions/answers.
- ✓ Know the company.
- ✓ Know the job description.
- ✓ Have positive answers to counter negatives.
- ✓ Get a good night's sleep.

It's important to remember that job interviews are not so much about you but about what you can do for the company. Think of it as a first date. If all you talk about is how wonderful you are in an attempt to impress your date, don't expect a second date. It's the same with interviewing.

THE FIRST IMPRESSION LASTS

- ➢ According to Stanford Graduate School of Business Professor Deborah Gruenfeld, research shows that "people decide how competent you are in 100 milleseconds."

Always remember that your first impression is likely the one that will last. Numerous research studies have proven that most people make up their minds about someone within the first five seconds of meeting. What's just as interesting is that in about 90% of the cases the first impression later held up as being accurate.

OPENING REMARKS

If you are comfortable with it, engage in a little light opening conversation. Avoid potentially harmful comments like "Boy, the Widget Corporation makes the last place I worked at look like a Siberian work camp." If you've done your homework you could say, "Mr. Roberts, thank you for seeing me today. I realize how busy everyone must be with the introduction of the Super Widget." This is a nice lead-in to an opening conversation and also demonstrates you've done your homework about their company.

If you have a chance to scan the room quickly, you can often pick up on a common area of interest to establish a personal rapport. If the interviewer has a photo on the wall showing him during his glory days playing football at Stanford, this could provide an opening. If you also went to Stanford or played football, a comment like, "You played football at Stanford? Why, that's where I got my PhD in widget design." You've just scored an interview touchdown. If you were also a halfback at Stanford, start thinking about your office decorations.

Of course you should have already done a significant amount of background research on every person who will be interviewing you—on internet search resources such as Google search, the company directory and website, LinkedIn, and Facebook. You want to know as much as possible about who you meet. I like to know where people grew up, who they are married to, where they live, how much they make, the schools they attended, hobbies and interests, and where they have worked previously. It's probably the kind of research they will do on you, so be sure to level the playing field. By doing in-depth research you'll feel more in control of wherever the interview process takes you.

PERCEPTION IS YOUR REALITY

"Chemistry is a huge factor in deciding who gets the job."
— Kenneth A. Heinzel, author of *Private Notes of a Headhunter: Proven Job Search and Interviewing Techniques for College Students and Recent Grads*

An interesting finding from Stanford research is the proportionate weight three key variables play in how you will be perceived.

1. The factor that influences your perception the <u>least</u> is words. Just 7% of the impression you make is a result of what you say and how you say it.
2. Presentation. How you look, dress, and carry yourself makes up 38% of your first impression.
3. And surprisingly, 55% of how competent you are perceived as being is a result of body language. Body language communicates non-verbally your power, status, and how approachable you may be. A 2010 survey of 2,500 hiring managers discovered that many job applicants blow their interview with poor body language:

- ✓ 38% didn't smile.
- ✓ 33% fidgeted.
- ✓ 33% had noticeably poor posture.
- ✓ 26% had a weak handshake.
- ✓ 21% crossed their arms over their chest.
- ✓ 21% played with their hair.

You'll also be judged quickly on weight, beauty, fingernails, height...even your hair style!

STUDY THE JOB DESCRIPTION AND QUALIFICATIONS REQUIRED

Be prepared to address any qualification or expertise needed in the job description. Know what you are going to say before the question is asked. "Winging" it just doesn't fly in the crowded airspace of 21st Century employment. Here are a few tips:

- **Come prepared**. Bring a slim black leather portfolio, a pen, and an extra copy of your resume.
- **Don't say "generic" things about yourself**. Always link comments to the job in some way. It's important to reinforce how you would add value to the company. If asked to describe yourself (a favorite interview question), tell how you are by nature a creative or energetic or organized person and then tell a story about how this admirable trait helped you increase the Acme Widget Corporation's sales by 1000% (just an example, don't actually say this).
- **People who listen well are judged more positively than those who speak well**. Focus on truly hearing what the interviewer is saying, not what you intend to say next. Studies show that people only retain 50% of what they hear. In an interview this could be disastrous. Your interviewer is likely providing many pieces of information that are important for you to respond to correctly. So, listen intently and ask clarification questions, if necessary, so that you understand completely what is being said to you. Don't feel as if you need to respond immediately. Take a moment to gather your thoughts…it shows respect for what the interviewer has said and indicates that you are giving some thought to it. Most importantly, if the interviewer wants to talk a lot…let her. In fact, encourage her to talk. Don't, under any circumstances, take up more than 60% of the conversation load.

In *Just Listen: Discovering the Secret to Getting Through to Anyone*, author Mark Goulston advises putting yourself in the other's shoes during a conversation. You'll be surprised at how the barriers to communication come tumbling down. Another tip from his book is to put PEP in your conversation: passion, enthusiasm, and pride.

- **Don't talk about your woes**. Sure, you're down to your last pennies, there's an eviction notice tacked to your door, and you're on food stamps, but do your best to channel Donald Trump instead.
- **Ask smart questions**. This means you will need to do some research on the company you are interviewing at (always a good idea). The stories HR managers tell about candidates who knew little or nothing about their company are incredible.
- **Don't get caught not knowing something on your resume**, especially dates.

THE MOST COMMON QUESTIONS YOU WILL BE ASKED IN A JOB INTERVIEW

Preparation and research are the two methods that will reap the most benefits in a job interview. Learn everything you can about the company, its competitors, and the key players. Then prepare answers to the most common questions asked in interviews.

1. Tell me about yourself.
2. Tell me about a challenge/success/failure and how you handled it.
3. Why do you want to work for us?

Of course, there are an infinite number of questions you could be asked. It's impossible to remember intelligent answers to them all. The best course of action is to prepare diligently. Keep in mind that every answer should relate back to the job description and show how you can fill the position successfully. For more information, read *301 Smart Answers to Tough Interview Questions* by Vicki Oliver or *101 Answers to the Toughest Interview Questions* by Ron Fry.

Since you will be judged within a few seconds of meeting, the job is yours to win or lose after that. If your first impression is a good one, simply try to do no harm afterward. If it was a bad first impression, then you sure better knock their socks off with great answers.

QUESTIONS TO ASK IN A JOB INTERVIEW

Most hiring managers are simply looking for a combination of traits, skills, and experience. They have one goal—to choose the best match from a field of applicants. To get hired, your job is to make this process easy for them. Remember, their job is on the line if they screw up. A bad choice could cost their company tens of thousands of dollars.

John Kador, author of *201 Best Questions to Ask on Your Interview*, says because of the Internet, there's really no reason to ask questions about the company. You should already know. It's better to put into the form of questions statements about who you are and what you can do. This is the way to advance your value as an employee.

If you ask questions, they should relate directly to your job performance at Acme Widget. In *Inc* magazine, columnist Jeff Haden lists three questions great job candidates ask.

1. **What do you expect me to accomplish in the next 60 to 90 days?** It shows you want to hit the ground running…and that they won't have to invest months in you while you get up to speed.
2. **What are the common attributes of your top performers?** The answer will help you determine if you're a good fit, and let the company know you intend to be a top performer.
3. **What are a few things that drive results for the company?** Great employees are those who know they must help their company succeed. Asking this question lets the interviewer know that you will contribute much more to their bottom-line than they are paying you (which makes them very happy).

Frame the questions you ask in ways that demonstrate that you are a serious candidate who wants to drill down to what it will take to help their company succeed. Next, transition your questions so that they promote your particular strengths in the context of how you are valuable to the company.

"What are some of the problems the company needs to solve in this position?"

"By what criteria will you select the ideal candidate for this position?"

"In my last assignment, I supervised 20 people. How would this skill translate to the requirements of this position?"

Questions like these put you in control of the interview—now you are asking the questions and the interviewer is responding with important information that will help you determine how to frame your responses. When you get close to an offer, begin pressing for a positive response.

"Is there anything standing in the way of us coming to an agreement?"

"This position sounds like what I'd like to do. Is there a fit here?"

"I'm very interested in this position and I realize your support is the key to getting it. Do I have your endorsement?"

For many job-seekers these questions may seem too bold and aggressive. But if there are two candidates equally qualified for the job and one asks great questions and the other doesn't, or one asks for the job and the other doesn't, who would you choose if you were the interviewer?

INTERVIEW FOLLOW UP

Within a day of your interview send a thank you note to everyone you interviewed with at the Acme Widget Corporation. In a line or two reiterate your interest and qualifications. If possible, include some new tidbit of information about how you can benefit the company.

If you haven't heard back within a week, it's appropriate to call and simply state you are following up on the interview. Ask if there is anything else you can provide while they are considering candidates. If all else fails, kidnap the CEO's wife and hold her for ransom (just kidding).

DON'T WANT THE JOB TOO MUCH… EVEN THOUGH YOU DO

Patti Wilson, who owns The Career Company, says it is important to tread a fine line between wanting a job too overtly and staying a bit aloof. It's human nature that people want what is difficult to have. This is where working with a good executive search consultant can be a great asset. She can do much of the follow-up for you. There's also a psychological advantage to having a recruiter bring you to a company rather than you soliciting them. You've been "discovered" and vetted by a professional. The hiring company knows that a recruiter will only bring qualified candidates to them…they're reputation is at stake.

DARWINIAN JOB INTERVIEW BLUNDERS

Interviewer: "Why did you leave your last job?"

Job Applicant: "It was something my boss said."

Interviewer: "What did he say?"

Job Applicant: "You're fired!"

Here are some of the world's dumbest interviewees. Perhaps it explains a lot about HR Directors and their attitudes toward job applicants (now I feel little bad about dissing them). If you recognize yourself in any of these—well, thank god McDonald's is still hiring.

"The well-dressed, attractive job candidate who—in mid-interview—jumped up and ran out, realizing she was at the wrong company."

"The guy who brought his mother to the interview to negotiate salary (she was good too)."

Here's one from former HR Manager Liz Ryan, writing for *Bloomberg News.*

"During a phone interview, the manager heard the distinct sound of a toilet flushing and couldn't stop himself from asking the applicant if he had just done his business. The applicant replied, "Yeah, Dude." Talk about a crappy interview.

And finally these classics.

"The applicant challenged me to arm wrestle for the job."

"The job applicant announced she was starving and hadn't eaten lunch, then proceeded to eat a hamburger and fries in the HR Director's office."

"The candidate stretched out on the floor to fill out the job application."

"One guy forgot to wear dark socks with his suit so he colored his ankles with a black felt-tip marker." At least give him credit for being resourceful.

"When I asked the applicant what person they would most like to meet, living or dead, her response was 'the living one.'"

It's hard enough to get a job if you have it all together. Don't blow it by making dumb mistakes.

NEGOTIATING A GOOD SALARY

For many people, negotiating a salary is the most difficult part of the hiring process. No one wants to screw up a job offer, and fear of doing that keeps many new hires from getting the best compensation deal. Remember, you're going to have to live with the deal you make for some time; better to start off with a good deal.

- A 2013 study in the *Journal of Organizational Behavior* determined that not negotiating a strong initial job offer could mean missing out on as much as $634,000 in salary over the course of a 40-year career. According to Career Builder surveys, 41% of all applicants make this mistake.

If a company really wants you they will be willing to pay fair market value. If they aren't willing to do that then perhaps this isn't the company or the job for you. If you want to find out what the value of your intended position is, and often what the company pays, you may be able to find this information at Glassdoor.com www.glassdoor.com or Salary.com www.salary.com. Both sites provide information on salary ranges for a variety of jobs in various industries and even at specific companies. Armed with this information, you are in a better position to bargain for an appropriate salary.

If you've gotten this far they probably want to hire you and a little money won't stop them. Asking for more money might even make you more attractive as a candidate; it shows you aren't a pathetic begging job-seeker like 90% of the others (even if you are too). You can always come down, but it's not so easy getting more once you've stated your price.

There are dozens of books on the art of negotiating, but the core of negotiation is presenting overwhelming evidence of why you are so damn valuable to the company that what you are asking for in compensation seems to be a bargain any fool would take. Two good books are *Negotiating Your Salary: How to Make $1,000 a Minute* by Jack Chapman, and *Salary Tutor: Learn the Salary Negotiation Secrets No One Ever Taught You* by Jim Hopkinson.

Life Rule: Remember, 90% of employers will pay more than the stated salary for a position…often significantly more. Give yourself a nice raise before your first day of work…negotiate.

JOB BOARDS, HR DIRECTORS AND RECRUITERS

Unless you decide to start your own business, have an uncle who is CEO or are just so darn capable that people are camping on your doorstep with job offers, you will inevitably need to deal with three of the established gateways in your path to career fulfillment: online job boards and sites, HR (human resource) directors, and recruiters. All can be helpful to your career—or impediments.

JOB BOARDS

The largest job boards—Monster, Indeed, Careerbuilder.com, and Simply Hired—are the "big ponds" of job opportunities. You dive in and immediately begin drowning in a vast sea of applicants. You will be welcomed with open arms—often for a fee. Their motto should be "Give me your tired, your naïve, your uninformed jobseekers desperately seeking to be hired."

Instead of throwing your carefully crafted resume into the giant black hole of applicants where it will immediately be consumed by a mysterious energy force never to be seen again, go niche. Niche job boards are the smaller, industry-targeted sites. They often include openings that seldom, if ever, show up elsewhere. Sometimes they even post the hiring manager, bypassing the dreaded HR Department entirely. Imagine getting your resume into the hands of someone you might actually work for someday.

Nearly every industry has a niche job board. Some began as community sites or blogs (or still are blogs) that list job openings—mainly because the site administrator could make a few hundred bucks off the job posts and advertising. That doesn't diminish their importance. As Ford Myers, a noted career coach and author of *Get the Job You Want Even When No One's Hiring* points out, simply applying for a job through a niche site shows that you are part of the industry, an insider.

You can use niche job boards as part of your overall job sleuthing plan to find out who the key players are at a target company—then do an end-run around the HR Department to the real hiring authority.

INHUMANE RESOURCE DIRECTORS

"Few great men could pass Personnel." — Paul Goodman

Like air traffic controllers who take naps on the job, there are some dirty little secrets about these folks. Here are a few confessions from real working HR Directors.

"Is it harder to get a job if you're fat? Absolutely. We don't hire anyone who is overweight."

"A lot of managers don't want to hire people with young kids, and they use all sorts of tricks to find out, illegally."

"If you've got a weak handshake, I make a note of it."

"People assume someone's reading their cover letter. I haven't read one in 11 years."

Oh, it gets worse. Much worse.

"If you are over 40 I won't hire you. My company doesn't care about experience or even your skills. It's all about filling positions at the lowest possible cost."

"Over 60? You have 0% chance of being hired."

"If you have been laid off or fired from your last job I probably won't consider hiring you."

"My boss only wants me to hire good-looking people. He says it's good feng shui."

"We hardly ever hire a man. Women are cheaper and less aggressive."

"We have two Asians, one African-American, a disabled person and a real Native American. Our equal opportunity requirements are met. Everyone else will be white."

Yikes!

One company regularly runs want ads (without identifying themselves, of course) for grand-sounding jobs at above-market salaries. They ask people to suggest solutions to a "hypothetical" business challenge and then steal the best ideas. Of course, they have no real jobs. Another company admitted to running "blind" ads for positions at their company...just to see if any of their own people apply for them. You can imagine their fate.

There are many professional HR Directors...and there are thousands of people who are doing it just because it's a job. Or they can't do anything else. Frankly, they are an impediment to their company—and to you. They screen out—often through the vile phone interview—otherwise great job candidates. How anyone can make an assessment of a candidate over the phone in five or ten minutes escapes me. If you've worked at a sex hotline you probably have a better chance than the typical Ph.D. of getting through the phone interview successfully.

The other way HR Directors miss good candidates is their often haphazard way of dealing with resume submissions or replies to job postings. Is the HR Director a little stressed today or trying to get away from work early to get together with friends? Well, let's just toss those last 50 resumes in the "round file."

Any company that relies on some minimally trained, inexperienced person to be responsible for their most valuable resource—their people—deserves what they get. How can an HR person with little or no business experience, little time in the HR business (the average is 3 years), much younger (average age is about 28) and of a different gender than many candidates (90% in Human Resources are female) be expected to judge what is best for their company?

If you're over 45 and have felt the job market deck is stacked against you, perhaps it has something do with the fact that nearly all HR Directors are young and female. If an open job has two candidates, one who is 30 years old, single, and female and the other is 50, married, and male, who do you think usually gets selected for the position? Not the candidate who is as old as the HR Director's parents. Not someone who they can't "relate" to at all. Not the "grey hair" who won't "fit the culture."

The ugly truth is that people hire people like themselves. Age discrimination by these HR "professionals" is one of the dirty, overlooked secrets in the job market. That's one reason why you see so many people in the work force who look as if they just got their driver's license in positions that once required some experience, training, and knowledge.

There are other shocking reasons why you might not get hired, even though your resume looks like a carbon copy of the job posting qualifications. I once heard a 26-year old HR Director say that she looks for candidates with very little career experience so they aren't "tainted and spoiled" by their previous employment. That's real smart, hiring people with no experience or skills.

Often job postings will go on at great length with a laundry list of requirements and qualifications that no living person on earth could ever match. In this way the HR Director can reject the candidates with 95% of the qualifications if she (or occasionally "he") doesn't like them.

HR will frequently rely on some computer algorithm to do the difficult candidate selection work for them. Or the ubiquitous (and infuriating to use) online resume submission services like Taleo. Isn't it nice to know your future (or your company's future) is in the hands of a computer software program? There was a time in America when the people who owned or ran companies hired their own people without a "gatekeeper" to make the initial decision for them.

Life Rule: Do whatever you can to do an "end run" around HR to contact the real decision-maker.

RECRUITERS

It's a smart career move to cultivate a strong relationship with two or three key recruiters. A good executive search firm provides many benefits to the job-seeker. Recruiters are in the business of finding qualified candidates for firms willing to pay to attract top talent. Think of them as career matchmakers. It's in their interest—and their client's interest—to make a successful match. No one wants to work at a job or company where they will fail. And if you fail, the recruiter may have to give back all or most of the fee they got for placing you.

Recruiters also have resources and knowledge about the job markets that are invaluable to job candidates. A good recruiter can help prepare you so that you're competitive in the job market. The key word here is "good." Good recruiters are as rare as wild Pandas. Again, it's a profession rife with people who are overworked, under-skilled, and unprofessional. A good recruiter can change your life. A bad recruiter is a waste of time.

RECRUITERS DON'T EXIST TO FIND YOU A JOB

Professional recruiters come in two sizes...retained recruiters are paid by a company to find specific candidates, and contingency recruiters who get paid when they fill a position. In either case, the recruiter is not in business to find YOU a job but to successfully fill a position for one of their clients.

Often you will be sought out by a recruiter who has found you through their personal network...usually on LinkedIn or through one of the employment services to which they subscribe, like CareerBuilder or Monster. The better recruiters will check out your background and job claims, contact your references...even test you on the capabilities you claim to have. Some may even coach you and help improve your resume.

Recruiting, like everything else, has changed in the past ten years. At the low end of the spectrum are younger, less experienced recruiters who have never learned how to creatively source candidates. They scan the job postings—both theirs and others—and respond to the "low hanging fruit." Since anyone can do this it's getting harder for these recruiters to find companies willing to pay them a fee for that kind of recruiting.

Nearly two dozen recruiting firms open in the U.S. every week. The Fordyce Letter, the country's foremost authority on the placement and recruiting industry, has a database of nearly 35,000 firms that do job recruiting. The average recruiter has been in their profession for three years. There are, as in any profession, some sleazy recruiters who will do almost anything to get a placement and get paid. Some provide poor follow-up. Others do little to provide a thorough description of the job and company. It's "churn and burn" for these types. There are unscrupulous recruiters who want you to pay a fee or a percentage of your salary (NEVER do this). But generally speaking, most recruiters are honest professionals. Just be sure to check qualifications. If possible, speak with someone who has worked with the recruiter.

You should be honest and forthright about your job qualifications, salary requirements, and education. Like with an attorney, never lie to them. Don't ever do an end-run around a recruiter and apply directly for a job, unless you haven't been submitted for some reason. And let the recruiter know if you are working with other recruiters.

Working with a recruiter does not forgo your responsibility in the job search process. You still need to do the work to prepare a great resume, be knowledgeable about the company you want to work at, be presentable, and, of course, be good at what you do. Recruiters are not miracle workers. They cannot guarantee you a job.

It's your responsibility to make it easy for recruiters to find you. As we've mentioned previously, you should create a rich presence on LinkedIn...good profile, professional photo, recommendations, keyword maximized description, testimonials, a job history that syncs up with your resume and expands upon it, and involvement in groups.

According to the 2012 Bullhorn Reach Social Recruiting Activity Report, the average recruiter has 616 LinkedIn connections...and 28% have a thousand or more. 1 in 5 recruiters has 50 or fewer connections. You want to work with recruiters who are well connected. Check out their LinkedIn presence. If the recruiter has hundreds of connections it shows he/she values networking...the source of most jobs.

WHY YOU DIDN'T GET THE JOB YOU WERE "PERFECT" FOR

Life often doesn't make sense. People behave in irrational ways. So, even though you are the ideal candidate for a job, you may not get it anyway. And you might be surprised by why you didn't get it.

One CEO told me why he didn't hire the perfect candidate for a VP position he was trying to fill. "The guy looked just like my first business partner—the jerk who ripped me off for $300,000. I knew I couldn't look at him every day without feeling the pain of that experience." Another person said she couldn't hire the perfect candidate for a job because he looked and acted like her ex-husband. "I could hardly wait to get him out of my office," she admitted.

Yet another CEO confessed that she didn't hire the SuperCandidate, as she called him, because she was afraid this person would make her look bad. According to one study, a fear of hiring someone who is "too talented" is a factor in more than 1 in 5 hiring decisions.

The point is...you may not get the job for the most inane reason imaginable. People are human. And humans often defy logic. Don't take it personally. Luckily, most successful bosses are happy to hire people better than themselves...because it makes them look good.

CREDIT REPORTS AND YOUR CAREER

The way you handle money can also impact your career. Your credit history and score is now as important as your resume in landing a good job. The Society for Human Resource Management estimates that 40% to 50% of employers, including the U.S. government, now run credit checks on potential hires. Unfortunately, it doesn't matter much if your credit score is low because of circumstances largely beyond your control (as millions of Americans have learned in the past few years). If it comes down to a contest between two closely matched candidates, and you are the one with the 500 credit score and foreclosure, you are Johnny Out-of-Luck.

Ironically, no clear correlation between performance and credit history has ever been proven, according to a 2003 study by Eastern Kentucky University. It's unfair—but it is what it is.

BACKGROUND CHECKS

Here's what the background check picture looked like as of 2010.

Screening method	% of employers using it	Increase in last 5 years
Some form of screening	93%	48%
Background checks	79%	51%
Drug tests	50%	54%
Percent of background checks showing red flags.		
Criminal records	9.5%	
Employment verification	48.1%	
Drug tests	3.3%	
Credit checks	42.9%	

Companies lose about 5% of their annual revenue—billions annually—to employee fraud, according to the Association of Certified Fraud Examiners. If you look at it through the eyes of employers, you can see why they run checks.

Life Rule: Keep a clean credit and background record.

THE OVER-40 CAREER REINVENTION PLAN

"The lack of respect for experience is a reality that older workers have to swallow." — Penelope Trunk, author of *Brazen Careerist: The New Rules for Success*

When you are over 40 and looking for a job for the first time in years, it can be a shock. Unreturned phone calls, resumes that disappear into the HR "black hole," and being "overqualified" for jobs you would love to have (even with the reduced pay) are the new norm in the workplace. At times you'll despair of ever getting a job. With another 40 years or so left to live, you may wonder how you're going to make it. Unfortunately, you've been "aged out" of the workforce.

Similar complaints by younger, inexperienced workers seem to indicate that your "best" career years are between 30 and 40. While this is not always the case, you will need a plan to successfully navigate the transition of your career into its mature stages.

OLDER...BUT NOT "OLD"

"The only source of knowledge is experience." — Albert Einstein

First, it's important to present yourself as experienced yet relevant, older but not "old," and with assets that would be hard, if not impossible, for anyone younger to have acquired. Emphasize those attributes that someone who is 26 years old would not likely have, such as advanced training or supervisory experience.

You may feel an impulse to "fit in" with younger workers by trying to be like them. This seldom works and rings false. Act and dress age appropriate...but not "stuffy." Adopt an attitude of equal collegiality and you'll usually be treated the same way in return.

One of the unspoken prejudices against older workers (and there are many) is the fear by younger workers of having someone report to them who is as old as their own father or mother. Perhaps the best stance to adopt is that of a trusted older advisor or senior counselor. Be willing to "mentor" younger staff members and support their career goals. If you are seen as someone who is not a direct competitor—or as the guy or gal who they can safely go to for advice, you will not only be welcomed, you could be the office champion.

You'll also need to look and act non-threatening to younger workers. If your co-workers dress down and seem to favor college dorm room garb, you'll probably not want to wear a dark blue suit, white shirt and tie. However, you would look ridiculous emulating their style. Stylish casual wear appropriate to your age works best.

Socializing with younger workers, who may still be into collegiate style binge drinking and chasing members of the opposite sex, can be problematic. Choose your socializing venues carefully. You don't want to be caught in awkward situations. Neither do you want to appear unsociable.

It's a shame that older workers—and the wisdom their experience can impart—are not valued more in our society. Everyone loses when there isn't a full integration of age, sex, and ethnic types.

YOU LOST YOUR JOB. NOW WHAT DO YOU DO?

OK, you just got your pink slip. You're in shock, angry, fearful, and feeling disconnected. How do you respond and recover?

First, don't take it personally, as hard as that is to do. Tens of millions of Americans have experienced the same thing in recent years...and most were doing a good job just like you. Take a deep breath and schedule a meeting with your HR Department or whoever owns the company. You want to negotiate the best severance deal possible. Realize that in many cases, perhaps yours, you may not be able to do anything other than pack a box full of belongings and exit the building. There may be no recourse. There may be no other option than to take what is offered and get on with the next chapter of your life. Before you leave you should attempt to get a commitment to provide a positive recommendation in the future... assuming you didn't get let go for stealing Widget secrets and selling them to the Chinese.

THE FIRST 60 DAYS AFTER LOSING A JOB ARE CRITICAL

While 7 out of 10 jobseekers think they know exactly what to do to get their next job, according to a survey by Right Management, a global outplacement firm, that figure drops to just 2 in 10 once they go through the outplacement process. What you do in the first 60 days after losing your job is critic

1. Utilize whatever outplacement services are available to you from your employer. These can range from classes, seminars, workshops, role-playing, resume evaluation, and networking events. If you are offered an outplacement consultant, spend time personally with her, don't just communicate online. The adjustment from job holder to jobseeker will be easier if you take proactive steps immediately.

2. If you have the means, go on a vacation or long weekend trip. You need time to settle your thoughts, regroup, consider options, and relax. Remember, you will be working hard to find a new job. And after you land the new job there likely won't be a real vacation for at least a year, so get some R&R while you can. Making important decisions when you are still in shock, angry, and stressed usually results in a poor outcome. This is the time to be clear-headed and focused.

3. Create a job search plan. Just putting down on paper all the action steps you will take to land a new job will give you a boost in confidence and energy. There's a lot you can do to improve your job hunting opportunities.

✓ Call friends and former colleagues to let them know you are actively looking for a job. A surprisingly large number of jobs are acquired through friends, relatives, and former co-workers.

✓ Sign up for online job boards. See if there are niche job sites in your industry.

✓ Schedule at least two lunch dates a week—one with a friend and another with someone who can help with your job search.

✓ Begin due diligence on companies that could be potential employers. Don't just take anything that comes along. Direct and control your search.

✓ Brush up on job skills that are important to your career. Now is the time to finally learn how to use PowerPoint or get that certificate in social media marketing.

✓ Review job recruiters and contact those you consider reputable. Recruiters can be extraordinarily helpful, so get on their radar screen.

✓ Set aside an hour a day to exercise—bike, swim, workout at the gym, play tennis, run; you'll feel more confident, look better, sleep better, and feel a sense of accomplishment at a time when you are most vulnerable to negative emotions.

✓ Begin a healthy nutrition program. You'll have more energy, lose a few pounds, and have a sense of purpose.

✓ Consider a change in direction. Now might be a good time to make a move into another area of your field. If all the marketing jobs are filled, try your hand at sales. Or consider starting your own business. Many entrepreneurs became one because they lost a job. It's tough work and risky but business owners can make considerably more money than employees. Try a part-time job in the business first to see if the change would be right for you. Want to open a coffeehouse? Go work for Starbucks as a barista first.

- ✓ Spruce up (or open up) your social media presence. If you don't have a LinkedIn, Twitter or Facebook account, get one. Learn how to fully utilize these to expand your network and create a dynamic online presence.
- ✓ Start a blog. Comment on the industry you work in. Do this one or two times a week. A blog can set you apart from other job candidates. It shows you're "current" and provides a forum to subtly promote your capabilities. For example, if you are an insurance claims adjuster you can post news, comment about developments in your field, and provide a forum for people to contribute suggestions to improve the claims adjusting practice.
- ✓ Freshen up your look. Have your hair styled professionally. Purchase a couple of killer outfits or suits. Get a professional manicure. Ladies, have an upscale salon do your makeup. When you know you are looking great your confidence level will rise a few notches at the interview.
- ✓ Track the progress of your job search plan daily. Keep all receipts and record all mileage...these are potentially tax-deductible.
- ✓ Apply for unemployment benefits immediately. You've paid into this fund all your life, now you deserve to get some of it back.
- ✓ Carefully craft a resume that is searchable online by keywords, has an attractive layout, is "lean and mean" with every word and phrase working to show why you are the best choice for the job. Be sure it's error-free.

If you haven't been nurturing your network of personal and professional contacts, now is the time to do some catch-up. Attend social networking events. Don't be shy about introducing yourself. You never know how a new personal connection can affect your career search.

Don't forget your alma mater. Colleges and universities have made tremendous strides in supporting the career goals of their grads—past and present. Many have their own online social networking presence. Most large schools have local chapters in major cities and host events for their grads. If the CEO or HR Director is a fellow grad of your school, you likely will have an advantage over other applicants.

Finally, join associations or trade groups in your industry. It will give you contacts at companies you may want to work at and provide built-in networking opportunities.

GET OUT OF THE HOUSE

"The wrong thing to do is sit at home in your pajamas and apply for jobs online. It's isolating and depressing." — Ford Myers

These days the personal touch in job search is disappearing faster than the arctic ice cap. Looking for a job is tough. When your ego is already scabbing up from all the rejection wounds it's easy to just hide behind the Internet and your computer. Many newly unemployed people are ashamed to face friends, so wrapped up is their identity in their job; they simply want to go into hibernation until that day when they can emerge with a newer and better job to show they're whole again.

But this is when you need to show what you're made of, so buck up and face the world. Attending conferences, networking functions, educational classes, donating time to charity, and having lunch or coffee with former and future colleagues will do more to get you a job than sending out hundreds of resumes.

Depression is a constant stalker of the unemployed. Getting out into the world, even if it's just for a tennis game or coffee with a friend, will buoy your spirit. So, unplug the TV, stop raiding the fridge, turn off the video games, and get out into the real world. Because that's where your next job awaits.

Life Rule: Formulate a job-search plan. Don't delay. Train for your next job.

THE FIRST 90 DAYS

OK, you prayed to St. Jude (and followed the advice in this book) and miraculously found the perfect job. Now what?

Your first 90 days, when everyone will be watching and evaluating your every move, are crucial to your long-term success in your new job. In *The First 90 Days: Critical Success Strategies,* author Michael Watkins points out that "small differences in your actions can have a disproportionate impact on results." The first 90 days are a particularly vulnerable time for a new employee, especially if you have executive decision-making responsibilities.

Corporate and business life are not the same as real life. You're a player in a game with other players of varying talents and ambitions. There are specific rules to the game that you must learn and follow. Like a soccer player you must always be on the move, watching the other players—both on the opposing team and your own. Former superstar hockey player Wayne Gretzky says his success is not being where the puck is, but where it's going to be. Think strategically about where you want to be in 90 days… start your new position with the end goal in mind.

➢ According to a study of 20,000 searches by executive search firm Heidrick, as reported in *The Financial Times*, more than 40% of senior executives leave a new organization or are fired within 18 months.

Often the reason a new hire fails is as simple as a poor cultural fit…something few people really evaluate before joining a new company. Whether or not your personality is a good match with the collective personality of the company is something that is hard to determine but important to your future success.

Here are some tips to succeed during your first 90 days.

1. Establish credibility

You may have the urge to bluff your way through some early interactions in your new job. Don't. You'll command more respect if you're honest and forthright. Admit it if you don't know something and ask for advice. People love to give it. And you'll seem more "human." Just be careful. There are some things you'll be expected to know from your first day.

Take extra care during your first 90 days to operate as error-free as possible. A faux pas that would be overlooked later in your career at the company can be deadly now.

2. Create some early wins

Find some tasks or projects that you can be sure to excel at during your first few weeks on the job. It doesn't have to be a major project. In fact, taking on something big in the beginning is very risky. Hit some singles before you try to go for a home run.

3. Build momentum

Don't rest on your early wins. Keep building upon them. Think of everything you do as concentric circles that keep expanding outward. Stay focused and keep working hard. If you lose momentum it will be hard to get it back.

4. Promote yourself

Without being tagged as an arrogant braggart, you need to quietly and subtly learn to blow your own horn. There's a real art to doing this well. It can be in the form of congratulating your boss or your team for doing such an outstanding job. In effect you are also congratulating yourself. Or you can be seen having lunch with the boss or a key client. Another way to raise your profile early on is to get published in the company newsletter or a trade publication.

5. Accelerate your learning

There's always a lot to learn at any new organization, much of it tied in with the company "culture." Be observant. Study company materials and systems. Become knowledgeable about the company's products and competitors. Not knowing something crucial about your company or its products/services during your first 90 days will telegraph to others that you aren't a company "player."

6. Communicate with your boss

Most people who join a new company think they work for that company. Well, yes and no. Technically you work for the company. But in reality you work for your boss. Keeping him/her happy is the key to success. Don't let anyone tell you otherwise. Just like in marriage "a happy wife, a happy life," in business "a happy boss prevents career loss."

7. Build your team

Most people like to work as part of a team, some don't. Get to know the personalities of your team and don't force them to do something that is against their nature. You are a new entity to them and there may be some initial resistance to your presence. Change isn't easy for many people. Be a clearheaded, logical, persuasive leader. Most people are willing followers and will support someone who has a logical plan. Get input from team members beforehand. It demonstrates that you value their expertise and enables them to feel "ownership" of your plans. If your team "has your back" your first 90 days will likely be successful.

8. Create supportive coalitions

Get out and about at your new company and develop a mutually supportive relationship with at least one key member in each department. Let them know you are there to help them make their jobs easier and more successful.

9. Support your co-workers

Support your co-workers ambitions and you will go a long way toward succeeding. Make them look good. Be a mentor. But ask for their advice and support when you need it. On the flip side, beware of the potential saboteurs who could torpedo you at the first chance.

10. Stay calm and balanced

A LOT will be coming at you during your first 90 days. Stay cool and calm at all times. Don't let anyone think you aren't in control. Losing your cool at this stage with the company can be disastrous. In your personal time make sure you get enough rest, exercise, and good nutrition. This is when you want to be at the top of your game.

Life Rule: You've got a lot to do when you're new. So you'll need to plan your transition and integration into your new job carefully. Remember, what worked for you before may not work at your new place of employment.

WORK VERY HARD

"The only time success comes before work is in the dictionary."
— Anonymous

The baseline for almost every successful individual is the ability and willingness to work hard. Very hard. Many people, realizing they are essentially too lazy to do the hard work required to build success, create elaborate excuses to cover their lack of ambition. I'm sure you've heard people proclaim they need "balance" in their life. That's why they only put in their 35 or 40 hours and refuse to ever work weekends. Balance is great. Rich people have it in spades. But they worked hard to get to that place.

Jack Canfield makes a great point in his bestseller "*The Success Principles: How to Get from Here you Are to Where You Want to Be.*" when he notes that mindset is a key ingredient in success. If you think you are worth $36,000 a year salary, that's probably the mark you'll hit. For many people this is OK. They really don't want to exert the sustained effort and focus it requires to be more successful in life.

People who hide behind excuses for their laziness frequently waste large segments of their life playing video games, watching TV or puttering around on the Internet. Successful people often watch little or no television, recognizing that their time could be put to more useful endeavors. Sure, you may find them on the golf course or sailing or traveling to Europe, but it's not often you will find them playing endless hours of Donkey Kong or Grand Theft Auto. Successful, wealthy people know how to use their time for maximum benefit. These are people who often work insanely hard—as much as 70 hours a week. Many travel 100 or more days a year on business.

"It takes about 10,000 hours to achieve mastery at anything."
— Malcom Gladwell, author of *Outliers, Tipping Point,* and *Blink*

Malcom Gladwell, author of *Outliers: The Story of Success*, makes the point that it takes about 10,000 hours practice to become truly proficient at anything meaningful. The Beatles, considered an "overnight success" by many, played 1,200 gigs before their first hit. Gladwell estimates the Beatles had played about 10,000 hours at that point.

Bill Gates began teaching himself about computer code and programming in 1968 when he was still in high school. Comedian Jay Leno worked more than 340 days a year for years before he hit it big. Even when he hosted the Tonight Show Leno continued to work more than 320 days a year, doing stand-up comedy on weekends all over the country.

"The first qualification for success is a good work ethic." — Henry Ford

In the 1970s there was a popular book sold through direct response ads in newspapers all over America called *The Lazy Man's Way to Riches* by Joe Karbo. It sold millions because most people (a) want to be rich, and (b) are lazy. Joe got rich but few, if any, who read his book did. Today, you can find dozens of schemes being peddled that promise great rewards for little work. This appeals to the average, rather lazy, American. Who wouldn't want to get rich without putting in all the effort required? That mindset also sells a lot of lottery tickets. And it's why gambling revenues are far greater every year than 401k contributions.

Work habits are often instilled by our parents and teachers at an early age. If your work habits are poor, learn to be more efficient with your time, create a plan, make frequent progress checks, and focus on the immediate task at hand. With good habits you should be able to create the elusive work/life balance. The "bibles" for learning good work habits are *Getting Things Done: The Art of Stress-Free Productivity* by David Allen, *First Things First* and *The 7 Habits of Highly Effective People* by the late Stephen Covey.

Life Rule: If you're lazy you won't succeed. Practice, study, visualization, and developing mental fortitude combined with focused work will lead to success.

WORK/LIFE BALANCE

Most people are much more productive when they take time to recharge their mental and physical "batteries" with vacations, weekend time, and family time during the week. About a third of all salaried employees work 41 to 50 hours a week, with overtime seldom being compensated. Even worse, Americans, who often only receive a two-week annual vacation, are taking less of their accrued time every year...a total of 577 million unused days (almost 1.6 million years total).

It's no wonder the Europeans call us the "no vacation nation." The French receive 5 weeks of paid vacation time...plus up to 22 days of RTT (reduction du temps) for employees who choose to work more than 35 hours a week (the limit is 39 hours). If the French take their vacation during the off-season they can earn bonus days of vacation.

- The value of all this unused vacation time to corporate America is $67 billion (2012), according to *CNN Money*. When was the last time corporations gave their employees that much money out of the kindness in their hearts?

According to a University of Pittsburg study, employees who took vacations suffered less depression, high blood pressure, and had healthier weight levels. Another study showed that people who take their vacation time are up to eight time less likely to develop heart disease. Numerous studies have proven the health benefits...as well as the productivity gains...derived from taking time off to regroup, refocus, recuperate, and reenergize.

➢ According to the *Austin Business Journal*, every $1 invested by companies in employee vacation time returns $3 in productivity.

It's simply good business to take time off. In fact, a comparison of European workers' productivity with American worker's productivity shows they surpassed us for 14 of the 19 years between 1981 and 2000. Yet Europeans take more than twice as much vacation time as Americans.

WORK TO LIVE, DON'T LIVE TO WORK

"There is no more fatal blunder than he who consumes the greater part of life getting his living." — Henry David Thoreau

✓ Nearly three quarters of all working adults say they have little control over their schedule.

✓ Only 29% of employed adults have access to flexible scheduling.

✓ A third of working moms have a schedule that's different from their husband.

Work is taking over our lives, when it should be making our lives better. It's instructive to hear the "regrets" that people on their deathbed share about their life. None say they wish they'd spent more time at the office working. But here's what they did say:

"I wish I'd had the courage to live a life true to myself, not the life others expected of me." This was the #1 regret in life.

"I regret not following my passion in life."

Life Rule: Do yourself (and your company) a favor...take all your vacation time. Work hard and smart...but take time to enjoy life too.

VISUALIZATION

"Go confidently in the direction of your dreams. Live the life you have imagined." — Henry David Thoreau

There's ample evidence that your mind has an amazing amount of influence over your actions, your success, even your health. Decades ago Wallace Wattles, in *The Science of Success*, said, "Whatever you habitually think yourself to be, that you are." There is scientific support for this belief.

Dr. Lynn Joseph, author of *The Job-Loss Recovery Guide: A Proven Program to Get Back to Work…Fast!*, developed a scientifically controlled program (endorsed by the U.S. Health and Human Services Department) that utilizes "mental imaging technology" to help people who have lost their job get back to work in about half the average time. www.drlynnjoseph.com

"The thing always happens that you really believe in; and the belief in a thing makes it happen." — Frank Lloyd Wright

Brain studies have shown that thoughts produce the same mental instructions to the body as actions. CAT scans show areas of the brain that are activated by visualization are the same as actually doing what is visualized. The consequences of visualization, both positive and negative, are apparent. It's important to control your thoughts and mental images since they influence behavior, action…and outcomes.

✓ Visualize your job interview.

✓ Visualize working in your new job.

✓ See yourself fulfilled in your career.

For more reading on the subject, start with Wayne Dyer's book *Wishes Fulfilled: Mastering the Art of Manifestation* and *Creative Visualization: Use the Power of Your Imagination to Create What You Want in Your Life* by Shakti Gawain.

Life Rule: Visualize the success you want to achieve.

WHY YOU SHOULD NEVER RETIRE.

"There's this American Dream to put enough away that you can golf and build a birdhouse or just be in a Barcalounger watching football all day. I'll never be that guy. And I'm not sure the people who have that are all that happy." — Kevin Bacon, actor

Retirement has had its 15 minutes of fame.

As a concept retirement is rather recent, dating back just 60 years to the early 50's. Before then people worked until they physically were unable to do so…or died. Retirement is a product of organized labor, longer lifespan, and the modern workforce.

The idea of working for 40 or 50 years and then quitting, despite the fact that you may have many productive years ahead, to play endless rounds of golf, travel for years or watch reruns of Seinfeld isn't relevant in the 21st Century. Even worse is leaving normal society to go live in an artificial, adult daycare facility, like Sun City, to frolic with other "seniors" in their Golden Years.

Numerous studies have proven that continuing to work, staying mentally and physically active, lengthens life and helps prevent age–related diseases and the decline of mental acuity.

RETIREMENT MAY NOT BE AN OPTION IN THE 21ST CENTURY

"34% of older workers don't plan to retire." — Charles Schwab

The economic meltdown of 2008 and its aftermath has dealt a serious blow to the retirement plans of many Americans. Retirement may no longer be an option for millions of people who have seen their savings and investments decimated.

It's baffling that so many people are fixated on the day when they will no longer work. Among many it's an obsession. Frankly, retirement is outdated, left–over thinking from the 1950's. Very little of it applies to 21st Century conditions. Economic instability, changing lifestyles, increased longevity, second families, new careers—the majority of Americans face one or more of these new realities.

Besides the likely necessity of creating additional income in the third part of their lives, most people are happier if they have meaningful work to do. In the last few years there has been a significant increase in the labor force participation rate among people 55 to 69. It's apparent that many Baby Boomers have a much different view of retirement than their parents. Although many are forced to return to the workplace as a result of the effects of the Great Recession, many want to continue working; it's just a matter of finding work that, well, works.

In a survey called "Rethinking Retirement," conducted by Schwab/ Age Wave in 2008, 40% of Americans surveyed said they "would like to go back and forth between periods of work and periods of leisure during retirement."

The key is to find work with a purpose. Unfortunately, thousands will be forced to work as Walmart greeters or at fast food restaurants—because they haven't planned for a second career.

DON'T COUNT ON SOCIAL SECURITY

Don't count on the paltry amount you'll receive from Social Security—or Social Insecurity as it should be called—to provide enough support while you figure out what to do during the last third of your life. According to the Social Security Administration, the average amount paid to recipients is just $1,269 a month...otherwise known as poverty level income. (2014)

- 51% of the workforce has no private pension coverage. (2014)
- 34% of the workforce has no savings set aside specifically for retirement. (2014)

If Social Security even survives longer than you, it will be radically different in the coming years. It's a simple matter of too little going in and too much coming out—and a long list of other economic priorities vying for the same funds. In other words, don't count on Social Security for your "retirement."

THE PLAN B CAREER

"Age is only a number, a cipher for the records. A man can't retire his experience. He must use it." — Bernard Baruch

It comes as a shock to people who have worked for 30 years and gained a considerable amount of experience to suddenly find they are no longer in demand. The harsh truth in America now is that most people over 50 are considered "dinosaurs." Their hard–earned expertise is devalued in favor of less capable younger job candidates. It can be a frightening prospect considering you will need to support yourself for another three or four decades in a world that only gets more expensive.

Unfortunately, this workplace dynamic isn't likely to change anytime soon. And even young people are finding the current workplace a challenge in the 21st Century. Your window of career opportunity now is somewhere between 30 and 45 years old. Below 30 you are likely finishing school, searching for a job, and establishing an independent life. After 45 you may already be considered "over the hill" in your career.

Fifteen years is not a lot of time to create success, especially when you are distracted by marriage, raising a family, buying a home, and making many of life's most important decisions. With this new and unsettling reality in mind, it's important to have a Plan B—your backup career path. It's a fact that most people will have more than one career during their life. The key is to build the skills that enable you to move into a new career path with as little transitional difficulty as possible.

The advice here is simple:

1. **Determine which skills can be easily transferred to a new career**. For example, expertise with accounting software such as Quickbooks can be invaluable in a variety of self–employment career paths.
2. **Do something you love and are talented at doing**. This can be a hobby (e.g. woodworking, photography) or just something you have a knack for doing well (e.g. accounting, teaching).
3. **Do something that has a reasonable chance of creating wealth**…at least enough to pay your bills.
4. **Create a lifelong plan to develop your Plan B skill**. Take classes, read books, make connections. study online educational resources…and practice, practice, practice.
5. **Start selling your skill in your spare time**. If it's photography, take wedding photos, help people with their headshots, enter photo contests.

If it's accounting, get your CPA credentials, work part-time during tax season, start a blog about some area of financial management.

6. **Consider working a second job**, part-time if necessary, in the field in which you are considering. You may find you hate it...or want to move more quickly into your new career path.

If you find yourself shut out of your primary vocation due to age, a shrinking or changing industry or personal circumstances you'll be able to slip effortlessly into your Plan B career.

Life Rule: Rethink 20th Century retirement to adapt to 21st Century reality.

FREELANCE, CONTRACT, TEMP AND "GIGGING" WORK

The rapid and pervasive restructuring of the American workplace has resulted in a huge increase in the number of workers outside the mainstream of full-time employment. Some might call this "underemployment" but others find working at temp jobs, freelance projects and contract "gigs" to be more attractive than a 40+ hour commitment to one employer. Going solo can be scary but the rewards are often worth the risk.

- 40% of America's workforce will be freelancers by 2020, according to research by NextSpace (from the *Rise of the Naked Economy* by Jeremy Neumer)

First, there's the freedom (most of the time) to control your own schedule. You can work mornings and be with your family in the afternoon. Or work a three-day week. You can work until 3am if you're a night-owl. Want to take a month-long vacation? You can—if you plan.

You also often have the freedom to work on what interests you—not just what you are required to do. Every study on the subject has found that people are happier and more productive when they work on things they find interesting, meaningful, and helps increase their knowledge.

Second, the financial rewards can be substantial. Many freelancers make more than they did in their previous fixed salary jobs. The sky is the limit on earnings.

Third, you save on commuting, lunches, dry-cleaning, clothes, and all the other "support" costs of working for a company. This can add up to a substantial amount—thousands of dollars each year.

Fourth, you are largely untouched by office politics, boring meetings, and abusive bosses. And if any of these things do become a problem—no problem—you simply go on to another "gig" or freelance project. With most temp or contract or freelance work, you are not perceived as a "threat" to anyone. So there's no one out "to get you." And you usually aren't around long enough to establish any negative relationships. Since nearly half of all workers say they don't like the company or the boss they work for, freelancing results in a major improvement in job happiness.

There are currently 40 million people in America who freelance—enough that there is a freelancers union with health care plans and other benefits www.freelancersunion.org. The number of freelance websites has grown rapidly to nearly a hundred (2013). Check out these top freelance resources:

www.freelance.com is the world's largest online outsourcing resource with more than 2.5 million freelancers and 500,000 businesses registered with the site for web design, data entry, content writers, and other jobs.

www.elance.com has more than 1.7 million members in a wide variety of industries.

www.oDesk.com for programmers, web designers, content writers, virtual assistants, and marketing professionals.

www.Guru.com for programmers, web designers, and content writers.

www.iFreelance.com for programmers, content writers, data entry, proofreaders, virtual assistants, writers, and web designers.

www.PeoplePerHour.com for programmers, content writers, virtual assistants, and graphic artists.

www.Fiverr.com for various jobs. Every gig is paid $5.

www.logomyway.com for graphic designers and artists.

www.99Designs.com for graphic designers. Dozens of designers bid for your job with spec work.

www.GetACoder.com for computer coders.

www.sologig.com is the place for IT and engineering professionals.

www.translatorcafe.com for typing jobs, medical translation, and other work-from-home jobs.

www.FreelanceWriting.com for people who can write quality freelance articles.

www.ProjectSpring.com for various projects, mostly programmers and web designers.

www.FreelanceJobSearch.com for content writers, graphic artists, programmers, and other jobs.

Additional resources: *The Wealthy Freelancer: 12 Secrets to a Great Income and an Enviable Lifestyle* by Steve Slaunwhite, Pete Savage and Ed Gandia www.thewealthyfreelancer.com or *Creative Inc: The Ultimate Guide to Running a Successful Freelance Business* by Joy Deanqdeelert Cho and Meg Mateo Ilasco.

Life Rule: Develop a second skill to earn extra money or a Plan B career.

YOU DON'T NEED NO STINKING COLLEGE EDUCATION

We've been raised to believe that a college diploma is an absolute necessity to career success. You may be surprised to learn there are some exceptional jobs that pay well, are in demand, and don't require a college degree. Here are twenty-five of the top-paying jobs that don't require a four-year degree and the average current salaries. Source: CBSalary.com and BLS 2011

1. Air Traffic controller $102,030
2. Funeral Director $79,030
3. Operations Manager $77,839
4. Industrial Production Manager $73,000
5. Transportation Manager $72,662
6. Storage and Distribution Manager $69,898
7. Computer Technical Support $67,689
8. Gaming Manager $64,880
9. Supervisor/Manager of Police $64,430
10. Nuclear Power Reactor Operator $64,090

11.	Computer Specialist	$59,480
12.	First-line, non-retail Supervisor	$59,300
13.	Nuclear Technician	$59,200
14.	First-line Supervisor Fire Fighting	$58,920
15.	Real Estate Broker	$58,720
16.	Elevator Installer and Repair	$58,710
17.	Sales Representative	$58,580
18.	Dental Hygienist	$59,790
19.	Radiation Therapist	$57,700
20.	Nuclear Medicine Technologist	$56,450
21.	Power Plant Distributor/Dispatcher	$57,330
22.	Fashion Designer	$55,840
23.	Ship Engineer	$54,950
24.	Detective	$53,990
25.	Commercial Pilot	$53,870

Many of these jobs do require some additional training. Obviously, you can't just begin flying commercial aircraft or hang out a sign saying you're a real estate broker. But none of these jobs requires a college degree.

Some of these positions can lead to extraordinary incomes. Top fashion designers make millions. A commercial pilot for a major airline with some seniority and advanced ratings can easily make a quarter million dollars a year. Even top funeral directors make $225,500 on average. And in sales, depending upon what you are selling, the sky is the limit.

According to the Department of Labor, nearly two-thirds of all job openings require only on-the-job training. There are roughly 50 million jobs in the marketplace that don't require a college degree and pay upwards of $40,000 a year.

MILLION DOLLAR IDEAS TRUMP MBA'S ANY DAY

You don't need a degree to get rich. What you need are great ideas—and the desire to succeed. Many million dollar ideas are staring you in the face. Just find a need and fill it well.

When David and Angie Porter developed the Furminator, they didn't have an MBA in business. He didn't have a college degree. But he saw a need (eliminating pet hair) and created a product to solve the problem. As a child I'm fairly certain he didn't say to himself, "When I grow up I want to invent a brush that removes dog hair." But when the idea came to him he acted upon it. Today the Furminator is a $25 million a year business.

Don't let the lack of a college degree become a stumbling block to achieving your dreams. There are plenty of people who did quite well without one. Here are just a few:

- Richard Branson — Billionaire owner of more than 100 businesses, including Virgin Atlantic.
- Coco Chanel — Founder of the House of Chanel, high-fashion clothes and frangrances.
- Mary Kay Ash — Founder of Mary Kay Cosmetics.
- Michael Dell — Billionaire founder of Dell Computers.
- Barry Diller — Billionaire broadcasting executive.
- Walt Disney — Billionaire founder of Disneyland, movies, cartoons.
- Henry Ford — Founder of the second largest auto company in America.
- Ty Warner — Billionaire creator of Beanie Babies.
- Frank Lloyd Wright — Iconic American architect.
- Sheldon Adelson — Former court reporter who built a multi-billion dollar casino empire.
- Ben Affleck — Oscar-winning actor, writer, producer, and director.
- Carl Bernstein — Famous journalist who uncovered the Nixon Watergate scandal.
- Sergey Brin — Billionaire co-founder of Google.

• John Paul DeJoria	Once lived in his car, now billionaire owner of Paul Mitchell, Patron brands.
• Thomas Edison	America's greatest inventor: phonograph, movies, light bulb.
• Larry Ellison	Billionaire founder of Oracle.
• F. Scott Fitzgerald	Famous American author.
• Harrison Ford	Former carpenter turned hugely successful actor.
• Benjamin Franklin	Founding father of the United States and prolific inventor.
• John Glenn	Astronaut and U.S. senator.
• Tom Hanks	Perhaps America's most successful modern actor.
• Quincy Jones	Musician and music producer.
• Thomas Kincade	Multi-millionaire American artist.
• Stanley Kubrick	Creative American film director.
• Ralph Lauren	Multi-billionaire former sock salesman and founder of Ralph Lauren company.
• Rush Limbaugh	Bombastic right-wing radio personality with a net worth of $300 million.
• Steve Martin	Famous American comedian, musician, and author.
• Steve McQueen	Iconic masculine American actor.
• Jillian Michaels	Multi-millionaire fitness guru.
• David Oreck	Inventor of Oreck vacuum cleaners.
• Joel Osteen	Multi-millionaire preacher.
• Larry Page	Billionaire co-founder of Google.
• Sean Parker	Billionaire co-founder of Napster, Airtime, and Plaxo. First Facebook president.

- Brad Pitt — Famous American actor and "sexiest man alive." Net worth $180 million.
- Wolfgang Puck — Multi-millionaire chef, restaurateur, and businessman.
- Vidal Sassoon — Billionaire founder of Sassoon salons, hair care line.
- Dave Thomas — Founder of Wendy's hamburger chain.
- Harry Truman — Former president of the United States.
- Mark Twain — Arguably America's greatest author and journalist.
- Orville Wright — Along with his brother Wilbur, invented the airplane.
- Jerry Yang — Billionaire founder of Yahoo!
- Mark Zuckerberg — Mega-billionaire founder of Facebook.
- Steve Jobs — Co-founder of Apple Computer and Pixar Animation Studios.

Convinced? This is only a small portion of the people who went on to great fame and/or fortune who did not earn a college degree. Of the 400 richest Americans, 63 did not graduate from college. What distinguishes these people from others is not the amount of education they attained, but the ideas they created or talent they developed.

Almost anyone with average intelligence and the means can be a college graduate. It is no formula for success…as many have discovered in The Great Recession. The multitudes of college grads who can't find a job, coupled with an outstanding trillion dollar student loan debt, will cause many to wonder whether college was a smart decision.

- More than 500,000 college grads are working as cashiers or waiters in 2013, as reported by Fox Business News. 46% are in jobs that require only a high school diploma.

Source: *How to Build a Successful Life Without a Four-Year Degree,* Blake Boles

Life Rule: A college degree isn't the only way (and may not be the best way) to make a living.

STARTING YOUR OWN BUSINESS

"There are some people who don't belong in a large organization."
— Peter Drucker

If the Great Recession has taught us anything, it's that job security working for someone else is history. If you're not going to have any job security, then take a shot at the gold ring and start your own business. After all, most millionaires who make it before age 40 did so with their own business.

Paradoxically, more businesses are started in recessions than during good times. Many of these new businesses are born of necessity—people who can't find work create their own. But many more are a result of the opportunities that arise during any period of change or chaos. One person's hard luck can be another's great fortune.

JUMP INTO ENTREPRENEURSHIP WITH BOTH EYES OPEN

"All you need is ignorance and confidence and the success is sure."
— Mark Twain

More than a million people will start a business in the next year. Sounds great, doesn't it? The hip new thing, especially among recent college grads, is to be an entrepreneur. Make scads of money and buy an Aston-Martin, a 180-foot yacht, and marry a supermodel. This actually does happen—to three or four people a year.

The reality is that 40% of all new ventures will be out of business before they reach their first anniversary. Within five years 80% will fail. And of the 20% that make it to the 5-year mark another 80% will fail within the next five years. Are you OK with those odds? Does it make you want to go running back to a comfy cubicle at the giant Acme Widget Corporation?

HEY, ISN'T FAILURE GOOD FOR YOU?

"Nothing succeeds like success." — Alexander Dumas

Despite all the rah-rah hype about how "good" failing is for you, how it builds character, and teaches you important lessons in life and business, the cold truth is that failing can often be a life-sucking, emotionally devastating, miserable experience that will take years to recover from personally and financially.

Many owners of failed businesses are forced into bankruptcy because new businesses are usually backed heavily with the entrepreneur's "skin in the game." Now you've got that albatross around your neck for at least seven years. Try to get a loan or a job or start another business and the old BK will come back to haunt you. It's like trying to run while wearing those ankle bracelets you see shackled to prisoners.

If you think failing is good for you, just see how your previously adoring bank treats you if you fail. Or the IRS. Or the BOE. Or the EDD. It doesn't matter if General Electric or Bank of America doesn't pay a cent in income taxes, the IRS will look the other way. But if YOU owe them $50 they will track you and hunt you down and harass you and add fines and interest and eventually seize the money from your bank account to get what you owe.

And that goes for your creditors too. Especially your creditors. It's OK for them to lose huge amounts of money on bad business decisions or investments that a monkey wouldn't make, but if you owe them money they don't see it the same way. You OWE them—and they will nag you a hundred times worse than your mom ever did to get their money back.

FAIL FAST, FAIL FORWARD...SOMETIMES

"It is hard to fail, but it is worse never to have tried to succeed."
— Theodore Roosevelt

Embracing the "fail fast, fail forward" philosophy so popular now in Silicon Valley is a little irresponsible since failure also harms other people as well as yourself. Investors lose money, suppliers don't get paid, and employees lose their jobs. There is no shortage of wise sayings about how much you will learn from your failures. You <u>will</u> learn a LOT. Just remember that others may pay dearly for your education.

SUCCEED FIRST, SUCCEED FAST

"Show me a good loser and I'll show you a loser." — Peter Thiel

Failing fast and failing often only works if you are testing out product ideas, debugging software or practicing jump shots...just don't embrace the concept in all areas of your life. Yes, failure is an inevitable fact of life, but your first responsibility is to do everything in your power to succeed. "Succeed first, succeed fast" should be your motto. It's a more positive approach.

RECOVERING FROM FAILURE

"Every perceived failure turns out to have a secret success, and every perceived success has some secret failing in it." — Ethan Hawke, actor

Since the near collapse of the economy in 2008, the repercussions have been severe for tens of millions of Americans. "Failure" in its many forms is pervasive...careers in ruin, homes lost, credit destroyed, evictions, repossessions, broken marriages, retirements on hold, savings and investments depleted, and dreams of a better future evaporated. With failure comes sleepless nights, stress, and depression. With failure comes fear; fear like you've never known in your life. Fear that causes you to do things you wouldn't ordinarily do. Fear that will make recovery even more difficult.

Re-evaluation and re-invention can come from an honest self-analysis of failure. "Sometimes our old self has to die for complete rebirth," says Julie Wainwright, former CEO of the now defunct Pets.com. "Remember, the best is yet to come." In her book *ReBoot: My Five Life-Changing Mistakes and How I Have Moved On*, Wainwright describes her own journey from public failure to depression to resurrection. She is now the CEO of a successful new startup The Real Real www.therealreal.com.

Realize that failure is simply part of life. A sucky part, but nonetheless a life experience that nearly everyone will experience. If you've failed in your life personally or professionally (or both), you're not alone, some of the most successful people in history have been repeat failures: Henry Ford. Walt Disney. Abraham Lincoln.

"Develop success from failure. Discouragement and failure are two of the surest stepping stones to success." — Dale Carnegie

According to former San Francisco Mayor Gavin Newsom, "Mistakes are the portals of discovery. I believe in failure in the context of learning from mistakes."

The advice columnist Ann Landers once said about life's "bumps" in the road. "If I were asked to give what I consider the single most useful bit of advice for all humanity it would be this: Expect trouble as an inevitable part of life and when it comes, hold your head high, look it square in the eye and say, 'I will be bigger than you. You cannot defeat me.'" After decades of dispensing advice on a daily basis, this is what Ann Landers considers the most important.

It may be difficult to see when you are in the midst of overwhelming trouble or experiencing soul wrenching failure, but these experiences are a natural—and important—ingredient in your personal growth. Faced with courage, honesty, and resoluteness you will emerge a better, smarter, and more confident person.

"If we don't succeed, we run the risk of failure."
— Anonymous (often attributed to Yogi Berra)

Bernie Siegel, the author of "*Love, Medicine and Miracles: Lessons Learned About Self-healing from a Surgeon's Experience and Exceptional Patients,*" talks about the "ying and yang" of life. "There are cycles of success, when things come to you and you thrive, and cycles of failure when they whither or disintegrate and you have to let them go in order to make room for new things to arise or for transformation to happen. If you cling and resist at that point, it means you are refusing to go with the flow of life, and you will suffer. It is not true that the 'up' cycle is good and the 'down' cycle bad—except in the mind's judgment." www.berniesiegelmd.com

Eckhart Tolle, author of *The Power of Now: A Guide to Spiritual Enlightenment* believes that dissolution is needed for new growth to happen…. that one cannot exist without the other. www.eckharttolle.com

"You always pass failure on the way to success." — Mickey Rooney

I've always liked the inspirational words of Theodore Roosevelt on failure:

"It is not the critic who counts; or where the doer of deeds could have done them better. The credit belongs to the man who is actually in the arena, whose face is marred by dust and sweat and blood; who

strives valiantly; who errs, who comes up short again and again, because there is no effort without error and shortcoming; but who does actually strive to do the deeds; who knows great enthusiasms, the great devotions; who spends himself in a worthy cause, and who at the worst, if he fails, at least fails while daring greatly, so that his place shall never be with those cold and timid souls who neither know victory nor defeat."

The "bad" times, the failures, the disappointments, the rejections, the losses, the inevitable negative stuff that is a natural part of life is an opportunity to change course, do something different, learn, and grow.

"I failed my way to success." — Thomas Edison

The life lesson here is that you can learn a lot from success *and* from failure. And failure may be the better teacher.

THINGS TO CONSIDER BEFORE JUMPING INTO ENTREPRENEURSHIP

Being good at something is great. But that's not the same as building a business to market that product or service. What is important is whether you have the smarts, the stamina, the mind-set, and the grit to operate and manage a business. The product or service isn't actually as important to your long-term success as you might think.

Are you the world's best pie maker? Does everyone salivate just thinking of your peach pie? Do your friends tell you all the time that you should start a business selling your wonderful pies?

Then why not offer them to the world and become a pie gazillionaire? Let's go! But wait. Do you enjoy accounting? Ordering and managing inventory? Hiring and firing people? Are you a great promoter? Does it excite you to think about cleaning your ovens? Do you enjoy working at 11pm doing the receipts for the day? Can't wait to get up in the morning to beg for money from your friendly local banker? Have you ever met one of the charming employees of the Health Department? What about that disgruntled whacko employee who takes you to court in order to extort money out of you to finance their pot-growing operation? Isn't it fun to pay $250 bucks a month to the pest control guy so your pie ingredients don't become infested with cockroaches?

Did your kid become a juvenile delinquent and you didn't even notice? Your husband says you haven't had sex with him in HOW MANY months... even though your apple pie scent turns him on? Do you mind spending EVERY FREAKIN' WAKING HOUR MAKING FUCKING PIES?

Say sayonara to all your important relationships—boyfriend, girlfriend, FRIENDS, wife, husband, kids, yourself—just about any other human being in your life other than those directly or indirectly involved in your wonderful business...like those employees who goof off half the time and steal from you when your back is turned? Or customers who complain because they think it will get them 10% off their order. Or suppliers who bitch because you're a day late paying them.

Do you like to work 80-hour weeks, seven days a week? That's what it will be like. Do you like to take vacations? Play tennis now and then? Read a fiction book? Meet friends for lunch. Forgeddaboutit! If you really believe you can take off time to lead a "balanced" life, then prepare yourself to be one of the above-mentioned business failure statistics.

This is the reality of being an entrepreneur—not the hyped up, trendy blather you hear so much these days about how "sexy" and "in" it is.

PARTNERS

But I'll get a partner you say. We will divvy up the work and it won't be so hard. Let me tell it to you straight—not the BS you'll find in your MBA classes or some blah blah blah business book.

When a partnership works out it can be a thing of beauty. But when it doesn't...think Steve Jobs and, what's his name? Oh yeah, Steve Wozniak. Or Bill Gates and the other guy, uh, Paul Allen. Or...you get the picture.

You can always fire a CEO or General Manager or anyone who works FOR you if things don't work out. But it's a different story when they work WITH you. The Lone Ranger worked well with Tonto. But I'll bet it wouldn't have worked out so well if there were two Lone Rangers (Dual Rangers?).

If you do start a business with a partner, at least make sure that every contingency is covered—in writing, witnessed and approved by a competent business attorney, and signed in blood by both of you (the same blood you'll likely be spilling soon). Take the time to talk frankly with your future partner about expectations, how the inevitable disagreements will be resolved, which responsibilities will be exclusive and which shared, how expenses and income will be divided, exit strategies for the business and for the partnership.

Then shake hands, have a celebratory drink or two, and begin the arduous task of building a business together. Hey, maybe it will work for you...it did for Hewlett and Packard, Larry Page and Sergey Brin (Google), Ben Cohen and Jerry Greenfield (Ben & Jerry's).

Just remember this...a bad partnership will make you wish you'd never gone into business, likely cost you money, and ruin your life. However...a good partnership can take your business to places you never dreamed it would go. Don't let my gloomy assessment of partnerships deter you from entering one; the statistics show partnerships work more often than going it alone.

According to the U.S. Small Business Administration, companies with multiple owners are more likely to survive longer than sole proprietorships...and had three times higher average revenues. A Darden School of Business study found that the single, common thread among successful entrepreneurs is their ability to compensate for their weaknesses by finding the right people to fill in the gaps.

In their book *The Power of 2: How to Make the Most of Your Partnerships at Work and in Life*, authors Rodd Wagner and Gale Muller utilize Gallup research data that shows the important ingredients in a strong partnership: complementary strengths, a common mission, fairness, trust, acceptance, forgiveness, communication, and unselfishness. They provide convincing data that people in collaborative relationships are happier and more successful in their endeavors. Yet, nearly 1 in 4 reported they had never experienced a great working partnership with anyone in their entire career!

Partnerships can reap huge rewards, but they're very hard work to get right. The bottom-line? Enter a partnership only if you're reasonably certain it will work...and then do the work to make it work. Remember, a partnership is like marriage...without the sex. Since marriages *with* sex only work out half the time, ask yourself how many would work if there was NO sex.

NOW THAT I'VE SCARED THE BEEJEESUS OUT OF YOU

Yes, going into business is terrifying. On the other hand. Done correctly...and with some luck and perseverance...you can create an exciting, satisfying—and financially rewarding—career by doing your own thing. Owning your own business is the surest path to wealth in America.

SOME PEOPLE SHOULD OWN THEIR OWN BUSINESS...SOME NOT

Blogger and Brazen Careerist www.brazencareerist.com co-founder Penelope Trunk believes that not everyone should run their own business. "Running your own business is very risky and makes each day full of disorder and uncertainty" and "puts your family on the line." But for those who understand the risks, and can reorder their life to build a business and still have a life, it can be the grandest adventure of their career.

A business of your own can have many rewards, including:

1. **No psycho boss** from hell...the bosshole...to deal with every day (nearly half of all employees dislike their boss).
2. **Freedom to work when you want** (even if that may be ALL the time).
3. **Freedom to work where you want** (Apple started in a garage and millions of businesses are run out of home offices).
4. **No commuting**. Many self-employed people work at home or close to their home (commuting is always at the top of the list of what people hate about working).
5. **No annoying colleagues**. Most businesses are one-person operations—which essentially solves the problem of annoying, backstabbing, gossipy, don't-pull-their-weight co-workers. And if you hire someone you can always fire them. Just make sure they are "at will" employees and cover your ass in writing anytime they screw up. One pissed off employee can ruin your business and years of hard work.
6. **The sky is the limit**. No tedious working your way up the corporate ladder of success for decades—only to get wasted in a corporate downsizing or buyout or bankruptcy. You can leapfrog your way to great success (if you're good, lucky, and the product/service you sell is wanted or needed by lots of people).
7. **There are many free or inexpensive resources available for entrepreneurs** to help you learn the ropes. The Small Business Administration

www.sba.gov conducts excellent classes (most are free—your tax dollars actually doing something good). SCORE www.score.org can set you up with a retired executive as a mentor. And dozens of sites online provide guidance, resources and support. In major markets there are dozens of startup and entrepreneur events to attend.

8. **You can do a lot with a little**. Unlike 20 years ago, the computer and Internet revolution makes it easy to set up and conduct business. A smartphone (about $300 for an iPhone or Android), a few free or low-cost apps ($60), a wi-fi enabled laptop (Toshiba or HP for about $500) a wireless printer/copier/scanner/fax (HP for about $200), a business license (about $200), a website you can create in a day from a template (less than $500) a business URL (about $20 at www.godaddy.com), logo design (about $150 at 99Designs www.99designs.com), incorporation (about $200 at www.legalzoom.com) plus setting up a business account at the bank and your wireless phone provider...and a few other incidentals like business cards www.vistaprint.com and, voila, you're in business for less than two thousand bucks. Of course you still have to either do (or make) something people will want to buy. Hopefully LOTS of people.

What do real entrepreneurs think about running their own business?

"Being the master of my own fate." Randy Hendrick, TRX

"Being able to create something magical and lasting." Larry Mindel, Il Fornaio Restaurants

"The freedom to do work I love and work with people I like." Suresh Kumar, Green Earth

"One reason to own a small business is the ability to direct the culture of your company." Kasey Gahler, Gahler Financial

"I love the pace and the challenges. I haven't had a dull day in six years." Christian Yanek, SurveyGizmo

"I can work from anywhere." Darin Kraetsch, Flip Flop Shops

"For me, it was a very conscious choice to make a living doing what I love." Trish Breslin Miller, This Little Gallery

"Continuing to learn new things." Jesse Lipson, ShareFile

Before you actually commit to opening a business, find out as much as possible about every aspect of operating a business. Begin by reading some of the excellent books on the market (there are hundreds), business websites, and blogs. Here are a few that come highly recommended.

- ***The e-Myth Revisited***, Michael Gerber www.e-myth.com
- ***Good to Great: Why Some Companies Make the Leap...and Others Don't***, Jim Collins www.jimcollins.com
- ***Influence: The Psychology of Persuasion***, Robert Cialdini. www.influenceatwork.com
- ***First, Break all the Rules: What the World's Greatest Managers Do Differently***, Marcus Buckingham, Curt Coffman.
- ***The Start-up of You: Adapt to the Future, Invest in Yourself, and Transform Your Career***. Reid Hoffman and Ben Casnocha. www.thestartupofyou.com
- ***The Art of the Start: The Time-Tested, Battle-Hardened Guide for Anyone Starting Anything***, Guy Kawasaki. www.guykawasaki.com
- ***Business Model Generation: A Handbook for Visonaries, Game-Changers, and Challengers***, Alexander Osterwalder, Yves Pigneur. www.businessmodelgeneration.com
- ***The Lean Startup: How Today's Entrepreneurs Use Continuous Innovation***, Eric Ries. www.theleanstartup.com
- ***A Whack on the Side of the Head: How You Can Be More Creative***, Roger von Oech.
- ***Made to Stick: Why Some Ideas Survive and Others Die***. Chip Health, Dan Heath. www.heathbrothers.com Also, ***Decision: How to Make Better Choices in Life and Work***.
- ***The New Leader's 100-Day Action Plan: How to Take Charge, Build Your Team, And Get Immediate Results***, George Bradt, Jayme Check, Jorge Pedraza. www.primegenesis.com
- ***See You at the Top***, Zig Ziglar. www.ziglar.com
- ***Awaken the Giant Within***, Anthony Robbins. www.tonyrobbins.com

- ***EntreLeadership: 20 Years of Practical Business Wisdom from the Trenches,*** Dave Ramsey. www.daveramsey.com

Read these books before starting a business...they're your learning baseline for success.

NOTE: If you don't have time to read them all, most are available in PDF or Slideshare form (just "Google" it). These "Cliff Notes" versions provide a topline of all the pertinent information in the books.

If possible, enroll in business courses at the SBA or your local college. You'll need some understanding of accounting, tax reporting, payroll, marketing, sales and employee management. There are exceptional facilities in most major cities. Many of the resources are free. www.sba.gov.

Stanford University offers more than 900 free lectures on entrepreneurship by over 100 top thought leaders, including Mark Zuckerberg, Elon Musk, and Reid Hoffman. Listening to these lectures is like getting a Ph.D. in entrepreneurship. For a chronological list of these lectures, go to www.APlanForLife.com.

Your location may be a factor in your eventual success or failure—especially if you're opening a retail business. Depending upon your business type you may want to consider shared offices or an incubator space. Rent is one of the big fixed expenses that you'll need to control. Check out www.hq.com or www.regus.com, both are nationwide shared space companies. There are also innovative startup shared spaces in most markets—such as RocketSpace in San Francisco where Zappos and Zaarly got their start. www.rocket-space.com

Be sure to have an attorney review your business documents—especially leases. Your location and the lease deal you put together can be one of the most important decisions you'll make. A bad lease can cost you a lot of money down the road. Just one poorly written line in a lease—one drawn up by an attorney—once cost me more than a half million dollars. So, double-check everything.

Find a successful businessperson who will help mentor you. A mentored business is five times more likely to succeed. It is invaluable to get advice from someone who has "been there" and can help you avoid painful and costly mistakes. The Service Corps of Retired Executives www.score.org is a good place to start.

Life Rule: Don't get so excited about going into business that you overlook doing your due diligence.

OPERATING CAPITAL

The single most frequent cause of business failure is not having enough capital. It is the lifeblood of business. You'll need money to get started. You'll need money to see you through the first years when income is often low and expenses keep mounting. And you'll need money to make changes after you're in business for a while, as well as to expand. I can't say this strongly enough…make sure you have the capital necessary to establish and grow your business.

Startup capital comes from several sources:

1. **Your own savings**. This is perhaps the best capital because you don't have to give up any equity or control. If you do seek out investors at some point, they will be impressed that you have "skin in the game."

2. **Friends and family**. The source of capital for many new businesses. Just make sure they understand the risks…or you risk losing important family relationships and souring long-time friendships.

3. **Angel investors**. There are more than 320,000 active angel investors in the U.S., some part of highly organized investor groups. In 2011 angels helped fund about 35,000 small businesses, many early-stage or start-ups, with a total of almost $23 billion in capital. Angels are often former entrepreneurs themselves. They love being "in the game" and provide much-needed mentoring, as well as funds, to new businesses. Angels also make far fewer demands on entrepreneurs than VC's (Venture Capitalists). Source: Jeffrey Sohl, "*The Angel Investor Market in 2011: The Recovery Continues*." Center for Venture Research, University of New Hampshire.

4. **Venture Capitalists**. Rather than use their own money, VC's invest pooled money from other people. Their investments are usually substantially higher than Angels, starting at $1 million. VC's typically ask for an equity interest and some control over the operation of the companies they invest in. VC's also are reluctant to invest in early-stage companies, preferring to invest in

expanding companies. About 1% of companies pitching VC's eventually obtain funding.

5. **Banks.** Ironically, banks are frequently the most difficult sources of start–up capital. As everyone has probably heard by now, banks don't like lending money to people who need it. While they don't seem to be risk–adverse to making their own investments with your money, they don't like you taking risks with their money. However, if you do have a long relationship with a bank, there are some that will take a calculated risk to help you start a new venture. Smaller community banks often know their customers on a first–name basis, may even attend the same church or be a neighbor. In these cases, the loan almost becomes a hybrid of Friends and Family and Angels.

RICHARD BRANSON'S TIPS FOR BUSINESS SUCCESS

Richard Branson started his first business at age 16…and dozens more in the years afterward. Now a billionaire, Branson enjoys sharing his wisdom with entrepreneurs.

1. Don't do it if you don't like it.
2. Be visible….sell yourself.
3. Choose your name wisely.
4. You can't run a business without taking risks.
5. First impressions are everything.
6. Perfection is unattainable.
7. The customer is always right (most of the time).
8. Define your brand.
9. Explore uncharted territory.
10. Beware of an "us vs them" environment.
11. Build a corporate comfort zone.
12. Not everyone is suited to be CEO.
13. Seek a second opinion…and a third.

14. Be a good listener.
15. Pick up the phone.
16. Be a leader…not a boss.
17. With mistakes, bounce back…don't fall.

The payoff from an intelligently planned and operated business can be life-changing, and the consequences for doing it poorly can negatively affect your life for years.

Life Rule: If you want more freedom and fulfillment in your career…and a shot at the "brass ring" of success…start your own business.

WRITE A BOOK

"The best way to become acquainted with a subject is to write a book about it." — Benjamin Disraeli

There's no faster way to become an acknowledged "expert" on a subject than to write a book about it. A book gives everything you do credibility and weight. Let's say you are a veterinarian. There's not a lot of difference in the public's eye between one vet and another. But if you are the author of *Keeping Pets Healthy: The Experts Guide*, you've got an immediate leg up on the competition…because you're now the expert on pet health.

- According to the Gallup Organization, it's estimated that 82% of America adults are capable of writing a book.

Rick Frishman and Robyn Freedman Spizman, authors of *Author 101*, say the best way for authors to strike it rich (since few books make money) "is to harvest other benefits from their books; for example, by establishing themselves as experts, becoming celebrities, getting wide media attention, boosting their businesses, and refocusing their careers in new, more lucrative directions."

One young marketing executive designed a seminar directly from the content of his self-published book. About once a month, he held his seminar for groups of thirty or forty people, all of whom paid $25 for the two-hours (plus a copy of his book). The seminars provided a steady extra annual income of nearly $1000 a month. The participants' feedback also provided him with additional material for the second edition of his book.

One evening his seminar was attended by an executive from a leading high-tech company who was so impressed she called the next day to offer him a top position at her company. He later learned the company received more than a thousand resumes applying for the position, one that he got without even trying.

"Writing a book is a tremendous experience. It pays off intellectually. It clarifies your thinking. It builds credibility. It is a living engine of marketing and idea spreading, working every day to deliver your message with authority. You should write one." — Seth Godin, author of *Linchpin: Are You Indispensable?*

Writing a book is also a great opportunity to build a website—both to promote the book you've written and enhance your business or career. If you have a KeepingPetsHealthy.com website, you can interact with customers, list your upcoming speaking engagements, talk about pet health issues that may attract more business, initiate interactive dialog with current or potential customers, build a database of names for a newsletter, display photos of the pets you've helped keep healthy—even sell pet products online to earn additional income.

Add a blog, a Facebook business page, a page on LinkedIn, and perhaps a Twitter presence and you'll have a set of contemporary marketing tools that reinforce each other. These can all be linked to your website.

If you think writing a book and getting it published is one of those impossible tasks that other people sometimes do but you could never accomplish, you should know it is easier today to get published than ever before. One of the major innovations of the 21st century has been the emergence of self-publishing as a viable, even attractive, alternative to traditional publishing.

"Prose writing has been of great use to me in the course of my life and was a principal means of my advancement." — Benjamin Franklin

Self-publishing actually offers several advantages over traditional routes:

- ✓ It's possible to get your book to market in weeks rather than months or years.

- ✓ You can revise your book quickly and easily in future editions.
- ✓ You retain ownership and control over your book.
- ✓ Best of all, you get to keep more of the revenue from the sale of your books.

Self-publishing has come a long way from the days of "vanity press" publishers, companies that often charged large fees and offered no pre-publication or marketing assistance. The publishing industry is going through major changes as print-on-demand (POD) technology and the Internet revolutionized the process of creating books. Much of the traditional publishing industry seems on life-support, clinging to an outmoded business model that is becoming less relevant every day. If you've ever encountered the insular, arrogant agent or publisher you understand how liberating it is to bypass these dinosaurs and publish your book another way. While there is still some cachet to having a big publishing house imprint, even that will be history in only a few short years.

You won't receive an advance self-publishing (although Amazon is experimenting with it), but you likely won't get one from a traditional publisher either. Few authors receive advances anymore. What you will get is as much as 70% of your books' revenue instead of only 15% with a traditional publisher. You also won't have to pay an agent's commission.

Traditional book publishing is often frustrating and time-consuming. While it's possible to sell directly to a publisher without an agent, in most cases you will have to secure an agent first. Agents, who become numbed by the thousands of awful manuscripts submitted to them, often seem to be more in the business of turning down authors than finding new ones.

Publishing houses all want the doctor or psychologist or talk show host or celebrity or head of a company to lend legitimacy to the books they publish. If you are simply a writer it isn't impossible to get a book published, just much more difficult.

Publishing houses assume complete control of your book. If they don't like the title—tough, your book will get a different title. They design the cover. They edit and change the copy to whatever they want and the author has little recourse. If it takes them a year or more to get it to market, that's how long you are forced to wait. In reality it's no longer your book, it's their product to do with as they please.

Many authors set up their own publishing imprint—literally their own publishing company. Decide what business entity you want to do business as (e.g. Sole Proprietor). Then file a Fictitious Name Statement with the county clerk (about $50) and post it in an approved local newspaper (about $50). You can then open a bank account under the name of your publishing company. There are several tax advantages to creating your own publishing company. Some authors who have done this will publish other writers' works under their imprint, becoming a bona fide publisher. It's smart to get the advice of a good attorney first.

As a self-published author you'll need to do your own editing, meaning you will have to hire someone to do it. Every author will tell you it's impossible to do it yourself, you are just too close to the work. Good freelance editors can cost between $1,000 – $3,000.

You will also need to market your book. Since traditional publishers won't even look at your book if you don't have a well thought out marketing and promotion plan, this is something you would have to do anyway. There are many good books and online resources to learn how to promote your book. You can begin with these resources: Penny Sensevieri at Author Marketing Experts www.amarketingexpert.com, Dan Poynter www.parapublishing.com, and John Kremer www.bookmarket.com. Penny makes a case for a book being the "new business card" that can lead to speaking engagements, visibility, and career success.

A book generally requires about 40,000 to 80,000 words, although there's no reason why it can't be more or less. There are thousands of books that are 60 to 100 pages in length. If you estimate that each page will contain about 300 words, an 80,000-word manuscript will result in a book that is 200 to 280 pages long, depending upon typeface, visuals, structure, and book size. If you write just 1,000 words a day you'll have a first draft manuscript finished in about three months.

If you are totally inept at writing, just put the words down in the clearest, most direct language possible—imagine you are talking to your wife or a friend. You aren't writing for a shot at a Pulitzer Prize or National Book Award, just to provide a service to your readers. As with giving a good speech, concentrate on giving your audience the information they want, not on your style. There are many good freelance book editors who will review your manuscript and help clean it up for publication.

Authors will tell you that publishing the book is only the beginning. Now you want people to actually read it. Which means they need to know about it. And that takes marketing. Consider joining the Author Marketing Club www.authormarketingclub.com. Pick up a copy of Jane Friedman's *Book Marketing 101.* Also follow Penny Sensevieri at Author Marketing Experts www.amarketingexpert.com. Who knows, perhaps you'll end up on the NY Times Bestseller list someday.

Additional Resources:

https://www.createspace.com
Createspace is Amazon's publishing and distributing book company. You can create a soft–cover print book in several sizes, Kindle ebook, DVD, CD, or audiobook easily and inexpensively through Amazon's vast resources. They offer editing services, book jacket and interior design, marketing.

www.Smashwords.com
Smashwords is an ebook self–publishing and distribution platform that converts files into multiple ebook formats for reading on various ereading devices.

www.lightningsource.com
Lightning Source, part of Ingram Content Group, is a printer and distributor of POD (print–on–demand) books.

www.blurb.com
Create and publish bookstore–quality books with free software for PC or Mac. Sell your book in the Blurb bookstore or make copies for yourself.

www.lulu.com
Self–publish books in any format, print only what you need, and have it available at Amazon, Barnes & Noble iBooks, and through Lulu.com. Professional support available. Lulu has published more than a million titles.

The best self–publishing guide I've found (and there are many) is *APE Author, Publisher, Entrepreneur How to Publish a Book* by Guy Kawasaki and Shawn Welch.

Career Life Rules to incorporate into your Plan for Life.

- Follow your passion or interest to a career you enjoy, excel at, and can earn an exceptional income.

- Get the best education or training possible…and engage in lifelong education to keep your skills relevant. Learn as much as possible about your career choices.
- Join LinkedIn and learn to use its range of career/business networking services.
- Become proficient in social media.
- Learn computer skills…and stay current with changes.
- Find a mentor.
- Join groups/associations that support your career goals.
- Craft an effective resume/cover letter.
- Learn how to interview well.
- Develop a personal "brand" that represents who you are…and ideally sets you apart.
- Develop emotional intelligence.
- Remember…first impressions count: smile, firm handshake, tasteful wardrobe, eye contact, listen.
- Develop a Plan B career.
- Consider going into business for yourself.
- Write a book.

Further reading:

How to Get a Job: Secrets of a Hiring Manager by Allison Green. www.askamanager.org

Promote Yourself: The New Rules for Career Success by Dan Schwabel. www.danschwabel.com

What Color is Your Parachute: A Practical Manual for Job-Hunters and Career-Changers by Richard Bolles. www.jobhuntersbible.com

The Brand You 50: Fifty Ways to Transform Yourself from an "Employee" into a Brand That Shouts Distinction, Commitment, and Passion! by Tom Peters. www.tompeters.com

The First 90 Days: Proven Strategies for Getting Up to Speed Faster and Smarter by Michael Watkins.

What Got You Here Won't Get You There: How Successful People Become Even More Successful* and *MOJO: How to Get It, How to Keep It, How to Get It Back if You Lose It by Marshall Goldsmith. www.marshallgoldsmithlibrary.com

True North: Discover Your Authentic Leadership by Bill George, Peter Sims and David Gergen.

Do What You Are: Discover the Perfect Career for You Through the Secrets of Personality Type by Paul D. Tieger and Barbara Barron–Tieger. www.personalitytype.com

Additional online resources:

www.linkup.com Available jobs from company sites.

www.jobshadow.com Interviews with people in various professions. Helps you choose the right career.

www.virtualjobshadow.com Allows you to "test drive" jobs through the experiences of people in those jobs.

www.dice.com Tech jobs.

www.snagajob.com Local jobs.

www.salary.com Use the Salary Wizard to find pay ranges for jobs.

www.jobhub.com 1,000,000+ job listings.

www.collegerecruiter.com Entry level work and career opportunities for recent grads.

www.indeed.com Millions of jobs from thousands of company websites.

www.idealist.org Non–profit jobs, internships, and volunteer opportunities.

www.glassdoor.com Insider tips on companies and job listings.

www.VetNetHQ.com A Google service to help connect military veterans to more than 1 million jobs.

www.talentzoo.com Marketing, advertising, new media, and creative jobs.

For more resources, go to www.APlanForLife.com

CHAPTER 4
LOVE

DATING, MARRIAGE, CHILDREN, AND DIVORCE—PRETTY MUCH IN THAT ORDER

"The most important career choice you'll make is who you marry."
— Sheryl Sandberg, CEO, author of *Lean In: Women, Work, and the Will to Lead*

Choosing a mate is arguably the most important decision you will make in life, and has a huge impact upon your chances of achieving life-long happiness, according to David Brooks, author of "*The Social Animal: The Hidden Sources of Love, Character, and Achievement.*" At the heart (literally) of marriage is love—at least in our Western culture.

It's a basic human need to want to be loved. As everyone knows, it can be the most exalted form of human interaction, and the lack of it can drive people to the depths of despair. There are many different types of "love," but for the sake of brevity we will talk about romantic love—from beginning to (unfortunately) end.

DATING

It's been said that dating is like test-driving a car before buying it. Wrong. Imagine testing out a new Mercedes or Ferrari that becomes a Honda Civic shortly after you buy it and bring it home. It's more like that. Then imagine driving that same car for the next fifty years.

Dating is almost nothing like marriage. And it's a poor indicator of what the relationship will be like once the knot is tied. Several surveys found that arranged marriages between two people who have never met (or hardly know each other) are just as successful as Western marriages between people who "fall in love." You know what happens when people "fall?" They often hurt themselves.

Many of the initial factors that attract two people are not the same things that contribute to a lasting married relationship. 89% say yes or no to a second date based upon physical attractiveness...but long-term relationship success depends upon shared interests and values.

WHAT ATTRACTS PEOPLE TO EACH OTHER?

"Guys go to a restaurant called Hooters. If there was a place where male waiters were dressed up to arouse women, they wouldn't be in Speedos. They would be in suits, carrying briefcases, and they'd be holding up their perfect credit scores." — Whitney Cummings, comedienne

In a study of 10,000 people in 37 countries, psychologist David Buss found that men consistently value attractiveness and youth in a mate. Women value ambition, status, and resources. Even in our 21st Century, mostly egalitarian society, these age-old preferences remain true. It's the way humans are genetically hard-wired. Yeah, yeah, yeah—I know we're supposed to be "equal" and all, but the truth is that women want faithful men with resources and men want, well, "hot" women they can sleep with who don't create a lot of "drama" in their life. If they're also smart, interesting, and have resources themselves...all the better.

Dating is supposed to be a sort of job interview to be a lifelong mate. Most sign up to find a mate, although many of the men simply *want* to mate.

HOW TO MEET SOMEONE

It always surprises me to hear a single person claim they can't find anyone to date. There are literally thousands of "places" to meet eligible members of the opposite sex. If you aren't meeting anyone it's likely more about you. Something about you is not attractive to potential mates. We'll discuss that more later.

The other reason is that you simply didn't make the effort to connect with the people you do meet. Nearly everyone has experienced meeting someone they found very attractive...and then did nothing to follow up on the initial contact. In love victory goes to those who take initiative.

The way people meet today is vastly different than the way people met just 20 years ago—and even more different than the way our grandparents met. And it's all because of technology...and the internet. Here are the primary ways people met in 2014.

1. Friends and family
2. Online
3. At work
4. By chance
5. A bar, party or club

Most people—about 1 in 3—meet the person they marry through friends and relatives. This has proven to be a fairly reliable method of meeting quality people. After all, who knows you better than your friends and relatives? Sometimes from their unique perspective they see things you may not see in another person. They also have a vested interest in seeing that you bring someone into the family or your close circle of friends who is compatible. So don't rule out your mom or best friend as a matchmaker.

Almost 1 in 5 people meet at their place of employment. With Americans spending more time than ever working, it's only natural that people who spend as much as 70 hours a week together end up romantically involved. Studies show that the more time people are around each other the more attractive they become. In the workplace you get a chance to see how someone reacts under pressure, treats others, their personality type, work ethic, and a host of other things that casual dating doesn't reveal.

Many workplace trysts evolve from this close association. Without the distraction of such things as children, taking out the trash, seeing what you look like first thing in the morning, or predictable sex—the "game face" of the workplace creates an image that is more attractive than the married reality. Most workplace romances are doomed to end in disaster, but while they are happening the people involved feel an excitement that is otherwise missing in their lives. The old saying, "Don't fish in the company pond" (or something like that) is solid advice, particularly if one party is married.

"Partying is such sweet sorrow." — Robert Byrne

About 12% meet their mate at a party, bar or nightclub. While not the most romantic way to meet, it's still the preferred place to meet for many young people. At these venues there is an enticing brew of alcohol, loud music, sexual innuendo, and lots of opportunity to "hook up" with someone (the current jargon for a one-night stand). Having sex releases a powerful brew of hormones that Nature designed to bond people together (especially for women). Sometimes these hookups result in romances. And sometimes they result in marriage. Sometimes they even last.

Nearly 1 in 10 meet "by chance." Chance meetings can be improved by being where you have the greatest opportunity to interact with people who share your interests and values. Good places include charitable or community activities, sports teams, church, and special interest clubs.

"On the Internet nobody knows you're a dog." — Famous viral cartoon

While friends and family are the best source for people to meet, online dating sites and social media now account for more than a third of all dates…35% – 40% according to a 2009 study by Stanford and the National Science Foundation. The figures skew dramatically depending upon whether or not you are in a heterosexual or same-sex relationship—24% for heterosexuals and 61% for same-sex.

The trend toward meeting online will only continue to increase as more people get comfortable with the idea.

MEETING PEOPLE THE OLD-FASHIONED WAY

"My wife and I were happy for twenty years. Then we met."
— Rodney Dangerfield

Meeting people in person during the normal course of your life is still the most prevalent way to meet someone. On the surface it seems like a poor way to go about it. After all, there are millions of potential mates in the world. In that giant pool of potential mates it's estimated that everyone has at least 30,000 "ideal" matches. These are people who are a perfect match for you in every way: looks, humor, personality, religion, attitudes, temperament, sexual orientation, career, and family. The problem is that unless you get very lucky the chance of meeting one of these "soulmates" is practically zero. Finding the perfect person is like a marriage lottery—with the same odds of success.

Even with all the changes in dating during the past couple of decades, the average person only goes out with about a dozen people before selecting a life–long (in theory) marriage partner. This isn't an ideal way to match up two people for life. Few couples are truly compatible when they meet by "accident." So marriage becomes a matter of compromise and unfulfilled needs. Under these circumstances it's amazing the divorce rate is only 49%, especially given the major fundamental differences between the sexes.

21ST CENTURY DATING

Dating in the 21st century is easier than ever before in history. Just 25 years ago the average person's dating pool numbered in the dozens, mostly from the local neighborhood or on the job…now it's in the millions and can be from anywhere in the world. The Internet has changed the playing field completely.

It's also now acceptable to be single at any time in your life and date many people. In 1960, 12% of men and 13% of women between 35 – 44 years old were unmarried. By 2007 these figures more than doubled to 31% for men and 28% for women.

THE NEAR PERFECT MATCHMAKER…THE INTERNET

There are more than a thousand online dating sites, including niche sites with very narrow targets such as WomenWhoLoveBarechestedConstructionWorkers.com (just kidding). Seriously though, there are dating sites for nearly every conceivable age, ethnic group, sexual orientation, and interest. There are even sites for people who are sick or suffering from a disease. One site www.prescription4love.com is the go–to spot online where singles who also happen to have diseases can meet (not as, uh, sick as it sounds).

Got genital herpes and worried no one will ever date you again? No problem, just go to www.herpespassions.com or www.herpessingles.com where the 1 in 5 adult Americans who has genital herpes can find a sympathetic soulmate. Lost an arm or a leg? These sites will lend a hand www.datingamputees.com, www.amputeedate.com, or www.disabledpassions.com.

There are niche dating sites for overweight people, Muslims, virgins, cat lovers, farmers, criminals, short people, tall people, people who like dressing up as dogs, pot smokers, farmers, vampire lovers, beautiful people, video gamers, and adults who enjoy wearing diapers (seriously). Here are a few:

www.farmersonly.com

www.fitness-singles.com

www.justsingleparents.com

www.tallfriends.com

www.shortpassions.com

www.thebigandthebeautiful.com

www.dating4disabled.com

www.theuglybugball.com

www.meet-an-inmate.com

www.glutenfreesingles.com

www.clowndating.com (I am not making this up)

There are also a couple of, shall we say, very exclusive sites:

www.darwindating.com
At Darwindating.com only the beautiful should apply. This site asks if you are "sick of dating websites filled with ugly, unattractive, desperate fatsos?" Seriously. The things that can exclude you from this site are daunting: saggy boobs, weird pubic hair, pasty skin, teeth that aren't white, mullets, acne, fat rolls, bald patches, gaps in your teeth, ski–jump noses, webbed toes, large hips, large ears, and so on.

www.nudistfriends.com
Nudists can expose themselves to thousands of potential dates on this bare bones site.

For people just interested in "hooking up" or finding a sugar daddy there are the "naughty" websites like www.AshleyMadison.com (for adulterers), www.adultfriendfinder.com (for married couples looking for other married couples, gays, escorts) www.whatsyourprice.com (women accepting money for dates), www.passion.com (for singles who just want to get it on), and www.SugarDaddyForMe.com or www.millionairematch.com (for women who want to be taken care of by a rich guy).

There's an entire industry now servicing people with specific sexual preferences, including cruises and resorts where gays, lesbians or swingers can meet. You can find out more at www.outtraveler.com, www.gaytravel.com, the International Gay & Lesbian Travel Association www.iglta.org.

Swingers can go to www.dreampleasuretours.com (specialists in bookings for two top swinger resorts...Desire and Hedonism). Other sites you might want to bookmark for your swinging and nude travel are www.toplesstravel.com, www.exotictravelservices.com, www.swingertravel.org, www.shoesonlytravel.net, and www.rightconnectionstravel.com.

THE TOP MAINSTREAM DATING SITES

Currently, these are the top mainstream dating sites:

www.Match.com
The big daddy of dating sites with more than 21 million members (2014). Dating via cellphone is offered. Notifies when profiles are read. Includes many options for finding suitable matches.

www.okcupid.com
Claims to be the fastest growing online dating site. Free. Takes a Web 2.0 approach. Has a couple of unique features such as MyBestFace, which analyzes your photos and tells you which ones are most likely to generate the most responses, and the Staff Blog, which provides insider tips on how to improve your dating odds.

www.maturesinglesonly.com
Claims 6 million members over the age of 40.

www.PerfectMatch.com
Uses an "advanced algorithm" to match members.

www.eHarmony.com
One of the Big 5 dating sites with millions of serious marriage-minded members. Uses a compatibility questionnaire (400 questions) to match members. Analyzes more than 600 variables, including your search habits on the site. Claims to be responsible for 120 weddings per day.

www.Zoosk.com
Caters to young singles. Is synced up with several social media sites. Provides daily matches. Has a good mobile app. The site claims 50 million members worldwide and operates in 24 languages.

www.Chemistry.com
Matches are based upon personality and interpersonal chemistry using a science-based algorithm. Relies on user feedback to refine searches. Free relationship advice. Best for singles over 35.

www.lavalife.com
Allows three different profiles, one each for their three sections: Dating, Relationships, and Intimate Encounters. Lots of options, including sharing personal photo galleries.

www.ChristianMingle.com
For singles who want to meet others with similar values and upbringing. Members call it "like a Sunday morning at church." All the "Godspeak" can be off-putting to more secular daters.

www.OurTime.com
A fast-growing site that specializes in the 50+ single crowd. You can search instantly without membership. Lots of advice from dating experts. Singles under 50 are allowed to register.

www.silversingles.com
For 50+ singles.

Each of these sites has more than a million members. Some have tens of millions (e.g. Match.com with 30+ million members). Most cost between $20 - $50 a month. You can also reach more than 20 million people on Yahoo Personals. Obviously, these sites open up your potential dating pool considerably more than just relying on friends and family or the local club.

There are also sites devoted to individual religions, if this is important to you:

www.CatholicMatch.com

www.jdate.com

www.LDSS.com

And ethnic groups:

www.BlackSingles.com

www.afrointroductions.com

www.asiandating.com

www.latinamericancupid.com

The online dating site industry is a $4 billion a year business. With hundreds of dating sites appearing in just the last few years, it's obvious that online dating is here to stay. Decide first what you want from the online dating experience and then review the sites to find one that matches your needs.

SOCIAL MEDIA AND DATING

- 75% of singles use social media and smartphones to find dates.

Social media has also enabled people to meet more easily. Facebook has resulted in many new romances. Sites like LinkedIn, Pinterest, and Twitter have resulted in offline relationships. Networking of any kind…online or offline…is about meeting people, and when people meet sometimes they are attracted romantically.

Even old relationships are being rekindled; the number of old flames reconnecting on Facebook numbers in the hundreds of thousands. Another popular site to reconnect with people from the past is www.Classmates.com.

While some caution needs to be observed…10% of sex offenders admit to using dating sites…this new form of dating is mostly a good thing. The more people you meet, the more likely you are to meet the right person. The defining factor in the success of online dating is search. It's now easier to find hard-to-find people. If your preference is different or narrow or outside the mainstream, you can find what you're looking for online with just a few keystrokes. It's why gay and lesbian use of online dating sites is much higher than for heterosexuals. Just 2% of all couples in the U.S. are same-sex, so niche dating sites are a viable alternative for them.

Another advantage with online dating is the ability to assess someone quickly by reviewing their personal profile. Unlike meeting someone at a bar or bar mitzvah, and learning after a couple dates that you have almost nothing in common, you can pre-screen dates online.

DATING SMART IN THE AGE OF THE INTERNET

It's important to do your "due diligence" when dating. Anyone who has been swimming in the dating pool for long has a story about the "psycho" date from hell. Unlike people you meet through friends and family or at work, online postings enable a person to control and manipulate their first impression. You inevitably will run across inflated profiles, Photoshopped pictures, invented careers, and phony education…and the occasional complete fabrication by a sociopath.

BACKGROUND CHECKS

It's good to do background checks on anyone who may affect your life in a significant way—bosses, new friends…and people you begin dating. This is especially important since surveys show that 33% of women have sex on their first online date, according to 2014 data from Statistic Brain. You don't want to get deeply involved with someone who could be a sociopath.

You might be surprised to learn that with just a few keystrokes you can find:

- Full name.
- Age.
- Photo.
- Address (including past addresses).
- Phone number.
- Email addresses.
- Online user names.
- Names of your relatives.
- When you purchased your home.
- What you paid for your home.
- Purchase history of your home.
- What your home is worth.
- A photo of your home and map to get there.

- Current value of your home.
- Size of your lot and square footage of your house.
- Number of bedrooms and baths in your home.
- Information about your neighborhood.
- Names of your neighbors.
- The value and price paid of your neighbor's homes.
- Whether you are married or not.
- Name of spouse.
- Spouses' age.
- How many children you have.
- Children's names.
- Children's ages.
- How many children are living at home.
- Profession (past/present).
- Past/present employers.
- How long you have worked at your last several jobs.
- Income.
- Credit score.
- Criminal record.
- Legal documents/lawsuits.
- Social networks (e.g. Facebook)
- Online profiles.
- Hobbies.
- The songs you listen to on Pandora.
- Your photos on Flickr.
- Other photos of you published online.
- The organizations you belong to now and in the past.

- Anything you have ever published.
- Mentions of you in traditional and online media.

Before the internet and "big data" even professional private investigators had difficulty finding out this much information.

Always do a Google search on your prospective date. Check out their social media sites, if possible. And consider signing up for an information service such as www.spokeo.com (currently $5 a month). Yes, it may seem a little creepy to check someone out this way, but people are not always what they purport to be.

In one study, more than 80% of people admitted to lying or embellishing information about themselves on a date (and those were just the people who admitted to it—if you lie about yourself to a potential mate, wouldn't you lie to the person doing the survey?). Men lie about age, height, and income. Women lie about weight, physical build, age. Source: Statistic Brain (2014)

Other investigative sites include Intellius www.intellius.com and Peek You www.PeekYou.com. For personal or business background information there's also www.BeenVerified.com. You can access the site's information free for seven days. If you sign up there's a charge for each background check, just $19.95 as of 2012

More than 1 in 3 women (and 1 in 6 men) report having been in at least one abusive relationship. With so many scam artists, cheats, and liars in the world, it's important to protect yourself.

SOULMATES

"88% of American men and women between the ages of 20 – 29 believe there is a soulmate out there waiting for them."

— Dr. Phil McGraw, citing a Louisiana State University study

Peter Todd, a psychologist and cognitive scientist at Indiana University, has developed a measure he calls "satisficing"—satisfying and sufficing. Satisficing involves setting a standard you want in a mate and then going about searching for this person intelligently.

You begin by dating a range of men or women to determine what you do and don't want. Maybe you like guys who take charge or perhaps this type seems like a "control freak" to you. Perhaps you like athletic, outdoorsy types. Or not—maybe you prefer a domestic, bookish, stay-at-home type. Do you like a person who is vivacious and outgoing? Does an intellectual appeal to you? What about their attitudes about being a parent? How do they handle stressful situations?

What is their family like? You can often "see" your spouse in the future by observing the mom or dad. There's some truth to the old saying "The apple doesn't fall far from the tree." What kind of relationship do they have with their parents and siblings? Poor relations with close relatives often is an indication the person's relationship skills are lacking. Or that they grew up in a dysfunctional environment.

How will you like their looks in 20 years when he's bald and she has gained 20 pounds? Women gain an average of about 20 pounds after marriage between the age of 30 – 50, according to a 2011 Ohio State University study. 30% of men are affected by baldness by age 30…and 73% eventually lose all or most of their hair. Will you still be attracted? It's often a shock when people look up their old girlfriend/boyfriend after thirty or forty years. My high school prom queen now looks nothing like in her glory days. I wouldn't have recognized her if we had been trapped in an elevator for several hours.

DECIDE WHAT YOU WANT BEFORE YOU MAKE ANY DECISIONS

"Choose a spouse in haste. Repent at leisure." — Harry Houdini

Decide what you find appealing, the values you must have, and the list of things that are non-negotiable in a mate. Set your baseline and start searching intelligently for someone who meets or exceeds it. There is someone, indeed many, absolutely perfect mates out there in the universe for everyone. Your job is to do the best you can to find one of them—or someone close.

WHAT TO LOOK FOR IN A MARRIAGE PARTNER

"Marriage is the most important decision you can make in life."
— R. James Woolsey

Popular blogger Eric Barker www.bakadesuyo.com compiled an excellent list of the key things you should look for in a marriage partner.

1. **Find someone who you idealize and who idealizes you**. Yes, when it comes to marriage it pays to be somewhat delusional.
2. **Marry someone with high self-esteem**. Look out for people who don't like themselves much. They will eventually convince you too.
3. **Find a spouse who will be actively involved with the kids**. Men of higher socioeconomic status are better at this.
4. **Men should avoid sexually passive and subservient women**...if they hope to have a sex life after marriage. In survey after survey, nearly all married men say they want more sex.
5. **Couples are happier when the wife is better looking**.
6. **Find a partner you can trust**. Women tell an average of 728 lies to their spouse in a year. Men tell 1,092. Source: One Poll and BMW Financial Services, 2012 Further reading: *The Honest Truth: How We Lie to Everyone—Especially Ourselves* by Dan Ariely
7. And this one from other sources...**be wary of your spouse's parents and siblings**. Children of divorced parents more often end up divorced themselves. Also, if there is any mental illness, substance abuse, and other harmful habits such as smoking, your new husband or wife is more likely to exhibit these too. Remember, your kids will inherit half the genes of your spouse. So, check the family out as carefully as you do your future spouse. You don't want to marry into the Addams family.

FIVE THINGS TO DISCUSS BEFORE GETTING MARRIED

If you walk down the aisle without discussing (and agreeing) on these five important issues, better have the name of a good divorce attorney.

1. **Children.** Do you want them? When? How will you raise them?
2. **Money.** What are your saving and spending styles? Who will earn the money? How will you use it? How will you save it? More couples divorce because of money issues than any other reason.
3. **Religion, morals, values.** Love conquers all...right? No, especially

when religious, moral or personal values conflict. Make sure you are in sync in ALL these areas.

4. **Disagreements.** A marriage without arguments and fights is...a fiction. The question is how you resolve your inevitable disagreements. Unresolved resentments are a cancer to relationships that often leads to the ubiquitous "irreconcilable differences" divorce.
5. **Deal breakers.** What are the "deal breakers" that you absolutely can't live with or without for, presumably, the rest of your life? Infidelity? Boring, infrequent sex? Addictions? Lack of ambition? Snoring? Obesity? Whatever it is that you just cannot bear to live with all your life, make sure you know about it before saying "I do."

LOVE AT FIRST SIGHT

"You are much more likely to have a satisfying marriage for a lifetime when you and your partner are fundamentally similar."
— *30 Lessons for Living: Tried and True Advice from the Wisest Americans,* Karl Pillemer Ph.D.

Don't discount the elusive "chemistry" element in a relationship. It's hard to define, but if it's there you'll know it. There's an old saying, "Love is blind." For 81% of men and 57% of women, when they met the person they formed a relationship with they said it was "love at first sight." Perhaps love isn't so blind after all.

While there aren't any solid statistics that indicate how successful these relationships are over the long run, the way to increase the odds is to marry someone of similar preferences, background, religion, and socio-economic status. While opposites may sometimes attract, it's the similarities that will ensure a solid relationship over time. As the years progress, the differences will become less easily tolerated but the shared interests will strengthen.

Most studies indicate there is a great deal of dissatisfaction in marriage. In a 2014 survey of 1,200 married men by *Men's Health* magazine, nearly 4 in 10 men said they aren't sure they married the right woman. 77% said "they want way more sex in 2014." 70% say they wish their wife was more sexually adventurous. 1 in 5 are having sex once a month or less. And more than 1 in 4 said they had cheated during their marriage.

Number of men who believe in "love at first sight." 48%

Number of women who believe in "love at first sight." 49%

Source: *Men's Health*, March 2007

Divorce rate: 49%

Hmmm.

21ST CENTURY MARRIAGE

Marriage is a constantly evolving institution.

- ✓ People marry later now.
- ✓ More couples than ever live together before marriage.
- ✓ Many couples never formally marry.
- ✓ Older women marry younger men.
- ✓ Same sex couples marry.
- ✓ Many married couples openly and freely engage in sexual relationships with other married couples.

Here's a statistical snapshot of where marriage is now.

- ✓ 27 – Median age women marry.
- ✓ 29 – Median age men marry.
- ✓ 21 – Median age women married 30 years ago.
- ✓ 65% of men and women live together before marrying.
- ✓ 40% who did so 30 years ago.
- ✓ 94% of women have sex before marriage.
- ✓ 96% of men have sex before marriage.
- ✓ 93% who did so 30 years ago.
- ✓ 1 in 6 divorces were people over 50 (2011)

Sources: American Psychological Association, 2004. National Center for Family & Marriage, 2002. *Bride* magazine, 2012. Guttmacher Institute, 2007, Census Bureau, 2011.

THE ODDS OF A GOOD MARRIAGE

"When two people are under the influence of the most violent, most insane, most delusive, and most transient of passions, they are required to swear that they will remain in that excited, abnormal, and exhausting condition until death do them part."
— George Bernard Shaw

If someone handed you a revolver loaded with one bullet and asked you to play Russian Roulette you would say they were crazy. Who in their right mind would take a one out of six chance with their life at stake? Now if you put two bullets in the revolver and left four chambers empty, only the truly crazy or suicidal would pull the trigger.

Every year millions of people take a chance with their life with worse odds: marriage. Approximately 4 in 10 marriages will eventually be killed off—through sexual infidelity, boredom, violence, changes in personality or life goals, and the ubiquitous "irreconcilable differences." It's like putting three bullets in the revolver and pulling the trigger. Yet millions of people, who only recently learned to drive, or were living with their parents, believe they have the life experience and skills to successfully mate with someone for the next, oh, *half century.*

- The United States has the fifth highest divorce rate in the world.

And if you think that marriage is better the second time around consider this, the failure rate for second marriages is even deadlier (65%) than first marriages. Obviously, people don't learn much from their experience with first marriages. It's why divorce is a $35 billion dollar a year problem in America.

➢ Couples who get married before the age of 25 have a 60% chance the marriage will eventually end in divorce, according to the National Center for Health Statistics.

WHY 40% OF AMERICANS THINK MARRIAGE IS "OBSOLETE"

In a survey of couples published in *Parade* (2008) the results painted a less than rosy picture of marriage:

- ✓ 44% said they might not marry the same person.
- ✓ 44% of women have thought about leaving their husbands.
- ✓ 31% of men have thought about leaving their wives.
- ✓ 31% of married couples have sex less than one time a month.
- ✓ 25% describe marital sex as tolerable or even terrible.
- ✓ 48% of men don't have sex more often because their spouse isn't interested.
- ✓ 19% of men have had extra-marital sex…and 1 in 6 women.
- ✓ Only 16% of men and 22% of women said they "definitely" would marry the same person again.

In his best-selling book *The Millionaire Mind*, Thomas J. Stanley PhD, writes "Can you live forever? Marry the wrong spouse and every day will feel like an eternity. Marry the right spouse and life will be a joyful and perhaps even rich experience." Choosing the right person to marry, and then doing what is necessary to keep the marriage strong and vibrant, is vital to lifelong happiness.

More than anything else in life, marriage will affect your future happiness, success, wealth—even health. Yet the majority of people buy a new car with more intelligent thinking than they use choosing a lifetime mate. Of the hundreds of millions of potential mates on the planet, the average person will make their selection from a dozen or so people met by random accident. In fact, 2 out of 5 people marry the first person they fall in love with.

MARRIAGE CHANGES YOU

"We marry for all the wrong reasons, and often we marry the wrong person as well. We marry to grow up, to escape our parents and to inherit our share of the world, not knowing who we are and who we will become." — Merle Shain

What few people consider when they meet someone, fall in love, and decide to marry is how much it will likely change them. You will both give up (and gain) things in your partnership. If you like to ski and your partner hates skiing, the chances of going on ski vacations together…or skiing at all…is slim. If you like adventurous sex, and your spouse is more conservative sexually, you will have to give up that interest. What if your wife is a left-wing liberal and you are a right-wing evangelical? How long do you think that relationship will last after the glow of falling in love/lust is over? What if you want children and he doesn't? You'd be surprised at how few discuss this fundamental ingredient in their future relationship.

SO WHAT GOOD IS MARRIAGE?

"The greatest pleasure of life is love." — Euripides

The flip side of what you potentially give up is what you can gain from marriage. Marriage can bring into your life entirely new activities and ways of thinking about life. I know couples who introduced their mates to new activities like horseback riding, travel, boating, and cooking. There are many people who have benefited from the exchange of different points of view. Some people marry into money. Or they discover a style of raising a family that was completely foreign to their own upbringing. Many married couples are open to their spouse's interests and grow because of it. Some women who were repressed sexually blossom in marriage. Many people grow in maturity during marriage.

Another style of marriage is to remain separate people with separate interests who remain together for reasons that are important to them both. In this kind of marriage a man may go hunting or bowling with his friends. A wife may belong to a book club or go surfing with her friends who share that interest. If a marriage can make room for these separate interests it can be a long-term success. Many experts believe this is the ideal form of marriage.

One of the biggest, and seldom discussed, problems married couples experience is the growing resentment they feel toward their spouse because of what they believe they are giving up as a result of being in the relationship. Other causes of resentment are annoying personality quirks—things that may have seemed "cute" when they were dating—that become much less cute over time. What often develops is a passive/aggressive attitude—feeling embarrassed to discuss the problem, but hoping that aloof or critical remarks will somehow encourage the other person to change. This indirect approach seldom works.

If the annoyance is something the other person can't easily change—perhaps your spouse hasn't aged well or gained a significant amount of weight and is no longer attractive to you—then you've got a serious problem. You may love the person, but no longer feel the excitement of being "in love" or physically attracted. Only honest communication or professional therapy can bridge this psychic chasm.

WHY MARRIAGES FAIL

Most marriages break up for just a few basic reasons: money, infidelity, boredom, abuse, and the ubiquitous "irreconcilable differences." Yet very few couples talk about these things seriously before marriage. A spendthrift who marries someone who is thrifty will have to find a common ground to avoid conflict. A woman who likes to "play around" sexually with other men could experience serious difficulties in her marriage if her husband wants total fidelity. A sports-loving guy may soon find his home-loving wife to be boring if she doesn't share his passions. If you simply have little in common with each other, this could be a problem. The initial glow of love and/or lust can cloud your mind to these harsh realities.

It's important to discuss these things openly and frankly before you tie the knot. If you aren't in agreement on the important stuff, then perhaps you should reconsider getting married.

WHY MARRIAGES SUCCEED

"The most happy marriage I can imagine would be the union of a deaf man to a blind woman." — Samuel Taylor Coleridge

Let's be honest, even in the "best" marriages the initial thrill and lust will diminish…if not disappear entirely. At some point the best most couples can hope for is to be great friends who enjoy each other's company, don't irritate each other too much, share the task of earning money and operating a home, jointly raise children, and have occasional sex together. The myth of undying love until "death us do part" is so strong that most people reading what I've just said will react strongly with protestations of denial. But ask any couple married for ten or fifteen years and they will likely nod in resigned agreement.

For the lucky ones this isn't a bad thing. Contrary to the Hollywood ideal of "love," this arrangement can provide a more realistic "love" and a wealth of understated satisfactions that make up a good life. Often, marriages enter a new phase of loving friendship and admiration after many years. There may even be a resurgence of sexual attraction.

I know a couple who have succeeded in achieving an ideal marriage. They are still very much in love, enjoy being together, and have built an interesting life. There are some lessons to be learned from how they were able to do it.

1. They are educated.
2. They have always been employed, earn an upper Middle Class income, have made sensible investments, and have no money worries.
3. They share many of the same interests.
4. Both come from "good" families who enjoy being with each other.
5. They each have their own friends separate from shared friends.
6. They are both physically attractive and have remained that way.
7. They value good health and exercise, eat well, and vacation often.
8. They are emotionally mature...neither have any bad habits or emotional "issues."
9. They have invested the time and resources to raise children who are well-rounded, successful, and independent.
10. They have been lucky so far to have avoided any unforeseen tragedies in life.

I'm convinced this is the recipe for a happy, fulfilling marriage.

The driving force behind most marriages is a fear of being alone. But as Gloria Steinem wrote, "The surest way to be alone is to get married." Nothing is lonelier than being in a bad marriage.

10 TIPS FOR A HAPPY MARRIAGE.

There are a few tips to keep your marriage healthy and strong that have proven to be effective:

1. **Frame your demands as requests or favors.** When people make demands upon their mate it leads to resentment. Resentment builds and in turn leads to passive aggressive behavior. Eventually each person begins withholding affection, attention, and sex as "punishment." Not good.
2. **Be appreciative and grateful.** When you express appreciation for your mate's good qualities it builds a reservoir of good will. One of the universal truths is that everyone wants to be acknowledged and appreciated for what they do.
3. **Frame your conversations as positive.** Constantly complaining, nagging, or tearing down your partner, your life, your kids, your circumstances is like an anchor on your life. Being positive is more likely to make positive things happen in your relationship than being negative.
4. **Focus on the good things in your marriage.** Every married couple can find something good about their relationship (if you can't, see a divorce attorney or therapist). By concentrating your energy on the good things in your marriage you are more likely to manifest more good things.
5. **Remember shared experiences.** Past shared experiences, even tough times you've weathered, can strengthen the bond between you and your spouse. There's a reason why soldiers who share training and combat together share a bond that often lasts a lifetime, a bond that is so strong a soldier will sacrifice his life to save his buddies. In the same way marriages go through both good and bad times—babies are born, jobs are lost, vacations are shared—that are unique to your married partnership. Recalling these helps remind you of your bond.
6. **Listen, be there for each other.** Sometimes you simply need to be a sounding board for your partner. Having someone to vent to, without judgment, and be supportive is one of the big benefits of marriage.
7. **Don't get too comfortable.** When you dated you were on your best behavior, looking your best, and just the nicest person to be with at all times. But once couples tie the knot they inevitably get comfortable being their authentic self with each other. Sometimes too comfortable.

Often the person you married looks and acts very different from that person you fell in love with a few years earlier. The happiest couples stay fit, well groomed, interesting, and as attentive as when they were dating.

8. **Establish shared rituals.** Couples who share rituals create stronger bonds. It can be an annual trip to the mountains, a special dinner on Sundays, or attending church or synagogue every week…these rituals reinforce the bond you share with your spouse.
9. **Be sensitive to your partner's needs.** In surveys, couples who notice and are sensitive to their partners' unspoken needs have the most lasting marriages by a factor of 3 to 1.
10. **Do the little, thoughtful things for each other.** Some women say that one of the sexiest things their husband does…is the dishes. Marriages with couples who share chores are more likely to succeed. Whenever you do something kind for your spouse, it makes an impact far beyond the effort it took to do it. A backrub when your wife has had a tough day, buying a book your husband might enjoy, or a card that simply says "I love you" can be the everyday glue that binds you both together.

SCIENTIFIC TIPS FOR A SUCCESSFUL MARRIAGE

Jeanna Bryner, Managing Editor of *LiveScience*, www.livescience.com posted recent scientific research about what makes a successful marriage (it's not always what you think).

1. **Marry a similar spender.** When it comes to money, opposites attract. Tightwads are more likely to marry people who are careless about spending money. When the University of Michigan School of Business analyzed surveys of more than 1,000 married and unmarried adults, they found that people tend to choose their spending opposites as romantic partners…to the detriment of their relationship.
2. **Have a LOT of sex.** Neurotic people are most often the culprits in screwing up a relationship. However, according to a study published in the 2010 *Social Psychological and Personality Science* journal, neurotics who had a lot of sex were just as satisfied with their marriages as non-neurotic couples. Of course, sex is the

cement for many relationships that holds together an otherwise dicey partnership.

3. **Show gratitude to your loved one.** Two words that go a long way toward creating marital bliss are "thank you." A study by Arizona State University in 2007 found that expressing gratitude for household chores resulted in less resentment over any imbalance in labor and more satisfaction with their relationships than people who felt gratitude but did not verbalize it. Studies confirm that expressing gratitude, appreciation, admiration, and using couple–focused words such as "we" and "our" boost relationship satisfaction. One study found that men who share chores equally with their spouse have more successful marriages…and more sex (where's the vacuum!!).
4. **What annoys you in the beginning only gets worse later.** Researchers found that people tend to view their spouse more negatively over time. However, according to Kira Birditt, a research fellow at the University of Michigan's Institute for Social Research, this pattern is normal for nearly all couples and is a natural part of an evolving relationship. If you realize this as fact, you can focus on the good things that attracted you in the first place…and ignore the little annoying things.
5. **Negative can be positive for some marriages.** University of Tennessee psychologist James McNulty found that some marriages actually thrive on negative behaviors. For unhappy and troubled couples it may be more effective being less forgiving, blaming each other for their problems, and telling the other person to change. Almost everyone knows a couple of Bickersons. Go figure.
6. **Work at it.** A 2009 study of 6,000 people, including new couples and marriages of at least 20 years, published in the journal *Review of General Psychology*, found that a surprisingly high number were still very much in love. Researchers drew a distinction between romantic love, which can endure, and the lustful, passionate love, which often fades quickly after the beginning of a relationship. The key to making it work is work. Couples who work on their marriage…resolve conflicts smoothly, care about the relationship, spend time together, and inject novel experiences into their life, create the most enduring marriages.

HOW TO LIVE HAPPILY EVER AFTER

What helps ensure a long, happy marriage?

Newlyweds who face marriage with realistic expectations rather than a fantasy image are most likely to maintain a healthy relationship, according to a study in the *Journal of Personality and Social Psychology*. It's important for couples to view their partner with a clear understanding of their strengths and weaknesses. Poor relationship skills coupled with high expectations result in a steep decline in marital satisfaction.

Here are some other tips from people who have been married several decades.

1. Fostering a constant curiosity about each other keeps relationships growing and strong.
2. Say to yourselves "Divorce is not an option." Commit to each other, no matter what.
3. Remember, there's no such thing as a perfect marriage…only perfect moments. Marriage is a "bed of roses, thorns and all."
4. Don't overestimate the seriousness of arguments. You can't have heat without friction. And you can't live with anyone for decades without disagreeing on something now and then.
5. Communicate. Talk to each other. Be honest about your feelings. Unexpressed frustration is death to relationships. As one married woman said, "Holding resentment is like drinking poison and expecting the other person to die."
6. Never stop dating. Get out and have fun.
7. Marriage is not 50/50…it's 60/40, no matter which spouse you are.
8. Don't get bogged down in routine. Life is short and most people on their deathbed say they wish they had done more in life. One woman said, "I wish I hadn't had so many 'headaches.'"
9. Always respect each other…and show it.
10. From Dr. Phil McGraw. "You don't fix things by fixing your partner."
11. Give each other frequent massages. It works!
12. Share the household responsibilities.

MARRYING FOR SEX

"The only time my wife and I had a simultaneous orgasm was when the judge signed the divorce papers." — Woody Allen

In her book *Why Him? Why Her?* author Helen Fisher reports that half of all middle-aged men say they are dissatisfied with the amount of sex in their marriage. Part of the problem is that men simply want more sex than most women. It's always been this way. If it wasn't, we wouldn't have prostitutes, porn movies, Hooters or randy politicians.

- 61% of men say that a good sex life is a major key to a healthy relationship. Only 47% of women feel the same way.

In one (admittedly non-scientific) survey, women said they preferred chocolate, a good night's sleep, and an interesting conversation more than sex. If men had been asked the same question I guarantee you the answers would be different.

A sociology professor caused a stir in 2012 when he labeled marriage as "forced sexual incarceration" for men (and presumably women too). He claimed that with longer lives and more sophisticated modern lifestyles, monogamy simply isn't viable any longer. With the amount of infidelity these days, it would seem to be true. Another critic of monogamy said the only reason there isn't more extramarital sex is lack of opportunity for many people. A 2013 study seemed to confirm this...74% of married men and 68% of married women said they would cheat if the opportunity presented itself—and they knew they wouldn't be caught.

A recent study found that among all modern industrialized nations, the amount of sex in marriage decreases in direct inverse proportion to the number of years of marriage. This was supported by a 2004 ABC poll that found both the quantity and quality of sex declines with the length of marriage. In other words, you likely won't be having sex with your husband or wife anywhere near as often after twenty years of marriage as during your first few years. And forget about those screaming, back scratching, orgasmic sex sessions...sex becomes, for most people, "medicinal." The only consolation is that single people report having even less sex.

Perhaps the worst reason to get married is because the sex is good. The feel-good hormone oxytocin, known sometimes as the "hug drug," literally drugs people into making poor decisions. Oxytocin suppresses the amygdala, reduces fear, and stimulates receptors in the hypothalamus. The hypothalamus releases sex hormones and stimulates a number of physiological reactions.

You know that warm and fuzzy "butterflies in the stomach" feeling? That's oxytocin at work. Oxytocin affects the feel-good neurotransmitters dopamine and norepinephrine that impact the reward centers of your brain. Combine this with testosterone and emotional neediness and before you know it you're getting deep into a relationship that likely will not have long-term prospects for success.

Women feel these effects more strongly than men because they also produce more estrogen, which is sensitive to oxytocin. For men, the neurotransmitter vasopressin affects bonding. While any bodily contact produces oxytocin, it is especially powerful when combined with sexual activity, excitement, and emotional need.

THE HORMONE THAT CLOUDS MEN'S MINDS

Immediately after meeting a beautiful and sexy woman, a man's testosterone can rise temporarily by 30%. The effect of this hormone on the brain's pleasure and decision-making centers can turn an otherwise intelligent man into a stupid, lying cretin. Strip clubs and advertisers know all too well that an aroused man is susceptible to suggestion.

In her book *Do Gentlemen Really Prefer Blondes?* author Jena Pincott quotes MIT behavior economists Dan Ariely and George Lowenstein who say "sexual arousal perversely affects men's decision-making skills and makes them more likely to engage in morally questionable behavior." Women need to realize that men often will do things for sex that they ordinarily wouldn't do when thinking straight.

Pincott makes a strong case for evolutionary biology being the base reason why men and women do almost everything in life, especially mating. Some findings:

- ✓ Men prefer women with symmetrical faces and a certain body type (it shows profundity).
- ✓ Semen from a partner inside their body can make women happy (it's a hormonal thing).

- ✓ Men have more casual sex than women (gotta spread that seed around and perpetuate the species).
- ✓ Your personal scent is as important as looks in attracting a mate (hormones again). And by "personal scent" we mean your natural scent… not cologne or perfume. In one study by the University of California at Berkeley, it was found that the smell of male sweat can spike a woman's arousal by 200% (during Roman times, gladiator sweat was in high demand).
- ✓ People can decide in less than one second if another face is "beautiful" or not (we're all programmed from birth with thousands of years of genetic preferences).
- ✓ When two people fall in love their brain scan patterns are indistinguishable from the clinically insane! (I'm crazy about him!)

It's humbling to think we are all at the mercy of our biological chemistry, but the science behind it is solid. If we've learned anything, it's that relationships—like people—are complicated. Hormones are just one of many powerful factors that influence attraction. In 21st Century society, relationships are beset by a deluge of often conflicting biological and social considerations and input.

MARRYING FOR MONEY

Good old American greed is alive and well—in fact thriving—in marriage. Women have always married men for their money. It's a simple fact embedded in their DNA. If Donald Trump sold vacuum cleaners and lived in a double-wide trailer, does anyone seriously believe he would be married to a gorgeous supermodel? I'm not dissing the Donald—except for the hair. With his forceful personality he would likely be the top vacuum cleaner salesman in his company. But married to a drop-dead beautiful former supermodel? No.

Ramit Sethi, author of *I Will Teach You to Be Rich*, writes in his blog that marrying for love is a deeply held "script" that is a recent development. "Throughout history, marriages were made for strategic alliances, economic gain, familial ties, and a variety of other unromantic reasons." In the 21st Century, when women list what they are looking for in a man, among the top attributes are ambition, success, and a good career...which decoded means "resources."

Women can't be blamed for marrying for money. There is a sizeable amount of science that proves women seek powerful, wealthy men for inbred biological reasons. When humans all lived in caves and hunted mastodons, it was the caveman who possessed the means to feed and protect his children best who cavebabes sought out as a mate. They needed the caveman's resources in order to raise their cavekids, something cavewomen were unable to do due to their poor saber-tooth tiger hunting skills.

If you're shaking your head and saying "This is the 21st century and women are equals with men, so there's no reason to marry for money anymore," just take a trip to your local upscale neighborhood. I live in one of the wealthiest towns in America. On an average day you will see more beautiful, physically fit women here than in a year in a poor neighborhood—or even a typical middle-class neighborhood. Not only are they attractive, these women are smart, educated, and accomplished. The fact that there isn't a single home in my zip code valued at less than a million dollars is no coincidence. Why are there so many top-tier women in Palm Beach, the Hamptons, Santa Barbara, Newport Beach, and Aspen? Because that's where the money is. The most attractive and desirable women flock to these places to be with or meet men with money.

The only difference now is that more men are marrying for money than ever before. As women become more educated (more than half of college students are women), climb the ladder of success, and take the reins of corporate power, their wealth increases as well. It's not unusual anymore for a woman to earn more than her husband. In fact, about 1 in 6 do. And in 2009 (for the first time in history) more women were employed in the United States than men.

For thousands of years men have earned more than women. So it's still a bit unusual for men to marry for money. But change is coming. In one survey of college-age men, a majority said that "potential future earnings" is an important consideration in their choice of a mate. As one man said, "Nobody wants to live poor. Both parties in a marriage have got to contribute. These days it takes two incomes to live well." Another said he would "be happy to be a stay-at-home-dad if he married someone who made substantially more than he did." One of my friends is married to a woman who is the CFO of a large company. She earns more than $400,000 a year. My friend takes care of the kids and home and hasn't worked in years (yeah, I know, raising kids and housework is work...I mean at a salaried job).

Nearly 9 in 10 marriages in India are still arranged by the families. In arranged marriages, money and other resources are a major consideration. How much of a dowry will the bride contribute? How much money will the groom earn in his career? What can the couples' relatives do to help support them? In most cases, love isn't even a consideration. Interestingly, these arranged marriages have a much higher success rate—about 90%—than marriages based on romantic love.

MARRIAGE AS A BUSINESS DEAL

"I don't think I'll get married again. I'll just find a woman I don't like and give her a house." — Lewis Grizzard

Marrying is a legal contract between two parties. In Western countries we've romanticized the deal to fit our notions of why people marry...love. But throughout most of history the "deal" has been based primarily on financial considerations. In modern America we still have marriages based upon money—the "trophy wife" syndrome—and there doesn't appear to be any difference in the success of these marriages compared with those based solely upon love.

If both parties are willing to agree to the terms of the deal, then so be it. I know a man who married a much younger woman, a former cheerleader, who fit every fantasy he ever had about women. His net worth is $55 million. The cheerleader came from a family of modest circumstances. She agreed to be his wife and lover and bear children with him in return for a list of non-negotiable demands. They must always live in a designer home no less than 5,000 square feet in size. They would have a full-time maid. She would never have to work. She would spend at least a month traveling every year—with or without him. A separate checking account in her name would be set up with $100,000 in it at all times.

If he ever cheated on her she would divorce him and he would agree to turn over half their assets with no questions asked. Also, she would keep the house and one of the luxury cars of her choice. The deal was struck, signed, sealed, and filed with the attorneys. They've been "happily" married for 15 years now and have three children.

Obviously, this is an extreme example of marriage as a business deal, but all marriages are a deal—a promissory note, if you will—between two people to abide by certain agreements (with "Til Death Us Do Part" being perhaps the most difficult to uphold). If the couple ever decides to break the agreement, the full legal repercussions of their marriage contract will become immediately apparent. So, before the deal is signed and witnessed and filed legally, a couple should carefully consider each point beforehand.

"TIL DEATH US DO PART" COULD BE 60 YEARS...OR MORE

Today people can expect to live a long life, perhaps eighty years or more. If you marry that hunky guy or that cute hottie at age 20, when your own brain has not fully developed yet, your hormones are raging, and you're just beginning a life in which you'll experience many significant changes, are you sure you'll still feel the same way more than half a century later?

Once the hormonal sexual attraction wears off (and it will), are there other qualities that so attract you that you are willing to commit your life to that person? Really think about this. What if the other person becomes ill? Are you going to stay the course In Sickness and in Health? I know an attractive, hip, successful couple who seemed to have it all...and then she was diagnosed with Multiple Sclerosis. As the disease progressed, the marriage disintegrated. I know a former beauty queen whose face was badly scarred in an auto accident. Her husband loves her more than ever. Could you remain true to your spouse if he/she suffered a stroke and was in a coma? It happens thousands of times every year.

If you've enjoyed, as many people do now, a robust sex life with several partners, will you be willing to Forsake All Others for the rest of your life? Our society is inundated with images of attractive people experiencing fun, romantic, adventurous lives. When you're trying to figure out how to pay the bills, take care of crying babies, deal with cranky in-laws, or going through a job loss, how exciting will you think your life is? How tempting would it be to go out and have some fun? Will you succumb to temptation and have an affair during your marriage, as 22% of men and 14% of women have admitted, according to the *Journal of Marital and Family Therapy* (2013)

Then there are the many other agreements in marriage. Will both of you work? How will you share household chores? Will you have children? If so, how many and when? How will you raise your children? How do you plan on handling finances? Where will you live? How will you worship? Are you a conservative or a liberal? What style will you furnish your home? Really. This was a deal-breaker for one couple I know. He just could not bear her taste for all blue and white furnishings (including blue and white tile on the floors).

And what about sex? Sure, when you first marry it's great and there's lots of it. But, I guarantee you this, in five years...not so much. There's an old saying that if you put a penny in a jar for every time you've had sex in the first year of marriage, and take one out for each time afterward, the jar will never be empty. How hot will you be for that significant other when he/she has gained 40 pounds, as 1/3 of all Americans do? Amazingly, fewer than 1 in 4 couples talk about these things before walking down the aisle.

With all the considerations that go into this complicated deal, it's a wonder anyone gets married at all. The point is this...in many ways marriage is a deal, a contract, much like any other. Be sure you know what you're getting into...and read the fine print.

MARRYING FOR LOVE

One of the best descriptions of Western married love is from Maureen Rice, the editor of the British magazine *Psychologies*. "A love story is still the best story. Divorce numbers may rise, we may slam doors and punch walls, but we go on believing in the power of love as the purpose and meaning of our lives. But every love story is written in chapters—there are the happy ones and the tense ones with cliffhanger endings, there are the wrong turns and obstacles, and the long, dry bits where we're tempted to skip a few pages and think about something more interesting. That's the reality of love. Happy couples are the ones who can turn the page and get back on track to the triumphant closing chapter."

Once the hormonal rush of early love/lust recedes, it must be replaced with the ingredients of lasting love: mutual admiration, shared experiences, friendship, genuine respect, devotion, and understanding. If you can traverse the minefield of temptations, frustrations, child-rearing, and change that characterizes most modern marriages, you may find lasting happiness.

THE BENEFITS OF A GOOD MARRIAGE

"Don't you see that there can't be any doubt in marriage? The whole thing's built on faith." — Cary Grant in the movie *The Awful Truth.*

Perhaps this happiness is one of the reasons why being married can extend your lifespan by as much as 7 years compared to those who remain single all their life, according to a 2006 UCLA study as reported in *The Long Life Equation.*

A good, committed marriage has tremendous benefits. David M. Buss, author of *The Evolution of Desire,* points out that from this unique alliance of two people comes the efficiency of acquiring complementary skills, a division of labor, a sharing of resources, a unified front against mutual enemies, a stable home environment for rearing children, and a more extended kin network. A sound, long-lasting marriage is one of the key building blocks of a successful life. However, to reap these benefits, people must be able to retain the mates they have won.

Those who fail to find a good mate or sustain a successful marriage suffer serious consequences—often affecting the quality of the rest of their lives. Children grow up in a painful, unstable environment. Finances are depleted. Careers are curtailed. Friendships lost. And future marriage prospects are compromised. Divorce is rarely easy or free of damage to either party. So it is to be avoided if at all possible.

MAKING THE RIGHT CHOICE

The average American dates a few dozen people at most. From this small group they will make the selection of a lifetime mate.

- The average man kisses just 21 women romantically before tying the knot for life.
- The average number of women that an American man has sex with before marrying is seven (women have sex with just five men).

It wouldn't be far wrong to say that people often choose a new car more carefully than a lifetime spouse. Yet, nearly every study on the subject indicates that the more experience a person has with the opposite sex before marriage, the happier the marriage will be.

If you were to make a list of all the things you would ideally like to have in a mate it might look something like this list a 36–year old single male friend of mine created. It represents the "perfect" woman to him.

- **Physically attractive.** Blonde hair. About 5 foot five inches. Pretty, large eyes. Slim figure. Nice hands and feet. Good legs. Full breasts. Since men are visually "wired" in their cerebral cortex to desire good–looking women, the common–sense response for women is to be as attractive as possible. Get fit, dress stylishly, learn to use makeup, find a great hairstyle.
- **Intelligence.** Interested in art, books, architecture. Well read. Excellent communication skills. A graduate of a good school. Curious. Smart men like smart women.
- **Emotional intelligence:** The ability to express love with kindness and feeling. Able to handle the ups and downs of life without becoming depressed. Free from off–putting idiosyncrasies. Loves her family. Has many good friends. Men hate "drama queens" and emotionally unstable women.
- **Interests:** Travel to south American and Europe. Bicycling. Tennis. Skiing. Helping poor children. Cooking. Dining out at gourmet restaurants. Fine wines. Health and physical fitness. If you want a man to spend time with you, it pays to have similar interests.
- **Family.** Wants one or two children. Has a great relationship with their own parents and siblings. Likes to celebrate birthdays and special occasions. Most men want a stable family life.
- **Marriage.** She is really "into" being married and does many special things to keep it alive and fresh. Sexually active and adventurous, uninhibited. Most men respond positively to women who demonstrate they really value their relationship.
- **Faith.** The same faith: Roman Catholic. Not overly religious but goes to church one or two times a month. Religious differences are frequently a cause of marital discord.
- **Career.** A creative person in some way—artist, writer or actress. Many men, especially younger men, want a woman with a career of her own.

- **Sensual.** Likes sex and a lot of it. Has a "sexy" persona. Willing to try "adventurous" sex. Guys are typically more "into" sex than women. It's just the way it is.
- **Personality.** Very charming and feminine. A great sense of humor. Steady and mature attitude. Able to relax when necessary and work hard when necessary. Vivacious. Loves dogs. . Is a loyal friend. In the end a man wants a friend who is easy to be with and makes life better because of her presence.

Now imagine a list that is ten times more detailed than this one. Maybe you like full lips. Or, if you're a woman, you prefer men with a mustache or tattoos. Perhaps you want the person to be between the ages of 25 and 35. Or he must be a fireman. What if you could make a list of two or three hundred things you would ideally want in a spouse—and could actually meet that person. Or several dozen people with exactly those attributes.

Out of the tens of millions of potential mates there are statistically several thousand that fit your exact specifications for the perfect mate. You just won't likely meet one. However, the online dating site eHarmony can help you get close to finding your ideal mate. They measure and match prospects using more than 600 variables…yours and your potential matches, including some you aren't aware are factored into the equation. The ability of online sites to help people drill down to exactly what you want is one reason why 1 in 4 marriages now begins at a dating site.

WHAT DO WOMEN AND MEN WANT IN A SPOUSE?

Looks may be what initially attract people to each other. However, as everyone knows, "looks don't last forever." Most people will look dramatically different at 60 than they did at 20 (even movie stars and models). Intuitively, most people know this to be true and account for it when evaluating a potential mate. They also typically don't choose someone who is outside their "norm" for looks. Research shows that people tend to choose a mate who is approximately on the same scale of attractiveness.

So what other attributes do men and women really want in a lifetime partner? You might be surprised.

A SENSE OF HUMOR

"Guys who think a sense of humor is important in a romantic partner...90%" — *Men's Health* magazine, 2009

A good sense of humor ranks near the top of almost every list made to determine what men and women want in a spouse. Don't be afraid to be funny. People are especially attracted to those who have a self-deprecating sense of humor. Humor shows off your humanity and that you aren't afraid to be vulnerable.

Women consistently report that the pick-up lines that work typically involve humor. Men regularly rate a sense of humor as more attractive in women than large breasts, great legs, a nice butt or a beautiful face. Everyone has met the gorgeous girl or handsome hunk with no sense of humor—and no personality. It negates all their other qualities.

So wouldn't it be smart to develop your sense of humor if you want to attract a mate? People will spend a fortune on clothes, cosmetics, working out, and other methods of attracting a mate, when all along a sense of humor would be more effective.

CONFIDENCE

"Our doubts are our traitors, and make us lose the good we oft might win, by fearing to attempt." — William Shakespeare

Asked what attracts them to the opposite sex, both sexes agree that "confidence" and a "self-assured" personality are at the top of the list.

Kent, a man in his early thirties said, "I've always been attracted to women who are confident in themselves. Two women who are equally beautiful can walk into a room. One is timid and shy, avoids looking anyone in the eyes and seems slightly fearful of the people in the room. The other strides in like she owns the place, head high, a cool smile on her face. That's the one I'm instantly attracted to."

"I like a man with a plan," said Katie. "He's got a solid idea of what he wants and how he's going to get it. That kind of confidence is very sexy."

Sara, a slim, pretty blonde in her early twenties said, "My dad was my rock. He always made me feel safe. I like that feeling and want it in a man. It's surprising how many men I meet are momma's boys or haven't grown up yet."

Another beautiful young woman, Emma, said, "My boyfriend's friends all wonder how he ended up with me. Roger isn't especially good-looking or talented. He isn't even as tall as me. But he knows who he is and isn't afraid of life. His take-charge attitude is a real turn-on. I like a man who acts like a man." Actress Vivica Fox said, "A great figure or physique is nice, but it's self-confidence that makes someone sexy."

Men like confident women too. My friend Jim told me that what attracted him to his wife first was her incredible self-assured personality. "There isn't anything she is afraid to do," he said. "That's very cool."

Confidence comes from mastery...being good at what you do. And belief in yourself. No less than president Theodore Roosevelt said, "Believe you can and you're halfway there."

SOLID VALUES

Values that rank highly in a potential mate include:

- ✓ Honesty.
- ✓ Responsibility.
- ✓ Intelligence.
- ✓ Supportiveness.
- ✓ Cheerfulness.
- ✓ Affectionate.
- ✓ Good manners.
- ✓ Unselfishness.
- ✓ Being capable.
- ✓ Appreciation.
- ✓ Kindness.

Other attributes that women and men say they find attractive include: good grooming/hygiene, assertiveness, a fit body, a good job, charming personality, respected by others, high self-esteem, a good conversationalist, an expressive face, positive attitude and zest for life, self-reliant and resourcefulness, smell good, and sexual prowess.

THE DEAL-BREAKERS

A poll of 1,500 people taken by big data company GLK Roper, commissioned by Divorce360, www.divorce360.com found that verbal or physical abuse was cited by more than a third of divorcing couples as a major cause of the break-up. Other oft-cited "deal-breakers" are addictions, adultery, and apathy. While adultery can be overcome, harmful addictions and physical abuse are grounds for immediate termination of the relationship. Indifference is a factor in a large percentage of divorces. No one should live in a marriage with a spouse who is disconnected emotionally. It's demeaning and humiliating.

MARRIAGE ISN'T FOR EVERYONE

Marriage isn't for everyone. In the 21st Century, with its myriad opportunities for friendship and companionship, near equality for women, and the endless number of interesting activities, living by oneself is a valid choice...for the first time in history.

There are nearly 102 million single people over the age of 18 in America...44% of the population, according to U.S. Census Bureau (2011). In 1950, according to Eric Klinenberg, author of *Going Solo*, the figure was just 22%. Fully 62% of single Americans have never married, 24% are divorced, and 15% are widowed. More than half (55%) are not seeking a relationship, according to a 2005 survey by Pew Research Center.

- More than 1 in 4 (27%) of all households are single people living alone...up from 17% in 1970, according to 2013 Census Bureau data."
- There are 88 single men for every 100 single women.
- Nearly 10 million single mothers and 2 million single fathers live with their children.

Committed single-life people point to the "limitless opportunities" their lifestyle affords, the ability to live on your own terms, and the "freedom" from the often stifling responsibilities of marriage as their reasons to go it alone in life. Modern life provides more opportunity to live on your own terms...if you think for yourself and break free from the ingrained restrictions of tradition, habit, and societal expectations.

DIVORCE

"I don't think marriages break up because of what you do to each other; they break up because of what you must become in order to stay in them." — Carol Matthau

Divorce is like a train wreck in your life. Nothing will ever be the same afterward. And if you have kids, their lives will never be the same. Divorce is quite simply one of the most devastating events in life…and to be avoided at all cost.

- Women marry believing their husbands will change. Men marry believing their wives will not change. Both are wrong.

The popular estimate is that almost half of marriages eventually end in divorce. In reality, no one actually knows…it's likely somewhere between 40% and 50%, according to marriage scholar and therapist Dr. William H. Doherty.

A snapshot of divorce:

- Every year there are nearly a million divorces in America—892,000 in 2011.
- An estimated 60% to 67% of second marriages fail.
- An estimated 70% to 73% of third marriages fail.
- Divorce in America costs $33.3 billion annually.
- Children of divorce are 50% more likely to divorce than children with intact parents.
- The average divorce costs $18,000.
- 30% of American divorces involve high conflict.
- 60% of American divorces involve medium to high conflict.
- Nearly 3 out of 4 Americans believe marriage should be a lifelong commitment.
- Divorced people have higher suicide rates than married, unmarried or widowed people.
- 40% of divorced women and 46% of divorced men later say it was the wrong decision.

Fatherless homes account for:

✓ 63% of youth suicides.

✓ 90% of homeless/runaway children.

✓ 85% of children with behavioral problems.

- ✓ 71% of school dropouts.
- ✓ 85% of youths in prison.
- ✓ 50%+ of teen mothers.
- ✓ Children in single parent families are twice as likely to develop serious psychiatric problems and addictions later in life.

Clearly, divorce carries heavy costs—emotionally and financially.

Sources: Center for Disease Control, National Vital Statistics Report, 2002, Institute of American Values, 2002, *DivorceMagazine.com*, 2003, Utah University Study "Consequences of Divorce", 2003, *The Lancet Medical Journal*, London, 2003.

MACRO FACTORS OF DIVORCE

The major factors associated with a high risk of divorce include:

1. Young age. 59% of marriages by couples under the age of 18 are doomed to fail.
2. Less education results in a higher divorce rate.
3. Less income translates to a higher probability of divorce.
4. Premarital childbearing. In the U.S., 1/3 of children are born to parents who are not married.
5. Parents' divorce. If you experienced a divorce as a child, your risk doubles. If your spouse also came from a divorced family, your risk more than triples.

"If you hire a divorce lawyer today, there's a good chance you will hire a bankruptcy lawyer within two or three years." — Gene Meyer

The two major causes of bankruptcy? Health problems. And divorce. A limited contested divorce can run from $15,000 to as much as $250,000 or more. And while a mediated divorce can cost 75% less, your finances will still likely take a serious hit. Actor Mel Gibson's divorce cost him a whopping $425 million.

Divorce can wreak havoc in your life. It tears families apart and affects everyone, especially the children. But it also can ruin your finances for years—even decades. Getting back on your feet financially may be a long arduous uphill battle. Your life may never be the same after divorce.

Dr. Thomas J. Stanley, author of *The Millionaire Mind*, points out that 92% of the millionaire households in America are composed of a married couple, and these millionaire couples have less than 1/3 the divorce rate of non-millionaire couples. A long, happy marriage is a critical key to a successful life.

THE "GOOD" DIVORCE

"Ah yes, divorce...from the Latin word meaning to rip a man's genitals out through his wallet." — Robin Williams

The devastation caused by a "bad" divorce is so severe that both parties ought to do everything possible to split up amicably. Chicago divorce attorney J. Richard Kulerski, author of the *Divorce Buddy System,* says that nearly all his clients tell him:

- I want what is best for the kids.
- I only want what is fair.
- I don't want to hurt my spouse.
- I want to avoid a court battle and all the legendary pandemonium.
- I don't want the divorce to drag on forever.
- I definitely don't want it to cost an arm and a leg.

Then they proceed to eviscerate each other, causing irreparable damage. A 2012 survey of therapists found that only 25% of divorces are amicable. Even if you don't get everything you want in a divorce, you don't want to sink your own ship. Bite your lip and compromise.

"There is nothing worse, for most children, than for their parents to denigrate each other." — *Sir Nicholas Scott*

WHY DO PEOPLE DIVORCE? FOLLOW THE MONEY

"Marriage is the chief cause of divorce." — Groucho Marx

The single biggest "practical" reason marriages fail are money problems. Lack of enough money causes enormous stress in a relationship. Too much money comes with its own unique set of problems. Different money styles—spendthrifts married to tightwads, for example—can be a constant source of friction.

Couples who are in financial distress usually cannot enjoy their life together. Everything becomes challenging and stressful. The stress may affect their sleep, health, and desire to make love. Their lives take on a negative focus. Often couples blame each other for their financial predicament. "If I was single and didn't have these selfish, costly kids I could be enjoying life, having great sex, driving a new sports car, and taking exotic foreign vacations." Or "if I hadn't married this loser I could have landed Bob, live in a big house and be the wife of a powerful, successful brain surgeon—–maybe even have an exciting career of my own."

SEX

Sex is either the glue that holds a marriage together during the tough times…or the wedge that drives couples apart. Most marriages begin with some heat and fire sexually. Inevitably this lessens over time.

- 70% of men surveyed report that they wish their wives were more sexually adventurous. Source: *Men's Health*, 2014 survey.

A 2012 survey of counseling professionals found that 74% agree that top predictors of divorce are kids, money, and/or sex, according to relationship site YourTango.com. Personal sexual preferences are so wide-ranging that it's rare for a couple to be completely in sync with each other. Sometimes a couple will expand each other's sexual repertoire. But too often one person in the relationship is rigidly attached to what they like and don't like. And this can lead to sexual frustration…and infidelity.

INFIDELITY

Peggy Vaughan, author of *The Monogamy Myth,* claims that 66% of men and 40% of women will cheat at some time during their marriage. And by "cheating" we mean getting naked with someone other than your spouse. Janis Abrams Spring, author of *After the Affair,* says that infidelity now affects 1 in 2.7 couples. The general consensus of most surveys indicates that 1 in 4 men and 1 in 6 women will have extramarital sex at least once during their marriage.

People commit adultery for many reasons. Excitement. Boredom. Lack of sex at home. Variety. Opportunity. Whatever the reason, it seldom ends well. One if four adulteries are discovered. Often the marriage has deteriorated so badly by this point that the cheating spouse actually wants to be found out. It's a way of forcing the inevitable. Only 20% of these marriages survive, even with counseling or therapy.

WOMEN CHEAT TOO

"The trouble with some women is that they get all excited about nothing—and then they marry him." — Cher

There's evidence that cheating by women is increasing. According to Dr. David Holmes, a psychologist at Manchester Metropolitan University, "women are having more affairs than ever." He estimates the figure at about 15%. The biggest difference is that women are much better at keeping their affairs secret than men...and other things. According to a 2006 survey, between 1.7% and 3.3% of fathers are unknowingly raising children fathered by another man.

In *Daring Wives: Insight into Women's Desires for Extramarital Affairs*, author Frances Cohen Praver, Ph.D., reports that many women have affairs because they feel trapped, bored, powerless, and lonely in their marriages. Like many men, they feel the quantity and quality of the sex in their relationship has seriously declined. But it's also often about the lack of passion in their relationship.

Ask.men.com listed the Top 10 Reasons Why Women Cheat:

1. Not enough sex.
2. Being the "bad" girl.
3. Self–esteem.
4. Revenge.
5. Lack of intimacy.
6. Feeling neglected, ignored, or underappreciated.

7. Your emotional withdrawal.
8. Bedroom boredom...monotonous sex.
9. Exit strategy...instead of breaking up with you, she cheats.
10. Revenge for your cheating.

These aren't exclusively female reasons for cheating, men cite many of the same reasons.

IRRECONCILABLE DIFFERENCES

"Irreconcilable differences" is code for changing priorities in life. As people mature they sometimes grow in different directions that are unacceptable to their spouse..."We just grew apart." This could be a change in religious beliefs or a new career direction...or simply a new life philosophy. Frequently the reason is one spouse spending more time away from the other...absence doesn't always make the heart grow fonder, frequently it's "out of sight, out of mind."

MENTAL HEALTH AND MARITAL HAPPINESS

Satisfaction in marriage is affected by the mental health of both spouses, according to a study in the October, 2005, *Journal of Consulting and Clinical Psychology*. The study involved 744 married couples and found that the level of anxiety and depression of each spouse was a reliable predictor of their own satisfaction with their spouse, with depression having a greater affect than anxiety (perhaps because most people are anxious). Depressed people often have a negative world view that includes marriage and their spouse.

If you, or a spouse, are one of the 1 in 6 Americans with a mental health problem, you need to get help. Common mental illnesses like depression, schizophrenia, and bi-polar disorder can be treated successfully.

Life Rules: Don't rush into relationships. Check a potential mate's background and family. Don't allow lust to cloud your thinking. Consider dating through online sites to find compatible matches. Discuss important issues in advance. Avoid divorce at all cost.

Further reading:

➢ ***Men are from Mars, Women are from Venus*** by John Grey.

- ***The Relationship Handbook*** by George Pransky.
- ***Relationship Rescue: A Seven–Step Strategy for Reconnecting with Your Partner*** by Dr. Phil McGraw.
- ***Relationships 101*** by John C. Maxwell.
- ***The Seven Principles for Making Marriage Work: A Practical Guide from the Country's Foremost Relationship Expert*** and ***Why Marriages Succeed or Fail: And How You Can Make Yours Last*** by John Gottman.
- ***Love Will Find You: 9 Magnets to Bring You and Your Soulmate Together*** by Kathryn Alice.
- ***Get the Guy: Learn Secrets of the Male Mind to Find the Man You Want*** and the ***Love You Deserve*** by Matthew Hussey.
- ***The Little Black Book of Red Flags: Relationship Warning Signs You Totally Spotted…But Chose to Ignore*** by Natasha Burton, Julie Fishman, and Meagan McCrary.

Online:

www.Lovepanky.com A guide to better love and relationships for both men and women.

www.JoyOfRomance.com Joy Nordenstrom blogs about how to bring romance into your life.

www.UnderstandMenNow.com Jonathon Aslay's dating and relationship coaching for women.

www.DrWendyWalsh.com The blog for *CNN's* resident dating and relationship expert.

www.DatingAdvice.com Dating tips for men and women, including gay and lesbian.

www.DavidWygant.com Dating tips for guys. Author of *5 Ways to Impress Women.*

www.DrKarenRuskin.com A range of marital, relationship, and family topics.

www.Lifescript.com Relationship site for women.

www.drtara.com Dr. Tara Fields on personal and relationship issues.

CHAPTER 5
EDUCATION

THE SMART DECISION

"If a man empties his purse into his head, no man can take it away from him. An investment in knowledge always pays the best dividends." — Benjamin Franklin

For most people, a quality education is the key to a better life. Of course, there are many examples of people with little education, who dropped out of high school or college, and went on to become wealthy and successful. Bill Gates, the world's wealthiest individual, is a college drop–out. Brad Pitt is a college drop–out. Sam Walton had only a high school diploma. But for most people more education translates into more money. A lot more money.

HOW TO MAKE A MILLION DOLLARS

"Who so neglects learning in his youth, loses the past and is dead for the future." — Euripides

Even with the rising cost of education, it's still a very good investment over the long run. The typical college graduate will earn 75% more than the average high school graduate. The difference adds up to about a million dollars more in earnings over a lifetime. A million dollars makes a big impact in the overall quality of life. It translates to better schools for your children, a better and safer neighborhood, interesting travel, business opportunities, a healthier lifestyle, and a longer life.

An advanced degree has an even more dramatic impact on wealth creation. People with advanced or professional degrees increase their average total lifetime earnings by as much as $2 million. A million dollars doesn't go as far as it once did, but just think for a moment what you could do with that much money. The approximately $55,000 the average public college education costs begins to look like a pretty smart investment (tuition, room/board, books for 2010–11).

According to 2012 U.S. Department of Labor statistics, here's how much you can expect to earn at various educational levels...and the percent who were unemployed.

Median Weekly Earnings by Educational Level		**Unemployment Rate (%)**
Less than high school diploma	$ 471	12.4
High school diploma	$ 652	8.3
Some college (no degree)	$ 727	7.7
Associate degree (two years)	$ 785	6.2
Bachelor's degree	$1,066	4.5
Master's degree	$1,300	3.5
Doctorate degree	$1,624	2.5
Professional degree	$1,735	2.1

If you're fortunate enough to attend a top–tier private school (just 0.4% of all students)your average earnings will be 20% higher, according to a study of 1980 alumni...although other studies conducted for more than two decades indicate that students' SAT scores are more predictive of how successful they will eventually be. Clearly, education equals more income and less chance of being unemployed.

"The direction in which education starts a man will determine his future life." — Plato

Most people can live comfortably on nearly $100,000 a year (residents of San Francisco or New York might disagree). But imagine living on just $21,600 or $30,800 or even $35,600. Not a pretty picture, is it? Yet, more than 1 out of 3 Americans (37%) fall into one of these average U.S. household earnings categories.

You'll find these people in jobs working at fast food outlets, as security guards or driving delivery trucks. While these are all necessary, respectable jobs they aren't aspirational jobs. No one sets out in life to work at a minimum wage job in a fast food restaurant. As a child no one says "I can't wait to grow up to drive a bus someday." People take these jobs because they have no other choice. They are then forced to live in homes they can barely afford—or worse. An estimated 20 million Americans live in mobile homes, according to the Census Bureau (2013).

These are the people who can't afford health care—and live shorter lives as a result. These are the people who suffer from more depression, whose children continue the cycle of poverty because their parents can't afford a good education for them, who end up in prison at six times the rate of more educated people.

- Often the under–educated live lives of "quiet desperation" just managing to survive from one week to the next...76% of Americans, according Bankrate.com (2013).

"Education is the best provision for old age." — Aristotle

If money isn't reason enough to go to school and stay there as long as possible, consider that the more education you get the longer you'll live. Every year of additional schooling adds approximately a half year of life. That may not make a great impression on a person when they're 20, but it's guaranteed to assume an inordinate amount of importance at, say, 70 or 80.

And not only are you likely to live longer, you'll probably live a healthier life too. The rates of most major diseases—from heart disease to cancer—drop as education rises. There are many reasons for this, including better nutrition, good health care, safer neighborhoods, and less dangerous work.

"Only the educated are free." — Epictetus

Getting an education isn't always easy. The costs keep rising each year faster than inflation, rising 6% to 11% annually in recent years. The average cost in 2013 was $15,000 to attend a public college, according to the College Board. The cost for the average private school was about double that much.

For many Americans the cost of an education seems an impossible hurdle to overcome. But if someone is truly motivated to get a good education there are many sources for financial aid. In fact, the amount of financial aid available is rising. In 2012, total aid to students rose to $185 billion dollars. That's right—billions.

Interestingly, there is so much financial assistance that even affluent families are able to qualify for it. Nearly half the families with household incomes of $80,000 or more qualify for aid. The more expensive the college the greater the amount will be awarded, especially if there is more than one child from a family attending college at the same time.

Aid is awarded for a wide variety of reasons ranging from scholastic aptitude to being a member of the Zuni tribe of Native Americans. It's safe to say that if you dig deep enough you can find a source of financial assistance to pay for an education. This is true for college students of all ages...even seniors.

Educational aid comes in many forms: tax benefits, Federal work study programs, Federal loans, institutional grants, state grants, federal grants, and even colleges themselves. Some aid also comes from private foundations and scholarships. Other sources include corporations, labor unions, credit unions, religious organizations, and interest groups ranging from the local Rotary Club to major sports teams.

YOUR TAX DOLLARS AT WORK

Your first stop on the way to financial aid should be the U.S. government. A variety of aid programs exist to help students in need. Go to www.studentaid.ed.gov first. Access the Federal Student Financial Aid Information Center. You can also call the U.S. Department of Education at 1-800-4FED-AID. Obtain a copy of their guide to federal aid called *The Student Guide.*

1.5 MILLION SCHOLARSHIPS

There are more than a million scholarships (1.5 million) available for everyone, whether you are a college freshman, Ph.D. candidate, or a returning adult. Scholarships are available for both merit and needs-based students, even at Ivy League schools such as Harvard and Yale. Likewise, if you want to attend a trade school to learn how to drive a truck, operate high-tech manufacturing equipment, or be a dental hygienist, there are scholarships for all these professions too.

Scholarships are offered for a wide range of reasons. There are scholarships for golf, rowing, and water polo. If you worked on your high school newspaper there are a long list of scholarships. If you were active in charitable or service organizations, there are thousands of scholarships from local and national organizations, including Dollars for Scholars, Kohl Cares, and Discover Scholarship Program. Government agencies such as VISTA and AmeriCorps offer scholarships. Industry groups from aviation to the auto industry provide funds for students.

The point is this...if you need money to go to college you can likely find it if you search for it.

Other places to begin searching include Fastweb www.fastweb.com. Here you'll find a scholarship matching service, as well as expert advice on financial aid. Another site that can help is Scholarships.com www.scholarships.com. You'll find links to scholarship providers, 500 videos describing various career subjects, and course outlines. From here you can also link to www.studentaid.ed.gov and www.college.gov.

CONSIDER STUDYING OVERSEAS

Another option is attending a university overseas. About 50,000 Americans are enrolled full-time at foreign schools. It frequently costs less to attend a prestigious school in Great Britain, France or Singapore than in the United States, according to Reuters. Plus, there's the added cachet of having an Oxford or Sorbonne degree. It's also an ideal way to become fluent in a language, an increasingly valuable asset in our global economy.

OTHER WAYS TO SAVE FOR COLLEGE

As the trillion-dollar student loan crisis has demonstrated, if there is any way you can avoid going into debt to pay for your education...do so. Starting life with debt will cripple your ability to move forward. This is especially true in the uncertain and rapidly changing 21st Century.

The most prevalent way to pay for college (after parents) is paying for it by working while attending school. Nearly 1 in 4 (23%) students work at least 20 hours a week while attending college. Here are some other ways to keep costs down:

1. Stay in state. The cost difference between out-of-state and in-state can be substantial.
2. Consider community college.
3. Keep your nose to the grindstone. Don't let partying or your job keep you from your studies. An extra semester or two can increase your costs substantially.
4. Stick to a personal budget. Don't get sucked in by offers from credit card companies that may result in racking up debts you can't pay.
5. Go online to find textbooks for less.
6. Learn about all the student discounts you are entitled to use.

TOP TIER SCHOOLS

Don't let anyone fool you into thinking that an education from a top-tier school is no different from a state college or university. A quick look at the educational background of America's CEOs, political leaders, and successful entrepreneurs shows that a Harvard, Yale, Princeton, MIT, Stanford or Vassar pedigree is a ticket to the top.

TOP SCHOOLS FOR FORTUNE 100 CEOS

1. Harvard
2. Cornell
3. University of Pennsylvania
4. Massachusetts Institute of Technology
5. Northwestern
6. Stanford
7. Yale
8. Columbia

9. Princeton
10. Southern Methodist University

Source: *Business Insider* (2013)

Unfortunately, most Americans are priced out of these schools, where an education often costs as much as a quarter million dollars for a Bachelor and Masters degree. However, most top-tier schools have enrollment goals that include a significant amount of diversity and merit-based students. Financial aid to meet these goals is available. So don't rule out an Ivy League or Seven Sisters education just because you're family isn't wealthy.

One of the benefits of going to a top tier school are the people you meet. As you will learn, success in life is largely dependent upon who you know. Every opportunity you will ever have will involve the support or cooperation of others. At top-tier schools you will meet more people who can open up doors for you after you graduate. If your college roommate's father is the CEO of IBM or the Secretary of Defense, you can bet that contact is more valuable than any you will find at a local community college. Top schools enable you to get a toehold into the elite circles that pretty much run the world.

IF YOU PLAN ON JUST GETTING A JOB, BE SURE TO TAKE THESE COURSES

"Some people 'go' through life and others 'grow' through life."
— Robert Holden, Ph.D.

For college grads with "light" majors...Liberal Arts, English, Philosophy... the increase in starting pay over a 2-year Associate degree is negligible. However, according to research published in *Forbes* magazine, just taking a few key courses can significantly increase your chance of landing a good job that leads to a lucrative career.

1. Economics, especially macroeconomics.
2. Statistics.
3. Computer programming, as long as it's something like Java, Python, C++ or Ruby on Rails

4. Calculus.
5. Communications.
6. Management and/or Financial Planning.

These courses provide useful knowledge that increase a grad's value. They show the prospective employer that the person who wants to work for them isn't afraid to take the harder courses. If in an interview you can say, "I love medieval history, but I can also take a derivative, calculate a standard deviation, and project an organization's costs two years out," the hiring manager will take notice and separate you from the dozens of other applicants.

A college education shouldn't be just a holding pattern in life during which you party and hang out for four years. As many grads are discovering, it's what you can offer to an employer that will help drive the success of their business that counts. While you are becoming an educated person, don't forget to learn some skills that are actually usable.

BUT WHAT IF I WANT TO BE A PLUMBER?

If you want to be a plumber or electrician or mechanic or computer repair technician, then do it. Despite our parents' insistence on a college education, it isn't necessary or even required to be a success. Education doesn't have to mean formal college education. The "trades" are a perfectly viable career path in the 21st Century, perhaps a preferred career path for most people.

"University administrators are the equivalent of subprime mortgage brokers selling you a story that you should go into debt massively, that it's not a consumption decision, it's an investment decision. Actually, no, it's a bad consumption decision." — Peter Thiel

American schools churn out millions of college grads, most with minimal usable skills, into the worst job market in decades…and with more than $26,000 in average student debt. The days of cushy white-collar jobs in middle management are fast waning. It's why there are so many grads serving coffee at Starbucks or working at $10 an hour jobs at Barnes & Noble. At the same time hundreds of thousands of skilled jobs go begging. At any given time there are about 3 million unfilled jobs in the U.S.

There is nothing wrong with pursuing a "blue collar" job—whatever that means in today's high-tech world. A trained Mercedes-Benz mechanic can make as much as $150,000 a year. A computer repair specialist or systems analyst can earn even more. Careers based upon job functions that are essential and specialized are needed more today than ever, while "white collar" jobs are increasingly being seen as expendable (not great news for the hordes of MBA graduates flooding the job market).

DOCTOR OR MECHANIC?

But what about financial success?

Well, let's look at the numbers. For argument sake, we'll compare an auto mechanic's career to that of a family physician. Let's say the Mercedes mechanic begins his career after graduating from high school. He or she will begin earning an income immediately while training on the job. By age 21 the mechanic will likely be earning about $60,000 a year. If the mechanic is smart he/she will save and put aside $10,000 annually in a safe, compoundable investment. Invest in an IRA early and consistently and it will likely grow to more than $1 million by age 60. This investment alone would cover much of the mechanic's retirement costs.

The future doctor is busy studying at college—and also racking up student loans. He/she has little or no income (there's no time for a job with the workload a pre-med student carries). After graduation comes medical school. Med school costs are astronomical and can easily exceed $200,000 over four years.

Meanwhile our mechanic has risen to the rank of Master Mechanic and is earning close to $100,000 a year by age 28. He has purchased a home and added a low-fee index stock fund with a balance of domestic and international stocks to his portfolio.

The mechanic takes a few thousand from savings and travels to Europe with his new wife. They visit Paris, Switzerland, and Germany. While in Germany they visit the Mercedes-Benz factory and museum in Sindelfingen. They are treated to a sumptuous lunch by the Mercedes staff. It's an experience that will help contribute to the mechanic's appreciation and understanding of Mercedes-Benz products.

After four grueling years of medical school our physician-to-be enters an even tougher stage of education—internship. For three or four years the intern works 70–hour weeks training to be a qualified physician, arriving home (a small apartment) exhausted each night. There is little time for any kind of social life. The internist takes out more loans to cover expenses while in training.

At age 32 our mechanic receives an offer from another mechanic to become partners in their own independent German car service and repair facility. With money from savings the partners open Krauthaus German Auto Repair near an upscale neighborhood. The demand for their expert service helps propel our mechanic's income to a new level. Even with the overhead costs, our mechanic is now able to take home $125,000 a year.

The mechanic is now earning more than a million dollars every decade. By age 35 he has already been working, accumulating income, building investments, and living a life without major debts (other than a home mortgage). He works five days a week from 8am to 5pm and takes three–week vacations every year with his family.

Our physician is finally setting up his practice (which involves incurring more debt), paying off more than $200,000 in student loans, and devoting 70 hours a week to his job. He's making $150,000 a year and will eventually earn $300,000 annually.

By age 60 both the mechanic and the doctor have arrived at about the same place in life financially. However, the mechanic decides to sell his share of Krauthaus German Auto Repair to his partner for $700,000. Physicians don't often sell their practice because they *are* their practice. If he's become part of a physician group he may sell out his interest and could realize as much from the sale as the mechanic did from selling his share of the business.

The point is not that one path is better than the other, but that either path is viable. Just because you don't acquire a college education or advanced degree does not mean you cannot be successful and fulfilled in your career. In *The College Myth* by Gene Kelly, he points out that many people with high incomes "had a head start making and investing money while doctors and lawyers spent many years in college and then spent the next several years paying off student loans." This is more true now than ever before.

So, why are the lifetime income disparities between high school grads and college grads so great? Because many of those who do not attend college also do not engage in any meaningful work. They are the "lost" percentage of our population, people with little education and no usable career skills. As the world becomes more sophisticated and automated, greater skills are required…and menial jobs become even less important. This trend will only accelerate in the future.

ONGOING EDUCATION

A college education is easy to come by, limited in its ability to truly educate, and largely wasted by those who get a degree. It's becoming a half–way house for teenagers where they can party (72% drink illegally/40% binge drink), away from the civilizing influence of their parents. Many students put in just enough effort to obtain the price of entry (the diploma) into a supposedly receptive work force and lucrative job.

Guess what? The unemployment rate right now is 50% higher for 20 - 26–year olds than the rest of the population. Why? Because few recent grads can add any real value to a company at a time when every new hire is being scrutinized carefully and expected to hit the ground running. Most recent grads haven't learned anything that is truly useful.

But it gets worse. Here's an astounding fact…1 in 3 college grads have not read a book in the past 12 months (fiction), according to the National Endowment for the Arts *Reading at Risk* report (2002). Read that sentence again and then tell me that these people are educated. Education isn't simply having a college diploma; it's an attitude, a belief in the value of learning.

"Formal education will make you a living, self–education will make you a fortune." — Jim Rohn

However, in America ignorance is often celebrated. Millions of people waste hundreds of millions of hours watching Swamp People, Redneck Island, Jersey Shore, Gator Boys, Honey Boo Boo and other equally idiotic TV programs. Americans are woefully unknowledgeable.

- ✓ Only 1 in 3 college grads can name all three branches of government.
- ✓ Just 1 in 16 people can find Pakistan on a globe if the countries aren't identified.
- ✓ This year, 1.2 million will drop out of high school, making themselves ineligible for 90% of jobs.

- ✓ 80% of U.S. families did not read or buy a book in the last year.
- ✓ 70% of U.S. adults have not been in a bookstore in the last five years.
- ✓ 1 in 7 Americans is illiterate, according to the U.S. Education Department.

If you expect to succeed in the highly competitive and ever-changing world of the 21st Century you can't stop educating yourself when you graduate from school.

- As author F. Scott Fitzgerald wrote in *The Great Gatsby*, don't be "one of those men who reach such an acute limited excellence at twenty-one that everything afterward savors of anti-climax."

A college degree is simply your launch pad, the rest of your life is the rocket.

LEARNING FOR LIFE

"Anyone who stops learning is old. Anyone who keeps learning is young. The greatest thing in life is to keep your mind young." — Henry Ford

The pace of change is exponentially faster every year. In order to adapt successfully to constant change it's important to continually update your knowledge and skills. To do this you must become an autodidact—a self-teacher. Some of the most successful people of all time were autodidacts, including Da Vinci, Benjamin Franklin, Henry Ford, Woody Allen, Maya Angelou, Walter Cronkite, Richard Branson, Ernest Hemingway, Tom Hanks, Abraham Lincoln, Walt Disney, Mark Twain, Bruce Willis, Walt Whitman, and Leo Tolstoy.

- As Brian Tracy has said, "Those people who develop the ability to continuously acquire new and better forms of knowledge that they can apply to their work and to their lives will be the movers and shakers in our society."

If there's one thing you can count on more than ever it's that change will happen—and happen more rapidly. Some experts estimate that one in five jobs that freshmen entering college will be competing for when they graduate doesn't exist now. So colleges are educating people for jobs with qualifications no one can even guess at today.

LIFE-LONG EDUCATION IS THE NEW NORM FOR SUCCESS

"I never let schooling get in the way of my education." — Mark Twain

In order to keep up with the change around you, it isn't enough to take a course or read a few books now and then. What's required is a semi-formal, long-term, structured course of study—similar to attending a real university. Life-long self-directed learning is more important in the 21st century than ever.

- In August 2012, Thomas Friedman, author of *The World is Flat*, wrote in the New York Times, "The truth is if you want a career that will lead to a decent life today you have to work harder, regularly reinvent yourself, obtain at least some form of post-secondary education, make sure you are engaged in lifelong learning, and play by the rules."

In the 21st Century, to thrive (and not just survive) you'll need to adapt to the macro changes that are affecting our very way of life. And that requires continuous retooling through an ongoing program of education and invention.

THE PLAN FOR LIFE YOUNIVERSITY...AN ONGOING EDUCATION FOR YOU, BY YOU

"Make the most of yourself, for that is all there is of you."
— Ralph Waldo Emerson

The Plan for Life Youniversity is your personal ongoing education plan for life.

The Plan for Life Youniversity is much like a normal school. You have courses of study and a curriculum. Homework. Books. Lectures. Even a Homecoming weekend, if you like. If you have enough space where you live, you might even want to set up one room as your classroom. Put up a blackboard for notes or brainstorming ideas. Install a desk for your computer and a bookcase for your course books. All the educational tools you would normally need in a regular school you will need in your Plan for Life Youniversity.

You can structure your Plan for Life Youniversity so that it adapts to changes in your life. When you have more time, add more study programs. If your interests or career opportunities change, change your curriculum. If your life has become so full that 24 hours doesn't seem to be enough time to get everything you need to do each day, cut back to just one core study program.

It's even possible to set it up so that you have fellow students to share the experience with—just like in a real college setting. Invite some friends to participate in their own Plan for Life Youniversity and plan it so that you study together...either online or in person. Research shows that if you study with a friend you'll learn more.

You might go so far as to give your Plan for Life Youniversity a name. In my case, Wentworth University sounds almost Ivy League. Or get creative and name your Plan for Life Youniversity something like Destination College or Success University or The University of Life Evolvement. It's your Plan for Life Youniversity, so name it whatever you want. If you really want to take this to the limit, have a sweatshirt or coffee cup printed up with your Plan for Life Youniversity name on it. www.customink.com www.zazzle.com www.vistaprint.com www.cafepress.com Make your Plan for Life Younuversity a real and tangible part of your life.

If you enroll in the extended education programs at your local university, or sit in on classes, you can align yourself with that school. Attend some on-campus events or go to the football games. For many people this may make their Plan for Life Youniversity seem more connected to traditional education.

An affiliation with a local college can reap many rewards over the years. One person I know felt comfortable enough at UCLA to begin teaching extended education classes, eventually enroll in a Masters program, and after retiring from a career as a writer, he was admitted as a full-time professor of creative writing at the school.

Resources posted throughout this book can help you create your own customized ongoing education program. You can find additional resources at our blogsite www.APlanForLife.com, our Facebook page or at LinkedIn, Pinterest, You Tube, and Twitter (@APlanForLife) under A Plan for Life.

CREATING YOUR PLAN FOR LIFE YOUNIVERSITY COURSE OF STUDY

"You need to be continually learning."
— Jim Collins, author of *From Good to Great* and *Built to Last*

What are the major areas of your life that you want to improve or expand? Are these professional or personal? Or a combination of the two? If you are in business for yourself do you want to learn more about accounting? Would knowing how to use QuikBooks be valuable to your business? How about dealing with employees? Or knowing more about the taxes small businesses must pay and how to minimize that burden? Would a course in public speaking, making presentations, or writing business correspondence improve your chances for upward movement in your career? Any of these, and many more, can be part of your curriculum.

What about personal improvement? Would you like to know about nutrition? Have you always wanted to speak a second language? Would you like to learn how to play an instrument? Or be knowledgeable about wines? Or have a deeper understanding of history? What are the things, both personal and professional, that will improve your life—or that you always wanted to know more about?

Here are a few categories to consider as you plan your own Plan for Life Youniversity curriculum.

COURSES

- ✓ Social media.
- ✓ Business.
- ✓ Literature.
- ✓ Nutrition/Fitness.
- ✓ Computer skills.
- ✓ Finance.
- ✓ Law.
- ✓ Art.
- ✓ Music.
- ✓ Language.
- ✓ Practical arts.
- ✓ Real estate.
- ✓ History.
- ✓ Interior design.

WENTWORTH PLAN FOR LIFE YOUNIVERSITY

I've created Wentworth Plan for Life Youniversity as closely to look like a real university as possible, given the limitations of my "campus"...my home. My Plan for Life Youniversity is named, appropriately enough, after me. I am, after all, the founder, chancellor. and student body of Wentworth University. So, I can do as I please.

I've designed my own tee-shirt with our family's real coat of arms and motto on it—"En Dieu est tout" (in God is all). It looks and sounds like an obscure, but expensive, Ivy League college. I've created a Homecoming Weekend (conveniently scheduled to coincide with my wedding anniversary in the fall) and Spring Break (Cancun, here I come!). Grading is on the curve so I should do well since I'm the only student. My professors are the Internet and every book or video ever made—as well as real people with the knowledge and experience in the subjects I'm studying. My study hall is the local library.

I expect to learn much more studying at Wentworth Youniversity than I would at any other school, be it Harvard, Stanford or Dartmouth. If you begin your own Plan for Life Youniversity after graduating from a standard university, you'll likely have about 60 years or more of schooling to look forward to in the future. Or the equivalent of 15 standard college educations. That ought to impact your life in a serious way.

Here is my Wentworth Youniversity curriculum for the next year.

➢ **Become more fluent in Spanish.**

✓ Check out Spanish CDs from library to play in car.

✓ Pick up Spanish phrase book to study at home.

✓ Add a Spanish vocabulary app to my iPhone.

➢ **Become more fluent in French.**

✓ Download French speaking course from Internet.

✓ Practice three times a week for 30 minutes.

✓ Add a French vocabulary app to my iPhone.

➢ **Become proficient in Adobe Creative Suite.**

✓ Take a course in Photoshop from Udemy.com (www.udemy.com)

➢ **Become proficient in Excel.**

✓ Read *Excel for Dummies* and practice on home computer.

➢ **Become proficient in PowerPoint.**

✓ Take PowerPoint classes offered by local library (free!).

✓ Read *PowerPoint for Dummies* and practice on home computer.

➢ **Study writing.**

✓ Listen to Stephen King's audio tapes on writing.

✓ Attend California Writers Club meetings.

✓ Attend Santa Barbara Writers Conference and the Maui Writers Conference.

✓ Sign up for writers groups on LinkedIn.com.

✓ Follow writing bloggers.

➢ **Join a health club and develop a fitness plan.**

✓ Join 24-Hour Fitness.

✓ Purchase weights and exercise bench to exercise at home.

✓ Work out with weights three times a week.

✓ Walk 50 miles a month.

✓ Add pedometer and tracking app to iPhone.

✓ Ride my bike 60+ miles a month.

✓ Do sit-ups and pushups every other day. Add pushup app to iPhone

✓ Follow a healthy, organic, non-GMO diet.

✓ Drink eight glasses of water a day.

✓ Take a multi-vitamin, a fish oil supplement, and extra Vitamin D daily.

➢ **Read one book a month:**

✓ Mystery genre: Michael Connolly, David Baldacci, Lisa Gardner, Robert Crais, Walter Mosley, Elizabeth George.

✓ Self-help genre: Jack Canfield, Tony Robbins, Brian Tracy, Eckhart Tolle.

✓ Classics: A Connecticut Yankee in King Arthur's Court, The Sun Also Rises, The Invisible Man, The Great Gatsby, Tolstoy.

An educational and self-improvement plan provides direction and structure to helping reach your goals…as well as enriching your life.

ONLINE EDUCATION RESOURCES

"Great minds have purposes, others have wishes." — Washington Irving

There are more online education resources than ever before. Now that the technical difficulties in streaming a "live" or recorded classroom experience have been largely overcome, the future of education will be democratized. There is no reason why, other than missing out on the campus life, that anyone cannot obtain a Harvard or Stanford education…at a fraction of the cost of typical tuition, books, room and board. Eventually, education for anyone, anywhere, may be offered free.

A big step in that direction is already underway. The online educational resources available now are impressive. Here are just a few examples of the kind of online educational resources available:

1. The MOOC list…Massive Open Online Courses www.mooc-list.com is a, well, massive list of free courses offered by top universities and other online entities.
2. www.lynda.com A wide range of online tutorial and training videos. Sign up for their Facebook page and receive occasional free courses.
3. www.ed2go.com Dozens of instructor–led courses costing about $99 on average. Includes business, college preparation, computer applications, design, legal, medical, teaching, technology, writing, and personal development. The courses are used at colleges and universities across America.
4. At Udacity www.udacity.com, world–renown university professors from top schools and industry experts teach their online technology students with challenging projects and "udacious" projects. It's free to take the courses, although there is an expanded version of many courses that costs extra (usually about $100). A Certificate of Completion is awarded upon completion of the course.
5. www.edx.org A new joint partnership by MIT and Harvard University to bring free online courses to the public.
6. www.fullsail.edu Online education in web, design, and entertainment.
7. www.usanfranonline.com Certificate course in social media. Also see

www.socialmedia-academy.com for social media certification courses.

8. www.udemy.com Learn from others or teach a course yourself. Some free, some paid. If you are an entrepreneur, there are more than 100 top thought leaders presenting more than 900 lectures on the subject through the Stanford lecture series…available here free. It's like a Ph.D. in entrepreneurship.
9. www.coursera.com Here's your chance to learn from top universities like Stanford, Princeton, the University of Michigan, and the University of Pennsylvannia. Courses include lectures, homework, grades, and certification. Subjects range from History of the World to Algorithms. More than 6 million students have studied online with Coursera.
10. www.academicearth.org Another valuable online source of educational classes and videos from some of the top colleges and universities. Subjects cover a wide range, including Business, Computer Science and Humanities.
11. www.OpenCulture.com 500 free courses by educators from schools such as Oxford, Stanford University, MIT, Carnegie Mellon, Tufts University, UC Berkeley, hundreds of free films and language courses.
12. www.grovo.com Grovo provides online video training with more than 3,500 bite–size lessons about how to use Internet tools (e.g. blogging, Google+, Feedly) and cloud services.
13. www.skillshare.com At Skillshare.com you can both take courses or teach them. Subjects range from film editing to fashion design. Most cost between $15 – $25. A monthly subscription for $9.95 accesses most of the courses for free, others at a 20% discount.

It's possible to "clone" an MBA degree by matching the course curriculum at a leading university with available free online courses from these resources. While you won't get the actual degree (yet), you will get the knowledge.

Here are some other online resource providers that you should bookmark for your Plan for Life Youniversity.

1. **Project Gutenberg**. Access more than 30,000+ ebooks about practically any subject you can imagine, great works of literature and texts. It's free. www.gutenberg.org

2. **Manybooks.net**. If you can't find a book at Project Gutenberg, try this site. It lists more than 25,000 ebooks—all free. www.ManyBooks.net
3. **PBS Video.com**. Stream video from their popular Nature and Nova series, as well as a wide range of other subjects. www.video.pbs.org
4. **DumbLittleMan**. www.DumbLittleMan.com Tips for living better.
5. **Mashable.com**. www.Mashable.com News and information about social media.
6. **Marc and Angel Hack Life**. www.marcandangel.com Practical and inspiring information on how to life a more productive life.
7. **Directory of Open Journals**. www.doag.org Categorized, searchable links to free, full text scholarly journals.
8. **TED lectures**. www.ted.com Watch one a week and watch your mind expand.
9. **Forum Network**. www.forum-network.org Free video lectures compiled by *PBS* and *NPR*. Also check out the Boston Forum Network at www.wgbh.org/forum for thousands more.
10. **iTunesU**. www.apple.com/apps/itunes-u The world's largest online catalog of free educational content from leading institutions.
11. **How Cast**. www.howcast.com Founded by former YouTube and Google staffers, the site features more than 7,500 instructional videos on everything from how to grill the perfect steak to how to fix a faucet.
12. **Wikipedia**. www.wikipedia.org Your online encyclopedia to find quick information on nearly anything. Over 10 million articles in more than 200 languages.
13. **eHow.com**. www.ehow.com Learn to do almost anything imaginable…short of brain surgery…at this huge compendium of instructional articles and videos.
14. **About.com**. www.about.com A resource for content that helps people solve the small and large needs of everyday life.
15. **Khan Academy**. www.khanacademy.org An online library of more than 3,000 videos covering subjects as wide-ranging as physics, finance, history and hundreds of skills to learn.

16. **Woopid**. www.woopid.com Free technology training videos.
17. **Zen Habits**. www.zenhabits.net Leo Barbauta's fascinating discussions of life, love, happiness, and other "life" subjects.
18. **How Stuff Works**. www.howstuffworks.com Thousands of topics, from engines to lock-picking, including videos and illustrations so you can learn how things work.
19. **WikiHow**. www.wikihow.com A wiki-based collaboration to create the world's largest online "how to" manual database. Want to know how to look like a cowboy? This is the place to go.
20. **VideoJug**. www.videojug.com Videojug asks "Want to get good at life?" And they deliver with easy-to-follow, expert "how to" videos on a wide range of subjects.
21. **Open Course Ware**. Search this subject to find dozens of courses offered online by leading learning institutions.
22. **LearningScience.** www.learningscience.org A free online resource for teaching kids at K-12 schools about a range of science subjects.
23. **BBC Languages**. www.bbc.co.uk/languages Free online language lessons, including courses, audio, video, and games.
24. **LiveMocha**. www.livemocha.com Learn a language and connect with native speakers for instructive help.
25. **IgniteShow**. www.igniteshow.com They're sorta like quickie TED talks. Thousands of five-minute videos recorded live at Ignite events held in more than 100 cities from O'Reilley Media.
26. **LifeHacker.** www.lifehacker.com This addicting site has thousands of tips on how to improve your productivity and get things done.
27. **Planet eBook**. www.planetebook.com Free ebooks of classic literature.
28. **eBooks Directory**. www.e-booksdirectory.com Categorized index of free downloadable online books and book reviews. Also, www.e-library.net for thousands of cheap and free ebooks for downloading. For Amazon Kindle users check out www.TheNovelsNetwork.com to get unlimited free ebooks.
29. **Teacher Tube**. www.teachertube.com An educator and student site

for sharing the best educational videos, docs, audios, and photos.

30. **WonderHowTo**. www.wonderhowto.com Free "how to" videos on a huge number of subjects from Minecraft™ servers to origami.

Stanford and MIT are pioneers in online education. Other big name universities are following in their footsteps. In 2013, UCLA announced expanded summer courses that even non–students and high–school students can take online and earn credit. Online education from respected colleges is a trend that will continue to grow. If you really want an education today, it's available…and often for free.

THE LIBRARY

Almost all the knowledge you could ever want to access is available for free from the network of 122,000 libraries in the United States. Nearly everything you can learn at Harvard or Stanford is available through your library. Most libraries have excellent internet resources, including computers available for free use. Soon there will be digital libraries where you will be able to take your smartphone, tablet, or laptop and download books and reference materials.

If you haven't made a trip to your local library in a while, you may want to visit and learn about the valuable resources there. At most libraries you can…

- ✓ Check out music and movies.
- ✓ Read the latest magazines and newsletters.
- ✓ Take classes.
- ✓ Attend book signings.
- ✓ Hear a lecture.
- ✓ Attend an artist reception.
- ✓ Download e–books.
- ✓ Access job postings.

At our local library you can warm yourself by a real fireplace as you look out on a marsh frequented by migrating birds while sitting comfortably in oversized upholstered chairs. There are plans to add more meeting rooms...even a coffee kiosk.

BOOKSTORES

Bookstores have become the retail libraries of the 21st Century as they strive to reinvent themselves to counter the digital reading revolution. From independent bookstores like Book Passages www.bookpassage.com in Corte Madera, California and Powells's www.powells.com in Portland, Oregon, to the large national chains like Barnes & Noble www.barnesandnoble.com and Books A Million www.booksamillion.com, the trend is to provide places for people to meet, have coffee and a light meal, relax with a book or magazine, and attend book–related events such as author signings and reading groups. Some bookstores even have kids' play areas. Bookstores have morphed into cozy community centers for people who love reading.

THE INTERNET

There's hardly a subject or fact or resource you can't find on the Web. Learn to do searches for the information you want. Study up on Boolean search techniques...combining words and phrases into search terms. The three key components to Boolean search are "or," "and," and "not." For a full explanation of how to use Boolean search, go to www.eHow.com.

If you have trouble finding something, you can always go to the Internet Archive WayBackMachine, a virtual archive of everything on the Internet since its inception…almost 4 petabytes of data since 1996. www.archive.org

The other resource to find great information on the Internet is Wikipedia, the Internet encyclopedia. www.wikipedia.org

Further reading:

Online Education for Dummies by Kevin Johnson, Susan Manning, Jonathon Finkelstein.

College Unbound: The Future of Education and What It Means for Students by Jeffrey Selingo.

The Higher Education Bubble by Glenn Harlan Reynolds.

Life Rules: Last–century rules don't apply to the 21st Century. The more education you get, the more money you are likely to earn…but it isn't guaranteed any longer. You may not need a college degree to succeed. Make learning part of your life forever. Consider creating A Plan for Life Youniversity to plan and schedule your ongoing learning.

CHAPTER 6
PLACE

WHERE YOU LIVE DETERMINES HOW YOU LIVE

Where you live may be one of the most important decision you will ever make. Your "place" includes:

- ✓ The state and city you live in.
- ✓ The house or apartment you call home.
- ✓ Your workspace.
- ✓ Your car.
- ✓ The clothes you wear.

Each of these personal environments will impact your life for better or worse. To a large degree, where you live determines how you will live. Choose your places carefully.

The Buddhist principle of "oneness" in self and environment…esho funi…means that life and environment are inseparable. Your "place" in life is an integral aspect of who you are and who you become. Physical environments reflect inner reality.

Some "places" have a more obvious impact on your life than others. If you are single and move to Atlanta the chances are high that you will marry a person currently living in Atlanta. In fact, approximately half of all marriages are among people who live near each other. And since a high percentage of relationships begin in the workplace, your choice of career may determine who you marry as well. You meet people where you are. So be in the places where the kind of friends, lovers, and mate you want can be found. Be where your best career opportunities are. And be in environments that reflect who you are...or want to be.

BORN TO SUCCEED...OR FAIL

Where you were born is one of the most important things that will happen to you in life.

- Dietary preferences and cultural attitudes about health vary widely from one place to another. Everything from the quality of schools, the purity of the air and water, the incidence of crime, all affect you from the moment of conception.
- Where you were born can affect how long you live by as much as ten years. What's more, even if you move you will carry some of the legacy of your birthright with you—both good or bad.
- Job opportunities, crime rates, weather...all vary widely from one place to another.

YOU ARE WHERE YOU ARE

"We have the power to control our environment." — Jack Canfield

The fact is that between 25 – 40% of what you are in life is a result of your genetics. The rest is environmental...including where you live. Yet, even though we're one of the most mobile populations on earth, nearly 50% of Americans live within 50 miles of where they were born.

The place you live—your home and neighborhood—not only affects who you meet but how you are perceived. Your personal environments say a lot about who you are—as every direct marketing company well knows. If you live in Palm Beach you will be initially judged by that place—just as your first impression would be impacted by living in Lubbock, Texas. People form an image of you based upon your tastes and lifestyle choices. The same is true about the home or apartment you live in, the car you drive, and the clothes you wear—your smaller "personal" environments. Every choice you make contributes to your persona—or personal "brand," as it is now widely described. All these environments will exert a strong influence upon your future, often in ways you never imagined.

Each "environment" you live in should be a conscious choice based upon who you are, what you want to be, and how you want the world to see and react to you. Choosing and shaping your environments to fit your personality and life goals is critically important to the success of your Plan for Life.

DISNEYLAND ISN'T THE ONLY HAPPIEST PLACE

"Dwell as near as possible to the channel in which your mind flows."
— Henry David Thoreau

Americans are promised "life, liberty, and the pursuit of happiness." Yet after more than 200 years following this doctrine, America fails to rank as one of the Top 10 Happiest Places on Earth, according to the 2013 World Happiness Report. The U.S. ranks #17, just after Mexico. Our particularly neurotic and stressful society is one major reason why true happiness seems to elude Americans. We may be pursuing happiness, but we sure aren't catching it.

Our neighbors to the North, who look and talk a lot like us, manage to pull off a #6 Happiness ranking among the nations of the world. So it must be us. Despite our "We're #1" arrogance, maybe it's time for America to take a long hard look in the mirror to see if what reflects back is what we really want to be. If the Canadians are happier than we are (despite the cold) then it must be something in our national culture that prevents us from achieving more happiness.

As for the Happiest Places, well, you will find them in countries that rank high on the dreaded (at least for Republicans) "socialism" scale. Places like Denmark and Norway. Our "high wire, no safety net" style of living isn't what the world seems to want these days.

Here's a look at the world's happiest countries:

WORLD'S HAPPIEST PLACES

1. Denmark
2. Finland
3. Netherlands
4. Sweden

5. Ireland
6. Canada
7. Switzerland
8. New Zealand
9. Norway
10. Belgium

One common attribute of happy countries is that none of them is at war. The United States, on the other hand, has been in six major wars and several minor military conflicts in just the past 70 years. Nations that are truly peace-loving are, well, peaceful places to live.

Most of the happy countries also have social support networks in place that make their citizens feel secure. America's individualistic national character creates an "every man for himself" competition that fosters a kind of neurotic instability.

The other common denominator among these places is the weather. They are not balmy, warm weather countries where you might expect living to be easy. Most are downright freezing cold most of the year. So what's to be happy about? Perhaps it's all that snuggling under the comforter. Or maybe they're just too damn busy staying warm to get into any mischief.

Sources: Organization for Economic Cooperation and Development (OECD), Gallup Poll of 140 countries measuring "life satisfaction." Courtesy of *Forbes.com.* United Nations Sustainable Development Soutions Network.

WHERE TO LIVE

Where you live affects nearly every important aspect of your life—career opportunities, the people who become your social network, who you marry, how long and healthy you live, and the options your family will have in the future. Your "place" must support your dreams.

Despite the fact that 40 million Americans move every year, it's usually with little or no thought about the long-term consequences. People move for a better paying job or an affordable house or to be with a boyfriend or for better weather. Few consider how the move will impact their overall life. Most people I've asked say, "I dunno. I just ended up here." Many people aren't even aware that it's an important choice that they have to make *consciously*.

There are many personal and professional factors that must come together in order to find the right place to live. For every person there will be some factors that outweigh others. It may be a smart move to pass on that $150,000 a year job if it's in Keokuk, Iowa. Then again, Keokuk is a nice town and $150,000 goes a long way there. And if that guy you're in love with insists you move to his city to live together (the case 80% of the time), maybe you should re-think the relationship—especially if his city isn't a good fit for you. The important thing is to find a place that provides the environment for you to achieve your life goals.

THE GREAT RECESSION AND ITS IMPACT UPON PLACE

When jobs are scarce financial considerations can be critical to the survival of your family. It's why people are flocking to North Dakota to live in dormitory housing where there are no social amenities and they have no friends—to work the booming oil fields...and make an average of more than $85,000 a year. There will be times when Place comes second to making enough money to secure some kind of decent future. I have one friend who has moved from Los Angeles to Florida to Seattle to Pittsburg...all within the past five years...to take a better job with each move.

The availability of jobs and cost-of-living are important factors to consider. Living in Cedar Rapids, Iowa, your income provides a 33.5% higher standard of living than Tampa, Florida, and a 78.4% higher living standard than Seattle.

Where you live can have dramatically different costs. I know this personally because the amount we pay for a 1,200 square foot, 1 bath home in one of San Francisco's most expensive neighborhoods would buy us a 7-room, 4-bath, Italianate villa on Lake Oswego in Portland, Oregon (a very nice town).

To show how dramatic the difference can be, here's a comparison of the cost of living between San Francisco and Minneapolis or Portland.

	Minneapolis	**Portland**
Groceries	- 7%	- 14%
Housing	- 57%	- 55%
Utilities	+ 3%	- 4%
Transportation	- 11%	- 3%
Healthcare	- 11%	- 16%

In this comparison, the only item that costs more than San Francisco in either city is for utilities in Minneapolis. If you're going to San Francisco be sure to bring enough money…you're gonna need it.

The difference in cost-of-living between the most expensive cities in America and the least expensive is significant.

Check out this website before you decide to move to another city… it compares the difference in standard of living: Sperlings's Best Places www.bestplaces.net. At this site you'll also be able to compare other key factors such as crime rates, climate, and quality of schools.

CITIES HAVE PERSONALITIES TOO

Over time cities develop their own distinctive personalities. A city's personality is a collective reflection of the people who live there and its unique history. Values, beliefs, attitudes, talent types, age groups, religions all cross-pollinate and create a culture that is distinctively representative of the city. Portland has a different "vibe" than New York. Miami is vastly different from Minneapolis. Las Vegas couldn't be more different from Salt Lake City. And San Francisco is about as far away (in every way) from Cleveland as you can get.

Professions (and their unique characteristics) congregate where the support services, jobs, and others in their profession are located. Investment bankers flourish in New York, musicians in Nashville, actors and filmmakers in Los Angeles, high-tech types in Silicon Valley and San Francisco, and so on. What makes Austin so radically different from most of Texas are the young, highly educated, entrepreneurial, technologically-hip people who gravitate to it. It's an island of progressiveness in a sea of conservatism. And the more like-minded people who move to Austin, the more its personality and character solidifies in its unique way.

To live somewhere other than among your peers can be career suicide. An actress in Omaha cannot go very far in her profession. A hedge-fund manager won't likely do well in Fargo. A computer design technician will find limited avenues for success in Baton Rouge. That's not to say those professions are absent from these cities, just that jobs and companies are few and there's almost no professional support network.

If you are young and single there are cities that cater to your interests more than others. Most large cities like New York, Chicago, Miami, San

Francisco and some smaller ones like Madison and Austin have large populations of single people. The opposite is true of markets like Cincinnati, Salt Lake City, Indianapolis, and Kansas City.

Since finding an ideal mate is both a numbers game and being around people who are similar, it makes sense to increase the odds by living in a city where you can find like-minded people. While opposites often do attract, nearly every survey ever conducted shows that most successful relationships are grounded in shared values, compatible backgrounds, and similar lifestyle preferences. After all, most people are simply looking for an opposite sex version of themselves, only a little better.

Gays and lesbians will likely gravitate to "Blue" states rather than more conservative, less tolerant and more religious "Red" states. Of course, San Francisco is famous for its large gay and lesbian population, but other cities gays find receptive to their lifestyle are Washington D.C., Boston, Los Angeles, New York, Madison, Boulder, and Santa Barbara. Being gay in Billings, Montana or Casper, Wyoming can be challenging.

YOUR NEIGHBORHOOD

Just as cities have distinctive personalities and styles, so do neighborhoods. In recent years the value of living in a neighborhood where one feels "at home" has become increasingly important. Especially valued are the neighborhoods that have matured into identifiable personalities that reflect their residents perfectly. I've lived in several of these neighborhoods over the years and find them endlessly interesting and charming. Places like Boston's Beacon Hill or Back Bay, the Near North "Gold Coast" or Lincoln Park in Chicago, Coral Gables outside Miami, Yorkville in Toronto, the Village in New York, and West Hollywood in L.A.

The Bay Area, where I live, is a patchwork quilt of neighborhoods, each with a distinctive flavor: Noe Valley, the Castro, Pacific Heights, SOMA, Chinatown, the Marina, North Beach, and Potrero Hill are all little cities within the city that is San Francisco. Outlying towns—Palo Alto, Berkeley, Mill Valley, Sausalito, Danville—all have distinct personalities even though some literally border each other.

People are usually happiest when they align their personality with the place they live. Before buying the cute Victorian house or renting an apartment that's less expensive—but in a neighborhood you're unfamiliar with—give it some thought. Spend time walking around the neighborhood. What are the people like who live there? Are the services you depend upon and like within easy reach? What's the overall vibe? Does it sync with your personality and what you want in life?

If you doubt the significance of where you live—or simply want to delve more deeply into the subject—read author Richard Florida's book *Who's Your City?: How the Creative Economy is Making Where To Live The Most Important Decision Of Your Life.*

CITY MOUSE OR COUNTRY MOUSE?

Whether you live in the city or a rural environment will affect how well you live.

- On average people who live in the country live two years longer than stressed out, crime infested, polluted city folks. But a lot depends upon the city and what part of the country you live in.

Residents of rural West Virginia, for example, suffer from a culture of poor diet. Their incidence of chronic diseases such as diabetes, stroke, cancer, obesity and heart disease are higher than most other areas of the nation. Their high unemployment and lower educational achievement creates stress and poor lifestyle choices. Good healthcare facilities are far away and the number of doctors and dentists is below the national average.

Meanwhile a city such as Boulder, Colorado ranks highly in healthcare, education, and has few pollutants. People enjoy a culture of exercise and outdoor activities. The temperate climate causes fewer health problems than areas of the country that endure harsh extremes of weather. Fresh, organic locally grown food is plentiful. And the number of fast food outlets is far below the norm in America.

So, while country life if often a better lifestyle choice, it's not always so.

BEST PLACES TO LIVE

Just for fun, listed below are the Top 10 Cities in varying categories gathered from published sources such as *Forbes.com, US News, Men's Health, AOL, CNBC, Bloomberg Businessweek,* and *Best Places to Live.* Some of the results are surprising—and surprisingly informative.

TOP 10 BEST LARGE CITIES IN THE U.S.

1. San Francisco
2. Seattle
3. Washington D.C.
4. Boston
5. Portland, Oregon
6. Denver
7. New York
8. Austin
9. San Diego
10. St. Paul, Minnesota

Source: *Bloomberg Businessweek* (2012)

TOP 10 BEST QUALITY OF LIFE STATES

1. New Hampshire
2. Hawaii
3. Vermont
4. Maine
5. Minnesota
6. North Dakota
7. South Dakota
8. Colorado
9. Wyoming
10. Utah

Source: CNBC.com, (2012)

AMERICA'S 10 MOST CRIME-RIDDEN CITIES

Nobody likes getting mugged or robbed. Or murdered.

1. Flint, MI
2. Detroit, MI
3. St. Louis, MO
4. Oakland, CA
5. Memphis, TN
6. Little Rock, AR
7. Birmingham, AL
8. Atlanta, GA
9. Baltimore, MD
10. Stockton, CA

Source: FBI crime data, (2012)

TOP 10 SAFEST CITIES IN THE U.S.

Some cities have almost no crime. Here are some of the safest.

1. Irvine, CA
2. Fremont, CA
3. Plano, TX
4. Madison, WI
5. Irving, TX
6. Scottsdale, AZ
7. Boise, ID
8. Henderson, NV
9. Chandler, AZ
10. Chula Vista, CA

Source: FBI crime data, *Business Insider* (2013)

The data used to determine the crime rate in a city you are interested in living in are available to anyone online at the U.S. Census Bureau website www.census.gov.

Often, cities in close proximity have radically different crime rates. The community I live in, Tiburon, California, has a very low crime rate. Just a few miles away across the Richmond Bay Bridge is Richmond, California, with an extremely high crime rate. Chicago's ritzy Gold Coast neighborhood is just a few blocks from one of the worst areas of the city.

Most locals know the differences between one community or neighborhood and another. But if you're just moving from another city or state, you may not know these differences in advance. So it pays to do as much due diligence as possible before deciding where to live.

TOP 10 METRO MARKETS FOR WOMEN'S WELL-BEING

Some cities are more supportive of women, which is why women flock to them.

1. Washington D.C.
2. San Francisco, CA
3. Boston, MA
4. Minneapolis, MN
5. New York, NY
6. Seattle, WA
7. Denver, CO
8. Baltimore, MD
9. San Diego, CA
10. Philadelphia, PA

TOP 10 UNHAPPIEST CITIES

Based upon statistics for depression, suicide, crime, divorce, unemployment and cloudy days, here are the unhappiest cities in America.

1. Portland, OR
2. St. Louis, MO
3. New Orleans, LA
4. Detroit, MI
5. Cleveland, OH
6. Jacksonville, FL
7. Las Vegas, NV
8. Nashville, TN
9. Cincinnati, OH
10. Atlanta, GA

Interestingly, Portland residents may be unhappy but the city frequently ranks among the top ten most desirable places to live. And I know people who are madly in love with New Orleans, which scores poorly on many rankings of livability.

AMERICA'S 10 MOST BORING CITIES

Having traveled a lot on business, I can assure you there are many cities and towns in America that could give these Top 10 Most Boring Cities a run for the (yawn) money.

1. Chula Vista, CA
2. Hialeah, FL
3. Mesa, AZ
4. N. Las Vegas, NV
5. Chandler, AZ
6. Santa Ana, CA
7. Bakersfield, CA
8. Aurora, CO
9. Gilbert, AZ
10. Henderson, NV

TOP 10 MOST ACTIVE CITIES.

If you're a sports–loving type, you'll love these cities.

1. Seattle, WA
2. San Francisco, CA
3. Oakland, CA
4. Washington DC
5. Salt Lake City, UT
6. Reno, NV
7. Portland, OR
8. Atlanta, GA
9. Denver, CO
10. Minneapolis, MN

Source: *Men's Health* magazine, 2012

AMERICA'S TOP 10 LAZIEST CITIES.

Based upon a variety of "laziness" factors such as the number of hours people work, how often they play video games, and the number of deep vein thrombosis cases (often caused by sitting), *Men's Health* magazine determined which cities are populated by "slugs" and which ones are the most active.

1. Lexington, KY
2. Indianapolis, IN
3. Jackson, MS
4. Charleston, WV
5. Oklahoma City, OK
6. Tulsa, OK
7. Little Rock, AR
8. Nashville, TN
9. Laredo, TX
10. Birmingham, AL

It's interesting to note how the "laziest" cities also are those with some of the highest rates of heart disease, diabetes, and cancer in America.

WORST WINTER WEATHER IN AMERICA

If you don't like snow, don't go.

1. Cleveland, OH
2. Boston, MA
3. New York, NY
4. Milwaukee, WI
5. Chicago, IL
6. Minneapolis, MN
7. Indianapolis, IN
8. Columbus, OH
9. Detroit, MI
10. Baltimore, MD

I've lived in Chicago and can attest to the weather—bitter cold in the winter, hot and muggy in the summer. Slight variations on this theme are true for all the other cities on this list. At least in some cities—like Minneapolis, Chicago, and New York—there are plenty of great places indoors to get away from the lousy weather. Minneapolis even has a pedestrian "freeway" system that crosses over streets, runs through retail stores, and has fast and slow lanes.

CITIES WITH THE WORST WEATHER IN AMERICA

For many people the weather is a major factor in where they decide to live. Here are the worst weather cities, based upon NOAA measurements of snow, heat, humidity, rain, and coldest temperatures.

Winter

1. Syracuse, NY
2. Duluth, MN
3. Casper, WY
4. Cleveland, OH
5. Detroit, MI

Summer

1. Miami, FL
2. New Orleans, LA
3. Dallas, TX
4. Mobile, AL
5. Corpus Christi, T

The funny thing about weather is that some people love weather that others hate. How else would you explain the millions of Americans who live in frigid Minneapolis, Minnesota and Portland, Maine; hot and humid New Orleans, Louisiana or Orlando, Florida; or other less than perfect weather cities such as wet Seattle, tornado prone Oklahoma City, and scorching hot Phoenix.

THE TOP 10 MOST MISERABLE CITIES IN AMERICA

Forbes magazine rated the Top 10 Most Miserable Cities in America, based upon a wide range of miserableness factors such as commute times, taxes, superfund sites, unemployment, violent crime, and weather.

1. Detroit, MI
2. Stockton, CA
3. Flint, MI
4. New York, NY
5. Philadelphia, PA
6. Chicago, IL
7. Los Angeles, CA
8. Modesto, CA
9. Charlotte, NC
10. Providence, RI

Now I'm sure to get mail about this list, especially from New York, Chicago and L.A. It's not MY list, it's from *Forbes*. Go complain to them. I've lived in all three cities and happen to like them a lot. So, don't kill the messenger.

TEN MOST EFFICIENT CITIES IN AMERICA

Real Simple magazine did a nationwide survey to determine which cities (over 200,000 population) were the most efficient (i.e. easiest) to live in. Using these criteria—commuting, walkability, sprawl, traffic congestion, doctor's appointment times, internet availability, biking, and non-car commuters—the editors ranked the most time-efficient cities.

Since time is as valuable a commodity in modern life as money, if this is a priority for you then these cities might be the right place to live.

1. Seattle
2. Portland
3. San Francisco
4. Boston
5. Minneapolis
6. Denver
7. Washington DC
8. Pittsburgh
9. Miami
10. Atlanta

AMERICA'S TOP 15 "WIRED" CITIES

Here's where to live if internet connectivity is important.

1. Seattle, WA
2. Atlanta, GA
3. Washington D.C.
4. Orlando, FL
5. Boston, MA
6. Miami, FL
7. Minneapolis, MN
8. Denver, CO
9. New York, NY
10. Baltimore, MD
11. San Francisco, CA
12. San Diego, CA
13. Los Angeles, CA
14. Portland, OR
15. Raleigh, NC

TOP 10 CITIES FOR DOG LOVERS

Americans love their dogs—all 43 million of them. More than 1/3 of all households (37%) have a dog in the family. Here are the cities with the most canine lovers.

1. Portland, OR
2. San Diego, CA
3. Seattle, WA
4. Austin, TX
5. San Francisco, CA
6. Albuquerque, NM
7. Tucson, AZ
8. Boston, MA
9. Phoenix, AZ
10. Minneapolis, MN

Source: *Huffington Post*, Estately.com (2013)

BEST-LOOKING STATES

I know most people aren't so shallow that looks would matter all that much in a relationship (yeah, right), but for my shallow readers here are the Top 10 Best Looking States.

1. Washington DC
2. Hawaii
3. California
4. Connecticut
5. Florida
6. New York
7. Massachusetts
8. New Jersey
9. Nevada
10. Rhode Island

Rhode Island?

You may agree or disagree with this list. I happen to think the women and men in Texas and Utah beat out New Jersey and Rhode Island, but these are the rankings as compiled by Gordon Patzer, Ph.D. from his book "*Looks: Why They Matter More Than You Even Imagined*." (2008)

Now you're probably wondering which states are the worst looking. And boy will I hear about this.

WORST LOOKING STATES

1. North Dakota
2. South Dakota
3. Mississippi
4. Nebraska
5. Ohio
6. Montana
7. Missouri
8. Vermont

9. Louisiana
10. New Mexico

I've met beautiful women in Missouri, Louisiana, and Mississippi. My gal pal Patricia extols the virtues of the handsome rugged cowboys in Montana. So, there are MANY exceptions.

TOP 10 BEST CITIES FOR MEN

Men's Health magazine listed the Best and Worst Cities for Men (2013) based upon a wide range of criteria, including unemployment, air quality, crime rates, commute times, cost of living, death rates, weather, and the ratio of single men to single women.

1. Boise, ID
2. San Jose, CA
3. San Francisco, CA
4. Plano, TX
5. Seattle, WA
6. Burlington, VT
7. Austin, TX
8. Salt Lake City, UT
9. Madison, WI
10. Portland, OR

TOP 10 WORST CITIES FOR MEN

1. Tulsa, OK
2. Detroit, MI
3. Columbia, SC
4. Cleveland, OH
5. Memphis, TN
6. St. Louis, MO
7. Toledo, OH
8. Charleston, WV
9. Philadelphia, PA
10. Birmingham, AL

LIMPEST CITIES IN AMERICA

The following cities were named "limpest" in America—and in need of Viagra. Criteria used to develop the list included percentage of smokers, obesity, number of urologists per capita, and erectile dysfunction prescriptions.

By the way, men who consume up to 3 alcoholic drinks a day have a 4.6% less likelihood of erectile dysfunction. So, if you're having problems downstairs perhaps all you need is a, uh, stiff drink.

1. Tulsa, OK
2. Lubbock, TX
3. Charleston, SC
4. Arlington, TX
5. Ft. Worth. TX
6. Oklahoma City, OK
7. Anchorage, AK
8. Bakersfield, CA
9. Modesto, CA
10. Omaha, NE

Hmmm. I guess things aren't always bigger in Texas.

AMERICA'S "HARDEST" CITIES

Conversely, the "hardest" cities in America are listed below (listen up ladies and other interested parties).

1. Boston, MA
2. Hartford, CT
3. Washington DC
4. Atlanta, GA
5. Burlington, VT
6. Durham, NC
7. Jersey City, NJ
8. Newark, NJ
9. San Francisco, CA
10. New York, NY

THE TEN FITTEST CITIES IN AMERICA

The success of every other key area in your life is dependent upon good health. So you may want to live where the environment is clean and the local population lives a healthy lifestyle.

1. Washington D.C.
2. Minneapolis/St. Paul, MN
3. Denver, CO
4. Boston, MA
5. San Francisco, CA
6. Seattle, WA
7. Portland, OR
8. San Diego, CA
9. Austin, TX
10. Virginia Beach. VA

Source: Forbes.com, American College of Sports Medicine (2011)

TOP 10 CITIES WHERE THE BREATHING IS EASY

You can breathe easy in these Top 10 Cleanest Air cities judged by Air Quality

Index, traffic congestion, and asthma rates as ranked by the Centers for Disease Control and Prevention Behavior Risk Factor Surveillance System.

1. Honolulu
2. Fargo
3. Lincoln
4. Corpus Christi
5. Fremont, CA
6. Cheyenne
7. Lubbock
8. Denver
9. Anchorage
10. Colorado Springs

TOP 10 WORST AIR QUALITY CITIES

The cities with the worst air pollution in America.

1. Detroit
2. Chicago
3. Pittsburgh
4. Bakersfield
5. Sacramento
6. Wilmington, DE
7. Milwaukee
8. Arlington, TX
9. Grand Rapids, MI
10. Atlanta

Source: *Men's Health,* 2006

TOP 10 "GREENEST" CITIES IN AMERICA

For those who are concerned about the environment, you may want to check out the cities listed below to find others who share your values.

1. Portland
2. San Francisco
3. Seattle
4. Chicago
5. Oakland
6. New York
7. Boston
8. Philadelphia
9. Denver
10. Minneapolis

Source: The SustainLane U.S. City Ranking, *How Green is Your City?* New Society Publishing.

Of course, being "green" requires more than just moving to a city where the people care for their environment. Consider these sobering facts about our world's wasteful practices.

- ✓ 48,000 gallons of oil consumed—every second.
- ✓ 150,000 Energizer batteries are discarded every 15 minutes.
- ✓ 2,000,000 plastic beverage bottles are discarded every 5 minutes.
- ✓ 1,140,000 paper bags are used every hour.
- ✓ 240,000 plastic bags are used every ten seconds.
- ✓ 1,140,000 brown paper bags used in grocery stores every hour.
- ✓ 410,000 paper cups discarded every 15 minutes.
- ✓ 50,000 pieces of plastic floating in every square mile of the world's oceans.
- ✓ In 1970 there were 40,000 tigers in the wild on earth, today there are fewer than 3,000.
- ✓ 2,400,000 pieces of plastic enter the earth's oceans every hour.
- ✓ 270,000 sharks are killed every day just for their fins.
- ✓ 260,000 gallons of gas consumed by cars in the U.S. every minute.
- ✓ 212,000 aluminum cans are used in the U.S. every minute.
- ✓ 200,000 packs of cigarettes are smoked (and 1/3 of the butts discarded as litter) every day.
- ✓ 20,500 tuna are fished from the sea every 15 minutes.
- ✓ 44,000 commercial jet flights in the U.S. every day.
- ✓ 15,000,000 sheets of paper are used every 5 minutes.

Source: The photography of Chris Jordon, Seattle, WA

www.chrisjordan.com.

THE TOP 10 "SMARTEST" CITIES IN THE U.S.

Portfolio.com ranked U.S. cities using census data by assigning point values to five levels of education ranging from high school dropout rates to holders of advanced degrees.

1. Boulder, CO
2. Ann Arbor, MI
3. Washington DC
4. Durham, NC
5. Fort Collins, CO
6. Bridgeport/Stamford, CT
7. San Jose, CA
8. Boston, MA
9. Madison, WI
10. San Francisco/Oakland, CA

TOP 10 LEAST INTELLIGENT CITIES IN AMERICA

1. Merced, CA
2. McAllister/Edinburg, TX
3. Brownsville, TX
4. Visalia, CA
5. Bakersfield, CA
6. Yakima, WA
7. Laredo, TX
8. Hickory, NC
9. Ft. Smith, AK
10. Modesto, CA

TOP 10 STATES FOR OVERALL HAPPINESS AND WELL-BEING

Happiness is important. One five-year study found a 35% decrease in the risk of dying among people who reported being happy, content or excited on a typical day, compared with those who were sadder or more anxious.

1. Utah
2. Hawaii
3. Wyoming
4. Colorado
5. Minnesota
6. Maryland
7. Washington
8. Massachusetts
9. California
10. Arizona

And now...

THE WORST STATES FOR OVERALL HAPPINESS AND WELL-BEING

1. West Virginia
2. Kentucky
3. Mississippi
4. Ohio

5. Arizona
6. Indiana
7. Missouri
8. Oklahoma
9. Tennessee
10. Michigan

The least "happy" states also are among the poorest, least educated, and unhealthiest states in America.

TEN BEST CITIES FOR FAMILIES

In 2012, *Parenting* magazine ranked the top 100 cities for families based upon a long list of family-friendly attributes such as educational facilities, healthcare, crime, cost of living, number of playgrounds and more.

1. Boston
2. Burlington, VT
3. Portland, ME
4. Austin
5. Cheyenne
6. Washington D.C./Arlington, VA
7. Minneapolis/St. Paul
8. Madison, WI
9. Omaha
10. Sioux Falls, SD

And the bottom ten cities from the list of Top 100 cities for families:

1. Los Angeles
2. Las Vegas
3. Bakersfield, CA
4. Detroit
5. Fresno, CA
6. Memphis
7. Chicago
8. Arlington, TX
9. Phoenix
10. San Diego

TOP 10 CITIES FOR STARTING A BUSINESS

The best place to start a business? Almost anywhere you have a good idea and a receptive customer base. If you look online at the 2013 Top 10 Places to Start a Business (*CNN Money, Forbes, Entrepreneur*, Motley Fool, Milken, *The Business Journals*) nearly every list is different. The cities that appear most often are:

1. Austin
2. Houston
3. Silicon Valley
4. Atlanta
5. Dallas/Ft. Wroth
6. Raleigh/Durham
7. Seattle
8. Des Moines
9. Salt Lake City
10. Dallas/Ft. Worth

TEN MOST EXPENSIVE CITIES

Cost of living is an important consideration when debating where to live. According to *Kiplinger* magazine, the ten most expensive cities in the U.S. (2012) are:

1. New York
2. San Francisco
3. Honolulu
4. San Jose
5. Stamford, CT
6. Santa Ana, CA
7. Washington DC
8. Boston
9. Oakland
10. Anchorage

TEN LEAST EXPENSIVE CITIES

The least expensive cities in the U.S., according to *Kiplinger* magazine.

1. Harlington, TX
2. Memphis
3. McAllen, TX
4. Fayetteville, AR
5. Temple, TX
6. Conway, AR
7. Pueblo, CO
8. Wichita Falls, TX
9. Springfield, IL
10. Winston-Salem, NC

TOP 10 PLACES TO RETIRE

Where to retire is a big decision for most people, since by definition it will likely be the last place they live. Many factors weigh into any retirement equation—weather, cost of living, proximity to close relatives, housing, healthcare availability, transportation, and cultural or sporting activities. As a result, there are literally dozens of Top 10 lists recommending places to retire.

Search on Google for Best Places to Retire and review the lists that appear. Here is a 2012 Top 10 list of best places to retire from *CNN Money*.

1. Albany
2. Portland
3. Louisville
4. Tucson
5. Austin
6. Winston/Salem
7. St. George
8. Traverse City
9. Cour D'Alene
10. St. Augustine

The lists of Top 10 cities and towns reveal surprising, as well as some predictable, findings. Emerging smaller cities could offer many opportunities as well as the pleasures and economies of small town living. Columbia, Missouri, appears frequently on top ten lists, for example. Other towns and cities you may hardly know exist, like Durham or Hartford, are worth exploring. Some towns—such as Taos, New Mexico; Aspen, Colorado; Seaside, Florida; Mill Valley, California—receive rave reviews from residents, but don't typically show up on any of the Top 10 lists.

I hope that reviewing these Top 10 lists has made you think more about the importance of "place" in your Plan for Life. Your choice of Place is important...but the importance depends upon your values, personality, and goals in life. As in all things, be true to yourself when choosing your Place in life.

THERE'S NO PLACE LIKE HOME

"Second only to our jobs in terms of identity we can place our homes, where we choose to live and how we live within it."
— Carmen Wong Ulrich, author of *The Real Cost of Living*

If you're like most people, you will spend at least half your life at home. It is your cocoon, your default refuge from the outside world. Whether it's a house, condo, apartment or houseboat, your home should also be a place that reflects your personality and supports your life goals.

THE STYLE OF YOUR HOME SAYS A LOT ABOUT YOUR PERSONAL STYLE

Once you decide upon a home, its style will impact your life in many subtle ways. Your particular taste in furnishings either serves to bolster your sense of self…or detracts from it. Spend a few minutes observing the furnishings and style of a person's living quarters and it will tell you a lot about the occupant.

Get rid of clutter. Don't allow boxes of papers or odds and ends to accumulate. Clear out your closets. Spend time setting up files and storage for the items you need to keep. Purge all else. Keep your "feng shui" simple, beautiful, and functional.

A disorganized home is often the sign of a disorganized life. Studies show that living an organized and uncluttered lifestyle contributes to success in other areas of your life. One efficiency expert said she can tell if a person is doing well in their career, or taking care of their finances wisely just by looking at their kitchen, bath, living room, bedroom, closet, and car. "I know with 95% accuracy what an individual's personality is like by seeing how they live."

- For guidance on how to maintain an efficient, uncluttered, attractive environment, check out *The Clutter Diet: The Skinny on Organizing Your Home and Taking Control of Your Life* by Lori Marerro. www.theclutterdiet.com

Ever spend an hour looking for something you know you have in your closet or storage room only to never locate the item? We all have. What if your home is destroyed by fire or a tornado? A Personal Inventory list is essential to locating items or validating their existence to insurance companies.

At KnowYourStuff.org the Insurance Information Institute has created an easy, secure method to keep an inventory of what you own online. As you list your possessions, make a separate list that shows exactly where in your home or storage each item is located.

MICRO ENVIRONMENTS...YOUR PERSONAL PLACES

Jack Canfield, author of *Success Principles: How to Get from Where You Are to Where You Want to Be*, says, "Make one change every day to improve your environment." www.thesuccessprinciples.com

Surround yourself with beauty and order. Carefully consider every purchase—furniture, paintings, dishes, flooring, paint. Does it add beauty and quality to your life? If not, pass on it.

Personal places that either enhance or detract from your life include the place where you work, your vehicle, even the clothes you choose to wear. You "reside" in all these places. Each is a reflection of who you are as a person.

Life Rule: Your places define who you are, so choose them carefully.

Additional resources:

www.bestplaces.net *Sperling's Best Places*, a compendium of resources to help you determine your best place to live.

www.bestboomertowns.com The top retirement places Baby Boomers.

Best Places to Raise Your Family by Bert Sperling and Peter Sander.

101 Best Outdoor Towns: Unspoiled Places to Visit, Live & Play by Sarah Tuff and Greg Melville.

Retirement Places Rated: Plan the Retirement You Deserve **and** ***Places Rated Almanac: The Classic Guide for Finding Your Best Places to Live in America*** by David Savageau.

Cities Ranked and Rated: More than 400 Metropolitan Areas Evaluated in the U.S. and Canada by Bert Sperling and Peter Sander.

The New Geography of Jobs by Enrico Moretti.

Life Rule: Your "places" exert tremendous influence upon what happens to you in life. Choose them wisely. Live in sync with environments that reflect your values and aspirations.

CHAPTER 7
YOU

YOU

"We are the CEOs of our own companies: ME Inc. The brand called YOU." — Tom Peters

All the advice from all the experts in this guide to creating a successful life will be ineffective unless you also work on YOU. You can have a Harvard Ph.D., but it won't do you much good if you are dishonest and deceitful. There are people in federal prison with Harvard degrees. It doesn't matter if you are talented or good–looking…if you have a negative, abusive personality. The world is full of talented and good–looking people who failed in life because no one wanted anything to do with them. Money, while important, isn't the key to happiness in life. You can have millions of dollars but never find true love. Or personal satisfaction.

"Dogs got personality. Personality goes a long way."
— Quentin Tarantino

You can be less than ideal in many areas of life if you have an engaging, outgoing, charismatic personality. A person with character and integrity. A person others like, want to be with, and help. A person who knows what they want out of life and how to get it.

YOU NEED TO KNOW WHO YOU ARE

"The worst loneliness is not to be comfortable with yourself."
— Mark Twain

"If you don't have any idea of what kind of person you want to become, it's all pointless," says Harvard Business School Professor Clayton Christensen, author of *How Will You Measure Your Life*. What is the purpose of your life? What is truly important to you...not what others expect of you? Without knowing this you're in a boat in the middle of the sea without a compass to get you where you want to go.

YOU are the most important ingredient in whether or not your life is happy and successful.

MANAGING YOUR STORY

"Make the most of yourself, for that is all there is of you."
— Ralph Waldo Emerson

One of the most insightful observations Tony Robbins www.tonyrobbins.com has made is the necessity of creating and managing your personal life story. The need to develop effective strategies...a Plan for Life...requires reaching a point in life where you will simply not settle for the status quo any longer, where your dreams become so important to your survival that you're ready to break the chains of past thoughts and actions. Whether it is in your career, health, finances, love life or personal development, you must have a strategy if you want to achieve success.

Robbins says we all have stories—narratives we tell ourselves about why we can or cannot do or achieve something in our lives. Your expectations then control your focus, perceptions, and the way in which you feel and act. Most people tell themselves a story that limits their chance of success because they are afraid of failure. So the story becomes self–fulfilling. Robbins points out that a disempowering story is one of the things that controls people and makes them hold on to beliefs that no longer serve them well.

DECISIONS, DECISIONS, DECISIONS

"How you come out of the womb has nothing to do with what kind of person you are. You decide what kind of person you're going to be."
— Warren Buffett

Your life will be the sum of your decisions...good and bad. So it is important to learn how to make better decisions. The guidance, tools, and resources in this book can help, but it's only a beginning. You'll need to constantly challenge yourself and dig deep into your own psyche to avoid the "cognitive biases" that make day-to-day choices so difficult.

In *Decisive: How to Make Better Choices in Life and Work* by Chip and Dan Heath, they outline the process for good decision-making.

1. **Avoid narrow framing.** For example, you may ask "Should I break up with my boyfriend?" Instead ask "How can I make this relationship better?" "Should I buy a new car?" can be reframed to ask "What is the best way to spend the money to support my family?"
2. **Don't succumb to confirmation bias.** This is the human tendency to make a decision based upon a "gut feeling" and then search for information to support that decision. Be open, get the facts, consider alternate solutions.
3. **Don't allow short-term emotions to rule.** For example, you are offered a job for more money in another city. Do you take it...and leave a city you love and your friends? Will the work at your new job provide as much fulfillment? Are you leaving a boss who is kind and supportive?
4. **Don't be overconfident.** Most people tend to be overconfident about the outcome of their decisions.

THE WRAP METHOD TO BETTER DECISIONS

The Heaths advise a four-step method to make decisions they call the WRAP method.

1. **Widen your choices.** Your first choice may not be the best.
2. **Reality-test your assumptions.** How would a trial lawyer argue against your decision?

3. **Attain some distance before deciding.** After the short-term emotional response has died down, what would you advise a friend?
4. **Prepare to be wrong.** Few decisions are black and white with guaranteed outcomes. Have a Plan B in case you are wrong.

Perhaps their best advice is to ask yourself, "What would have to be true for this to be my best option?"

Finally, while there is no magic formula to decision-making, it's good to know the process...so much in life depends upon your ability to make sound decisions. A classic book on decision-making is *Smart Choices: A Practical Guide to Decision Making* by John Hammond, Ralph Keeney, and Howard Raiffa. Their explanation of decision theory, practical tips, and psychological pitfalls will greatly improve your ability to make better choices.

5 STEPS TO BETTER DECISIONS

Decisions are often made haphazardly, infused with emotion and stress, and with very little due diligence. Here are five more ways to avoid potentially disastrous mistakes when making decisions.

1. Plan ahead whenever possible.
2. Gather as much information as you can...both pro and con.
3. Use your intuition (as well as your intellect) but don't make decisions emotionally.
4. Ask others...but decide on your own.
5. Sleep on it...then make your decision in the morning when you are fresh and rested.

PERSONAL BOARD OF ADVISORS

Most corporations, sports teams, clubs, trade associations, and magazines create an Advisory Board to help provide expert advice and direction.

Building a Personal Advisory Board will be vital to your success in life. I can say without qualification that had I reached out to people with more experience, more wisdom, and a different point of view, my own life would be dramatically different. No matter how smart you are and how hard you work, getting another person's perspective or advice helps decision–making.

Look for people who are in your field of endeavor or who have a particular expertise that could be of value to you, and begin building a mutually respectful and rewarding relationship. In areas of your life that require specialized expertise (e.g an attorney), find reliable people before you need them.

Don't forget to add a friend or family member to your Personal Advisory Team…one you can count on to provide honest feedback. Friends and family are the people who have the most interest in your welfare.

YOUR PERSONAL SUPPORT TEAM FOR LIFE

There are several key professionals with the expertise to support you in the smooth functioning of your life.

1. Professional coach/mentor
2. Doctor
3. Lawyer
4. Dentist
5. Accountant
6. Auto mechanic
7. Priest/therapist
8. Electrician
9. Plumber
10. Handyman

In most cities you can find guides such as www.AngiesList.com or Yelp www.Yelp.com that will steer you to reputable people who are recommended by actual users. It's like having a few dozen friends recommend the same person. Of course, you can ask people you trust who they use.

- Create a list of qualifications, personal attributes, price, and any other criteria important to you. Use this as your baseline qualifying test to evaluate your Support Team.

The key is due diligence…you want to judge each person on the basis of recommendations, a personal interview, and as much background research as possible. You do not want to make mistakes in choosing your support team. Take the time to do it right.

While very few people make the effort to build a Personal Support

Team, it will be one of your most important decisions in life, affecting everything from your health to your wealth.

YOUR PERSONAL "BRAND"

In 21st Century America it's important to manage your public persona—your personal "brand." More than ever perception is reality. This may not be the way it should be, but it's the way it is. The sooner you realize this and accept it the faster you will achieve what you want in life.

What other people think of you will largely determine your future. We all depend upon others as much as ourselves for success. 80% of the opportunities—jobs, new clients, promotions—will be a result of others helping you in some way.

In order to create the person you want to be—and you want others to see—you must define who it is you are. The first step to creating your public image is to create a personal brand for yourself based in reality. Personal branding expert Dan Schwabel, author of *Me 2.0: Build a Powerful Brand to Achieve Career Success*, says that personal branding is about unearthing what is true and unique about you and letting everybody know about it. Creating a personal brand that is not of truth will certainly fail over time. Take time to perform an honest evaluation of yourself.

Make a list of your assets.

- ✓ What are your natural talents?
- ✓ What are your personality strengths?
- ✓ How much education do you have?
- ✓ How much and what kind of experience do you have?
- ✓ What skills do you offer?
- ✓ Are you creative or analytical?
- ✓ What kind of personal style do you have?
- ✓ Do you have a wide network of personal and professional contacts?

List your disadvantages.

- ✓ Are you physically or mentally challenged in some way?

- ✓ Do you have little in the way of skills or experience?
- ✓ Are you an introvert or socially awkward?
- ✓ Do you have a criminal record?
- ✓ Are you lacking education?

Honestly think of every negative about yourself and what it will take to overcome them. What improvements do you want to make? Are they achievable?

- ✓ Can you get the skills, training or education you need?
- ✓ Are you willing to do the work to get fit and healthy?
- ✓ Is there a personal coach who can help you be more socially adept?
- ✓ Are you willing to invest in new clothes, hairstyle, makeup…and find someone who will help refine your unique personal style?
- ✓ What "rough edges" do you need to remove from your personality?

What impact do you want your image to have on others? And what do you want to accomplish by shaping a definable image? At the very least you want an image that sets you apart in some memorable way—that uniquely reflects who you are.

Find a niche where you are the acknowledged expert and master. "Own" what sets you apart, what makes you desirable, what gives you "value." Above all, your personal brand must be authentic.

To manage your image you'll need to manage your public exposure. Consistency is important. You don't want to purport to be an intelligent, mature, and dependable person and then post naked photos of yourself on the Internet. If your co-workers see you as a bright star, it only takes one DUI to blow that impression.

Decide what is true for you, create a style and "brand," and then stick to it. Otherwise you'll lack definition and substance. You're just another face in the crowd that lacks any hard description.

BE DIFFERENT

It's a lot easier to develop a unique personal image if you <u>are</u> unique. Think for a moment about the great personalities of our time—Truman

Capote, George Plimpton, Dorothy Parker, Ernest Hemingway, Pablo Picasso, Somerset Maugham, John Kennedy, Katherine Hepburn, John Wayne, Ronald Reagan, Coco Chanel, and William F. Buckley. They combined talent, creativity, charm, charisma, confidence, an ability to connect with people, and a distinct personal style into something uniquely their own.

Perhaps you'll never develop a style or personality that's as easily recognizable as Hemingway or Bogart, but you can create a persona that's uniquely yours and different from anyone else. Just don't be beige, invisible or insignificant in life.

MANAGING YOUR PERSONAL "BRAND" ONLINE

In the 21st Century you'll need to manage your personal brand both offline and online. Increasingly, what appears online defines you in the eyes of others. Your first step is to claim your "space" online.

GOOGLE PROFILE

On Google Profiles you can set up your profile so that when your name is "Googled" by anyone your profile will be displayed at the bottom of the search results.

If you don't have one already, set up a Google account. Use your complete name when registering so that you can get a vanity Google profile URL. Remember to check where it says "Display my full name so I can be found in search." Fill out as much of the requested information as possible so that your rank will be higher. Include links to your blogs and social networks.

SOCIAL NETWORKS

Find out if you can reserve your personal brand name on the social networking sites. Go to www.namechk.com or www.knowem.com to see where it's possible to claim your name on dozens of social networking sites, including the big ones like Facebook, Twitter, LinkedIn, Google+, Flickr, Delicious, Stumbleupon, You Tube, Tumblr, Vimeo, Pinterest, and Blogger. You don't need to register with every available site, but by reserving your name on the biggest social networks and the ones that pertain to your interests or profession, you protect your personal brand from being hijacked by others of the same name.

CREATE A PERSONAL BRAND "HUB"

Establish a central "hub" where all your social networking profiles, blogs, and websites can be gathered under a single domain name (yourname. com). You can then use this one website for your resume, business cards, literature, and as the link to everything online about you.

There are dozens of good resources to build your own website. Popular free website building sites are www.wix.com, www.webnode.com, www.moonfruit.com and www.weebly.com. You can create a free blog using Google's Blogger www.blogger.com or the microblogging platform Tumblr www.tumblr.com.

Another popular choice to build your own blogsite is Wordpress. This requires a bit of work on your part, but it isn't brain surgery...millions have created blogsites with Wordpress. There are two forms of Wordpress, the hosted and non-hosted type. www.wordpress.com.

Most professionals use the hosted version...Wordpress.org. Go to www.wordpress.org for more information about how to create your own site, select and purchase a URL (about $12), choose an appropriate design theme (many are free), and find a good hosting company (about $5 a month). Popular hosting companies are Go Daddy www.godaddy.com, Bluehost www.bluehost.com or Host Gator www.hostgator.com.

If you have some tech savvy, you can likely build your blogsite without a designer (although I don't recommend it). Many hosting companies now have "one click" installations of Wordpress and good service departments to help you get going with your blogsite. To self-educate yourself about Wordpress the *Wordpress All-in-one for Dummies* book contains virtually everything you need to know (885 pages, $34.99).

Graphic designers to help build your blogsite can be found online at 99Designs www.99designs.com, eLance www.elance.com, iFreelance www.ifreelance.com, PeoplePerHour www.peopleperhour.com, and Freelancer.com www.freelancer.com. It's possible to get a great-looking basic site design for less than $500.

GET A GOOD HEADSHOT

You want to present your best image online. So don't skimp on your headshot photo. Get one taken by a professional. Make sure the photo isn't so "posed" as to look unnatural. Have a photo taken that shows what you really look like...at your best of course. Also, don't make the mistake of using a great photo taken 15 or 20 years ago in the hope that it will make you seem younger or more "hip." You'll only embarrass yourself.

ONLINE PHOTOS

Before posting any kind of photograph of yourself online, consider what impact it will have now and in the future. You don't want unflattering photos permanently out there in cyberspace just waiting to sabotage that perfect job you're interviewing for or screw up the relationship with the gorgeous, charming, talented guy/gal you just met. Managing your visual presence online is vitally important to the long-term success of your personal brand.

One college student posted a gag photo of himself on Facebook showing a cop handcuffing him at the beach during Spring Break. It wasn't a real cop and the student hadn't done anything wrong. It was just a bone-headed joke—one that unfortunately soured when the HR Director of a large company happened across it during a routine online background check. Guess who isn't laughing now?

By carefully choosing the photos you allow online you also control your image. One physical therapist I know posts photos during her treks through Africa, on 100-mile bike races, and climbing Mt. Whitney. It reinforces her brand personality as an active, fit person.

MEDIA EXPOSURE

Nothing promotes your personal brand and reaches as many people as favorable articles in the media. If you plan it intelligently, your offline/online media exposure can have significant impact upon your career and personal life.

With the expansion of media to the web, there are now literally thousands of potential points of media exposure you can utilize to further your interests. Reporters, bloggers, and web content managers are always looking for pieces that provide informative or interesting reading/viewing for their audience. Approach them with a good story they can implement easily and your chance of being given exposure are excellent. Start with Help A Reporter Out. www.haro.com

Put yourself in the mind of the journalist. They aren't particularly (or at all) interested in promoting you, your "amazing" service or widget. Frame your pitch to the journalists' self–interest, not yours. What will interest his/her audience?

Always approach the journalist using their preference for contact: telephone, email, skype, twitter, etc. If you can't determine what this is, simply call or email. Have a Twitter length "elevator pitch" ready to catch the interest of the journalist. They will know (and tell you) within 30 seconds if they want to continue to learn more about what you are pitching.

DON'T JUST EXIST...LIVE

"Those who believe they can move mountains, do. Those who believe they can't, cannot. Belief triggers the power to do."
— David Schwartz, author of *The Magic of Thinking Big.*

One of my favorite websites is Marc and Angel Hack Life: Productive Tips for Productive Living www.marcandangel.com. I suggest bookmarking their site and subscribing to the RSS feed. It will become one of your Plan for Life support resources.

They've listed 15 ways you can approach life so that you aren't just one of those people "leading lives of quiet desperation," as Emerson said, but truly living.

"The proper function of man is to live, not just exist." — Jack London

1. **Appreciate the great people and things in your life.** You never know how much you have until you lose it. Be grateful for what you have, the people who love you, and your potential in life. Daily and continuous gratitude will change your life.
2. **Ignore other people's negativity.** Be confident and secure in yourself. Don't let other people's opinions shape your existence.
3. **Forgive those who have hurt you.** People hurt others for a multitude

of reasons, and often they are unaware they've hurt someone. You allow your life to be defined by resentment if you harbor hurt and think thoughts of revenge. You don't have to trust or like someone who has hurt you (especially if they aren't sorry), but don't let them have control over you. Be the first to forgive…then move on.

4. **Be who you really are.** Be your authentic self. Don't try to fit into someone else's idea of who or what you should be, you'll only feel like a fraud and appear phony to others. It's better to live as you truly are, with all your genius, foibles, faults, and unique attributes.

5. **Choose to listen to your inner voice.** Human beings have developed instincts over the last hundred thousand years or so that enable us to know what is right or wrong in our lives…if we just learn to listen. That "gut feeling" about a decision or course of action is usually correct, even though we have no idea where it emanates from…it's hardwired into our DNA.

6. **Embrace change.** If there is one constant in 21st Century life, its change. Adapt to it, use it to your advantage, and experience what unfolds. Look at life as an adventure, including both the good and the bad.

7. **Choose your relationships wisely.** Much of the good (and the bad) that happens in life is a result of the people you allow into it. Don't trust too quickly. Don't rush love because you're lonely, infatuated or feel you have to be in a relationship…wait until you are ready and the right person comes along. Be a good friend, but don't get into a toxic relationship because you want to have friends…and be ready to dump anyone who is negative or untrustworthy. Work with people you respect.

8. **Recognize those who love you.** People often ignore or don't appreciate those who love them the most. This is especially true during the narcissistic years of youth, when parents and friends may run against your desires. The most important people in your life will be those who loved you most when you were not being very lovable. Revere those who care enough about you to love you.

9. **Love yourself.** The majority of people find fault with themselves… often to the point of self–loathing. Learn to love yourself as the

unique person you are...faults and all...because all growth begins with self-love.

10. **Do things your future self will thank you for.** Your life, both good and bad, is the result of every decision you make. Learn to make those decisions as wisely as possible, even if it hurts now. Good decisions are like contributing money every day to a high-interest savings account... someday your life will be rich.

11. **Be thankful for the troubles you don't have.** Recent years have seen millions of people encounter difficulties they never imagined could happen. When you have troubles, it's easy to focus on them and begin a downward spiraling "pity party." If you've just lost a job or a boyfriend, know that there are people who have lost a son or daughter, been wiped out financially, learned they have a terminal illness and have just months to live or have been in an accident and are paralyzed for life. Put your troubles in perspective. Better yet, get out and help those less fortunate than you are...it's the best therapy for putting your own difficulties in perspective.

12. **Allow time for fun.** Life is to be enjoyed. In fact, it may be our primary purpose in life. Life itself, and the amazing world we inhabit, is a precious gift. Don't squander it with endless work, worry, hatred or a boring existence. Get out and enjoy the world.

13. **Enjoy the little things.** Someday you will look back and realize it was the little things in life that made it meaningful. The beauty of a sunset, playing with a baby, hiking in Yosemite, laughing with friends, watching the ballgame, a great bowl of chili. These are the things you don't want to take for granted, but revel in.

14. **Don't let the past steal your present and future from you.** Learn from the past but don't be enslaved by it. What exists is now...and the potential in your future. That's where you need to focus your thoughts and energies.

15. **Let go when you must**. As surely as change is inevitable, some things in life will no longer serve you in the present or future. Be honest and brave enough to recognize these things...change, start over or move on.

YOUR ATTITUDE IS YOUR ALTITUDE

"Man is made or unmade by himself." — James Allen

A positive, optimistic attitude about life—despite its inevitable travails—is an important ingredient to attaining success in all things you pursue. This is, of course, easier said than done. With all the negativity in the world, being optimistic can be a challenge.

A great deal is being written currently about how the mind influences outcomes in life. While visualization is a valid and important element in achieving what we want (athletes and performers rehearse in their minds all the time—and clinical studies show it works), it's simplistic to think we can attain what we want in only this way. If everyone could think their way into a Lamborghini, a mansion in Malibu, a supermodel girlfriend or a movie actor husband, then possessing these things would be commonplace. Millions of people also pray for world peace at church every weekend and we're no closer to achieving it than we were fifty years ago. Wishing something is so won't make it so. You need to combine action with belief.

"Belief creates the actual fact." — William James

Taking action is what this book is all about. And action combined with continual focus and visualization can result in the magic of manifestation, that elusive phenomena that produces what we want in sometimes unexplainable ways.

There are several excellent books that can help you with visualization, focus, and manifestation.

1. ***The Magic of Thinking Big***, David J. Schwartz, Ph.D.
2. ***The Power of Intention: Learning to Co-create Your World Your Way***, Wayne Dyer
3. ***Manifest Your Destiny***, Wayne Dyer www.drwaynedyer.com
4. ***How to Win Friends and Influence People***, Dale Carnegie
5. ***Awaken the Giant Within***, Anthony Robbins www.tonyrobbins.com
6. ***The Power of Positive Thinking***, Dr. Norman Vincent Peal
7. ***The Success Principles: How to Get from Where You Are to Where***

You Want to Be, Jack Canfield www.jackcanfield.com

8. ***The Aladdin Factor***, Jack Canfield and Mark Victor Hansen
9. ***Reinvention: How to Make the Rest of Your Life the Best of Your Life***, Brian Tracy www.briantracy.com
10. ***Goals: How to Get Everything You Want—Faster Than You Ever Thought Possible***, Brian Tracy www.briantracy.com

For about $150, you can tap into the wisdom of many of our greatest personal development thinkers.

The books on this list have helped hundreds of millions of people. Buy them, read them, and refer back to them often. Build your Personal Success Library around these books.

TOP TEN WAYS TO MAKE YOURSELF MISERABLE

It isn't hard to make yourself miserable; people do it all the time. If you want to make your life a miserable waste of space on earth, here are the Top 10 ways to do so:

1. Live in the past.
2. Think constantly about missed opportunities.
3. Always think the grass is greener somewhere else.
4. Remember when you've been mistreated.
5. Worry about possible future mistreatment.
6. Focus on what is missing in life and don't be grateful for what you have now.
7. Stress over everything (not enough money, nobody loves me, I'm too fat/thin/old/young/ugly, people don't like me, I'm not too bright, where did I put my keys, I hate my (insert insecurity here), everyone is out to get me, is my husband/wife cheating, I hate my thighs/my job/my life).
8. Think about money (making it/financial ruin/what to do with it).
9. Gossip and complain.
10. Believe your current circumstances are hopeless and won't change.

Life Rule: What goes into your brain is perceived by the brain as real. Discipline yourself to banish negative, destructive thoughts and replace them with positive, constructive thoughts.

POSITIVELY RID YOURSELF OF NEGATIVITY

"The greatest discovery of my generation is that a human being can alter his life by altering his attitudes of mind." — William James

You can easily get caught up in negative thinking, especially when hit by a series of problems or challenges. It's human nature. Over time you unconsciously train your mind to react negatively and it becomes habit. That's why it is important to never let a bad day go by without a course correction. When something negative intrudes on your life, repel it with something positive. If you allow negative thinking to gain control of your subconscious you'll find yourself spinning out of control in a downward spiral.

Go for a walk. Ride your bike a few miles. Or go pump some iron at the gym. Exercise helps stimulate positive endorphins, clears your mind, and defuses stress. Then give yourself a pep talk by tuning into the wisdom of people like Jack Canfield, Tony Robbins, and Dale Carnegie.

Review the Plan for Life chapters and your own Personal Plan. Stay focused and on track. Whatever negative thing that happened to you is a speed bump…don't let it become a roadblock.

MANAGE YOUR ENERGY FIELD

My good friend Ron Nash, author of TheInAcademy www.TheInAcademy.com, always includes a discussion of a person's personal energy field when he conducts a seminar. People get jobs, find ideal mates, and experience manifestation in their lives when they manage and control their personal energy. It's something that others react to either negatively or positively, depending upon what you project.

When life is going well this is easy to do, but when you are experiencing difficulties, setbacks or hardship, managing your personal energy is challenging. There are several techniques for keeping your energy positive.

1. **Get out in nature**. A walk in the woods or by the seashore "grounds" you to the earth and usually infuses your senses with mood-improving negative ions.
2. **Listen to music**. Find a signature song that makes you feel good and play it often.
3. **Hang out with your more positive-minded friends.**
4. **Laugh.** Go to a comedy club, watch a funny movie or check out a website that posts funny videos.
5. **Meditate.**
6. **Exercise.** Exercise reduces stress and infuses your body with positive hormones.
7. **Keep life in perspective**. Remember that as bad as it seems now things will get better. Many others have been in worse circumstances and risen above them to emerge in a better place.

NOT EVERYTHING WILL ALWAYS GO AS YOU PLAN

"There is one thing about which I am certain, there is very little about which one can be certain." — Somerset Maugham

Most of the inspirational books will tell you that you are the sum of the decisions you make in life. You are solely responsible for what becomes of you. While this is true, it's also true that sometimes bad things happen to good people.

You may make great decisions 100% of the time. You may be responsible and hard-working. You may be generous and kind-hearted. And you may still lose your job, suffer a stroke or be hit by a drunk driver. There will also be times when the planets all line up just right and you get lucky. A chance encounter leads you in a new, exciting, and rewarding direction. Life falls neatly into place. Or what seemed like bad luck at the time turns out to be the best thing that could have happened.

As much good "luck" will occur in your life as the opposite. It's how you handle each that counts. Weathering the down cycles with grace, courage, and a positive attitude will minimize their impact upon your life.

DISCIPLINE

"Life is tons of discipline." — Robert Frost

Discipline is the one area of life that most people fail at miserably. For Americans it's a word with immediate negative connotations…like hard work, deprivation, delayed gratification, and making tough choices instead of easy ones.

Americans make goals but don't stick to them.

- More than two-thirds of New Year resolutions have been broken by March.
- Only 13% of the people who begin working out at a health club are doing so six months later. Health clubs know this and thrive because of their members' lack of discipline.
- Study after study shows that 95% of the people who lose weight gain it all back within a year. Why? Because they don't have the discipline to keep working toward a goal over an extended period of time.

In his book *Getting It Done: The Transforming Power of Self-Discipline*, author Andrew J. DuBrin Ph.D. quotes President Theodore Roosevelt, "With self-discipline, all things are possible. Without it, even the simplest goal can seem like the impossible dream."

Durbin describes the self-discipline of the late author Michael Crichton, who produced dozens of best-selling books and movies during his career. Crichton's favorite line was "butt to chair." When he was working on a book or screenplay, Crichton woke at 4 a.m. to drive to his office in Santa Monica, California, and focused entirely on his work until 5:30 p.m. when he returned home for family activities. As Durbin points out, "I suspect the extraordinary fame and income Crichton derived from his self-disciplined activity contributed immensely to his sense of happiness and well-being."

World-renown cognitive scientist, author, and Harvard psychology professor Steven Pinken believes that "together with intelligence, self-control turns out to be the best predictor of a successful and satisfying life."

Jim Rohn, author of *7 strategies for Wealth & Happiness: Power Ideas from America's Foremost Business Philospher*, said in recent years there have been a number of books which promote the idea that if one verbally affirms what one wants on a daily basis, success will magically emerge. "I'm completely opposed to this mode of thinking." He sums it up by saying, "Discipline is the foundation on which all success is built. Lack of discipline inevitably leads to failure."

"Laziness travels so slowly that poverty soon overtakes it."
— Benjamin Franklin

In her book *The Willpower Instinct: How Self-Control Works, Why It Matters, and What You Can Do To Get More of It,* Kelly McDonigal Ph.D. provides empirical evidence that two ways to improve self-discipline are through exercise and meditation. Both help provide the necessary positive feedback required to maintain continued positive action. Following a plan with benchmarks and interim goals also can help you stay disciplined and on track.

Life Rule: Sometimes discipline is simply forcing yourself to do what is unpleasant or difficult, knowing that it will lead to success.

ENTHUSIASM

"Nothing great was ever achieved without enthusiasm."
— Ralph Waldo Emerson

Enthusiasm creates a self-perpetuating circle of energy that expands exponentially. People with enthusiasm and a positive personality make positive things happen. The more things go your way the more confident you become. The more confident you become the more you make happen. And making things happen that you want in your life is a sure road to greater happiness.

"Energy and persistence conquer all things." — Benjamin Franklin

Enthusiasm is the fuel that drives charisma. And people with charisma can overcome many other deficiencies in their personality, physical ability, talent, education, upbringing, financial circumstances or social status. Enthusiasm combined with confidence, courage, and intelligence creates legends. Teddy Roosevelt, Henry Ford, and Oprah Winfrey...all achieved greatness through enthusiasm, a positive outlook on life, and charisma

"Success is the ability to go from one failure to another with no loss of enthusiasm." — Sir Winston Churchill

Enthusiasm is energy. And energy is what drives success in life. The highly regarded psychologist Martin Seligman of the University of Pennsylvania, said "Biographies of great achievers often note their subjects' remarkable levels of energy, far more crucial to their success than any raw ability."

Life Rule: This is important. Energy alone trumps talent, education, and connections. Enthusiasm is energy in action.

WHY YOU'RE HAPPY—OR NOT

"Most people are about as happy as they decide to be."
— Abraham Lincoln

In the *Review of General Psychology* (2005) a study found that 50% of how happy a person feels is determined by genes. Everyone has a happiness "set point." Another 40% of how happy people are is a result of the things they choose to do—exercising, setting goals, leisure activities, relationships, and sex. Just 10% of what makes people "happy" is based upon circumstances such as age, race, gender and financial status.

LOVE = HAPPINESS

"Happiness is not something ready-made. It comes from your own actions." — Dalai Lama

Loving relationships can make you happy. Nobel Prize–winning economist Daniel Kahneman, who has researched the subject of happiness for decades, says the surest path to "happiness is the experience of spending time with people you love and who love you." Love and relationships rank highly on every measure of happiness ever done.

SEX MAKES PEOPLE HAPPY (DUH)

You'll be glad to learn that sex is one of the things that makes people happiest. It ranks fairly high on most surveys. I once asked an 88–year old man what he would do more of if he could live his life over and his immediate answer was, "I'd have a lot more sex." It's difficult to understand why people don't have more sex. It's free (usually). It feels great. It's good for your health. And it's good for your emotional well-being. If you created a pill that did all this everyone in the country would be taking it. Yet, the number of Americans who live lives without any sex is substantial.

In general Americans are having less sex...just 85 times a year now on average compared to more than 120 times just 20 years ago. Other countries have more sex than we do. Greeks, for example, have sex 164 times a year. It's no wonder that fewer than half of Americans (48%) say they are happy with their sex life, according to a comprehensive *ABC-TV* poll (2004).

There are huge differences between men and women in their sexual preferences. Men tend to want more sex, more adventurous sex, and more partners. A 2013 survey found that 1 in 10 men would have sex with a robot! (some married men claim they already make love with robots).

There are men who purchase robot "dolls" www.realdoll.com and have sex with them. Buyers can customize their doll to their specifications, even adding a penis if desired. Prices start around $5,000. Some experts predict that robot sex will become widespread within the next 30 years.

THE SMARTER YOU ARE THE HAPPIER YOU ARE

People who are smarter also report being happier. As IQ increases so does happiness. When people attain more education, they also gain more happiness. More education usually translates to career success which in turn creates financial success and marital success (which also increases happiness).

- Happy people are 73% more likely to experience positive outcomes in their career and personal life.

A LIFE OF PURPOSE AND MEANING

"Many persons have a wrong idea of what constitutes true happiness. It is not attained through self-gratification but through fidelity to a worthy purpose." — Helen Keller

Living a life of purpose and meaning is a key ingredient in achieving happiness. Spending money on helping others creates more "happiness" in people than spending money on material things. People who volunteer their time to worthy organizations and causes report being happier than those who do not. Living a life of purpose is a fundamental human desire.

EXPERIENCES MAKE PEOPLE HAPPIER THAN THINGS

Experiences, especially with family or friends, provides more lasting happiness than buying things. A new car soon becomes just another mode of transportation, but the memories of a vacation in Paris with a loved one improves over time. When asked, most older people say they wished they had spent more of their money on experiencing life rather than accumulating stuff.

Hobbies and leisure activities also provide a great deal of happiness to most people. A great game of golf, tennis with friends, travel, painting, music...what we do to enjoy being alive generates emotions that last a lifetime and create a "happy" life.

CIRCUMSTANCES AFFECT HAPPINESS

One reason why Americans are so unhappy now compared to other developed nations is our normally optimistic expectations for a better future have been squashed by the unrelenting and unprecedented difficulties we've all faced since the dawn of the 21st Century. This disruption is likely to get worse...especially if the nation slips back into serious recession, as many predict.

Personal happiness in the future will need to depend less on the trappings of our consumerist society and more on core values.

TOP 10 HAPPINESS LIST

1. Family.
2. Love.
3. Sex.
4. Spirituality.
5. Hobbies.
6. Relaxing/vacations.
7. Achievement.
8. Socializing with friends.
9. Financial security.
10. Helping others.

A DOZEN WAYS NOT TO FIND HAPPINESS

"Oh what a bitter thing it is to look into happiness through another man's eyes." — William Shakespeare

There are many ways people sabotage their own happiness.

1. **Not being grateful.** Not just the big things, but the little things too.
2. **Allowing others to define who you are.** You must lead your own authentic life and not let others lead it for you. Develop a solid self–concept…and stick to it.
3. **Taking your life too seriously.** A sense of humor seems to be on the endangered list of personal attributes these days. Take time to laugh. Drop the seriousness. Smile more…it can change how you feel about the world and how the world feels about you.
4. **Being a control freak.** There are some things you can influence (not control) and other things over which you have little or no control. Focus on what you can do to improve your life and the lives of others.
5. **Allowing stress to rule your life.** Stress can literally be a killer. In modern life there are a million things that can potentially stress you out. But being stressed not only harms your health, it can also lead to poor decisions and reduced productivity. Get out in nature, read a book, see a movie, sign up for a yoga class, work out or go for a run, get a massage…it can save your life.
6. **Letting the past control your present and future.** What is done is done. All we really have is the present and the promise of the future. Stay in these areas exclusively.
7. **Missing out on life's journey.** It's the journey, not the destination, that ultimately provides the most satisfaction. Don't miss out on all the wonderful things life offers because you are too focused on getting to your end goal.
8. **Not being flexible.** Even the most well thought out plan needs to incorporate flexibility. Resisting or avoiding something in life draws energy to it…what you resist, persists. Have a plan, but allow for the natural flow of life.

9. **Letting consumption consume you.** True happiness comes from experiences and relationships, not giant homes, expensive cars, or huge flat screen TVs.

10. **Allowing adversity to crush your spirit.** Failure is a part of the natural order of life. Don't allow failure to define who you are. Keep your best thoughts about yourself in mind, and banish all negative thoughts.

11. **Not living an authentic life.** When you don't pursue your dreams, when you allow yourself to be something others want you to be, and when you live according to others rules, you invalidate yourself. Only you should decide how you are to live.

12. **Being afraid of change**. Change is inevitable. Today there is more dramatic change than any time in recent history. Some of it is only dimly understood. It can be frightening. To be happy you must embrace change, adapt to it, and find the opportunities change always brings.

"Generally, when you are unhappy you will discover it's because you want something you don't have, have something you don't want, or are simply too attached to something you do have."
— Dennis Merritt Jones, author of *The Art of Being*

PERSEVERANCE

Through perseverance many people win success of what seemed destined to be certain failure." — Benjamin Disraeli

When Jack Canfield and Mark Victor Hansen looked for a publisher for their book *Chicken Soup for the Soul*, they met with almost universal rejection…123 publishers turned it down. Not giving up, they went to the American Bookseller's Association convention. Patiently they walked the floor, meeting with as many potential publishers as possible. Eventually they approached the booth of HCI, a small publisher from Deerfield Beach, Florida. The folks at HCI loved the book and decided to take a chance on it. *Chicken Soup* went on to become a bestseller—selling more than eight million copies. The *Chicken Soup* books (there are now over 200 versions) have since sold more than 100 million copies and made Canfield and Hansen multi-millionaires.

As Jack Canfield relates, "Mark and I are big believers in perseverance. If you have a vision and a life purpose, and you believe in it, then you do not let external events tell you what is so. You follow your internal guidance and follow your bliss."

The point here is to not take any rejection or setback personally. Most rejection has nothing to do with you personally. The decision-maker may not be very smart, have ego issues, is dealing with another major decision and is distracted, gets bad advice, is afraid to risk, the timing isn't right—the reasons are myriad and often hard to understand. Just know that the old maxim about "one door closing opens another" has the ring of ancient wisdom about it.

PERSEVERENCE + OPTIMISM = SUCCESS

"Ambition is the path to success. Persistence is the vehicle you arrive in."
— Bill Bradley

You have to keep moving forward when faced with adversity. The capacity to persevere through repeated setbacks and obstacles is associated with a 31% more optimistic view of life and a 42% greater level of satisfaction in life.

Perseverance, grit, persistence, and determination lead to optimism… and when combined these personality traits are a powerful engine of success. "Failure devastates us," says Martin Seligman Ph.D., author of *Learned Optimism: How to Change Your Mind and Your life*. "Optimists bounce back and begin trying immediately; defeat is temporary and achievement is assured. Pessimists, on the other hand, are defined by their failures." When the going gets tough, the strength, courage, and resilience to keep moving forward… perseverance…will reward you in more ways than you can imagine.

One tried and true quote that sums up the role of persistence in life is this one attributed to President Calvin Coolidge:

"Nothing in the world can take the place of persistence. Talent will not; nothing is more common than unsuccessful men with talent. Genius will not; unrewarded genius is almost a proverb. Education will not; the world is full of educated derelicts. Persistence and determination alone are omnipotent."

DON'T BE AFRAID OF FEAR

"Do one thing every day that scares you." — Eleanor Roosevelt

"We have nothing to fear but fear itself," said Franklin D. Roosevelt to the nation during the dark days of the Great Depression. It's true. What you fear either doesn't usually happen or isn't as bad as you expected. But fear itself can be immobilizing.

What you fear is what you often attract…when you dwell upon your fears you end up manifesting exactly what you don't want. That's because you tend to attract what you think about most. So, even in your darkest hours, visualize overcoming your obstacles, creating the success you want to achieve, and experiencing the pride in obtaining the goals you've set for yourself. Fight fear with faith that you will succeed.

Fear is a driver of everything negative that will happen to you in your lifetime. Fear can also motivate success, but more often:

- ✓ Fear paralyzes.
- ✓ Fear creates debilitating stress.
- ✓ Fear impairs sound thinking.
- ✓ Fear is the reason you may find yourself living in opposition to your own beliefs.

"Your attitude is everything and determines how you experience every aspect of your life." — Jerry Jampolsky, M.D. and Diane Cirincione, Ph.D., authors of *Change Your Mind, Change Your Life*

In *Letting Go of Fear* my friend Gerald Jampolsky, founder of The Attitudinal Healing Center, writes "The world we see that seems so insane is the result of a belief system that is not working. To perceive the world differently, we must be willing to change our belief system, let the past slip away, expand our sense of now, and dissolve the fear in our minds." www.jerryjampolsky.com

Your ego creates fear to keep you small and impotent. Fear of failure, rejection, humiliation, mistakes…they all can be overcome by simply feeling the fear, then doing it anyway. What you feared is almost never as bad as you imagined it to be. However, you will feel liberated and joyful by confronting your fears.

"Fear defeats more people than any other one thing in the world."
— Ralph Waldo Emerson

The best way to overcome fear is to walk directly into it. This takes some courage but by approaching your fears you will discover that they likely aren't so scary—and you will develop tactics to deal with fear. The antidote to fear is action.

Remember, everyone is fearful of the very same things you fear. Knowing you are not alone helps mitigate fear. Approach your fears as opportunities for growth. The old sayings "Nothing ventured, nothing gained" and "No guts, no glory" are solidly based on the principle that if we don't stretch ourselves we won't grow.

Most of the world's greatest inventions and breakthroughs were not developed by those credited with inventing them, but instead by people who were not afraid to "go for it." The light bulb was actually "invented" by Sir Humphrey Davy in 1802 but he didn't take the idea to commercial completion. In 1840 James Bowman created a light bulb but was afraid to go further because of the cost involved in completing the design. Thomas Edison bought the previous patents, experimented with thousands of filament materials, and eventually created a light bulb that lasted 1,200 hours. He then wasn't afraid to go commercial with his idea. Those who conquer their fears will profit from their victory.

CONFIDENCE

"Self-confidence is the first requisite to great undertakings."
— Samuel Johnson

Everyone loves the confident person. Confidence is one of the top attributes mentioned time and again in studies of what makes a person attractive. However, confidence is elusive for millions of people.

- More than 15 million Americans suffer from social anxiety disorder, according to the Anxiety Disorder Association of America.

General anxiety disorders affect 40 million American adults, with women likelier to experience anxiety than men (60% to 40%). Of those people diagnosed with anxiety disorder, nearly 3 in 4 treat it with some type of prescription drug.

"If I have lost confidence in myself, I have the Universe against me."
— Ralph Waldo Emerson

For many people there are no underlying physical or mental reasons for feeling a lack of confidence. But 21st Century life can be a constant challenge. There are dozens of things to face every day that sap your confidence. The media flaunts people who are better looking, richer or more successful. There are the constant daily injustices and indignities, from getting a parking ticket to being scolded by your boss. It takes mental fortitude to maintain confidence.

HOW TRUE CONFIDENCE IS ATTAINED

"The man who has confidence in himself gains the confidence of others."
— Hasidic maxim

While drugs and therapy may alleviate the symptoms of social discomfort, there isn't a legal drug that will make you feel confident. The surest path to achieve confidence is through competence, mastery, and achievement.

As you become more educated, more physically fit, more skilled, and more attractive, a natural sense of confidence emerges. You instinctively know that you can handle what life throws at you. You have the ability to make things happen, to turn a lemon into lemonade, and to continually move forward and upward in life. All this feeds upon itself and every success helps create the conditions that will cause more success to happen. Each success is like throwing another log on the fire—you keep getting hotter and your flame burns brighter. And with this success comes financial security, an important ingredient in a confident persona.

Authentic confidence is a product of mastering life.

BEGIN BUILDING CONFIDENCE NOW

Great, you say, but how do I get confident as I'm working on all these things? Try these steps:

1. Remind yourself every day of all the good things about yourself.
2. List all the skills you have developed and the things you are naturally talented at doing. Nearly everyone has something that sets

them apart—even if it's simply being a good friend or parent (a pretty valuable skill actually).

3. Focus on the positive aspects of your looks and personality. No one is perfect (unless heavily Photoshopped). If you don't like what you see, begin a diet and nutrition program. Build some muscle tone with regular exercise. Treat yourself to a new wardrobe, hairstyle, and professionally applied makeup. Just taking these proactive, positive steps will generate confidence. Look at the "before" and "after" photos of people who have successfully lost weight or buffed up by exercising diligently. The "after" photos always show a transformed person brimming with confidence.
4. Examine your personality objectively. If this isn't possible, you may want to ask a close friend or relative to help. What are your "rough" spots? Begin changing them. Where can you improve? Use the resources in this book to smooth out the rough spots and become a more appealing person.
5. Make a plan...A Plan for Life. Just beginning a program of self-improvement will increase your confidence. Sure, you're not where you want to be now...but you're moving in the right direction.

SEIZING THE MOMENT

"You only go around once in life. So grab all the gusto you can get."
— Schlitz Beer commercial

If you look back on your own life you will almost certainly remember small, almost inconsequential, moments that changed the direction of your life forever. Donald Trump relates the story of how one chance occurrence completely changed his life. And how he almost missed it.

When Trump was a billion dollars in debt and his real estate interests were imploding around him, he faced the very real prospect of bankruptcy. Walking along the street in Manhattan one day he stopped to give a homeless man a couple dollars and commented to his wife Ivana, "That man is richer than me."

"How can you say that? We live on Park Avenue and dine at wonderful restaurants and dress in designer clothes."

"Yes, but he's not a billion dollars in debt."

A while later Trump was mulling over whether or not to go to a bankers convention dinner he had been invited to attend. At that moment there were many bankers who weren't particularly fond of Trump. They stood to lose a lot of money with him. Word had gotten out that he was in trouble. It sounded like a boring dinner. Plus, he would have to put on his dinner jacket. He decided it would be much more comfortable to just stay home.

But something made him change his mind. Maybe it would be a show of confidence to dine with the bankers, he thought. At the last moment he decided to go. Trump arrived at the dinner late and his seat was taken. He looked around and sat at the first available table. During dinner he engaged in conversation with his tablemates—all bankers. They took an interest in his dilemma, liked his confident style, and invited him to meet with them.

The meeting resulted in a huge loan that saved the Trump organization and put it on the road to success. Later, when he was a bona fide billionaire again, someone asked how he had done it. "He was lucky," said an observer. Yes, but Trump had made his own luck by going to the dinner, engaging in conversation, and projecting confidence even when he was on the verge of bankruptcy and a billion dollars in debt.

"The biggest adventure you can ever take is to live the life of your dreams." — Oprah Winfrey

Sliding Doors is one of actress Gwynth Paltrow's first movies...and one of the most intriguing. In an early scene she misses a subway by a matter of two or three seconds. The scene is then repeated and this time she makes it on to the subway, again by just a second or two. From this point forward the film shows in parallel scenes how the life of Paltrow's character takes radically different paths—one good and the other not so good. Like the film, real life can be propelled in dramatically new directions by a seemingly minor, chance incident.

In his book *Sixty Seconds: One Moment Changes Everything*, author Phil Bolsta relates how little moments can reroute the course of our lives. In an instant everything can change. If you step outside the frenzy of modern life and pay attention to each moment, the revelations can be life-changing and transformative.

Dr. Dean Ornish talks about how just a few words, spoken in the right way at the right time, pulled him out of a suicidal depression. Lives can be changed, even saved, by the right words at just the right time.

A woman relates how she was about to end her life by jumping from the Golden Gate bridge. As she walked toward the center of the bridge she passed another woman sobbing. She stopped and asked what was wrong. The woman related how she had just lost both her parents to cancer and then her husband and son were killed in an auto accident. "There's no reason to go on," she cried.

Suddenly feeling foolish about her own problems, she invited the woman for a cup of coffee so they could talk. The two became good friends and formed what they called their "mutual admiration society." Later they went into business together, were successful, and built wonderful, fulfilling lives. Their children (who would never have been born had their moms committed suicide) also went on to lead happy, successful, meaningful lives.

Chance encounters like these happen all the time. Some call it destiny. Others call them miracles. The writer Allen Wright calls them "God Moments."

Sometimes these chance occurrences carry us in new directions without our immediate knowledge and without our ability to resist it or change it. But if you are an aware and sensitive person, you can sometimes recognize these catalytic moments in life and use them to advance toward your goals. For a deeper understanding of the dynamics of "being in the now" and "mindful living," read *The Power of Now* by Eckhart Tolle.

HOW TO BE LUCKY

"1 in 5 super-rich people said that luck played a significant role in their success." — From *The Millionaire Mind* by Thomas Stanley, Ph.D.

"Some people get all the lucky breaks." You've heard this (or perhaps said it) hundreds of times. Some people just seem to be born lucky. They get the best jobs. They attract the quality guys or girls. Money–making deals seem to fall into their laps. Yet, there is no discernable difference between you and them.

Or is there?

In one research study, a person who had identified himself as lucky and another who said she was definitely "unlucky" were presented with identical scenarios. Both were instructed to go to a café at different times and wait for a person who would tell them about an interesting research project they might be asked to participate in. Both subjects would be exposed to the same "chance" opportunities at the cafe.

A five-dollar bill was left on the sidewalk outside the café. Inside the café, actors were placed at each of the tables. One of the actors would play a "millionaire." All of the actors would behave in exactly the same way when the "lucky" and "unlucky" subjects entered the café.

The "lucky" subject immediately spotted the five-dollar bill as he walked up to the café. After entering, he sat next to the "millionaire" actor, introduced himself and offered to buy a round of coffee. Soon he and the "millionaire" were involved in a conversation about business. The "lucky" subject left with the future possibility of exploring a joint business deal with the "millionaire."

The "unlucky" subject didn't notice the five-dollar bill when she walked up to the café. She too sat next to the "millionaire" but didn't acknowledge or say a word to him. Nor did she engage any other customer or employee of the café.

Later when both were asked to describe what their day had been like, the "lucky" subject said it had been a great day—and very lucky. He'd found some money and met a fascinating person who might be a collaborator on a business project. The "unlucky" subject reported that it had been a rather uneventful day.

British psychologist Richard Wiseman, author of *The Luck Factor: Changing Your Luck, Changing Your Life, The Four Essential Principals* posits there are steps you can take to become luckier. He claims that people who consider themselves lucky think about their past and view their future in terms of successes rather than failures. Other happiness experts agree. According to Shawn Achor, author of *The Happiness Advantage*, if you see the world in positive terms, your brain identifies similar positive opportunities. www.goodthinkinc.com

LUCKY PEOPLE CONNECT WITH PEOPLE

"Chance is always powerful. Let your hook be always cast; in the pool where you least expect it, there will be fish." — Ovid

Lucky people get involved—they aren't afraid to engage people. In Jean Chatzky's book *The Difference*, she makes an excellent case for the power of connections and their relation to luck. She cites Richard Wiseman, a professor at the University of Hertfordshire, who conducted an experiment in which he asked people first to tell him whether they were lucky, unlucky or neither. Then he gave them a list of fifteen last names common in the United Kingdom and asked if they were on a first-name basis with at least one person with each last name. Nearly half the "lucky" people had eight or more of the last names on their list of personal contacts, compared with one-quarter of the "unlucky." www.jeanchatzky.com

Why did the "lucky" ones know more people with last names on the list? Because they were open to new experiences and new acquaintances who may at some point turn into contacts, mentors, or friends.

"Lucky" people also:

- ✓ Project confidence.
- ✓ Are typically in a good mood.
- ✓ Have a positive attitude.
- ✓ Notice their surroundings and reflect upon them.
- ✓ Focus on what they're doing, yet see the bigger picture.
- ✓ Are living in the moment and aware of their environment.
- ✓ Are socially well adjusted.

Numerous studies have shown that being socially adept is more important to future success than school grades, IQ or educational level.

"It's rare that an individual becomes successful without the assistance of others," writes Thomas Stanley in *The Millionaire Mind.* It makes sense, people like to be with, do business with, and help people they like. Likeable people are lucky people. www.thomasjstanley.com

Lucky people are frequently charismatic. When they speak, people listen. And follow. Others want to be with them. They make people feel good. And people want to support them.

Lucky people often seem to manifest their desires without any direct correlation between cause and effect. But it's the openness and awareness of their surroundings that enables lucky people to see and then act upon opportunities, when most others are not even aware of them.

On the other hand, unlucky people:

- ✓ Are often distracted, depressed, and afraid.
- ✓ Don't take an interest in their surroundings or people.
- ✓ Aren't mindful.
- ✓ Life is to be endured, not experienced.
- ✓ Often are self-centered and narcissistic.
- ✓ Lack confidence.
- ✓ Are frequently distant, introverted or cold. People are simply not attracted to them.

Unlucky people miss the opportunities that do come their way because they are unaware of them. Even when they do notice a potential opportunity they often lack the resolve or confidence to act upon it. It's said that most people have life-altering opportunities in their life—and most are completely clueless they have been presented with them.

INCREASING YOUR LUCK WITH PREDICTIVE ENCODING

"You have brains in your head. You have feet in your shoes. You can steer yourself any direction you choose. You're on your own. And you know what you know. And YOU are the one who'll decide where to go."
— *Oh, The Places You'll Go!* by Dr. Suess

In a process called "predictive encoding," you can increase your ability to be "lucky" and manifest what you want in life by as much as 50%. Predictive encoding is a deep visualization process—envisioning what you want in great detail, even rehearsing out loud scenarios and conversations that lead to your desired outcome. Doing this programs your subconscious mind to discern patterns that your conscious mind might miss. Since you have nothing to lose but a few minutes of time each day (and it's free) why not try this technique?

"Unconscious assumptions (There is never enough money. Life always lets you down. I don't deserve love. I don't deserve abundance) create emotions in the body which in turn generate mind activity and/or instant reactions. In this way you create your personal reality."
— Eckhart Tolle, *A New Earth Awakening* www.eckharttolle.com

If you want to be lucky, you must do all you can to develop the personality traits and thought processes that lucky people share. You can improve your luck by simply training yourself to be more self-aware, to notice what is happening around you—and be more confident, positive, cheerful, outgoing, and more decisive. The percentage of Americans living a life that is superficial, desensitized to all but the most obtrusive events, and fearful of any decisive action is enormous. Luck comes to those who are aware it exists, prepare for it, are aware of it when it happens, and then act upon it.

According to *Get Lucky: How to Put Planned Serendipity to Work for You and Your Business*, authors Thor Muller and Lane Becker say that "luck" presents itself as moments of serendipity, a time when preparation meets opportunity. In order to make this happen you must be motivated, prepared, committed, connected, and create attraction. In other words, luck isn't something that just happens, you make it happen.

FOCUS

THE "LAW" OF ATTRACTION AND MANIFESTATION

"No great man ever complains of want of opportunity."
— Ralph Waldo Emerson

Kevin Hogan, www.kevinhogan.com author of *The Science of Influence: How to Get Anyone to Say "Yes" in 8 Minutes or Less,* has come up with what I think is the best solid explanation of how and why "manifestation" works. In 1991 he coined the phrase The Law of Expectancy. It's "expectancy" that is the key to attracting or manifesting your desires.

To demonstrate what this "law" means, he points to a 1968 study where researchers divided students into two groups—High IQ and Low IQ. The teachers at the school were told which group they were given at the beginning of the year. Everyone else, including the parents, were not informed their child was in one or the other group. Only the teachers knew.

After eight months the High IQ group, as might be expected, did remarkably well. Conversely, the Low IQ group performed poorly. This is logically what you would expect from the two groups of students. Just one problem. The researchers assigned the students to one group or the other *randomly*. In reality there wasn't a High IQ group or Low IQ group.

The students didn't know which group they were in. The parents were unaware which group their child was in. No one except the teachers knew which students they *thought* were in their class. The study was halted prior to completion because *expectations* of student performance by the teachers were leading to unhealthy changes in behavior in the children. The Power of Expectation—which is <u>not</u> visualization or affirmations or an attitude—created real, definable changes.

The key to The Law of Attraction and the Power of Manifestation is EXPECTANCY. The teachers simply *knew* their students were either superior or inferior because they believed the researchers at the beginning of the school year. No one ever doubted what they were told or questioned it based upon their own observation.

This certainness—knowingness, if you will—that what you want is both right for you (at least at that point in your life) combined with the expectancy that it will happen is a powerful subconscious force. It filters your thoughts and actions in innumerable small and large ways to bring about the desired outcome.

In the study, the teachers performed countless little interactions with their students that influenced the students' behavior—and their own self-confidence or feeling of self-worth. The teachers' lack of confidence in their students created a negative environment for the students. And they performed as they were expected to perform.

Similarly, focus draws energy to some things while excluding other things. Those things that receive focus are amplified while other things decrease and fade from relevancy. Teachers unconsciously reinforced positive outcomes with their "high IQ" students and the opposite occurred with the students judged as having low IQs.

There is a BIG difference between hoping that something will happen and expecting it to happen. Hoping does not set into motion the complex social and biological experience that expectancy does. Expectancy supports focus and action. Hope just allows life to happen without direction.

THE POWER OF INTENTION

One ancillary element of The Power of Expectancy is the Power of Intent. Combined, these two create a powerful force that can manifest almost anything in life. In *The Power of Intention* and *Wishes Fulfilled: Mastering the Art of Manifesting*, Dr. Wayne Dyer talks about the remarkable power of intent. It's as if you magnetize your desire, bringing people, circumstances, and the means to its creation. If you then achieve the certainty of expectation, the powers are in place to create manifestation.

- The vehicle of manifestation is expectancy. The engine is focus. The fuel is intent. The gas pedal is action. High gear is confidence. And you are the driver.

LEARN THE ART OF ACTIVE LISTENING

"When people talk, listen completely. Most people don't listen."
— Ernest Hemingway

Listen actively.

✓ Pay attention to what the other person is saying...rather than concentrating on what you want to say next.

✓ Reinforce your listening with eye contact, body language, and occasional comments that show you want to really hear what the other person has to say.

✓ Clarify their statements with questions such as "If I'm hearing you right..." or "Are you saying...."

These active listening techniques engage the other person and lead to a real conversation, not just two people talking "at" each other. The average time someone listens in a conversation before interrupting is just 17 seconds.

Remember that a constructive conversation is one that both parties benefit from...and that means you must allow the other person equal time, truly listen, and don't just think about what you're going to say next.

Keep in mind that the words LISTEN and SILENT contain the same letters …it will help you remember to refrain from interrupting until the other person has had a chance to communicate what they want to say.

"I've found that when I talk, I'm simply repeating things I already know. When I listen, I learn." — Amy Frost

Stephen Covey, author of *The 7 Habits of Highly Effective People: Powerful Lessons in Personal Change*, says that "most people don't listen with the intent to understand; they listen with the intent to reply." Try listening with the sole purpose of truly hearing what the other person is saying… with absolutely no thought to how you will respond, only to understand their point of view. As G.K. Chesterton said, "there's a lot of difference between hearing and listening."

Finally, numerous studies indicate that the #1 way to get people to like or think positively about you is the ability to listen well.

Resource: If you want to learn how to connect with people, read *Just Listen: Discover the Art of Getting Through to Absolutely Anyone* by Mark Goulston M.D.

Life Rule: Learn to listen well if you want to be heard.

DIG YOUR WELL BEFORE YOU'RE THIRSTY

One of the greatest books written about networking and its power to transform your life is *Dig Your Well Before You're Thirsty* by Harvey Mackay. At the time the book was published in 1997 Mackay wrote "Since 1979, more than 43 million jobs have been lost in America. Though a greater number more than that have been added, many are at lower pay. Among those people who have been laid off and have found new jobs, two-thirds are earning less." Sounds eerily familiar, doesn't it? Job loss and job restructuring continues to this day as businesses grapple with the new realities of a changed world and economy.

Surviving and thriving in the turmoil of a chaotic job market (and life) requires constant focused effort. As Mackay points out, "Talent alone will not save you in today's economy." In fact, even additional training and education may not save you. Competition for available jobs hasn't been this fierce in more than 70 years.

It's been demonstrated time and again that about 4 in 5 opportunities are found through personal contacts and connections. Every job seeker should start first with their family and friends, a surprisingly large source of job leads. And today it is also vitally important to build a network on social media sites like LinkedIn, Twitter, and Facebook.

In love, the more people you connect with the more likely you will be to meet the ideal person. The Internet has been a huge help bringing tens of thousands of potential mates to your attention. Online dating sites, once scorned, are now an accepted form of meeting...and the source of 1 in 4 romantic relationships.

Throughout your life there will be people who will have a profound effect upon who you become, where you live, how much money you'll make, and every other aspect of living. Meeting the right people, and building rewarding relationships with them, should be one of your primary goals.

YOUR *METWORK*

A *Harvard Business Review* article featured a study that set out to learn what attributes the 15% to 20% who are identified as "stars" differ from the average performers. The bottom-line? The "stars" built a network of people who had an integral influence upon the direction of their life.

A critical component of your Plan for Life must be to create a rich and rewarding network of your own—your Metwork. Almost every person you've ever met can potentially become part of your ever-expanding social support network. Your Metwork includes co-workers, friends, relatives, role models, professional providers, links to others on social networking sites, the maitre'd at your favorite restaurant, your kid's teachers, the author you met at a bookstore—the thousands of people you meet during the course of your busy life.

The people in your Metwork will advise you, connect you, refer you, comfort you, provide you with financial assistance, collaborate with you, entertain you, and make your life meaningful. Without these valuable people in your life it will be very difficult to find a job, make a sale, get quality healthcare, buy a house, decide on a school for your kids, meet your husband or wife, fight a lawsuit, manage your finances, have fun, and provide emotional support when you need it.

Nothing much in life happens without the support, acceptance, or involvement of other people. As Harvey Mackay teaches, "No matter how smart you are, no matter how talented, you can't do it alone."

WORK YOUR METWORK LIKE LINKEDIN

The professional online networking site, LinkedIn, has many great features. But one I like the most is their Recommendations feature. With this feature you can recommend someone you have worked with in the past. On LinkedIn, these recommendations are a vital ingredient in the overall impression a hiring authority makes when reviewing possible candidates for a job or project.

In 2012 LinkedIn added another feature, Endorsements. This feature allows people in your primary contact network who have knowledge of your various skills to endorse those skills, essentially providing a stamp of approval. On LinkedIn you can claim any skills and attributes you want, but the verification of a third-party endorsement by someone who knows you provides validity to your skillset.

In real offline life, you can do the same. Remember always to recommend people in your Metwork if you come across something that might help them in their career or life. Do it with no expectation of return. "Paying it forward" is a great concept for living in general and if everyone did it the world would be an infinitely better place. In reality, your thoughtfulness will likely come back to benefit you in some way in the future. People naturally want to return favors. It's human nature.

Get to be known as the person who is "connected." Be the catalyst for helping others. Of all the success strategies posited by everyone from Norman Vincent Peal to Tony Robbins, a large and well-maintained network of contacts is the most important. Your Metwork will be the source for most of the best things that happen to you in life.

EVERY YEAR YOU HAVE A CHANCE TO MAKE A POSITIVE IMPRESSION

"There comes a time when you should stop expecting other people to make a big deal about your birthday. That time is age 111."
— Dave Barry, author of *You Can Date Boys When You're Forty*

A powerful way to make a lasting impression is to remember birthdays. From the time we are infants birthdays are treated as special days of remembrance. It's always a little surprising to me how positively others react from a simple card or email saying "Happy Birthday." Perhaps it's a subliminal reminder of our childhood. Or maybe it's just that someone cared enough to remember. Find out and write down the birthdates of your family, friends, and acquaintances. Then send them a birthday greeting. I think you will be amazed at the response. Facebook, LinkedIn, and Google make this easy by sending you notices of impending birthdays among your contacts (as long as the data is entered first).

When you see that one of your contacts has been promoted, changed jobs, won an award, gotten married, had a baby, lost a loved one—send them a personal note. These simple, thoughtful gestures have a profound effect.

Building a network of friends and business contacts is all about caring and thoughtfulness. And as the old saying goes, "What goes around comes around." If you show care and concern for others it will come back to you.

CONNECTING WITH PEOPLE—TIPS FROM PRESIDENT CLINTON

Sean Stephenson, author of *Get Off Your "But": How to End Self-Sabotage and Stand Up For Yourself*, worked in the Clinton administration. He observed first-hand the magic that Bill Clinton performed on people he met. He called it the Clinton Car Wash. Sometimes people would come into the White House angry or bitter opponents of Clinton's policies. By the time Clinton worked his charm on them, they left smiling and shaking his hand enthusiastically.

Clinton has often been called a great communicator. Stephenson says it was more than that, Clinton connects with people. Stephenson carefully watched his boss many times as he met people. Here's what he observed:

TELL STORIES

Clinton often framed his discussion with a story, making what he said more personal. These stories were both memorable and helped humanize Clinton's outsized personality.

THE POWER OF TOUCH

Clinton made physical contact with people, touching their shoulder or placing his hand on their forearm. He wasn't shy about hugging people who needed comfort. He frequently told those he met under unfortunate circumstances, "I feel your pain." And they believed him. And when he wanted to seal a physical connection, he would hold on to a person's hand after shaking it. Clinton knows the power of touch to create a connection.

➢ Research by Matthew Hertenstein, a psychologist at DePauw University, shows that touch is capable of communicating multiple positive emotions: joy, love, gratitude, and sympathy.

- To learn more about the importance of physical contact, read *The Power of Touch: The Basis for Survival, Health, Intimacy, and Emotional Well-Being* by Phyllis Davis.

REMEMBER NAMES

Remembering names is also one of Clinton's strengths. When someone who meets thousands of people is considerate enough to remember your name, it makes a strong impression. Clinton repeats the name of the person he is speaking with many times during a conversation. Not only does it help him remember the person's name, people love hearing their name—especially when said by a president.

If you want to improve your ability to remember names, two good books to read are author Jerry Lucas' *The Memory Book: The Classic Guide to Improving Your Memory at Work, at School, and at Play* and *Moonwalking with Einstein: The Art and Science of Remembering Everything* by Joshua Foer.

MAKE EYE CONTACT

If you watch Clinton meeting someone new or speaking to an old friend he always makes deep eye contact. After speaking with Clinton people often say that "he made me feel as if we'd know each other my whole life" or "I felt as if he really cared about what I said."

Clinton's facial expression conveys his emotions and his voice modulates to heighten the empathy he projects. He can go from elder statesman to good 'ole southern boy in a flash. He laughs a lot. Although his temper is legendary, he is careful to keep it in check while out in public.

SHOW GENUINE INTEREST IN THE PEOPLE YOU MEET

Clinton also asks the opinion of people he meets, whether it's a visiting head of state or the local pizza parlor owner. This not only makes the person he is speaking with feel valued, it allows the president to adjust his response to each individual.

COMPLEMENT YOUR INTERACTION WITH COMPLIMENTS

Finally, Clinton often praises people in public. He knows the power of recognizing a person's value. Compliments are often remembered for decades, if not a lifetime.

Bill Clinton has personal weaknesses, as everyone knows. But his power to connect with others has enabled him to overcome his faults to become one of the most admired and loved people on the planet.

EMOTIONAL INTELLIGENCE

"Emotional intelligence is the strongest predictor of job performance."
— Ernest O'Boyle, *Journal of Organizational Behavior.*

The difference between being a "star" or just another average schmo is not necessarily academic IQ, but emotional IQ. In his book *Emotional Intelligence, why it can matter more than IQ*, author Daniel Goleman relates the findings from a ground-breaking study of personal performance conducted by Bell Labs, the world famous think tank. When the "stars" were compared with everyone else, what emerged was how little difference there was between the two groups. There was virtually no difference in innate abilities. The study also found that academic achievement or IQ isn't necessarily a good predictor of job performance, productivity or success. What is important are the connections and networks people develop—and how they relate to them...emotional intelligence.

When a high degree of education, skills, and experience have set the bar high in life, the differentiating factors are the "soft skills" that comprise emotional intelligence. In the 21st Century, this is what will often determine success or failure.

ASK AND YOU SHALL RECEIVE (AT LEAST MORE OFTEN THAN NOT)

"One of the greatest lessons you'll ever learn is how to ask for what you want." — John Gray, author of *How to Get What You Want And Want What You Have* and *Men Are From Mars, Women Are From Venus*

You'll never get anything you want in life if you don't ask for it. Sure, there will be times when something just falls into your lap or someone gives you something without your asking. But 99% of the time what you get in life you must ask for first.

When asking it is important to be very specific about what it is you want—whether you're asking another person, the Universe, or yourself. Specify How Much and When you want what you want. Be perfectly clear.

Don't ask for what you don't want. Instead of saying, "God, please don't give me cancer" say "I'm going to lead a healthy life, do healthy things, and stay in peak condition." You've probably heard people phrase questions like this: "You don't have a socket wrench, do you?" Huh? What kind of question is that? Starting off with a negative is a sure way to increase your chances of getting a negative response. Always be positive, expecting a positive outcome.

Say "I want to be promoted to Vice President of my company by June 1" and not "I don't want to be overlooked for promotion to Vice President." Guys who want a positive response say "Will you marry me? They don't say "You wouldn't want to get married to me, would you?" If you put a negative thought into your mind it doesn't process the information any differently than a positive thought. Your mind does what you tell it to do.

HOW TO ASK FOR WHAT YOU WANT

Here's how to ask for what you want.

1. Ask repeatedly.
2. Appeal to the other person's self–interest.

3. Stay calm.
4. Don't create resistance to what you want.
5. Ask with confidence and authority.
6. Be gracious in accepting a no—it sets the stage for a possible yes in the future.
7. Ask what you can do in the future to receive what you want.

ASK FOR WHAT YOU WANT KNOWING YOU WILL GET IT

If you ask for what you want with the expectation of getting what you want you'll project confidence—and people tend to give others what they want when they ask with confidence. When you ask with the confidence that you will get what you ask for it will affect your voice, your posture, and your choice of words. All these will contribute to a successful outcome.

ASK, ASK, ASK, ASK, ASK...AND THEN ASK SOME MORE

Whatever you want in life—ask for it. Ask for more money. Ask for a better price on something you want to buy. Ask out the person you want to meet. Ask for a loan. Ask for a promotion. Ask for the sale. Ask for a better seat. Ask to be on the team. Ask for cooperation or support. Ask for sex. Ask for help. Ask someone else to treat you better. Ask for investment capital. Ask for time off. Ask for whatever you want. Ask. Ask. Ask. Ask. Ask with the expectation you will get what you ask for—but don't allow the rejection of your request to affect you one way or another.

- For more on the power of asking for what you want, find a copy of *The Alladin Factor* by Jack Canfield and Mark Victor Hansen. This book is so valuable that I recommend purchasing the audiobook version (about $60) so that you can listen to it frequently.

Life Rule: Ask for what you want in life.

CHARM AND CHARISMA

Charm and charisma are important factors in personal power. Charismatic individuals generally project unusual calmness, confidence, assertiveness, dominance, authenticity, and focus—and almost always possess superb communication skills. Ronald Reagan, John Kennedy or, more recently, Barack Obama are all charming, charismatic leaders. In a study conducted by the University of Waterloo, 85% of the participants (both men and women) expressed that charm was the principle reason for their attraction to an individual.

Some people develop charm naturally—it's simply part of their natural personality. Although rare, natural charm is the most beguiling and attractive. It's an elusive combination of physical looks, self-assuredness, and an often quirky life view. A unique talent or personal style is frequently part of the equation. People with these attributes are often described as "magnetic." We're drawn to them and their individuality.

Perhaps you won't ever have the charisma of the Dos Equis Most Interesting Man in the World (his charm is so contagious they invented vaccines for it), but you can develop your personal brand by accentuating your uniqueness, learning to communicate well, and facing life with confidence.

FIRST IMPRESSIONS

First (and lasting) impressions are made within 7 seconds, according to body language expert Carol Kinsey Goman. Studies by New York University show that people make eleven major decisions about a person in these first crucial seconds of meeting. Are you trustworthy, competent, likeable, confident—someone to be avoided or embraced? A Princeton study published *in Psychological Science* found that people decide within a tenth of a second whether a person is attractive and trustworthy simply by looking at their face.

This research demonstrates that humans may be hard-wired to make these instantaneous judgments. While rational assessments are the function of the prefrontal cortex, first impressions may bypass this part of the brain and default to the amygdala, a fear-based part of the brain that existed for millions of years before the prefrontal cortex evolved.

No one knows what kind of face makes a good or bad impression. Some studies indicate that symmetrical features are judged to be more appealing. There are steps you can take to mitigate a less than appealing face, such as dressing well, smiling, body language, and tone of voice. Just know that impressions are made quickly...and are hard to change.

According to Ann Demaris Ph.D. And Valerie White Ph.D., authors of *First Impressions: What You Don't Know About How Others See You,* the first impression you make on someone is critically important to what happens next. "The first impression people get about anything—a person, a place, an idea—–influences the way they process later information." In other words, it will be very difficult to change how you are first perceived.

Here are a few tips to keep in mind when meeting someone for the first time.

1. Don't go into a meeting with a confrontational, angry or uptight attitude. People pick up on your attitude immediately. Adjust your attitude first. Smile. Think positive thoughts. Take a deep breath and tell yourself how great the interview will be.
2. Your first step to a successful first meeting is a big smile and a good handshake.
3. Lean in slightly to establish rapport and show you're interested.
4. When meeting someone, you are likely to start off on the right foot if you keep that person to your right side, according to research studies.
5. Make eye contact and open your eyes slightly more than normal...the "eyebrow flash" that is a universal sign of recognition and greeting.
6. Stand tall, pull back your shoulders, and hold your head straight. Status and personal power are transmitted nonverbally by your posture.
7. Dress in colors that complement your skin tone, hair color, and eyes.
8. Body weight influences how you are perceived. If you are overweight, dress in darker colors and well-tailored clothing.
9. Wear good quality, stylish clothing.
10. Project a relaxed confidence, don't speak too fast or slowly, and don't slouch.

YOU'RE LOOKS ARE JUDGED IN LESS THAN A SECOND

Research by Florida State University found that men and women judge other people's attractiveness in less than half a second. The study also showed that when people meet attractive people their attention is temporarily riveted to them—they literally cannot take their eyes off the person. Women were just as fixated on handsome men as men were with beautiful women.

Attractiveness is important to self-esteem. If you've ever looked "hagged over" because of a poor night's sleep or had a bad hair day or couldn't get your wardrobe together for a special occasion, you know how it can negatively affect your confidence level and mood. Research has shown that when people feel attractive they perform better—on the job, on tests, even in the bedroom.

Generally speaking it's true that good looks will give you an advantage over someone who isn't as handsome or beautiful. Part of the reason is because your looks are tied directly into self-esteem and that in turn affects your attitude and actions. So it becomes an endless loop of either feeling good (or bad) about oneself—and realizing the consequences.

GOOD LOOKS ARE BECOMING A COMMON COMMODITY

Compared to generations past, contemporary humans (at least in the U.S.) are significantly more attractive. If you look at photos of men and women taken in the 1880's you'll be hard-pressed to find a Christie Brinkley, Angelina Jolie or Victoria Secret supermodel. Among men the difference isn't as dramatic, but most men from 1880 pale in comparison to Tom Cruise or George Clooney.

With each successive generation meeting more people, marrying the best-looking people they can attract...and with the advances in diet, exercise, and styling...we've arrived at a point where beautiful women and handsome men are abundant.

Most Americans do what they can to improve their looks in the 21st Century. Humans naturally know that looking good is important now to success. What is difficult to understand is why so many people seem to do their best to look as unattractive as possible. The dramatic "before and after" makeovers that are frequently in beauty magazines show what is possible for nearly everyone.

With diet and exercise nearly everyone can transform their body in less than 18 months into something attractive. Add to that the magic of a good hairstylist, professional makeup (for women obviously), and a stylish wardrobe, and often it's hard to even recognize that it's the same person as before the transformation.

Clothing alone can make a big difference. A dramatic example of this are the elderly men of Italy who continue to dress stylishly despite their age. I once overheard a young woman in Bologna remark that a well-dressed man of about 75 looked "sexy." It's all about fashion and quality...better to carefully select a few extremely well made and beautiful items than have a huge wardrobe of cheap stuff.

If being better looking could draw more attractive people into your life, improve your sex life, earn you more money, and boost your self-esteem... why wouldn't you want to do it? Yet millions of people are horribly out of shape, dress like they bought their clothes at a flea market, and spend little time or attention to their face and hair.

BUT DO LOOKS REALLY MATTER?

- Americans spend $33 billion on beauty products and $10 billion on plastic surgery.

Beauty is only skin deep...right? Even though you might like it to be this way, most people instinctively know that how you look definitely plays a role in whether or not you achieve success in life. Oftentimes, it's all that matters. Martha Beck writes that "good-looking individuals are treated better than homely ones in virtually every social situation, from dating to trial by jury." In a 2010 CBS report of a study by Cornell University on the role looks play in the sentences given to legal defendants, it was found that unattractive defendants are 22% more likely to be convicted than good-looking ones. And the unattractive defendants also got slapped with harsher sentences...an average of 22 months longer.

The way people treat plain people is, well, just plain ugly. Research shows that an attractive man or woman will likely earn an average of nearly a quarter million dollars more during their lifetime than similarly intelligent and educated homely people. One study on the influence of looks found that more attractive NFL quarterbacks earn $300,000 more than their stats would predict. In job interviews good-looking candidates get called back 10% more often. If you are a good-looking or handsome man you can expect to earn 17% more than the least fortunate males—those who are plain or homely. Good-looking or beautiful women earn 12% more than below average females.

Obviously there are many exceptions. Bill Gates, Warren Buffett, and Oprah Winfrey don't spring to mind immediately when people are asked to name someone beautiful. They are obviously successful. But these variations from the norm generally compensate with some other attribute that makes their looks a secondary factor in their success.

In his book *Beauty Pays: Why Attractive People Are More Successful*, author Daniel Hamermesh says that the perception of beauty is fairly universal. When shown photos of people and asked to judge their beauty or handsomeness on a 1 to 5 scale, there was very little variation. Even babies are attracted to prettier faces, as described in research done by Nancy Etcoff, author of *Survival of the Prettiest: The Science of Beauty.* For better or worse the love of beauty is part of our evolutionary genetic makeup.

If you're wondering, the distribution of looks in the U.S. follows a bell-shaped curve. 1% of men and 2% of women are considered homely. Another 11% of men and 13% of women are judged to be quite plain. At the other end of the spectrum 2% of men and 3% of women are judged as strikingly handsome or quite beautiful. A larger group are considered good-looking—27% of men and 31% of women. That leaves the largest group in the middle—the average-looking for their age and sex. 59% of men and 51% of women are judged to be in this group.

So, let's dispel that old myth (you know, the one in the Declaration of Independence) that all men are created equal...they're not. Both men and women believe attractive people are:

- ✓ More successful.
- ✓ More intelligent.
- ✓ Better adjusted.
- ✓ More socially adept.
- ✓ More interesting.
- ✓ More poised.
- ✓ More excited.
- ✓ More independent.
- ✓ More charismatic.
- ✓ More sexually competent.
- ✓ Have happier marriages.
- ✓ Are more successful professionally.

With preconceptions like these it isn't surprising that attractive people generally lead more fulfilling lives. Expectations, as we discussed earlier, have a significant influence on how people evolve.

Research shows that people are drawn to and will pay more for beauty—whether it's a home, a car, clothing or people. It's called the "beauty premium" by economists. This beauty premium is coupled with a distinct bias against unattractive people. For every preconception listed above you can apply the opposite to unattractive people.

In a study of 737 male and female MBA graduates from between 1973 and 1982, results indicated that more attractive men had higher starting salaries and they continued to earn more over time. By 1983, men were found to earn $2,600 more on average for each unit of attractiveness (on a 5-point scale) and women earned $2,150 more. Another study found that salary goes up 8% with each standard deviation increase in facial symmetry—a universal determinant of beauty.

SURPRISE—MEN AND WOMEN ARE DIFFERENT

The perception of attractiveness and its affects upon potential income are drastically different depending upon whether you are male or female. Tall men earn considerably more money throughout their lives than shorter co-workers, with each inch adding about $789 more a year on average, according to research by Timothy Judge, a University of Florida management professor, as reported in the *Journal of Applied Psychology*. Tall men (6' or more) earn nearly $6,000 a year more than men under five feet, five inches tall (or about $800 an inch). Who says size doesn't matter?

Unfortunately being tall doesn't translate into more money for women. In fact, there is a slight income penalty for women who are extremely tall.

While thin women earn substantially more than their more endowed sisters, the opposite is true for men. A man who is 30 pounds under the average weight for men will earn about half as much as a man who is 70 pounds over the average.

So hit the chips and guacamole dip and knock back some brewskies this weekend guys, you have nothing to fear! Consider it an investment in your career. However, you poor ladies will have to live on water and air; a woman who is 30 pounds under the average weight for all women earns more than twice as much as a woman who is 70 pounds over the average. For men weight is great—but for women thin is in.

WE'RE NOT MAKING THIS UP

In psychological tests, women who wear makeup are perceived as being more competent, likeable, attractive, and trustworthy. The innate knowledge of this perception by most women, combined with a degree of insecurity, is at the core of the enormous "looks" industry. What is surprising is how many women don't take advantage of using makeup to improve the impression they give others. You may have valid intellectual reasons not to use makeup, but our human preference for a woman wearing makeup is rooted (as many things are) in our distant past as a species. What's fascinating is that this preference for makeup only applies to women and not men. Since this is the way it is, and preferences are not likely to change in our lifetime, women should either decide to take advantage of using makeup or suffer the consequences.

WHY GOOD-LOOKING PEOPLE *ARE* BETTER

In numerous studies it's been found that attractive people earn more, achieve more, and generally lead more successful lives. I know I've found this to be true (just kidding!). The reason for this phenomena is early discrimination and bias by authority figures. Parents favor their good-looking offspring. In one study, attractive children are 11 times more likely than their least attractive sibling to get buckled into shopping carts. Yikes!

Good-looking children receive more attention and support than their homely brothers and sisters. But parental preference is only the beginning. School teachers favor attractive children. Aggressive acts are thought to be less naughty when done by attractive children. Unattractive kids receive lower grades for the same work, receive detention more often, and are called on less by teachers. Teachers also assume that unattractive students are dumber than their good-looking students and treat them differently. This divergence of preference based upon looks continues throughout all the school years.

- In one study it was found that unattractive college students did better when the professor couldn't see them.
- In another study, students ranked "4" for attractiveness performed 36% better than those ranked "2."

This preferential treatment has an enormous impact upon a person's self–esteem and available opportunities. Is it any wonder that after graduation the attractive people get better job offers, make more money at age 25, and over a lifetime earn substantially more: $78,927 vs. $50,323. (2008) Early bias and prejudice becomes part of the good–looking or unattractive person's personality—and a self–fulfilling prophecy.

IT'S GOOD TO BE GOOD–LOOKING

Good–looking people are smarter than average looking people. Not just perceived as smarter, but actually smarter. In a London School of Economics research study of 17,000 men and women from Great Britain and 35,000 from the United States, good–looking men averaged 13.6 IQ points higher than those rated less attractive. Good–looking women scored an average of 11.4 IQ points higher than average–looking women. When people comment on how "smart–looking" an attractive person is, they are closer to the truth than they realize.

The bottom–line. It's unfortunate that our society places an unusually high premium on looks. But knowing this you can now feel comfortable about doing whatever it takes...a diet, a stylish wardrobe, good haircuts, makeup...to make yourself as attractive as possible.

WEIGHT, WEIGHT—WHAT'S WRONG WITH ME?

"Order is the shape upon which beauty depends." — Pearl Buck

People who are seen as being overweight are judged harshly by others. Thin is often equated with attractiveness in America. Advertising in particular, promotes the good life with near–anorexic models purporting to be real people. As this American ideal becomes increasingly unattainable, its value rises. Being slim, fit, good–looking, well–dressed, and confident is our national goal—one that is frequently well compensated in every way.

One telling example of this trend is in broadcast journalism. In the past it was important to be a good journalist first and looks were a distant second on the list of attributes. But those days, and broadcasters, are waning. Morley Safer, Mike Wallace, Charles Kuralt, Walter Cronkite, Roger Mudd—none of these old–line journalists could have posed for a fashion advertisement. But the typical TV journalist today is runway handsome or beautiful. The reality in media hyped American right now is that looks do matter.

If you think there isn't much hope to improve your looks, almost every women's magazine has featured a "before and after" article showing the dramatic difference hairstyle, makeup, and flattering clothing can make with women considered "plain," even by themselves. Most men are just as clueless when it comes to their looks, often not progressing much from their college jeans and sweatshirt/cheap haircut days. While not everyone (in fact, very few) are born naturally good-looking, there are many things you can do to improve your looks.

1. Lose weight. Everyone looks better at their proper weight.
2. Get fit. Exercise improves your body and your mind…and gives you a healthy "glow."
3. Smile, be outgoing, practice optimism, be confident. This alone improves your "looks" 100%.
4. Invest in a professional haircut or style.
5. Invest in body flattering, top-quality clothing.
6. Take care of your skin. Use sunscreen and moisturizer.
7. Invest in dental care and practice good oral hygiene.
8. Take care of the little things…moles removed, manicures, trim nose hairs, use contact lens or fashionable eyewear.
9. Get plenty of sleep…it restores your body, slows aging, and improves energy levels.
10. Avoid stress and/or practice yoga or meditation. Stress causes premature aging.

Maybe Nature didn't bless you with supermodel or superhunk looks, but that doesn't mean you can't be attractive.

YOUR SIGNATURE SCENT

"The best smell in the world is that man that you love."
— Jennifer Aniston

Scent is one of the most powerful emotional connectors between humans. It is the one sense that is directly connected to the limbic region of the brain, our "old brain" that controls emotions and memories. According to the Smell and Taste Treatment and Research Foundation, www.smellandtaste.org smell is the most important sensory organ. It has the power to instantly bring back memories as nothing else can. And it is a key ingredient in attracting the opposite sex.

Scent has the power to make you happy or sad. It can trigger physiological responses such as calmness or sexual excitement. In tests on subjects exposed to various scents, Dr. Alan Hirsh, Director of the Smell and Taste Treatment and Research Foundation , Ltd., found that a combination of pumpkin pie and lavender increased blood flow to men's genitals by 40%, nearly as much as some pharmaceuticals. Vanilla and cinnamon scents also increased blood flow substantially.

For women the blood flow increase to their genitals was less, but still an impressive 11%, although the combination of Good and Plenty candy with cucumber performed best (13%). Men's cologne had almost no effect (a slight decrease in arousal of 1%). Perhaps a bowl of Good and Plenty candy should be a bedroom accessory for the man who wants to get lucky.

"Smell has the power to unleash memories in a way nothing else can."
— *Forbes* magazine

Everyone has (or should have) two scents...your natural personal scent and the one you choose to identify yourself. Your personal scent is a product of DNA and the physiological makeup of your body. It's as unique as a fingerprint.

Every time you smell something, microscopic solid particles register in the nose, on the tongue, and pass down your throat. When you smell someone, you literally take them in. Men prefer the scent of young women, perhaps because in our caveman past a young woman was associated with fertility. But men don't have nearly as sensitive a sense of smell as women.

Even with cologne, research shows that a man's personal, natural scent cannot be easily masked. According to *Psychology Today*, a man's allure depends upon how many immune system genes he shares with a potential mate. If the scent isn't a good match it can be a deal–killer.

"I judge people by how they smell, not how they look." — Jennifer Lopez

A person's scent can vary depending upon the circumstances. A woman's scent during the days she is ovulating is more powerful, the better to signal to a compatible mate that it is possible to impregnate her. Women can often smell fear or illness in a man. Powerful, confident men exude a more attractive scent than do weak men. Again, this is a signal to women that he may be a better father and protector. Women can also often smell a man who is sexually aroused.

To the right woman, no cologne is sexier than Eau de You. Going au naturel may be a man's best scent if the aim is to attract the right women. Many women report that they knew a man would be their future husband as soon as she smelled him. Men too are powerfully affected by a woman's scent. Some men become aroused and may actually ejaculate from the scent of a woman. When returning from battle, Napoleon would send a messenger ahead to tell Josephine not to bath.

In these modern times we've done everything possible to mask natural scents. And sometimes these are warranted. A well-chosen cologne or perfume worn consistently is as much a personal signature as your hair color. A powerful reminder of you is a scented pillow case or tee shirt sent to your lover. Years after your relationship has ended, your scent will still evoke the memory of you. Smell is hard-wired into our brains.

When you select a personal scent, try several first to see how the ingredients react to your unique chemistry.

APPRECIATION, GRATEFULNESS, GRATITUDE, AND THANKFULNESS

"Gratitude bestows reverence, allowing us to encounter everyday epiphanies, those transcendent moments of awe that change forever how we experience life and the world." — John Milton

What exactly is gratitude? It's many things—appreciation, recognition, thankfulness, and acknowledgment of the good in life. Gratitude should be given without expectation of personal benefit. However, with gratitude often comes good fortune, happiness, and abundance.

Researchers at the University of Missouri asked people to count their blessings or visualize the best possible future for themselves for one month. "The subjects who counted their blessings saw an immediate improvement in their moods," said Kennon Sheldon, Ph.D., co–author of the study. "Those who visualized their best future selves saw an even more significant upswing." Upon receiving an Oscar for Best Actor in 2014, Matthew McConaughey told the audience that he got to this place in life by aspiring to be the person he saw himself as being in ten years.

Author Robert A. Emmons, in his book *The Psychology of Gratitude*, writes that gratitude is a deep, complex phenomena that plays a critical role in human happiness. His scientific research, in collaboration with Michael McCullough, a psychologist at the University of Miami, made several important discoveries about gratitude and its affects upon people who practice it regularly. What they discovered was that gratitude has a number of measurable benefits—psychological, physical, and interpersonal. Gratitude was the reason for transformative change in people's lives.

Just as important, their research found that family, friends, partners, and others who interacted with people who practice gratitude said they seemed significantly happier and more pleasant to be around. Often people report that when they incorporated true gratitude into their life it led to near miraculous positive changes.

Journalist Deborah Norville writes of the many benefits of gratitude in *Thank You Power: Making the Science of Gratitude Work for You*, Her book reports findings of studies on gratitude reported by some of the nation's top researchers in leading psychology publications.

- ✓ You'll be more optimistic.
- ✓ You'll exercise more.
- ✓ You'll think more creatively.
- ✓ You'll be less intimidated by challenges.
- ✓ You'll have higher immune response.
- ✓ You'll be more alert and interested.
- ✓ You'll be more adventurous.
- ✓ You'll live longer.
- ✓ You'll be more likely to help others.

- ✓ You'll be more likable.
- ✓ You'll be more tolerant.
- ✓ You'll be a better boss or team leader.
- ✓ You just might do better on a test.

"Reflect on your present blessings, of which every man has many, not on your past misfortunes, of which all men have some."
— Charles Dickens

Here are some simple ways to begin incorporating gratitude into your life:

- ✓ Keep a gratitude journal.
- ✓ Remember birthdays.
- ✓ Tell one person a day how much you appreciate them.
- ✓ Always say "Thank You" when someone does a courtesy for you.
- ✓ Once (or more) a day, think of something you are grateful for in your life.
- ✓ Do something kind for another person every day…pay it forward.

"Gratitude is not only the greatest of virtues, but the parent of all others." — Cicero

You'll start to see the benefits…both for others as well as yourself… almost immediately.

Economist, actor, and author Ben Stein summed it up nicely, "I cannot tell you anything, that in a few minutes, will tell you how to be rich. But I can tell you how to feel rich, which is far better, let me tell you first-hand, than being rich. Be grateful…it's the only totally reliable get-rich-scheme." www.mrbenstein.com

CREATIVITY

"Imagination is more important than knowledge."
— Albert Einstein

By some measurements the number of people who are considered "creative" is low…fewer than 15%, although 25% self-identify as being creative. According to social scientist and economist Richard Florida, author of *The Rise of the Creative Class*, the "creative core" of the U.S. population comprises about 12% of the workforce. These are people who are fully engaged in the creative process.

"Because we live in a world where whatever can be done will be done, the most important competition today is between you and your imagination." — Thomas Friedman, author of *The World is Flat*

While the trend is to consider creativity to be a collaborative process involving several people, the truly breakthrough creativity is usually done in solitude. According to blogger Leo Barbatua www.zenhabits.net, "creativity flourishes in solitude. With solitude you can hear your thoughts, you can reach deep within yourself, you can focus." Many of the most creative minds in history…Einstein, Kafka, Hemingway, Goethe, Picasso, to name a few…insisted upon solitude in order to create. Picasso said, "Without great solitude no serious work is possible." Value your time alone as an opportunity to create.

A distracted or stressed mind is hard–pressed to do the kind of inner mental work necessary for lateral thinking, connecting disparate dots, and making the jumps required to break out of conventional patterns of thought. It's why so many people say they get their best ideas in the shower…sometimes the only place in our busy world a person can be alone.

Meditation and yoga can spur your creativity too. Both have significant calming effects upon the mind. Another way to find the solitude necessary for creativity is cycling or running. Plus, the increased blood flow from anaerobic exercise improves brain function..

"In order to be open to creativity, one must have the capacity for the constructive use of solitude. One must overcome the fear of being alone." — Rollo May

Creative people are defined by certain characteristics. While some people are born with many or all of these characteristics, they can also be developed. Try doing more of the things that describe the creative person and see if you don't become more creative too.

1. Curiosity.
2. Unafraid of problems.

3. Place a high value on new ideas.
4. Embrace challenges.
5. Good at finding connections.
6. Able to reframe things differently.
7. Enthusiasm.
8. Persistence.
9. Frequently dissatisfied.
10. Optimistic.
11. Able to let go of an idea.
12. Likes to go for the kill.
13. Not afraid to failure.
14. Knows the environment in which they are most creative.
15. Able to make intellectual leaps.

I've found during my career in the advertising business that the most creative people often had all, or most, of these characteristics. But almost anyone can make the personal changes necessary to develop them as part of their own personality.

MUSIC

"Music gives soul to the Universe, wings to the mind, flight to the imagination." — Plato

Music has the unique ability to engage and stimulate our brain in ways that produce a variety of mental and physiological results…mostly positive. Incorporate it into your life whenever possible.

When Thomas Jefferson was composing the Declaration of Independence, he would frequently play his violin in order to help his brain find the right words to put on paper. Albert Einstein was considered "slow" by his teachers. He credits learning to play the violin with his prodigious mental achievements.

Learning to play an instrument has been proven to reorder the brain's neural structure, making it easier for many people to learn other things, such as computer programming. It "rewires" the brain. The corpus collusum, the cluster of fibers connecting the right and left hemispheres of the brain, is more developed in professional musicians. Like learning a second language, music has the ability to make your brain more fully functional.

Music has been used to help people recover from brain injuries. Congresswoman Gabrielle Giffords, who suffered a traumatic gunshot wound to her brain in 2011, was able to learn to speak by singing sentences. Sufferers of Parkinson's disease have found music helps them retain their ability to speak. Autistic children can often learn to speak through song. Human beings come hard-wired for both speech and musical ability, two separate but overlapping—and mutually supportive—capabilities.

The human response to music is easily detected and measured. Classical music, especially baroque, can slow heart rate, decrease blood pressure, and relax the body, enabling the mind to concentrate more easily. Listening to Mozart, with its 60 beats per minute pattern, activates both hemispheres of the brain, maximizing learning and retention. According to The Center for New Discoveries in Learning, learning can be increased by a factor of five times with this musical pattern.

In numerous studies it's been found that music facilitates learning and recall of information. Composer Frederick Handel wrote his Water Music to help King George I of England overcome problems with memory loss and extreme stress.

Music's physiological effects impact body chemistry, including levels of testosterone (aggression and sexual arousal), cortisol (stress and arousal), and oxytocin (affecting nurturing) have been thoroughly documented. Music can affect the release of endorphins (a natural opiate that reduces pain) and dopamine (a neurotransmitter that helps control the brain's reward and pleasure centers). Most people have experienced the phenomena of exercising strenuously to music and finding their discomfort reduced.

Several studies have shown that music affects your immune system. Measurable increases in recovery from a wide range of physical maladies, such as heart disease, lung ailments, and viral infections have been aided by music therapy. Music reduces stress levels and raises immune markers, creating disease-fighting antibodies. Many hospitals play soft music to sooth surgery patients or premature babies. Music helps newborn babies gain weight faster and leave the prenatal unit sooner.

Since music engages both sides of the brain, reduces stress, increases neurotransmitter activity, and aids in memory retention, you can actually become smarter listening to certain kinds of music. It's been called the Mozart Affect (sorry, there's no evidence of a Red Hot Chili Peppers Affect).

Music, as everyone instinctively knows, has been proven to improve your mood. A Penn State University study, published in *Psychology and Education: An Interdisciplinary Journal* (2003), found that listening to music caused subjects to feel "more optimistic, joyful, friendly, relaxed, and calm. They were also less pessimistic and sad."

Marketers have long understood this affect. That's why so many retail stores play music—their customers purchase more (and are happier with their purchases)—than in stores without music.

Experiments have shown that people work more efficiently, are more productive, and finish their work faster when they listen to music. In *The Psychology of Music*, author Teresa Lesiuk found that without music the quality of work was lowest and time on task was longest.

Music is especially beneficial during times of prolonged stress…as millions in the U.S. are experiencing during the challenging first years of the 21st Century. In tough times music can help brighten your mood. Every human culture in the past 50,000 years has enjoyed music. It's in our genetic makeup. And it should be part of your life.

BEWARE OF SOCIOPATHS AND PSYCHOPATHS

Most of the opportunities that come your way in life are the result of well-meaning actions by good people. We need people to succeed in our dreams and aspirations. But people will also be the cause of most of the misery in your life. Much of the serious harm is caused by sociopaths… people who lack a normal conscience.

- It's estimated that **approximately 1 in 23 people is a sociopath and 1 in 100 is a full-blown psychopath**, according to *The Sociopath Next Door* by Martha Stout, Ph.D., and *Without Conscious: The Disturbing World of the Psychopaths Among Us*, by Robert Hare, Ph.D.

On the average air flight there will be at least ten sociopaths sharing your space. In your child's classroom there is a good probability that he/she will interact with at least one or two sociopaths. In a typical day you will likely cross paths with one of these toxic people. How many psychopaths do you think were in the crowd at the last concert you attended? More than a hundred, according to statistical estimates. Kind of creepy, isn't it? As M. E. Thomas writes in her book *Confessions of a Sociopath: A Life Spent Hiding in Plain Sight*, sociopaths are your neighbors, co-workers, lovers, family, and friends.

While many social scientists use the terms interchangeably because of similar behaviors, there are differences in the two disorders. A sociopath is partly shaped by societal factors and living in a dysfunctional environment. But sociopaths are also unlucky enough to be born without a conscience. You may hate them for the harm they do, but it isn't entirely their fault—just as you can't hate a bee for its sting.

Psychopathic disorders are a result of biological and genetic factors. Both sociopaths and psychopaths have no conscience. But the way psychopaths manifest their disorder is more pronounced than the sociopath—and often violent or depraved.

Brain scans have shown a significant difference in the way sociopaths and psychopaths are "wired" that affects their ability to feel true emotion. The signs of a sociopath are often detectable as early as age five. There is no cure for a sociopath or a psychopath and drug therapy has met with limited success.

Sociopaths can (and do) function very well in society—especially in a world with values that are often in sync with the sociopath. Sociopaths are frequently quite charming, glib, and cunning. Their risk-taking behavior and fearlessness can be exhilarating. They often have quick wits, cunning intelligence, innovative thinking, and supreme self-confidence. In *Confessions of a Sociopath*, Thomas writes that high-functioning, non-criminal sociopaths are often quite successful. Thomas makes the case that in today's narcissistic, greedy, materialistic society, there's often a fine line between sociopaths and "normal" narcissistic people.

The sociopath doesn't value the feelings or rights of others. They see their self-serving behavior as permissible. They're only interested in others in respect to how the relationship promotes their own interests. Their bête noir is exploiting the trusting and forgiving nature of most people. In

Almost a Psychopath, Harvard researchers and authors Ronald Schouten, MD, JD and James Silver, JD, point out that their glibness and superficiality, and the propensity to lie to get whatever they want, enables the sociopath to effectively manipulate and con others for their own gain.

The sociopath intuitively knows how to "play" relationships to their advantage. They are masters of manipulation. Lovers, friends, co-workers—they are just avenues for the sociopath to get what they want. It's all a game to these dysfunctional people.

In *The Wisdom of Psychopaths: What Saints, Spies, and Serial Killers Can Teach Us About Success,* author Kevin Dutton says that certain fields of work are more likely to attract psychopaths (and sociopaths) than others:

- ✓ CEO.
- ✓ Lawyer.
- ✓ Media (TV/Radio).
- ✓ Salesperson.
- ✓ Surgeon.
- ✓ Journalist.
- ✓ Police Officer.
- ✓ Clergy.
- ✓ Chef.
- ✓ Civil Servant.

Want to avoid psychopaths and sociopaths? Stick with doctors, teachers, accountants, therapists, nurses, charity workers, and beauticians.

I once worked for a sociopath who cheated on his wife with prostitutes, stole money from his clients, and yet was so personable he charmed everyone into giving him whatever he wanted. His outgoing personality and Johnny Carson-style gift of gab was legendary. When it was discovered he had stolen more than a million dollars from his employer, he talked his way out of prosecution. The firm just let him go and absorbed the loss to avoid bad publicity. He ran the same scam at the next company he worked at and got away with it there too. Eventually he was caught (and prosecuted) for bilking yet another company out of hundreds of thousands of dollars. The resulting legal action ruined him financially and destroyed his family.

Sociopaths have a complete inability to love anyone…except themselves. They may fake love, but they can't feel love. They are so manipulative and convincing that it often takes years for a spouse to realize they've married a sociopath.

Chronic lying is another sign of a sociopath. In recent years we've been charmed (and lied to) by seven-time Tour de France winner Lance

Armstrong and Senator John Edwards. Both lied repeatedly and very publicly, thinking (as sociopaths do) that they were smarter than everyone else and could get away with their lies.

A sociopath experiences absolutely no remorse, shame or guilt. They only see people as a means to an end—their end. And the end always justifies the means for a sociopath. They let nothing stand in their way.

Sociopaths can mimic emotions to get what they want but they can't authentically feel emotion. The sociopath is sometimes admired for having a cool, calm personality. They are often such good actors that a spouse can live with a sociopath for years before discovering the truth. It's the sociopath's inability to experience authentic love that frequently trips them up.

Promiscuity, gambling, and other stimulating and risky behaviors are common among sociopaths. They are often sexual addicts, rapists, child abusers, and adulterers. Because they have a total lack of emotional empathy, a sociopath will have no hesitation in embezzling funds from their company, ousting a trusting business partner, breaking up with a loving spouse with a text message, or conning thousands of people out of their life savings. If caught, they will try every way possible to blame their actions on others (often the victims of their actions), avoid punishment, and continue their dishonest activities. Ironically, their lack of fear and love of risk can also be the reason many sociopaths are successful in business, politics, and religion.

Sociopaths can reinvent themselves at will to create an entirely new, and just as phony, persona that meets their new circumstances in life. They are easily bored, require instant gratification, do little planning for the future, and live for the moment. Sociopaths can be authoritarian, smug, contemptuous of others, secretive, paranoid, and controlling.

It's not stretching reality to say that many of the problems today—the economic meltdown, abusive religious leaders, scandal-ridden politics, and a breakdown in trust—is a result of sociopaths and psychopaths in our society.

Don't try to reform or "fix" a sociopath/psychopath—they're extremely resistant to change, even with professional therapy.

15 WAYS TO SPOT A SOCIOPATH

Some of the characteristics of the psychopathic/sociopathic personality include:

- ✓ Frequently bored.
- ✓ Excitable.
- ✓ Parasitic lifestyle.
- ✓ Poor behavior control.
- ✓ Exceptionally glib.
- ✓ Irresponsible.
- ✓ Grandiose sense of self.
- ✓ Liar.
- ✓ Manipulative.
- ✓ Does not experience guilt.
- ✓ Sexually promiscuous.
- ✓ Impulsive.
- ✓ Charming.
- ✓ Lacks empathy.
- ✓ Blames others for their mistakes.

TOXIC PEOPLE

I'm convinced the nation is roughly divided into two halves…fairly normal folks who mostly enrich our lives by their presence…and toxic people who are an anchor on society. If you haven't already met a toxic person (unlikely) you eventually will. These are the nut jobs who make life difficult with their screwy behavior…the back–stabbing co–worker, boss from hell, liars, con artists, religious fanatics, dopers, welfare cheats, racists, criminals, and narcissists. They are the lower–functioning humans who cost those living on a higher plain our money, time, energy, and health. They impede progress. They leave destruction in their wake. They suck the life out of society like leeches.

The best advice is to avoid toxic people at all costs. Allowing them into your life will only cause harm— harm that may last a lifetime. If it isn't possible to avoid them, then you must draw a line in the sand and make it perfectly clear that you won't tolerate it being crossed. Clearly spell out the consequences if it is crossed…even once. These people deserve NO second chance. Then you must be willing to follow through on the consequence, even if it means disrupting your own life. The damage will be less than if you allow a toxic person to inflict their poison on you.

ANGER MANAGEMENT

"If you are patient in one moment of anger, you will escape a hundred days of sorrow." — Confucius

We seem to live in an angry world. The wars, violent crime, political rhetoric, rudeness, road rage, abuse, and name–calling produce a level of anxiety in daily life that can be emotionally debilitating. And it can be deadly.
In a typical year more than a hundred million Americans are on the receiving end of someone's anger.

- ✓ Every 9 seconds a woman is the victim of domestic violence.
- ✓ More than 300 incidents of road rage leave someone injured or dead each year.
- ✓ There are 1.8 million assaults requiring emergency room treatment each year…most due to uncontrolled anger.
- ✓ 1 in 5 people report ending a relationship because of an angry confrontation.
- ✓ 1 in 20 have fought with a neighbor.
- ✓ More than 1 in 4 (28%) say they worry about how angry they get sometimes.
- ✓ 45% have lost their temper at work.
- ✓ Mass shootings average about one per month in the U.S.

"Speak when you are angry and you will make the best speech you'll ever regret." — Lawrence J. Peter, author of *The Peter Principle*

It's important to a successful life to learn anger management. Here are 10 tips from the Mayo Clinic to help you control your anger.

1. Take a time out. Count to 25. Remove yourself from the scene.
2. Once you've calmed down, express your anger in a non–emotional manner.
3. Get some exercise. Exercise helps calm anger and frazzled emotions
4. Think before you speak. Words said in the heat of anger can have lifelong negative effects.
5. Focus on an intelligent solution rather than demands made with anger.
6. Say "I" not "you." Don't start the blame game but say how you feel.
7. Don't hold a grudge or become resentful. No one (including you) ever

does exactly what others want them to do. Learn to forgive mistakes and transgressions.

8. Use humor (but not sarcasm) to lighten the mood.
9. Practice relaxation skills. Put on some music…it's hard to fight when Tony Bennett is singing "I Left My Heart in San Francisco."
10. Know when to seek help. Anger often is the result of pent–up frustrations, emotional problems, a chemical imbalance, or psychological disorder. You may need professional support if you, or someone close to you, is unable to overcome anger issues. Cognitive restructuring (psychologist–speak for changing the way you think) is often very successful if guided by a trained anger management consultant.

ANGRY CITIES

Some places are angrier than others. Here are the ten angriest places to live in America, according to a 2011 ranking by *Men's Health* magazine.

1. Detroit, MI
2. Baltimore, MD
3. St. Petersburg, FL
4. Las Vegas, NV
5. Newark, NJ
6. Charleston, WV
7. Dallas, TX
8. Houston, TX
9. Philadelphia, PA
10. Miami, FL

Looking for a serene, mellow place to live? Try Burlington, VT, Lincoln, NE, Fargo, ND, Colorado Springs, CO or Madison, WI.

While there are millions of victims of anger…from road rage to domestic abuse to murder…people who can't control their anger also eventually hurt themselves.

Start by educating yourself about anger management with these two books, *Anger Management for Everyone: Seven Proven Ways to Control Anger and Live a Happier Life* by Raymond Tafrate, Ph.D. and Howard Kassinove, Ph.D. or *Anger Management for Dummies* by W. Doyle Gentry.

Learning to deal with stress will also help control your anger. Exercise, get plenty of sleep, try meditation, enroll in a yoga class…and, if this fails, get professional help. You'll find a directory of anger management consultants at the National Anger Management Association website www.namass.org.

PORN FREE

The Internet is porn's best friend. One–third of all data transmission on the internet is porn. Porn sites get more visitors than Netflix, Amazon, and Twitter...combined. The leading porn site, Porn Hub, gets 1.68 million visits per hour...more than 1.7 billion in 2011.

- According to a 2010 article in *The Week*, 25% of all search engine requests are for porn sites.
- There are now more than half a billion pages of porn on the Internet.
- 266 new porn sites are added *every day*.
- 1 in 8 websites on the Internet is devoted to sex.
- Worldwide, porn is a $100 billion industry.
- In the U.S. there are more than 75,000 porn sites and a new one is produced on average every 39 minutes.
- By age 18 an average of 96% of men and 30% of all women view porn at least once a month.

PORN IS CHANGING HOW WE HAVE SEX

It's said that porn is responsible for changes in sexual activity. Anal sex, a popular activity on porn sites, is now practiced by approximately a third of the population. Fifty years ago few people engaged in it.

Women now routinely shave their pubic hair, a practice that is almost universal among porn stars. According to a survey by Vagisil, a quarter of women either shave their pubic hair completely or trim closely. There are even "personal" razors being sold to accommodate this new trend. "Manscaping" is practiced by nearly 2 in 3 men, according to a 2011 survey by Flinders University in Australia.

➢ *Atlantic* magazine reported in 2011 that "pubic hair in America is on the road to extinction." Nearly 60% of women 18 –24 and 25% of women 25 – 29 have bare vulvas, according to Indiana University research.

The millions of pages of porn are populated with a seemingly endless supply of men and women doing almost unimaginable things with each other. For a country with a deep history of sexual repression, the Internet has tapped into a hidden well of sexual interest of every imaginable type.

Some couples use porn as a stimulant to their sex life. It's a safe way to vicariously indulge their fantasies and can make sex more exciting. But porn can be harmful to a relationship as well. Sometimes men view their wives more critically after watching porn. Or they want to take extreme sex from fantasy to reality. Sexual activity with their spouse, rather than enhanced by porn, is then diminished. Often, normal sexual activity disappears in place of masturbation to highly unrealistic porn images.

Supermodel Christie Brinkley's husband admitted to an online porn habit that cost several thousand dollars a month—and led to an affair with their babysitter. Actor David Duchovny confessed to being a sex addict while married to the beautiful Tea Leoni. Now if a supermodel and a gorgeous actress can't compete with porn, who can? Men will defend their actions by saying their sex life at home is boring or practically non-existent. In reality, porn is the "perfect storm" of variety, frequency, excitement, and easy access for men.

Porn affects women in other ways too. Many feel as if they can never measure up to the porn models' looks or behavior (just as most men haven't the equipment or stamina to keep up with the male models). But for women the rejection by their husbands and boyfriends leaves them feeling unattractive and rejected.

About 20% to 35% of all therapy sessions and divorces involve sexual problems, many exacerbated by porn. A divorce can cost you plenty—your home, your fortune, and your children. Is looking at porn worth that to you?

Even worse, children are exposed to porn at an age that is much too young for them to process intellectually—about 10 years old on average. By some estimates 90% of our pre-teen children have been exposed to porn.

If you're worried about declining testosterone levels, you should know that the National Institutes of Health found that men who refrain from masturbating for one week saw an average increase of 45.7% in their testosterone levels (2007).

Life Rule: If you have a porn habit, have the discipline to break it—if not for your spouse's sake, then for your children. If you simply view porn occasionally to rev up your sex life, be discreet. And put some easily installed parental controls on your computers.

GRANDMA, IS THAT YOU IN THE GANGBANG?

Tens of thousands of people post their "amateur" sex videos online. It would seem that nearly every attractive (and quite a few not so attractive) woman or man in America has been photographed naked and/or having sex.

What people who take part in these things don't think much about is the fact that the internet is forever. The young couple having sex with each other, or several others, may have a change of heart down the road about what they are doing. Then what? Want to run for office? Not if you've been in a gangbang. You just know that will make front-page news in the *National Enquirer.*

Want to marry that gorgeous (and chaste) soulmate you've been seeing? What will she think when she learns about (and sees) your 23 sex videos. Want to have kids someday? Boy, will they be surprised to see naked mommy having oral sex with daddy. And just wait until mom and dad see their little girl taking on three guys at the same time.

ONLINE IS ABOUT AS PERMANENT AS CARVING IT IN STONE

Thousands "sext" naked photos of themselves every day on their smartphones (hey, Brett Favre, Congressman Weiner, Tiger Woods, Rihanna, Kim Kardashian, and Paris Hilton, are you reading this?).

- According to a recent survey reported on *CBS-TV*, 1/3 of adults 18 - 24 have sent or received sext messages, with slightly more women than men sending nude or sexually suggestive photos.
- 22% of teen women have posted nude or semi-nude photos or video online, according to Safe Communications, Inc. www.safeco.com (2013)

Yes, there's nothing like putting your stupidity out there into cyberspace for anyone in the world to retrieve someday. A former Miss California was bounced out of competition when sexts of her appeared on the internet.

It's a free world and you can do whatever you want so long as it doesn't hurt anyone. But the person you may hurt is yourself...and your family. So, be discreet. Just remember, diamonds are forever. And so is the Internet.

CULTIVATE HUMOR

"A sense of humor is part of the art of leadership, of getting along with people, of getting things done." — President Dwight Eisenhower

Every credible health organization from the Mayo Clinic to the National Institutes of Health have weighed in on the benefits of humor, especially laughter.

As reported on *ABC-TV* in 2005, a study of 20 men and women by the University of Maryland School of Medicine presented to the American College of Cardiology, discovered that 95% of the volunteers experienced increased blood flow while watching a humorous movie, such as "There's Something About Mary," while 74% had decreased blood flow during a more serious film, such as "Saving Private Ryan."

Others studies have verified that the body's natural "killer cells" are activated by humor, kicking the immune system into high gear. Humor also has been reported in numerous studies to decrease disease-related symptoms, especially pain.

Humor therapy has become an accepted part of medical care. There are even trained "laughter leaders" who work in hospitals, retirement homes, and with mental health professionals. Memorial Sloan-Kettering Cancer Center includes Dr. Stubbs the Clown (Michael Christensen) on its staff. He founded the Big Apple Circus Clown Care Unit. Since 1986, the program has sent dozens of clowns to hospitals around the country and made hundreds of thousands of bedside visits.

Laughter as health therapy first came to the attention of the medical community when the author Norman Cousins was fighting ankylosing sponsylitis, a potentially deadly disease of the joints and connective tissue that left him in excruciating pain and with few treatment options. Cousins documented the results of his laughter therapy in the book, *Anatomy of an Illness*. A ten-minute "belly laugh" would give him two hours of pain-free sleep.

There's even a professional organization dedicated to the therapeutic effects of humor, the Association for Applied and Therapeutic Humor www.aath.org. Here you can take a course in therapeutic humor and even be certified.

If you have chronic pain, like millions of Americans, or suffer from depression or insomnia, or simply need a boost from the incessant negative news today, try a little humor. Laughter is the best medicine.

A sense of humor is also cited as one of the top personality traits desired by both men and women in a spouse…and by employers in job candidates. Humor is a social indicator of character that is likely embedded in our DNA. Humor is assumed to be the ability of an intelligent person, and intelligence is ranked highly as a desirable quality in a mate. Intelligence is a good indicator of how successful a person will be…and success is also rated as a highly desirable ingredient in a good mate. Potential employers see job candidates in much the same light.

While surveys show that about 90% of men and women think they have a good sense of humor, what they often mean is that they like other people's sense of humor. The actual figure is closer to 10% of those who have a developed sense of humor. Either way, developing a sense of humor or finding humor in others will add greatly to your life.

REJECT REJECTION

"We have nothing to fear but fear itself." — President Franklin Roosevelt

Fear of rejection is one of the biggest reasons people don't achieve what they want in life. Ironically, the fear of rejection creates the very failure people fear. Ralph Waldo Emerson said, "Do the thing you fear and the death of fear is certain." Action dissipates fear. And while it may not entirely rid you of fear, it can keep it at a manageable level.

Most fears are the product of an active mind that is focusing on the worst that could happen. A lot of books suggest that you ask yourself "What's the worst that can happen?" This isn't good advice, although it's become a cliché recommendation. The fact is, the worst could truly be disastrous. It's why you must carefully and dispassionately weigh the pros and cons of any major decision.

In most cases, people fear failing to get something they don't currently have but want. So, looking at the situation logically, if you are rejected and don't get what you want you haven't really lost anything. You are where you began.

Some men discover this early in life when they shed their fear of being rejected by girls and approach any girl they think may be interesting. They learn what every good salesman eventually learns—that every "no" puts them just one more person closer to a "yes." Who cares if you ask 100 beautiful girls out and 99 say "no" if just one says "yes." You now have a beautiful girl. Without 99 rejections you'd have nothing.

My friend Jack was lusting after a pretty blonde he met at a party. From the moment he saw her he was smitten. But he thought she was "out of his league." When they did have a chance to talk she was always friendly enough. But Jack decided she was just being kind and wasn't really interested in him, so he never asked her out.

Four years went by and Jack ran into the pretty blonde's brother at a convention. He asked about her. "Oh, my sister just got married to a guy she met a year ago. By the way, Suzie always wondered why you didn't ask her out. She was crazy about you, you know. Suze has always been a little shy but she is really a great gal when you get to know her."

Jack never forgot the missed opportunity. And never let it happen again.

Think of rejection as your friend. Without it you can't achieve much in life. And what you do achieve won't have as much value because it came too easily. There's nothing like the feeling of overcoming a fear and succeeding. But you'll never know that feeling if you don't overcome the fear of rejection and take the necessary action and risks.

And like every successful actor who has endured hundreds of auditions, don't take the rejection personally. You are a better person, not worse, because of the rejection. You've learned what doesn't work. At the least, you can pat yourself on the back for having the courage to try.

"You miss 100% of the shots you don't take." — Wayne Gretzky

Think about what you want now. Have you taken any action to get it? Why not? Are you afraid? Are you waiting for the right time. As Napoleon Hill said, "Don't wait. The time will never be right."

If you want anything in life you must accept that part of the process is <u>not</u> getting what you want sometimes. There isn't a salesperson or actor or entrepreneur alive who hasn't been rejected numerous times on the road to success. Each rejection is an opportunity to learn, to strengthen your resolve and get closer to eventual success.

It's been estimated that 99% of all the bullets and bombs used in World War ll failed to hit their target. But the 1% that did were responsible for millions of deaths. Remember the 99% rule. It only takes 1% success to make a huge difference. If you make 100 sales calls but one results in millions of dollars in business you'll be considered a huge success, not a failure—-even though you did fail 99% of the time.

LEARN TO SPEAK WELL IN PUBLIC

"The voice is a second face." — Gerard Bauer

The ability to speak well has been the signature element of success for many of our greatest leaders. Barack Obama, John Kennedy, Martin Luther King, and FDR are all outstanding speakers. In everyday life, few people have the oratory skills these exceptional speakers have, but the ability to speak articulately and communicate effectively is one of the most often cited reasons for success.

Your voice can help define your personality. Many people can be immediately identified by their unique vocal style. John Wayne, Humphrey Bogart, Christopher Walken, Morgan Freeman, Jimmy Stewart, Walter Cronkite, Bill Clinton, JFK, Katherine Hepburn and, of course, Marilyn Monroe all had distinct voices. Close your eyes and you can "hear" their voices in your mind.

Monroe even had two styles of speaking, her "public" voice (breathy and sexy) and her private voice, of which there is little recorded but was more average in tone and modulation, according to reports from her friends. If you naturally have a distinctive voice, use it to your advantage. If not, learn to speak in a style that flatters you. Your voice is potentially one of your most powerful tools in developing a distinctive and effective personal style.

Of all fears, public speaking ranks at the top. But it's easily mastered and can have an outsized impact upon your future success.

A few tips for successful public speaking include:

1. Arrive early and become familiar with the room, podium, and sound system.

2. Look professional and be well-groomed. You'll be perceived as more capable by the audience.
3. Create a strong title. Engage your audience.
4. Know your material. Prepare. Practice. Visualize giving your talk in advance and you'll likely do better.
5. Focus on your message. If your talk improves your audience's life is some way, you will be appreciated.
6. Know your audience. Greet audience members before your presentation. What do they want from you?
7. Be passionate. Don't shrink onstage..expand your gestures. Be animated, speak to the person in the last row, pause for effect, and smile.
8. Be concise. Don't ramble on or belabor a point.
9. Divvy up your talk into 10 minute chunks. People have trouble remembering anything longer.
10. Don't worry about being perfect. Some of the most influential speakers were not technically very good speakers. Some, like Winston Churchill or Barbara Walters, even had speech impediments. Speak to the audience as you would to a few close friends. You're being judged by what you say, not how you say it. Be relaxed and laugh about your mistakes.
11. Don't get bogged down in data or too much information. Less is more.
12. Provide a recap printed piece of the highlights from your talk.
13. Thank your audience.
14. Answer questions.

In *Talk Like TED: The 9 Public-Speaking Secrets of the World's Top Minds* by Carmine Gallo, the presentation ingredients of the top speakers included (1) being passionate, (2) telling three stories to illustrate points, (3) practice relentlessly, (4) teach your audience something new, (5) deliver a jaw-dropping moment, (6) use humor without telling a joke, (7) favor pictures over text, (8) be authentic and vulnerable, and (9) keep your talk to 18 minutes.

Here are additional tips to become an effective speaker in one-to-one interactions:

1. Be a good listener. Provide time for your listener to respond. And don't ignore what they are saying because you're trying to think of what you want to say next.
2. Look the person in the eyes…but don't stare.
3. If appropriate, you can make a strong connection by touching the other person's arm or shoulder to make a point.
4. Show you are listening by occasionally adding a thought or by nodding.

The Toastmasters www.toastmasters.org is an international organization that helps people learn to speak effectively in public. Founded in 1924, Toastmasters now has more than 270,000 members in 13,000 clubs in 117 countries. Famous past Toastmasters students include astronaut James Lovell, author/speaker Harvey McKay, and motivational pioneer Napoleon Hill.

For more tips, read *The Presentation Tips of Steve Jobs: How to be Insanely Great in Front of Any Audience* by Carmine Gallo, *136 Effective Presentation Tips* by Tony Jeary or *Presentation Skills 201: How to Take It to the Next Level as a Confident, Engaging Presenter* by William Steele.

THE TIME OF YOUR LIFE

"Dost thou love life? Then do not squander time, for that's the stuff that life is made of." — Benjamin Franklin

"Where does the time go?" "The time just flew by." "I need a 48–hour day!"

In the hectic, jam–packed, constantly changing, digital–age 21st Century, the way you manage and utilize time could be your key to success. Or not.

AMERICANS ARE GOOD AT WASTING THEIR TIME

"Lost time is never found again." — Ben Franklin

Americans waste enormous amounts of time. It's estimated that during the first week following the release of the video Grand Theft Auto IV in 2008, more than 3 million days of time were spent playing this game. By another estimate a total of 600 years of time was spent (as of 2011) playing World of Warcraft. *Time* magazine reported in November, 2011 that 200,000 years of combined time was spent playing the smartphone game Angry Birds during the first two years after its release. Imagine what could have been accomplished if the time had been used productively.

In order to get back in touch with many of the things that make you a well-rounded, fully-functioning human it makes sense to go on a media "diet." This may sound Draconian to many people, especially the hyper-connected under-30 age group, but it won't hurt to try it. You may just realize how many benefits there are to reducing your media consumption.

I'm not advocating getting rid of TV altogether—only reducing and controlling its usage. Watching a baseball or football game with friends, watching a movie with your family, and viewing educational programs can be valuable. But 95% of what is on TV is simply a waste of time, "mindless" entertainment. Watching the inane antics of Honey Boo Boo, Real Housewives of Atlanta or Swamp People is not a good investment of your time...if you want to accomplish anything in life. The eyes are a pathway to the brain. What you send to your brain should be positive, uplifting or informative.

AC Nielsen estimates that the average time spent watching TV in America is 4 hours and 49 minutes a day—an all-time high (in 2008/2009). Many people will spend a decade of their life in front of the TV (the average is about 9 years)

Watching too much TV can do more harm than just waste time. Here are a few other downsides to TV viewing:

- People eat 71% more food on average while watching TV.
- Type 2 diabetes increases 141% among heavy TV watchers (14+ hrs a week).
- Obesity increases 91% on average among heavy (no pun intended) TV viewers.
- Erectile dysfunction increases 30% on average among men who view 17+ hours a week (turning off the tube can be a turn-on).
- Insomnia increases an average 105% among those who view 21+ hours a week.

Managing your time is one of the most important things you can do in your life. Reducing the amount of time you spend in front of the TV is one big step toward that goal.

WHY DON'T WE VALUE TIME?

Every year you will have 8,760 hours to do all that you want or need to do (doesn't seem like much in hours, does it?). Most people assume they have an abundant amount of time and therefore don't put a great value on it. The truth is no one knows how much time they have. If you knew you had just ten days left to live, time would become very valuable. Every minute would count.

The first step to using time wisely is to realize its value in your life. There will never be more of it, only less. Every moment you are alive the value of time increases. So use it wisely.

LEAKING TIME

Few people are aware of how they use or misuse the time in their lives. Time "leaks" are the major cause of wasted time.

- The average time spent on Facebook by the 1.1 billion users (as of 2013) is 32 minutes a day.

Many people spend dozens of hours a month just texting. Here's how many text messages the typical smartphone user sends/receives every month, according to Experian and Pew Research studies (2011).

Age	Send	Receive
18 – 24	2,022	1,831
25 – 34	1,110	1,130
35 – 44	831	726
45 – 54	525	473
55+	247	244

By one estimate, approximately 80% of all text messages are essentially meaningless…just "chatter" by overly connected users.

Other time leaks include:

- ✓ Errands.
- ✓ Standing in lines.
- ✓ Shopping trips.
- ✓ Video games.
- ✓ Email.
- ✓ Household tasks.

Americans mismanage their time by frittering it away…time leaks. As a result, the things that we say are most important to us get what time is left—often none at all.

- ✓ 80% say they aren't satisfied with how much time they have with their spouse.
- ✓ 70% aren't happy about how much time they engage with their children.
- ✓ 53% see their friends less than once a month.
- ✓ Nearly 4 out of 5 people report being "busier" today than just five years ago and unable to keep up with things in their life.

"A man who dares waste one hour of time has not discovered the value of life." — Charles Darwin

Time Masters know that controlling their time involves making only a few adjustments. A friend reduced his TV viewing from approximately 24 hours a week to just four. He began taking the ferry instead of driving to work—and used the time to brush up on his Spanish and make phone calls. He disciplined himself to use his computer only for business and essential communication—and saved another five hours a week. Finally, he hired a housekeeper to clean his house, do his laundry, and pick up groceries. The $100 a week she charged saved him about ten hours a week. Altogether these few simple changes in lifestyle saved him slightly more than 40 hours a week—about equal to his workweek

My friend was now able to find restorative time in his schedule, including more time with family and friends, exercising, reading, going to movies and plays, hobbies, visiting the local museums, and getting more sleep. This new-found restorative time made him significantly more productive and resulted in a nice promotion and more money. He also felt more in control. Life began to have more meaning. All his social relationships improved. Not a bad return on a minor investment in time management.

KEEPING TRACK OF TIME

Be vigilant about the use of your time. Keep a time diary. Write down everything you do for two weeks and how much time you spend doing it. What can you reduce or eliminate? How can you do tasks more efficiently? Who can you delegate or hire to do repetitive or mundane jobs?

If you want to get serious about focusing your time usage, check out RescueTime www.rescuetime.com . With their software you can track time spent at websites, on applications, meetings, phone calls, and track offline activities. You get detailed reports of your time usage and a weekly summary by email. You can set goals and track your progress, block distracting sites, and even get a "productivity score" in pre-defined categories to see how you're doing and make adjustments.

TIME MASTERY

"Revel in the gift of time, for every year brings the magical opportunity to write a new chapter in the book of life." — Isadora James

According to business expert Peter Drucker, "The management of your time is the foundation for your effectiveness."

The main reason most often given for not exercising, not achieving a goal or not developing a talent into a lucrative business is "not enough time." Yet many people with the same amount of time (we all get the same 168 hours a week) achieve great things while others accomplish little.

In an analysis of the amount of time spent at the office, a large percentage of "work" time was actually spent on socializing, surfing the Internet, and doing personal tasks. For more than 1 in 5 workers the amount of paid working time spent on non-work activities amounted to about half their time on the job.

- Surfing the Internet has become such a problem for employers that 54% of companies with more than 50 employees block the use of social media sites like Facebook and Twitter, according to *Wired* magazine (2011).

- A report publicized in *PC World* magazine (2011) found that more than 3 in 4 companies monitor their employee's internet usage.
- According to a 2011 survey by AOL and Survey.com www.survey.com, America's workers waste 2.09 hours a day on average. That's about 1 ½ weeks every month.

Here's how it adds up:

44.7% Surf the web

23.4% Socialize with co-workers

6.8% Conduct their own business

3.9% Are "spaced out" or daydreaming

3.1% Run errands off-site

1.3% Are applying for other jobs

1.0% Arrive late

1.0% Plan personal events

- A study by DeskTime found that employees spend an average of 65 hours a month on social media sites.

Let's compare the way a Time Waster and a Time Master use their weekly allotment of time.

BE A TIME MASTER NOT A TIME WASTER

"We must use time as a tool, not as a crutch." — John F. Kennedy

#1 Time waster: Television

The average American watches 4.6 hours of TV a day. This largely wasted time amounts to 1,679 hours a year (70 days). Or 210 eight-hour work days.

The 21st Century equivalent is surfing the Internet. According to an eMarketer report, Americans spend an average of 23 hours a week emailing, texting, surfing the web, and on social media (14% of total time). Eight hours is spent with email, 7 hours on Facebook, and 5 hours on You Tube.

Imagine what you could accomplish with this much time devoted to something that adds real value to your life?

#2 Time waster: Commuting

Tens of millions of cars head out on the road every day so that people can put in their 8+ hours of work. A 25-minute commute (the U.S. average) adds up to more than 200 hours (about a month of 8-hour days) a year of mostly wasted time.

The negative consequences of commuting aren't often considered when deciding on a job or where to live, but there are many:

1. People who commute 45 minutes or more are 40% more likely to divorce.
2. Commuting causes significantly more stress.
3. Commuters have less sex.
4. Commuters exercise less.
5. Commuters sleep less.

It's even worse for the 3.5 million "extreme commuters" who commute 90 minutes are more each way to work.

For many people a commute is unavoidable. But there are ways to make your commute bearable.

1. Bike to work. You'll get some quality exercise and save money.
2. Take public transportation. Trains, ferries, and buses are very efficient in most large cities.
3. Walk to work. When you buy or rent a home, consider how much time it takes to get to work. Live near where you work and you can save thousands of dollars and hours of time. And the exercise will help keep you healthy.

#3 Time Waster: Waiting in line.
The average American spends three hours a week just waiting in line. If that doesn't sound like much, consider this—it adds up to almost seven 24-hour days a year…a full week. What could you do with a week of extra time? Read a book (this book?). Call people you haven't spoken to recently? Do your taxes? Write a good Plan for Life? Anticipate waiting in line and be prepared to use it wisely.

#4. Time Waster: Errands

Running errands absorbs a huge amount of available time for most Americans. To reduce this Time Waster make a list of your errands at the beginning of the week and combine as many as possible. Better yet, find someone you can pay to do your errands. Consider this…if you earn $50,000 a year your time is worth about $25 an hour. If you can devote more time to earning money rather than Time Wasters, then you come out ahead.

THE TIME MASTERS' CREDO

Time Masters use time the way they use money…wisely. Before you buy anything it's a good idea to stop for a moment and ask yourself if it's a "need" or a "want." Limiting your spending primarily to "needs" is a good way to stay financially sound. In the same way, people who utilize their time productively always ask themselves if what they are doing is going to contribute to reaching the important goals in life such as building a business, getting fit, having more time for family and friends, or getting more sleep. Everything in life is a trade–off…you'll need to decide what are your priorities and act accordingly.

PRODUCTIVE TIME

1. Exercise.
2. Creating multiple sources of income.
3. Working on a personal project.
4. Helping kids with homework.
5. Keeping the house, cars, yard maintained.
6. Improving a skill.
7. Education.
8. Doing meaningful work.
9. Networking.

RESTORATIVE TIME

1. Reading.
2. Travel.
3. Sex.
4. Relaxing.
5. Meditation.
6. Family dinner.
7. Playing with the kids.
8. Visit to a local attraction.
9. Lunch with friends.
10. Time in the outdoors, hiking, fishing.

OUTSOURCING

Consider doing what most of the Fortune 500 companies are doing and outsource your work. Two resources are Brickwork www.brickworkindia.com and Your Man in India www.yourmaninindia.com. Lifestyle Design advocate Tim Ferriss, author of *The 4-Hour Workweek*, swears that both of these companies have made his busy life manageable.

Need to get your personal finances in order? A Personal Assistant at Brickwork will set up a Quicken program for you and input all your data, providing you with regular updates online. Would you like to build a list of providers in your industry? Outsource the task to Your Man in India.

If working with someone halfway around the world makes you anxious, find someone local to help you. In many major markets you can post your needs on TaskRabbit www.taskrabbit.com. It's a great place to find help immediately on a variety of tasks from accounting to dog walking. The service is so popular that many competitors have popped up in the past couple of years: www.thumbtack.com, www.zaarly.com, www.zaask.com, www.airtasker.com, www.fiverr.com, and www.gigwalk.com (smartphone app).

The Life Rule about time usage is all about comparative advantage. There is an opportunity cost for everything. If you have a higher value activity that utilizes your core competency to advance your goals, and if you have funds to support it, then outsourcing and delegating mundane tasks will help you create success more quickly than if your time is devalued.

THE POWER OF LESS

"A simple life is its own reward." — George Santayana

In order to create more of what you want in life it's important to lead a life with less. This seeming contradiction is at the heart of many of the problems Americans grapple with every day. Yet for approximately 10% of the population the power of intelligent frugal living has led to increased happiness, more time, less stress, improved health and financial freedom. You simply need to give up the American lifestyle of more and more STUFF.

Americans buy too much, eat too much, have too much debt, and keep too much stuff. We have so much stuff that we don't even have room for it in our already overstuffed homes. The personal storage business is a $22.6 billion industry in America…bigger than the motion picture industry.

As a result, Americans have less time and money for the things that truly matter—family and friends, productive work, hobbies, leisure time, education, reading, and sleep. Setting limits on everything from what we buy to how we allocate our time lessens stress, improves health, increases focus, and creates the framework of a successful life. Realizing the value of less can be the key that unlocks your life.

Start by asking these questions of yourself:

- ✓ What is most important to you?
- ✓ What activities have the most meaningful impact upon your life?
- ✓ What are your core needs and what are your wants?
- ✓ Of the wants, what can you do without?

If you're like most people you probably have never slowed down long enough to consider what it is in your life that really matters. You may crave a new Jaguar convertible, but just how necessary is it that you get one? What will you have to give up to own one…and is what you give up worth it? What if it means working longer hours and not spending time with family or friends? Or not taking that three-week European vacation? After all, a Jaguar is a car. Its purpose is to get you safely and reliably from one place to another—in the same way a much less expensive (and frankly more reliable) Honda Accord does.

Or is the Jaguar a want? If so, why do you want it? Of course, part of why you want it is its beauty. A Jaguar is a gorgeous car. But a Honda Accord is very good-looking too. Do you want it because it will impress your friends? Or because it reinforces an image you have of yourself? Or to bolster your self-esteem? Ask yourself if someone's car has made you think differently of them. If you are operating from a place of truth in your life, the answer would be "no."

Why do you lust after a large home? The average size of a home in the U.S. has gone from about 1,500 square feet in 1970 to more than 2,400 square feet by 2005 while the average household size has decreased from 3.5 to 2.1 average members. Most experts agree that 1,500 to 2,000 square feet is the optimal size for a home. Anything larger is simply excess.

There's a trend beginning in America toward smaller "tiny" homes, some just 400 square feet. They're charming, efficient, and usually cost less than $20,000. In many cases they are even portable. For thousands of tiny home enthusiasts, it's more important to live simply and without large home expenses.

The desire for more and bigger is almost endless. Walk-in closets are an invention of modern American life. More than half the homes in the U.S. have three or more TV sets. The average woman in the U.S. owns 19 pairs of shoes (but wears only seven). In a classic case of obscene excess, singer Mariah Carey owns more than 1,000 pairs of shoes and several houses, including one that cost $125 million and has more than 70 rooms. America is a nation defined by over-consumption.

- More than 21 million American households have more than two cars...and 2 million have more than five, according to *Motor Trend.*
- There are nearly 3.4 million second homes.

SIMPLIFY – DECLUTTER – GET ORGANIZED

Too much stuff—clutter—is bad feng shui...it impedes life rather than adding to it. Too much stuff is like too much body fat. It slows you down, making life less healthy. And like anyone who has been overweight and taken the necessary steps to get slim, fit, and healthy, if you do the same with your possessions you'll feel reborn.

A good place to begin de-cluttering and organizing your life is with Lori Marrero's book *The Clutter Diet: The Skinny on Organizing Your Home and Taking Control of Your Life* www.theclutterdiet.com and Ciji Ware's *Rightsizing Your Life: Simplifying Your Surroundings While Keeping What Matters Most.* www.rightsizingyourlife.com.

According to Ware, your goal is to "create a living environment filled only with the household goods—as well as people and activities—that we love, along with surroundings that suit our stage in life." Keep only the best, highest quality, most meaningful things. Instead of twelve pairs of mediocre shoes, own three pair of stunning shoes. Instead of sixteen dress shirts, choose five that work with your suits and sport coat. Wear less, use less, eat less, and spend less. But when you do buy anything, buy quality. This is the key to "less is more."

You don't need to live in a 5,000 square foot home. Most families are fine with a home of 1,200 square feet. The mortgage, taxes, utilities, and maintenance will be far less. With the tens of thousands—even hundreds of thousands—you save you can invest in your future security, take a few fabulous vacations, earn an advanced degree or take up a new hobby. These are the things that create true happiness…not more stuff. You don't need a bigger, newer car. You don't need more clothes. You don't need to replace a perfectly fine TV set with a new one. Learn to live on less and you will learn to live more.

Take one month and go through your closets, drawers, garage, pantry, files, car trunk, attic and aim to get rid of all the unnecessary items you have stored. If you have the guts, try to aim for removing at least 50% of what you own. Sell it on eBay, Craigslist, or at a garage sale. Or donate it to charity.

Set up a simple filing system for your paperwork (see sample below). Then go through it regularly and discard anything that isn't necessary. Most items that are two years old or older can be tossed out. Keep tax records for seven years or longer, real estate papers, investment docs, passports, titles, birth/adoption/death certificates, military records, insurance policies, your will, and power of attorney paperwork.

Think about keeping some or all of these in a bank safe deposit box. If a fire, flood, tornado, earthquake or hurricane hit your home—as it did for tens of thousands last year—it would be difficult or impossible to replace these valuable papers.

FILE SETUP

- ✓ Family documents.
- ✓ Tax records (state, federal, real estate).
- ✓ Bills to pay.
- ✓ Paid bills.
- ✓ Auto expenses.
- ✓ Credit cards (with a separate file for each card).
- ✓ Investments.
- ✓ Charitable donations.
- ✓ Medical.
- ✓ Dues/memberships.
- ✓ Utilities (separate file for gas, electric, telephone, water, etc).
- ✓ Home expenses, including mortgage.
- ✓ Insurance (home, auto, health, etc.).
- ✓ Social security.
- ✓ Travel.
- ✓ Entertainment.
- ✓ Education.
- ✓ To Be Filed.

- More than 90% of all papers that go into a file are never looked at again. Before adding anything to your file (or life) ask yourself, "Do you really need it?"

Further reading:

Organizing From the Inside Out: The Foolproof System for Organizing Your Home, Your Office, and Your Life by Julie Morgenstern.

Taming the Paper Tiger by Barbara Hemphill.

Clutter Control: Putting your home on a Diet by Jeff Campbell.

Unclutter Your House: 7 simple steps – 700 tips and ideas by Donna Smallin.

***The Paradox of Choice: Why More is Less*: How the Culture of Abundance Robs Us of Satisfaction** by Barry Schwartz.

The Power of Simplicity by Jack Trout and Steve Rivkin.

Online resources:

www.messies.com

If you're one of the estimated 6.5 to 15 million hoarders in the U.S., know that 75 cities now have task forces dedicated to helping you clean up your home. There are a number of private services you can call to help clean up your home (or a loved one's). In California call 1-800-HOARDERS. Other services include www.americanhoarders.com or www.clutterhoardingcleanup.com.

Life Rule: KISS…Keep it simple stupid.

SPIRITUALITY

"We are not human beings on a spiritual path, but spiritual beings on a human path." — Dr. Lauren Artess

Religion and spirituality seems to be ingrained in the human DNA. Archeologists have discovered evidence of religious artifacts dating back to the Stone Age…at least 50,000 years ago. By some estimates, more than 20,000 religions or spiritual beliefs have been practiced by mankind.

- Nearly half of Americans, about 43% attend church regularly (2009).
- ➢ According to a 2009 *Newsweek* poll, a third of Americans said they are "spiritual" but not religious.
- ➢ A 2012 Pew poll found that 20% of Americans say they are not religious, including 6% who are atheists.
- ➢ According to a U.S. Federal Bureau of Prisons survey, just 0.02% of prisoners are atheists. (2013)

While formal religion seems to be on the decline, belief in some form of spirituality continues to rise. And while the world is embroiled in religion-based conflicts and rampant prejudice, there are positive aspects to believing in a higher power or being spiritual. Viktor Frankl's research of Nazi death camps found that those who had found meaning in their life were most likely to survive, not necessarily the youngest or strongest.

Most likely, religion fulfills a complex array of human needs. And while most of the tenets of nearly every religion is to do good, there is almost always a side to religion that isn't so good. From molesting priests to racist evangelists to Aztecs who sacrificed virgins by cutting out their still beating hearts, religion mirrors the dual nature of mankind. Most wars have a religious component.

TANGIBLE BENEFITS OF BELIEF

People with religious beliefs tend to live longer and have slightly happier marriages than non–believers. A 9–year study of 21,000 Americans found that religious attendance at least once a week resulted in 7 additional years of life expectancy, even after adjusting for social and health factors. Religious belief and affiliation also helps boost the immune system and lower blood pressure.

No doubt some of this can be accounted for by the "placebo" affect…if you believe something to be true it is often experienced as true. Nonetheless, it is a real benefit of religion. The social network that organized religion provides is also comforting psychologically to many people. People who give back to their communities by volunteering to help improve the lives of others also report positive benefits in their own lives.

- Slightly more than 1 in 4 Americans volunteer at least once a year, according to the Bureau of Labor Statistics.
- In 2012, approximately $300 billion was donated to the 1.8 million charities in the U.S., according to a report from the Giving USA Foundation and the Center on Philanthropy at Indiana University.

If you want to check out the viability of any particular charity online, go to www.CharityNavigator.com or www.charitywatch.org.

People engage in religion, charitable activities, and volunteering for many reasons. The bottom–line is it makes them feel good about themselves. But if that also translates to doing good for the world, we're better off for it.

Life Rule: Give back.

YOU ARE A LIFELONG WORK IN PROGRESS

Living a complete and fulfilled life isn't easy. It requires constant work and maintenance. In order to achieve a life you can look back on someday with pride and pleasure you will need to be a lifelong student of all that makes a good life. And you'll need to incorporate what you learn into actions that guide your course through life.

Life Rules:

- ✓ Make health your foundation for success.
- ✓ Make wealth your engine of success.
- ✓ Engage in lifelong ongoing education to expand your skills and knowledge.
- ✓ Choose a career that you love…and can make money.
- ✓ Live in a place that is in sync with your personality and goals.
- ✓ Constantly work to improve who you are as a person.
- ✓ Love smart.

Further reading:

The Power of Self-Confidence: Become Unstoppable, Irresistable, and Unafraid in Every Area of Your Life and ***No Excuses! The Power of Self-Discipline*** by Brian Tracy.

The Time Trap: The Classic Book on Time Management by Alex Mackenzie and Pat Nickerson.

Learned Optimism by Martin Seligman.

The 4-Hour Workweek by Timothy Ferriss.

The Art of Happiness by the Dalai Lama.

Feel the Fear and Do It Anyway by Susan Jeffers, Ph.D.

CHAPTER 8

A SAMPLE PLAN FOR LIFE

Start now by using the information, tools, and resources in this book to begin your successful Plan for Life. It's important to begin immediately… the changes that are coming in the next few years will be massive. Plan out a direction that will prepare you to navigate the future successfully.

Everyone will use the information in this book differently, according to your goals, lifestyle, age, sex, and personal preferences. However, to give you an idea of what a Plan for Life looks like, here is one for a fictional young woman named Angela Jones.

ANGELA JONES

Age: 35

Single

Height: 5' 6"

Weight: 162

College degree in marketing from the University of Illinois

Currently living in a small city in Illinois

Many of the same elements apply whether you are younger or older, male or female. Take what is offered in this book and build your own Plan for Life. While Angela's plan isn't overly detailed, if you prefer to include specific action steps, due dates, and resources…all the better.

ANGELA JONES PLAN FOR LIFE

MAJOR GOALS

1. Lose weight (135 target).
2. Get fit and healthy.
3. Earn my MBA.
4. Find a job as a Marketing Manager/Director at a hospitality company.
5. Get married by age 30 and be a good spouse.
6. Have two children and be a good parent.
7. Own a home by age 35.
8. Live in San Diego.
9. Travel to Europe, New York, and South America.
10. Expand my network of personal and professional contacts.
11. Begin an ongoing structured learning program.
12. Save 10k% of my income…$50,000 by age 30.
13. Learn to be a great speaker.
14. Create a second income stream as a marketing writer and publish a book by age 30.
15. Create a stylish home and wardrobe.

HEALTH

Goals: Lose 30 pounds. Reduce BMI, cholesterol, and blood pressure to healthy level. Run a 10k race. Eat healthy foods only.

1. Revise diet to include mostly organic, raw foods (vegetables, fruit, fish, grass-fed beef). Go to the farmers markets.
2. Join the YMCA and use their gym equipment and exercise classes. Find an exercise partner. Track progress—including caloric intake, weight, blood pressure, cholesterol levels, and body mass index.
3. Reduce weight from 163 to 130 within one year (July 2013)
4. Target blood pressure…from 160 over 100 to 120 over 80 by July, 2013.

5. Reduce cholesterol level from 240 to 180 by end of year 2013.
6. Reduce BMI from 35 to 24 by end of year 2013.
7. Lose weight by keeping daily calories to 1500 or less. Use CalorieTracker app to track exact calories consumed.
8. Begin walking/jogging.
9. Take a yoga class or do daily 15 minutes of meditation. Decide by March 15.
10. Purchase a water filter and drink only filtered water...either Brita or H2O.
11. Eliminate cakes, cookies and doughnuts from diet, except as rare treat.
12. Eat fast food only once a week (or less) instead of ten times a week.
13. Reduce/eliminate processed foods...fresh, fresh, fresh and raw.
14. Upgrade bedding, make bedroom more attractive, get to sleep by 10pm. Take a bath before bedtime. Buy down pillows and a lightweight comforter.
15. Quit smoking with supervised smoking cessation program (Smokenders?).
16. Reduce alcoholic beverage intake to two glasses of wine or beer a week.
17. Laugh more...see funny movies, go to the comedy club, see the humorous side of life.
18. Purchase a Basis health tracker wristband to monitor my daily activity.

WEALTH

Goals: Begin a retirement savings program. Save $5,000.

1. Begin tracking expenses and income daily with monthly recaps. Save all receipts. In a binder, put all invoices and correspondence for expenditures in tabbed categories (banking, healthcare, gas, auto expenses, etc). Mark all invoices when paid with check number and amount. Put everything in a manila file folder with amounts and dates under each category. Chart on Excel spreadsheet.

2. Save 10% of income. Adjust by eliminating cigarettes, sweets, and impulse buys. See if the company I work for can deduct it automatically into my savings account.
3. Start a Roth IRA. See Richard, my accountant.
4. Select a low–cost index stock fund. Research.
5. Babysit on weekends for neighbors to earn extra cash. Put ads up at the library and YMCA. Contact the daycare centers. Put out the word with friends and neighbors.
6. Purchase a good security system for my home. Put locks on all windows. Get timers for indoor and outdoor lights. Select a new password with nine letters and numbers, including one character and one capital (change every six months).
7. Order a copy of my credit report every six months. www.annualcreditreport.com

CAREER

Goal: A better, higher paying job.

1. Begin researching higher paid jobs in Chicago and Indianapolis. Check out LinkedIn, Craigslist, industry job boards, and find a couple of good recruiters. NETWORK!! Start with friends, family and former co–workers and supervisors.
2. Read the all–time best–selling career guide What Color is Your Parachute?
3. Open a LinkedIn account and begin building a targeted network. Join industry and alumni groups. Ramp up LinkedIn knowledge quickly by enrolling in TheInAcademy www.TheInAcademy.com.
4. Bookmark career blogs, read daily.
5. Become active in the alumni association.
6. Get testimonials and references lined up.
7. Find out what skills are in demand in my industry.
8. Write a killer resume.

EDUCATION

Goal: Work toward a Masters Degree in Marketing. Become more knowledgeable about social media and business software programs.

1. Take an online accredited social media marketing course.
2. Prepare documents to submit to attend graduate school online (either University of Chicago, University of Illinois, or Northwestern). Research school programs and costs.
3. Learn to use Excel, Powerpoint, Microsoft Office, and Quicken. Check out online resources and books at library. Commit to one hour a night to study at Jones Academy. Ha!!
4. Become proficient in social media: Facebook, LinkedIn, Google+, Twitter, Pinterest.
5. Plan out an ongoing education program to acquire the skills/knowledge I want over the next five years.

PLACE

Goal: Move to a place more in sync with who I am…and with better career opportunities.

1. Research career opportunities, cost of living, culture, and climate at major market cities. First choices: Chicago, Indianapolis. Second choices: Milwaukee, Minneapolis. Why? To be near friends/family and familiar Midwest surroundings. Also, look into warmer climate cities: Miami, Atlanta, Austin, San Diego, San Francisco. Why? Hate cold weather. Plan to move within six months.
2. Find an affordable one-bedroom apartment in a neighborhood that has charm, nightlife, good access to transportation, and is safe. Check out rentals on Craigslist.
3. Decide on style of furnishings (shabby chic?).
4. Build a professional and casual wardrobe within my budget ($2,000).

LOVE

Goal: Find a good boyfriend that leads to marriage.

1. Join alumni social groups, if available where I move.
2. Consider joining match.com, eHarmony.com or chemistry.com to try online dating.
3. Decide what I want in a man and a relationship…and don't get sidetracked by the bad boys!

YOU

Goal: Become a better me.

1. Work on being the best me I can be…smooth out the rough spots: don't be too serious…have fun/be funny, don't be clingy…be independent but not aloof, work on being sexy, do well in my career and keep learning, reduce my self-induced stress, keep my anger under control, be a good friend, listen instead of talking so much, and don't accept anything that isn't right for me.
2. Don't get lazy about how I look when I go out…always dress your best! Buy fewer things…but the best quality. Plan out my wardrobe so I don't waste money.
3. Keep my natural red hair instead of coloring it (since everyone says I look better that way). Get it professionally styled.
4. Learn to be a good public speaker. Join Toastmasters.
5. Get out and meet people, remember them, and stay in contact…build my Metwork!

CREATE THE LIFE YOU'VE ALWAYS WANTED

I highly recommend including specific Action Steps with Completion Dates to keep you firmly committed to your Plan for Life. Refer to your plan often. Revise it as circumstances change. Be disciplined and consistent and work hard to make it a reality. It's important work…because it is your one life to live, and if you don't live it the way you want…someone else will live it for you.

Good luck!

ONE MORE THING

Life is complicated in the 21st Century. There's much more to know and learn in order to manage it well. Due to space limitations, I couldn't include everything I wanted in this book to help you...it would have run more than 1,500 pages. But if you go to the companion website www.APlanForLife.com, I'll post what I couldn't put in the book...as well as new information to help you take control of your life.

A PLAN FOR LIFE
REFERENCE

A Plan for Life is the product of extensive research, numerous interviews, and review of more than 500 books. Here are several books that I found useful in developing the content for A Plan for Life.

BOOKS

- Ageless Body, Timeless Mind | Deepak Chopra
- Addict Nation | Jane Velez-Mitchell
- After the Affair | Jamis Abrams Spring
- The Aladdin Factor | Jack Canfield, Mark Victor Hansen
- Anger Management for Dummies | W. Doyle Gentry
- Anger Management for Everyone: Seven Proven Ways to Control Anger and Live a Happier Life | Raymond Tafrate, Ph.D., Howard Kassinove, Ph.D.
- Anti Cancer: A New Way of Life | Dr. David Servan-Schreiber
- Dr. Bob Arnot's Guide to Turning Back the Clock | Dr. Bob Arnot
- A Random Walk Down Wall Street | Burton Malkiel
- The Art of Being | Dennis Merritt Jones
- The Art of Happiness | Dalai Lama
- The Art of the Start: The Time-Tested, Battle-Hardened Guide for Anyone Starting Anything | Guy Kawasaki
- Awaken the Giant Within | Anthony Robbins
- Beauty Pays: Why Attractive People are More Successful | Daniel Hamermesh
- Best Places to Raise Your Family | Bert Sperling, Peter Sander

- Beyond Addiction: How Science and Kindness Help People Change | Jeffrey Foote, Ph.D., Carrie Wilken, Ph.D.
- The Blood Sugar Solution | Dr. Mark Hyman
- The Brand You 50: Fifty Ways to Transform Yourself from an "Employee" into a Brand that Shouts Distinction, Commitment, and Passion! | Tom Peters
- Body Revolution | Jillian Michaels
- The Bogleheads Guide to Investing | Taylor Larimore, Mel Lindauer, Michael LeBoeuf
- The Bogleheads Guide to Retirement Planning | Taylor Larimore, Mel Lindauer, Michael LeBoeuf
- Career Success Without a Real Job: The Career for People Too Smart to Work in Corporations | Ernie Zielenski
- Change Your Mind, Change Your Life | Jerry Jampolsky MD, Diane Cirincione, Ph.D.
- Chicken Soup for the Soul | Jack Canfield, Mark Victor Hansen
- Clark Howard's Living Large for the Long Haul | Clark Howard
- The Clash of Generations: Saving Ourselves, Our Kids, and Our Economy | Lawrence Kotlikoff, Scott Burns
- The Clutter Diet: The Skinny on Organizing Your Home and Taking Control of Your Life | Lori Marrero
- Clutter Control: Putting Your Home on a Diet | Jeff Campbell
- The Coffeehouse Investor: How to Build Wealth, Ignore Wall Street, and Get on with Your Life | Bill Schultheis
- College Unbound: The Future of Education and What it Means for Students | Jeffrey Selingo
- The College Myth | Gene Kelley
- Confessions of a Sociopath: A Life Spent Hiding in Plain Sight | M.E. Thomas
- Creative Inc.: The Ultimate Guide to Running a Successful Freelance Business | Deanqdeeleert Cho, Meg Mateo Ilasco
- The Art of Happiness, How to See Yourself as You Really Are | Dalai Lama
- Daring Wives: Insight Into Women's Desires for Extramarital Affairs | Frances Cohen Praver, Ph.D.
- Decisive: How to Make Better Choices in Life | Chip Heath, Dan Heath
- The Difference: How Anyone Can Prosper in Even the Toughest Times | Jean Chatsky
- Dig Your Well Before You're Thirsty | Harvey Mackay
- Disease Proof | Dr. David Katz
- Divorce Buddy System | J. Richard Kulerski
- Do Gentlemen Really Prefer Blondes? | Jena Pincott

- Do What You Are: Discover the Perfect Career for You Through the Secrets of Personality Type | Paul D. Tieger, Barbara Barron-Tieger
- Do What You Love, The Money Will Follow | Marsha Sinetar
- Drinking Water to Lose Weight | Lexi Burke Alexander
- Eat This Not That! | David Zinczenko, Matt Goulding
- The E-Myth Revisited | Michael Gerber
- In Defense of Food | Michael Pollan
- EntreLeadership: 20 Years of Practical Business Wisdom from the Trenches | Dave Ramsey
- The Evolution of Desire | David M. Buss
- Fast Food Nation: The Dark Side of the American Meal | Eric Schlosser
- Fat Chance: Beating the Odds Against Sugar, Processed Food, Obesity, and Disease | Robert Lustig
- Feel the Fear and Do It Anyway | Susan Jeffers, Ph.D.
- The 15 Invaluable Laws of Growth: Live Them and Reach Your Potential | John Maxwell
- First Things First | Stephen Covey
- The First 20 Minutes: Surprising Science Reveals How We Can Exercise Better, Train Smarter, and Live Longer | Gretchen Reynolds
- The First 90 Days: Proven Strategies for Getting Up to Speed Faster and Smarter | Michael Watkins
- First, Break All the Rules: What the World's Greatest Managers Do Differently | Marcus Buckingham, Curt Coffman
- Food Rules: An Eater's Manual | Michael Pollen
- The 4-Hour Work Week | Tim Ferriss
- Garage Sale Tips and Treasures | Sherie Le Masurier
- Generation Debt: Take Control of Your Money | Carmen Ulrich Wong
- Get Lucky: How to Put Planned Serendipity to Work for You and Your Business | Thor Muller, Lane Becker
- Getting It Done: The Transforming Power of Self-Discipline | Andrew J. DuBrin, Ph.D.
- Get Off Your "But": How to End Self-Sabotage and Stand Up For Yourself | Sean Stephenson
- Get the Job You Want Even When No One is Hiring | Ford Myers
- Getting Things Done: The Art of Stress-free Productivity | David Allen
- Goals: How to Get Everything You Want-Faster Than You Ever Thought Possible | Brian Tracy

- Going Solo | Eric Klinenberg
- Good Calories, Bad Calories | Gary Taubes
- Good to Great: Why Some Companies Make the Leap…and Others Don't | Jim Collins
- The Great 401k Hoax | William Wollman
- The Healing Power Within: How to Tap the Infinite Potential Within Yourself | Ann Wigmore
- The Higher Education Bubble | Glenn Harlan Reynolds
- How to Build a Successful Life Without a Four-Year Degree | Blake Boles
- How to Find Your Dream Job…Even in a Recession | Ron Nash
- How to Get a Job: Secrets of a Hiring Manager | Allison Green
- How to Get What You Want and Want What You Have | John Gray
- How to Master the Art of Selling | Tom Hopkins
- How to Win Friends and Influence People | Dale Carnegie
- How Science and Kindness Help People Change | Jeffrey Foote Ph.D., Carrie Wilkens Ph.D., Nicole Kisanke Ph.D.
- Index Mutual Funds: How to Simplify Your Life and Beat the Pros | Dale C. Maley
- Influence: The Psychology of Persuasion | Robert Cialdini
- Innovation in a Reinvented World | Dee McCrorey
- The Investment Answer | Daniel Goldie, Gordon Murray
- Irrational Exuberance | Robert Schiller
- I Will Teach You To Be Rich | Ramit Sethi
- The Job-loss Recovery Guide: A Proven Program to Get Back to Work…Fast! | Dr. Lynn Joseph
- Job Searching with Social Media for Dummies | Josh Waldman
- Just Listen: Discovering the Secret to Getting Through to Anyone | Mark Goulston
- Just Start: Take Action, Embrace Uncertainty, Create the Future | Charles F. Kiefer, Paul B. Brown
- Learned Optimism: How to Change Your Mind and Your Life | Martin Seligman, Ph.D.
- Let's Eat Right to Keep Fit | Adelle Davis
- Let's Get Well | Adelle Davis
- Leveraging LinkedIn: The Essential Guide to Building Your Career Network | Ron Nash
- Linchpin: Are You Indispensible? | Seth Godin
- The Little Black Book of Red Flags: Relationship Warning Signs You Totally Spotted… But Chose to Ignore | Natasha Burton, Julie Fishman, Meagan McCrary
- Living the Good Life | Scott Nearing, Helen Nearing

- The Little Book of Common Sense Investing | John Bogle
- The Long Life Equation: 100 Factors that Determine How Long You'll Live | Dr. Trisha Macnair, Dr. Olga Calof
- Looks: Why They Matter More Than You Even Imagined | Gordon Patzer, Ph.D.
- Love, Medicine and Miracles: Lessons Learned About Self-healing from a Surgeon's Experience and Exceptional Patients |Dr. Bernie Siegel
- Love Will Find You: 9 Magnets to Bring You and Your Soulmate Together | Kathryn Alice
- The Luck Factor: Change Your Luck, Change Your Life, The Four Essential Principles | Richard Wiseman
- Luck is No Accident: Making the Most of Happenstance in Your Career and Life | John Krumholtz
- Made to Stick: Why Some Ideas Survive and Others Die | Chip Heath, Dan Heath
- The Magic of Thinking Big | David J. Schwartz Ph.D.
- Manifest Your Destiny | Wayne Dyer
- Maximum Strength: Get Your Strongest Body in 16 Weeks with the Ultimate Weight Training Program | Eric Cressey
- Me 2.0: Build a Powerful Brand for Career Success | Dan Schwabel
- The Memory Book: The Classic Guide to Improving Your Memory at Work, at School, and at Play | Jerry Lucas
- Men are from Mars, Women are from Venus | John Gray
- The Millionaire Makers Guide to Creating a Cash Machine for Life | Lorel Langemeier
- The Millionaire Next Door | Thomas Stanley Ph.D., William Danko
- The Mind Body Prescription | Dr. John Sarno
- Mindless Eating: Why We Eat More Than We Think | Brian Wansink Ph.D.
- The Monogamy Myth | Peggy Vaughan
- MOJO: How to Get It, How to Keep It, How to Get It Back if You Lose It | Marshall Goldsmith
- Moonwalking with Einstein: The Art and Science of Remembering Everything | Joshua Foer
- The Most Effective Ways to Live Longer | Dr. Jonny Bowden
- A New Earth: Awakening Your Life's Purpose | Eckhart Tolle
- The New Geography of Jobs | Enrico Moretti
- Negotiating Your Salary: How to Make $1,000 a Minute | Jack Chapman
- The New Leader's 100-Day Action Plan: How to Take Charge, Build Your Team, and Get Immediate Results | George Bradt, Jayme Check, Jorge Pedraza

- Simple Secrets for Becoming Healthy, Wealthy & Wise | David Niven, Ph.D.
- The Omega-3 Connection | Dr. Andrew Stoll
- The Ominivore's Dilemma | Michael Pollan
- Online Education for Dummies | Kevin Johnson, Susan Manning, Jonathon Finkelstein
- The Only Investment Guide You'll Ever Need | Andrew Tobias
- 101 Answers to the Toughest Interview Questions | Ron Fry
- 101 Best Outdoor Towns: Unspoiled Places to Visit, Live & Play | Sarah Tuff, Greg Melville
- 136 Effective Presentation Tips | Tony Jeary
- The 150 Healthiest Foods on Earth | Dr. Johnny Bowden
- The 150 Most Effective Ways to Boost Your Energy | Dr. Johnny Bowden
- Organizing from the Inside Out: the Foolproof System for Organizing Your Home, Your Office, and Your Life | Julie Morgenstern
- Outliers: The Story of Success | Malcom Gladwell
- The Paradox of Choice: Why More is Less: How the Culture of Abundance Robs Us of Satisfaction | Barry Schwartz
- People Are Idiots and I Can Prove It: The 10 Ways You Are Sabotaging Yourself and How You Can Overcome Them | Larry Winget
- Pinched: How the Great Recession has Narrowed Our Future and What We Can Do About It | Don Peck
- Places Rated Almanac: More than 400 Metropolitan Areas Evaluated in the U.S. and Canada | David Saganeau
- The Power of Habit: Why We Do What We Do In Life And Business | Charles Duhigg
- The Power of Intention: Learning to Co-Create Your World Your Way | Wayne Dyer
- The Power of Now: A Guide to Spiritual Enlightenment | Eckhart Tolle
- The Power of Passive Investing | Richard Ferri
- The Power of Positive Thinking | Dr. Norman Vincent Peale
- The Power of Self-Confidence: Become Unstoppable, Irresistible, and Unafraid in Every Area of Your Life | Brian Tracy
- The Power of Simplicity | Jack Trout, Steve Rivkin
- The Power of Touch: The Basis for Survival, Health, Intimacy, and Emotional Well-Being | Phyllis Davis
- The Power of 2: How to Make the Most of Your Partnerships at Work and in Life | Rodd Wagner, Gale Muller
- Power Sleep: The Revolutionary Program That Prepares Your Mind for Peak Performance | David Axelrod

- Presentation Skills 201: How to Take it to the Next Level as a Confident, Engaging Speaker | William Steele
- The Presentation Tips of Steve Jobs: How to be Insanely Great in Front of Any Audience | Carmine Gallo
- Prescription for Nutritional Healing | Phyllis Balch
- Private Notes of a Headhunter: Proven Job Search and Interviewing Techniques for College Students and Recent Grads | Kenneth Heinzel
- Promote Yourself: The New Rules for Career Success | Dan Schwabel
- The Psychology of Gratitude | Robert A. Emmons
- The Psychology of Music | Teresa Lesiuk
- Psychology of Success: Finding Meaning in Work and Life | Denis Waitley
- The Power of Focus: What the World's Greatest Achievers Know About The Secret of Financial Freedom and Success | Jack Canfield
- The Real Age Makeover | Dr. Michael Roizen
- The Real Cost of Living: Making the Best Choices for You, Your Life, and Your Money | Carmen Wong Ulrich
- Reboot: My Five Life-Changing Mistakes and How I Moved On | Julie Wainwright
- Recover to Live: Kick Any Habit, Manage Any Addiction | Christopher Kennedy Lawford
- Reinvention: How to Make the Rest of Your Life the Best of Your Life | Brian Tracy
- Relationships 101 | John C. Maxwell
- Relationship Rescue: A Seven-Step Strategy for Reconnecting with Your Partner | Dr. Phil McGraw
- The Relationship Handbook | George Pransky
- Retirement Places Rated: Plan the Retirement You Deserve | David Savageau
- Rich Like Them: My Door-to-Door Search for the Secrets of Wealth in America's Richest Neighborhoods | Ryan D'Agostion
- Rightsizing Your Life: Simplifying Your Surroundings While Keeping What Matters Most | Ciji Ware
- Rise of the Naked Economy | Jeremy Neumer
- Salary Tutor: Learn the Salary Negotiation Secrets No One Taught You | Jim Hopkinson
- See You at the Top | Zig Ziglar
- The Science of Influence: How to Get Anyone to Say "Yes" in 8 Minutes or Less | Kevin Hogan
- Seven Strategies for Wealth & Happiness: Power Ideas from America's Foremost Business Philosopher | Jim Rohn
- The Science of Success | Wallace Wattles

- The Secrets of the Millionaire Mind | T. Harv Eker
- The 7 Habits of Highly Successful People | Stephen Covey
- The Seven Principles for Making Marriage Work: A Practical Guide from the Country's Foremost Relationship Expert | John Gottman
- The Seven Spiritual Laws of Success: A Practical Guide to the Fulfillment of Your Dreams | Deepak Chopra
- Sixty Seconds: One Moment Changes Everything | Phil Bolsta
- The Slight Edge: Turning Simple Disciplines into Massive Success and Happiness | Jeff Olson
- The Smartest 401k Book You'll Ever Need | Daniel Solin
- The Smartest Investment Plan You'll Ever Need | Daniel Solin
- The Social Animal: The Hidden Sources of Love, Character, and Achievement | David Brooks
- Social Networking for Career Success: Using Online Tools to Create a Personal Brand | Miriam Salpeter
- The Sociopath Next Door | Martha Stout, Ph.D.
- Spend 'til The End: The Revolutionary Guide to Raising Your Living Standard–Today and When You Retire | Lawrence Kotlikoff, Scott Burns
- The Start–up of You: Adapt to the Future, Invest in Yourself, and Transform Your Career | Reid Hoffman, Ben Casnocha
- The Success Principles: How to Get From Where You Are to Where You Want to Be | Jack Canfield
- Survival of the Prettiest: The Science of Beauty | Nancy Etcoff
- The Stress of Life | Hans Selye
- Take Control of Your Money | Carmen Wong Ulrich
- Talk Like TED: The 9 Public Speaking Secrets of the World's Top Minds | Carmine Gallo
- Taming the Paper Tiger | Barbara Hemphill
- Thank You Power: Making the Science of Gratitude Work For You | Deborah Norville
- Think and Grow Rich | Napoleon Hill
- Think Big: Unleashing Your Potential for Excellence | Ben Carson
- The Time Trap: The Classic Book on Time Management | Alex Mackenzie, Pat Nickerson
- The Ultimate Secrets of Total Self–Confidence | Dr. Robert Anthony
- 30 Lessons for Living: Tried and True Advice from the Wisest Americans | Karl Pillemer Ph.D.
- 301 Smart Answers to Tough Interview Questions | Vicki Oliver

- True North: Discover Your Authentic Leadership | Bill George, Peter Sims, David Gergen
- The Twitter Job Search Guide: Find a Job and Advance Your Career in Just 15 Minutes a Day | Susan Britton Whitcomb, Chandless Bryan
- The Ultra Mind Solution | Mark Hyman
- 301 Best Questions to Ask on Your Interview | John Kador
- The Wealthy Freelancer: 12 Secrets to a Great Income and an Enviable Lifestyle | Steve Slaunwhite
- What Got You Here Won't Get You There: How Successful People Become Even More Successful | Marshall Goldsmith
- Why Him, Why Her? | Helen Fisher
- Why We Get Fat: And What To Do About It | Gary Taubes
- Without Conscious: The Disturbing World of the Psychopaths Among Us | Robert Hare, Ph.D.
- The World is Flat | Thomas Friedman
- A Whack on the Side of the Head: How You Can Be More Creative | Roger von Oech
- The Willpower Instinct: How Self-Control Works, Why It Matters, and What You Can Do To Get More of It | Kelly McDonigal, Ph.D.
- The Wisdom of Psychopaths: What Saints, Spies, and Serial Killers Can Teach Us About Success | Kevin Dutton
- What Color is Your Parachute? | Richard Bolles
- Who's Your City? How the Creative Economy is Making Where You Live the Most Important Decision of Your Life | Richard Florida
- Why Marriages Succeed or Fail: And How You Can Make Yours Last | John Gottman
- The World is Fat | Barry Popkin, Ph.D.
- Wrong: Why experts* Keep Failing Us-And How to Know When to Trust Them | David Freedman
- Your Money or Your Life: 9 Steps to Transforming Your Relationship with Money and Acheving Financial Independence | Vicki Robin, Joe Dominguez
- Yoga Cures: Over 50 Simple Routines for Radiant Health | Tara Stiles
- YOU! The Owner's Manual | Dr. Michael Roizen, Dr. Mehmet Oz
- Water: For Health, for Healing, For Life: You're Not Sick, You're Thirsty! | Dr. F. Batmanghelidj

Made in the USA
Lexington, KY
15 November 2019